From Prejudice to Destruction
Anti-Semitism, 1700-1933

From Prejudice to Destruction
Anti-Semitism, 1700–1933

Jacob Katz

HARVARD UNIVERSITY PRESS
Cambridge, Massachusetts
1980

Copyright © 1980 by Jacob Katz
All rights reserved
Printed in the United States of America

Library of Congress Cataloging in Publication Data

Katz, Jacob, 1904-
  From prejudice to destruction.

  Includes bibliographical references and index.
  1. Antisemitism—History. 1. Title.
DS145.K354   305.8'924   80-14404
ISBN 0-674-32505-2

Preface

PREJUDICE TOWARD JEWS—anti-Semitism in modern parlance—has been strangely persistent ever since its first appearance in ancient times. The force and universality of the anti-Jewish animus attracted the attention of observers even before its deadly culmination in the Holocaust. Since then it has become the subject of extensive historical, sociological, and psychological research and of intensive theological and philosophical inquiry. Most of these intellectual endeavors were prompted by the desire to find an answer to the gnawing question of how this inhuman event, unique in its mass dimensions and abysmal evil, could have occurred.

The present study has a less ambitious objective: to show how the anti-Jewish animosity grew in strength, paradoxically just when in the wake of the Enlightenment and modern rationality one might have expected it to disappear. I do not claim that such historical investigation will satisfy the quest for ultimate explanation. It may, however, pave the way for it or at least prevent the creation of myths, which is the easy way to avoid facing hard facts.

I have made use of previous research undertaken for my book *Exclusiveness and Tolerance: Studies in Jewish-Gentile Relations in Medieval and Modern Times* (1961), and I have had at my disposal the best possible collections of source material. Besides the great treasures of the Jewish National and University Library in Jerusalem, I consulted for over a decade materials in the British Museum and the Wiener Library in London, the Bayerische Staatsbibliothek in Munich, and the Zentralbibliothek

Preface

in Zurich. During the years 1973-1975 I enjoyed, as visiting professor, the hospitality of the university libraries of Harvard and Columbia. Some results of my research I have published in learned periodicals; here I have presented the conclusions most relevant to the overall trend of my studies.

The book appears almost simultaneously in Hebrew (Am Oved, Tel-Aviv) and in English—both versions composed by the author, the English with the gracious assistance of Rabbi Arthur Super and others.

A research grant from the American Jewish Committee facilitated the accomplishing of the project.

J. K.
The Hebrew University of Jerusalem
1980

Contents

Contents

Introduction

THE TERM ANTI-SEMITISM was introduced in Germany at the end of the 1870s to describe the negative attitude toward the Jews held by a part of the population at that time.[1] Needless to say, hostility toward Jews was hardly an unprecedented phenomenon in Germany or elsewhere. Why, then, was there a need for a new term? To gain an answer, even if it be a tentative one, we must examine the conditions that prevailed when *anti-Semitism* took its place in the modern vocabulary.

At the time, the process of legal emancipation of Jews was being completed in Germany and Austria-Hungary, two countries where Jewish affairs had occupied government and public opinion since the end of the eighteenth century. The question was whether to leave the Jews in their former condition as aliens or half-citizens or to extend them full citizenship. The same question faced all the Western countries that had abandoned the feudal structure for one in which all citizens were equal before the law. Would this equality apply to all the citizens of the state, including the Jews? Or should that minority that had always been exceptional both by its own choice and the will of others continue to hold a special position in the future? At first sight, the answer should have depended on the new constitutional state's relation to the institutions of the Christian religion, from which the Jews were dissociated by mutual consent. To define the state as Christian in any sense of the word would have been sufficient reason to exclude Jews from full citizenship. If, on the other hand, the state was explicitly secular, any religious criterion would disappear, and no distinction should have obtained between Jews and others. However, religion alone

1

did not always determine the status of the Jew. The name "Jew" aroused abundant associations—mostly negative—in the minds of most Europeans; and it was easy to find pretexts for the exclusion of the Jews without explicit reference to religious arguments. Consequently, naturalization of the Jews was never a smooth process; indeed, a stormy controversy accompanied emancipation everywhere.[2] In the course of this controversy, which occurred repeatedly over a period of ninety years, from 1780 on, the fitness of Jews for citizenship was continually discussed. In the process, various claims were made for and against them. The arguments against them included not only prejudices inherited from the Middle Ages, but also new indictments that emerged during the struggle over emancipation.

Throughout most of the struggle, the opponents of emancipation appeared to be fighting a losing battle: the naturalization of Jews was making progress. In France, it was achieved in 1790-1791, during the Revolution; in Holland and the western parts of Germany (the Rhineland, Frankfurt, and Hamburg) after the French conquests of 1796-1808; in Prussia, in 1812, as a part of the general reform; and likewise in Bavaria a year later. This emancipation, which was not yet called by that name, but by such cumbersome expressions as "the civic betterment of the Jews,"[3] was hardly complete: nowhere did it gain the Jews absolute equality with other citizens, nor did it always last. In some places it was withdrawn. In particular, the period from the fall of Napoleon until the 1830s was one of reaction—the name by which it is known in general German historiography. The process of naturalization was interrupted and even reversed; rights that had been given to the Jews were limited or canceled. But, with the rise of liberalism in the thirties, the struggle was resumed and the status of the Jews improved rapidly. In the revolutionary years of 1848-1849, the principle of absolute equality for Jews was declared in all of Germany and Austria-Hungary; and even though the leaders of the revolution did not succeed in realizing their principles, there was no return to the status quo ante, even after the failure of the revolution. The foundations of the reactionary regime were shaken, and the authorities were forced to initiate reforms and grant civil liberties to their citizens. Progress toward parliamentary rule and the constitutional state had an effect on the Jewish question as well.

Full emancipation was achieved in the states of northern Germany that were united under Bismarck's leadership after the Prussian victory over Austria in 1866. The 1869 constitution of the united state provided that the rights of the citizen did not depend on his adherence to any particular religion. With the creation of the Reich in 1871 the principle of equality was extended to all of Germany. The unification of Germany came about with the severing of the political ties that had connected Austria-Hungary with the German states. Both Austria and Hungary, which operated independently in internal affairs, had already granted the Jews emancipation in 1867. In France and Holland, emancipation had been a fact for three generations. In England, the first Jew entered Parliament in 1858. This marked the end of the basic political disability of the Jews, a limitation that had stemmed from the close connection between church and state.

Anyone examining the position of the Jews in the 1860s, when all these events took place, could have reasonably concluded that European Jewry was becoming completely integrated. He could have viewed the accusations made by those opposed to emancipation as the last flare of a dying fire that would gradually burn itself out once Jewish naturalization became a fact in every country. Indeed, most enlightened observers at the time, Jews and non-Jews alike, saw the situation just so. For precisely this reason, it came as a terrible shock when writers, politicians, and scholars in the 1870s, again attacked Jews and found their onslaught so well received by the general public that an entire movement sprang up, one openly proclaiming its opposition to Jews. The movement sought to achieve its aims by creating local parties and international organizations. In one specific respect these renewed attacks against the Jews were much more ominous than those of previous generations. When Jews lived in the ghetto, and immediately after they left it, accusations against them came from citizens who enjoyed a legal status denied to Jews. These accusations were designed only to justify and reconfirm the status quo and provide a rationale for keeping Jews in an inferior legal and social position. Now, however, the accusations were leveled by citizens at citizens who were equal before the law, and the purpose of these indictments was to show that Jews were unworthy of the legal and social position conferred upon them.

The movement's followers came from diverse ideological backgrounds—Christian, secular, and even racial—and they differed also in their views of the movement's necessary sociopolitical objectives. Some sought to turn back the clock and rescind emancipation; others simply wanted to exclude Jews from certain social positions and restrict them to certain professions. Several individuals went so far as to explicitly demand the elimination of Jews by any means possible.[4] Whatever the case, they all saw themselves as entering a political or social struggle in order to change the status quo. For this they enlisted arguments used in polemics and disputes in the past. These were adapted to the contemporary situation with the incorporation of new accusations. Of course, the new movement did not want to appear to be regurgitating old ideologies or pursuing outdated objectives. On the contrary. It wished to demonstrate that it was aroused to react to a situation newly created and was indeed employing new thinking in line with the new situation. The proponents of the new movement rejected the charge that they were only carrying over from past Jew-haters. They claimed that the basis for the former opposition to Jews and Judaism had gone. Previously, religion had constituted the factor dividing Jews and Christians and causing alienation and hatred. Now, the influence of religion had weakened considerably or disappeared completely. There were anti-Semites who confessed Christianity, but these, too, wanted to appear as supporters of the principle of religious toleration, this being a universally accepted principle. The spokesmen of the new movement searched for new catchwords that would express the modernity of their approach. The adoption of the name "anti-Semite," rather than anti-Jew, was meant to suggest that it was not the Jewishness, that is, the religion, of the Jews that aroused opposition, but some aspects of their character that found expression in their behavior.

This simplified survey of the process that brought about the rise of the anti-Semitic movement that emerged in Germany in the late 1870s—spreading from there to other European countries or awakening in them independently through similar causes or circumstances—leads to the conclusion that even if modern anti-Semitism has distinct historical antecedents, when and where it arose it came as a surprising innovation, indeed a shocking one for those directly affected, who were mainly, but not exclusively, Jews. If "shock" means the sudden awareness of a negation of accepted ideas and conventions, the anti-Semites themselves must be included among the shocked. They found themselves, overnight as it were, possessed by a vision entailing the diagnosis of the illness of their time and proclaimed their discovery of the cure at the top of their lungs. The panic of the Jews, whose confidence in the civil equality they had achieved after so long a struggle was undermined, is hardly surprising. It seemed to them as if the clock had been turned back and the evil spirits which they thought had vanished completely from the world had come back to life.

The reaction of the Jewish community to the wave of anti-Semitism came on two levels, the practical and the theoretical. A full-scale political and legal defense campaign, together with an appeal to public opinion, was waged in Germany, Austria-Hungary, and France in the decades after 1880. On the political plane, the idea was to strengthen the parties and the public bodies that opposed anti-Semitism.[5] Sometimes the actions of anti-Semites constituted a violation of the rights of individuals or of the status of the Jewish community. In these cases, recourse could be had to the courts.[6] Concurrently, Jewish organizations, some of them established especially for this purpose, attempted to refute the arguments of the anti-Semites. These attempts depended, of course, on a certain theoretical

Introduction

grasp of the anti-Semitic phenomenon. The apologists had to understand the phenomenon they were combating. Moreover, people of intellectual bent tried to come to terms with the reality they encountered, some developing complete theories on the cause, or causes, of modern anti-Semitism.

Two fundamental concepts developed, reflecting the social and political positions of the theoreticians. One concept saw in anti-Semitism an anomaly, a kind of social disease which the parties involved could have avoided with caution and which, even after its eruption, could be cured or at least alleviated. The proponents of this concept sought to locate the causes of the disease in every sphere of life: economic—the competing of Jews for a livelihood with their Gentile counterparts; social—the eagerness of Jews to gain new social positions; religious—the persistence of Christian hostility, consciously or unconsciously, even after the principle of religious toleration had been accepted. Sometimes these explanations had moralistic overtones, suggesting that if those involved would act properly—if the competitors of the Jews would control their jealousy, if the Jews would be less ambitious, if the Christians would practice genuine tolerance—there would be no place for anti-Semitism. This approach was predominant in the Jewish community in the first generation of the rise of anti-Semitism and continued to be held by all those who did not give up hope of ultimately achieving good relations between the Jewish minority and the non-Jewish majority by removing the burden of the past.

The second theory about the cause of anti-Semitism was the Zionist hypothesis. Despair of ever seeing Jews integrated fully into Gentile society as equals was a central factor in the formation of the Zionist movement. This despair was the outcome of a new evaluation of the nature of anti-Semitism. It no longer appeared to be a passing affliction, an illness that time would heal, but was conceived of as a chronic condition inherent in the very constitution of the afflicted. A stateless ethnic group living in the midst of a foreign people was diagnosed as the cause of the illness; and the only remedy was surgery, that is, emigration to a state that would have to be founded for that purpose. This was the view that Theodor Herzl arrived at after the Dreyfus trial in France in 1895; Leo Pinsker had proposed the same diagnosis and recommended the same therapy after the pogroms in Russia in 1881.[7]

To these two basic theories one must add a third: the socialist hypothesis. This looks upon anti-Semitism, like all other modern social ills, as an outcome of the essential nature of the capitalist system, in which Jews fill a highly visible role as investors of funds and commercial intermediaries, benefiting from the system so long as it functions smoothly. When the cracks in the system showed in the form of economic crises, the

5

Jews, as its most obvious representatives, became a target for criticism and accusation. Another version is that anti-Semitism was created deliberately as a means of defending the capitalistic system by diverting public attention from those cracks that heralded its demise. According to both these versions, anti-Semitism would disappear with the establishment of the hoped-for socialism.[8] Although anti-Semitism was not among the factors that generated socialism, once socialism emerged it not only evolved a theory to explain anti-Semitism but also suggested a solution to it.

Any theory that attempts both to explain a social phenomenon and to propose, on the basis of this explanation, a program of action for the future assumes the nature of an ideology, which is prone to blur the distinction between the facts themselves and their evaluation. Indeed, neither the concept of anti-Semitism expressed by the assimilationists, nor that of the Zionists, nor that of the Socialists is the product of disinterested examination, not to mention objective historical or sociological research. However, later, more detached thinkers and scholars have dealt with the subject of anti-Semitism without relating their explanations to a social or political program of action. Numerous essays and studies have been written by perceptive intellectuals who examined the phenomenon of anti-Semitism as they would any other historical or social phenomenon worthy of inquiry and understanding.[9] The advantage of the scholar over the ideologist—assimilated Jew, Zionist, socialist, Christian missionary, or anti-Semite—is that while the latter purposely merge their assertions regarding the present and the past with their expectations and programs for the future, the scholar tries to distinguish between them. Whether and to what degree he succeeds depends on the effort he makes and his talent—that is, his ability to criticize and control the thought patterns and research patterns he is using. Even if the norms of his discipline do not save the scholar from subjectivity, they clearly distinguish him from the blatant ideologue.

Research has enriched our knowledge and understanding of anti-Semitism. Sociologists and psychologists have pointed out the social and personal factors that permit both masses and individuals to succumb to anti-Semitic slogans and prejudices. Sociological and psychological studies have revealed the response patterns of the prejudiced toward those whom their prejudices teach them to scorn and have helped explain the process by which the majority assumes social reservations toward the minority and how ideological and even spiritual approval is granted ex post facto to such discrimination. The analysis of these tendencies in the present is applicable to the study of the past and in particular to the history of anti-Semitism.

Nevertheless, pertinent understanding of the past comes only from following the development of events and the course of the historical pro-

Introduction

cesses, and that depends on direct examination of historical sources. Many historical surveys have been conducted in the last two or three generations in order to uncover the roots of the behavior of non-Jews toward Jews. We are aware today of the negative formulations current in the ancient world concerning the Jewish people—a people bewilderingly different in its beliefs and rituals, comprising whole communities that dwelt among the Gentiles but did not mingle with them.[10] Jewish singularity stood out even more when the surrounding world was conquered by Christianity, a religion that had grown out of Judaism itself, but which the Jews refused to accept and recognize as spiritual truth. There is no question that the Christian reaction—from the polemics of the Church Fathers against the Jews to the precepts of the medieval synods requiring suppression and exclusion of Jews—is important in establishing the practical and emotional relation of the non-Jewish world to the followers of Judaism. Christian teachings and theories lowered the stature of the Jew, obstructing his access to many sources of income, denying his citizenship and degrading him to the position of a barely tolerated resident in need of special protection from the ruler, emperor, bishop, or magistrate. The marginal occupations he was permitted and the inferiority of his political and social position made the Jew a convenient object for discrimination, mockery, and prejudice, so that in the popular mind his image became that of a satanic, subhuman monster. This creature, whose humanity was doubtful, was ready and willing to commit any abomination—deceit, infanticide, and desecration of objects sacred to Christianity; as such, he risked losing the right to be treated like other human beings.[11]

The low social and political standing of the Jew, and the profoundly negative opinion that the non-Jew held of him, had reinforced each other since the Middle Ages. His low status seemed to be warranted by his observance of a despised and worthless religion, and his being of that low status invited aspersion to be cast on his faith and character. However, this vicious circle appeared to be breaking at the end of the eighteenth century—and even earlier among the enlightened—when writers and thinkers began to expose the accepted opinions regarding the Jews, and, simultaneously, statesmen took an interest in improving their social and political lot. As states gradually completed reforms, making Jews equal citizens, the web of damaging opinions and prejudices that had come to surround the Jew might well have disintegrated and vanished, for two reasons. First of all, ideology had lost its function of explaining the Jews' inferior position. Second, ideology had lost its credibility. Ultimately, the point of departure for disqualifying the Jews was religion, or Christian theology, and these now found only modest support in contemporary thinking. The question, then, is how did the anti-Jewish conceptions retain

7

their force and tenacity? How were they passed down and transmuted into terms consonant with the new social reality and intellectual environment? These questions are the subject of this book.

A clue to the answers is inherent in the process of emancipation, as described above. Jews were emancipated only after several generations of public debate. Throughout the polemic, opponents of emancipation argued against the full integration of Jews into a state and society that were not theirs. The old accusations, which had justified the degradation of the Jews from a religious and theological point of view, were unsuited to the new situation. Advocates of emancipation relied on the principles of the Enlightenment: rationalism, humanism, and universalism. Rationalism declared reason the highest authority, and reason did not permit an individual's status to be based on religious tenets, which were by nature irrational. Humanism demanded respect for the human element in every man, including the Jew. Universalism prescribed that the rights of men be determined by uniform criteria. The adversaries of emancipation responded to these principles by contending that though the ideals of the Enlightenment may be valid, they were not applicable to Jews. In the new anti-Semitic teachings, the Jews were denied any share in the rights inherent in rationalism, humanism, and universalism. This denial would seem to be illogical. However, in ideological arguments, logic and consistency are hardly decisive; the train of thought is not guided by the quest for truth but by the need to justify prior beliefs. Those opposed to the Jews attaining equal political or social status were fierce in their determination; and this determination, not logic, was crucial in their argumentation.

Indeed, the flaws in their arguments clearly revealed themselves, but not so much for their logical vulnerability as for their conflict with contemporary political and social trends. From the 1780s on, the old social and political patterns were in a process of disintegration. The state based on late feudal estates and guilds or corporations gave way to one of independent citizens under direct jurisdiction. In this state there was no place for the familiar type of Jewish community structured like a corporation, albeit the lowliest of corporations. The Jews confronted the state and its institutions as individuals; it was essential to confer citizen status upon them if they were not to be removed from the state. The formation of the new state and its relations with its citizens was accompanied by broad and varied ideological support—from eighteenth-century rationalism to nineteenth-century liberalism. Likewise, the movement for the naturalization of the Jews relied on ideas taken from these schools of thought. Conversely, ideological objections to the new development seemed to contradict reality, and the patterns of thought behind them were deprecated as reactionary. This accounts for the disparaging attitude of the supporters of

Introduction

emancipation toward their opponents, whom they regarded as backward. And indeed, so they were at that time.

However, the struggle did not end with the achievement of formal emancipation. The hope, or perhaps more accurately the social utopia, that was intertwined with the attainment of civil rights for Jews—that the Jews would no longer be differentiated from other citizens except by their faith—was not fulfilled. The Jews remained a distinct social group—by virtue of their marriages, their concentration in certain professions, their social cohesiveness, their maintenance of particular cultural patterns, and their denial of the predominant religion—even after their naturalization.[12] Barely had one generation of emancipation passed before the critics of the Jews began to claim that the Gentiles had got a bad bargain. These views were expressed first in Hungary, by the Liberal member of parliament Gyözö Istoczy in 1875, and after a few years by Adolf Stöcker and his comrades in Germany. Even in France, where emancipation had been a fact for more than three generations, the same accusation was heard; and as the enormous circulation of Drumont's book *La France Juive* in 1886 indicates, the general public was not disinclined to listen to such views. Not all the accusers drew equally radical conclusions. Some demanded the repeal of emancipation, others sought to have Jews restricted in their choice of occupation lest they infiltrate governmental and juridical positions or take over the economy, the stock market, and the banks. Stöcker even turned to the Jews themselves, asking them to examine their actions and to moderate their passion for power and their eagerness for social advancement. Simultaneously, the call went out to the Christian community to band together into political parties and organizations to protect its interests and to restrict Jews from places where they were unwanted.

The rise of anti-Semitism was not a matter of the dissemination and acceptance of ideas on a purely intellectual level. It was rather by virtue of their inherent political and social challenge that these ideas prevailed. They were not expressed for the sake of perception and understanding, but in support of a stand and a corresponding course of action in the political and social sphere. And this fact has implications for the methods to be used in the historical research and presentation of the anti-Semitic movement. It is, of course, important to know the sources of anti-Semitic ideologies, how their ideas were passed down from one source to the next, who was influenced by whom, and the like. However, the more significant question is what were the social intentions and political goals that motivated the ideologues to use these ideas, and how did they adapt them to the needs of the situation at each particular time.

I shall begin with a summary of the opinions on Judaism and the Jews expressed at the end of the Middle Ages, particularly by one of the great

Introduction

students of Judaism in the seventeenth century, Johann Andreas Eisenmenger, who was concurrently the greatest contender with the Jews. Afterward I shall describe the rationalists' view of the essence of Judaism and their description of the Jew, concentrating particularly on one writer who stands out among the rationalists, both in his importance and in his antagonism to the Jews: Voltaire. When the possibility of emancipation later arose, the foes of the Jews were to quote and paraphrase both Eisenmenger and Voltaire abundantly. Of course, neither writer imagined that their writings would be used in this way; their words were revised by later polemicists and incorporated into arguments that they had never considered. As issues concerning the Jews arose time and again throughout the generations of the emancipation, the social image of the Jews alternately rose and fell in the eyes of their contemporaries; this process of ascent and descent will be traced until the end of the period of emancipation, when, after apparently declining, the old historical hatred returned, reviving itself in the form of modern anti-Semitism.

Part I: Background, 1700-1780

1 | The Christian Tradition: Eisenmenger

THE PHENOMENON OF MODERN anti-Semitism cannot be fully understood by reference to contemporary data only, whether sociological, economic, political, or ideological. A heavy hereditary burden, going back to the Middle Ages and ancient times, has loomed over the relationship between the Jew and the non-Jewish world. This heritage was partly accountable for the enmity that broke out just when one might have expected it to have been eradicated by the change in historic circumstances. How far must we traverse the past in our search for the roots of this enmity? Do we have to accompany the Jewish communities from land to land and trace their transmutations and those of the prejudices that clung to them?[1]

Although an investigation of the relation between the Jewish community and the surrounding society in the different eras is valuable in itself, the study of a subject with such historic continuity should focus on that era of change in which a definite release was attained from the inherited burden of the past. Fate decreed that a certain Christian writer, Johann Andreas Eisenmenger, should have arisen at just that moment in the history of anti-Semitism and concentrated the tradition of medieval anti-Jewish doctrines in his great work *Entdecktes Judenthum.*[2] The conceptual structure of Eisenmenger and his motives for writing his book are rooted in the spiritual world of the Middle Ages. With the rise of rationalism it was possible to view *Entdecktes Judenthum* as the last flare-up of denunciation based on the traditional Jewish-Christian schism; and this is how it looked to many people.[3] However, rationalism did not bridge the

13

schism, but succeeded only in changing its character, and so the denunciations of Eisenmenger did not drop out of sight for more than a brief period. They kept coming up, and his book nourished the anti-Semitic movement directly and indirectly at all stages of its development.

Eisenmenger was born in 1654 and the book, to which he had devoted twenty years, was printed in 1700. However, the actual publication was delayed a further ten years. The Jews of Frankfurt induced the court agents Samson Wertheimer and Samuel Oppenheimer to influence the Hapsburg emperor to distrain the copies of the book. Eisenmenger appealed, and litigation continued for decades. The writer died in 1704 and his heirs on the one hand, and those who would have the book banned, carried on the struggle. Before the trial ended, Eisenmenger's book found a royal patron elsewhere. Frederick I, King of Prussia, helped the heirs to reprint the book in Berlin. The frontispiece states that the book was printed in Königsberg, a city outside the jurisdiction of the emperor.[4]

The obstructions that Eisenmenger's book encountered indicate that it was recognized immediately as a work detrimental, and possibly dangerous, to the Jews. The title, "Judaism Uncovered," discloses its purpose: Eisenmenger claimed to expose the secrets hidden in the books of the Jews and thereby uncover their true image. His book was impressive both on account of its size—some 2,120 pages in two volumes—and its tremendous erudition. Eisenmenger was well versed in Hebrew, Aramaic, and Arabic. He quotes from about two hundred books: legal works (Halakoth), homiletics, cabala and philosophy, popular ethical works, polemics against both Christianity and Islam. In short, Eisenmenger was acquainted with all the literature a Jewish scholar of standing would have known. He had learned to use these books partly through contacts with Jewish scholars in Frankfurt and Amsterdam; rumor has it that he passed himself off as a potential convert to Judaism.[5] In fact, it was not unusual at that time for non-Jewish scholars to take an interest in the literature of the Jews.[6] However, Eisenmenger surpassed his predecessors in his mastery of the sources and his ability to interpret them tendentiously. Contrary to accusations that have been made against him, he does not falsify his sources. He quotes them in full and translates them literally into German. Nevertheless, Eisenmenger's presentation of the beliefs and opinions of the Jews reveals an image of Jewish thought that is a far cry from the actual attitudes of those Jews who studied and lived by that same literature he uses.

Eisenmenger's declared purpose, as explained in the last chapter of his book, is to help the Jews to recognize their error and acknowledge the truth of Christianity. In order to divert the Jews from their religion, Eisenmenger suggests several concrete steps: restricting of their economic freedom, limiting their rights, prohibiting them from writing against Christianity, and proscribing their synagogues and law courts. Above all, Eisenmenger wants to point out to the Jews the folly and blasphemy of the beliefs and opinions expressed in their writings and the immorality of their laws, especially those laws determining behavior toward Gentiles. Indeed, the description Eisenmenger gives as he presents the fundamental beliefs and laws of the Jews leads one to the conclusion that Judaism is a combination of foolish beliefs and wicked laws. In the sphere of theology, he accuses the Jews of gross anthropomorphism and distortion of the divine attributes; in the ethical sphere he attacks them for condoning deceit, theft, and even murder of non-Jews. The question is how did Eisenmenger arrive at so darkly a negative picture of Judaism while quoting its sources unadulterately?

In order to understand Eisenmenger's method, we must first examine the nature of the Jewish sources and the exegetical system by which the Jewish community understood them.[7] In the course of its long history, the Jewish tradition adopted diverse methods in attempts to express the divine essence in a way that all could grasp: mythical images, metaphorical expressions, and anthropomorphic descriptions. Likewise, Israel and its relation to the nations were conceived sometimes in historical terms and at other times in legendary concepts. These elements stemmed both from the thought of individuals, on the one hand, and from popular creativity, on the other. The situation was not dissimilar with regard to the practical guidance, legal and ethical, to be found in Halakic literature. Opposing opinions are often presented on the same subjects, sometimes as a controversy between contemporaries and sometimes as the result of conflicts that came about with the change of conditions. After all, the Talmudic tradition is itself the result of a thousand-year development—from the Persian period in the fifth century B.C. to the end of the Roman Empire in the fifth century A.D. The whole corpus of this tradition was sanctified by later generations who ignored the difference between early and late or between that which was derived from the teaching of the sages and that which evolved from popular sources. That is not to say that every point in the tradition exerted an equal influence. In matters of law, a system of interpretation developed by which ancient disputes were resolved. Sometimes explicitly and at other times unconsciously, laws were rejected and views were abandoned if they clashed with positions that had meanwhile been formed. The formation of new positions was sometimes the product of internal development and sometimes the result of shifts in the position of the Jewish community. The Biblical and Talmudic Judaism that had developed in the ancient world had to adjust to the atmosphere of Medieval Europe. Unlike a people in its own land or a community living in provinces where Jews were the majority, as in Babylonia, the Jews in Europe found themselves a small minority dependent on the few occupations allocated to them. From a religious and cultural point of view, the environment had also changed: in the place of idolaters, the Jews found themselves opposite Christians and, later, Moslems, peoples believing in religions that had developed out of Judaism and subsequently broken away from it, competed with it, and at times combatted it. Both Christians and Moslems were, on the one hand, closer to Judaism than the ancient pagans had been, and, on the other, more inclined to be resentful toward it. The patterns of thought and behavior that had determined the relation of Judaism to the pagan did not meet the conditions of their new environment. And indeed, many laws that were practiced regarding pagans were allowed to lapse in relation to Christians and Moslems. Jews did business with Gentiles throughout the year, including the days of non-Jewish festivals. They borrowed from them and lent to them, employed them in every occupation — in contradistinction to the Mishnaic and Talmudic regulations that restricted these activities in order to keep the Jew away from anything that had to do with pagan ritual and to minimize his social contact with non-Jews.

Such transformation occurred also with regard to the place of the Jewish community vis-à-vis the peoples of the world. The classical view conceived the Jews as a separate nation absolutely different from the others. Israel and the nations appear as two worlds in confrontation, without distinction between nation and nation and different non-Jewish religions. However, this generalization retained its force only in theory. Faced with concrete problems in their relations with Christians and Moslems, the solution of which depended on the evaluation of their religion, Jews differentiated between them and the pagans. Nevertheless, the Bible and the Talmudic literature, ancient sources that lacked these distinctions, retained their standing and authority. At best they might be reinterpreted in the light of new conditions and concepts that had come into being.

For this reason, the study of the writings of the Jews alone could not reveal what part of the legal and intellectual tradition was valid for later generations. Indeed, many sections of their books and even entire chapters were no longer regarded as valid and binding—not literally, at any rate. Dialectic and homiletic exegesis enabled those who grew up on Jewish sources to maintain the sanctity of the entire tradition on principle, despite the astounding laws and bizarre legends that were included. The Mishnah and the Talmud did not serve as guides for the daily behavior of the Jews, but as books for study. For guidance in daily life, the Jew relied on what he had been taught by his parents and teachers and on recent legal codes that adapted the requirements of the law to contemporary conditions and dominant ethical views. In the matter of theoretical concepts, beliefs, and opinions, no binding principles were ever established, although there were certain dogmatic assumptions the violation of which was considered heresy. Within the constraints of those assumptions, the faithful were free to interpret the tradition themselves; indeed, preachers in every generation devoted unbounded energy to making the sources— even the most bizarre legends to be found in them—correspond to the demands of reason. One may conclude that in the realm of law and in the realm of doctrine alike, the Jewish sources were complemented by an institution that reconciled and adapted them—that is, the authority of exegete and preacher to discover in the writings of his predecessors that which seems to him to be the requirement of reality, the dictate of reason, and the obligation of pure faith.

The exegetical-homiletical method is the total opposite of the historical approach that tries to understand the sources in the light of the time and circumstances of their emergence. The historical approach consciously ignores whatever later generations read into the earlier sources, seeking only the original meaning intended by the writers. On the surface, Eisenmenger did likewise, casting aside the interpretations accepted by his contemporary Jews in his quest to reconstruct the world of Judaism by studying the sources themselves. In fact, Eisenmenger did not possess the slightest element of historic sensitivity; his way of thinking resembled the exegetical-homiletical pattern of the Jewish scholars from whom he learned. Only the assumptions on the basis of which each proceeded distinguished Eisenmenger from the Jewish scholars. The Jewish scholar of the seventeenth century accepted the opinions prevalent among the Jews regarding right and wrong, true and false, the permitted and the prohibited—and sought to justify those opinions in the sources; Eisenmenger accepted the opinions about Jews prevalent in the hostile Christian society and was guided by them in his study of the same sources. Since, according to the Christians, the Jews suffered from spiritual blindness and were incapable of seeing the truth of Christianity, any concept falsifying the divine essence could be legitimately attributed to them. Legends that describe God studying the Torah, wrapping himself in a prayer shawl, or wearing phylacteries—legends which the Jews who studied them understood perhaps as designed to exalt the commandments or perhaps as clues to hidden secrets, but never literally—served for Eisenmenger as proof of the grossly anthropomorphic view the Jews held of God.[8] Eisenmenger gathered legends of this type in order to prove the vulgarity of the Jewish concept of the divine. Other folk legends, such as fantasy stories of Rabbah bar bar Hana,[9] recognized by Jewish authorities as such ever since, are quoted in order to prove the worthlessness of the Talmud to which the Jews attribute religious authority close to that of the Bible. Five chapters are devoted to Jewish beliefs regarding the Messiah and to eschatology and resurrection.[10] All this is intended to prove that the Jews are ingrained with superstitions and illusionary conceptions.

However, Eisenmenger attacks Judaism principally for its attitude toward other religions and their adherents. The point of this attack is to show that the Jews are commanded by their religion to abuse that which is sacred to all other religions, and above all that which is sacred to Christianity.[11] The Jewish tradition prohibits robbery, deceit, and even murder only in relations between Jews, while the property and even the life of the Christian are as good as outlawed. If that is the tenor of the tradition into which Jews are initiated from childhood, one should not be surprised by their actual behavior should they be found abusing articles of Christian worship, that is, desecrating the host, or be caught in deceit, robbery, or even murder.[12]

The nature of the Jewish tradition, its earliest strata reflecting the conditions of the ancient world, enabled Eisenmenger to prove such theses. The legal and ethical systems of the ancient world were dualistic. They were intended primarily to regulate relations between members of the group—tribe, people, or community. The protection of the property and even the life of the stranger who was outside the group had to be determined by special amendment. Such amendments never achieved absolute universality. In the period of the Mishnah and Talmud, the question of whether the property of non-Jews was protected by law was still under dispute. Certain individuals who were considered subversive—idol worshippers and the like—remained outside the absolute protection of the law even in matters of life and death. Regarding some of them, the saying "Neither raising up nor lowering down" applied—that is, they were not to be killed, but they should not be helped when in danger. To others, the *minim* (sectarians, infidels), the applicable expression was "Lowering down but not raising up," that is—one should actively work toward their deaths.[13] According to the law, there was one people Jews were obligated to destroy: since the Torah says (Deut. 25:19) that Amalek's memory is to be blotted out, this blotting out was regarded as a positive commandment. In treating these issues, the later exegetical and homiletical literature generally did not draw conclusions relating to concrete conditions that faced contemporaries. They dealt with laws relating to these matters in the same way as with legal and other ritual problems whose true background was in the ancient world and were "at the present time" nothing more than theoretical material, or at best, a pretext for raising purely symbolic concepts. For example: blotting out the memory of Amalek finds a ritual men-

18

tion when the relevant portion of the Torah is read on the Sabbath nearest to Purim. The reason was that tradition identified the wicked Haman of the Book of Esther that tells the story of Purim with the seed of Amalek.[14]

What characterizes the method by which the Jewish tradition was adapted to new conditions is that the most far-reaching changes in the content of this tradition were achieved by leaning on its authority. The tradition was reinterpreted but never deprived of its force. As conditions changed—that is, as the Jews were transformed into a minority and the Gentiles abandoned idolatry—the exegetes reinterpreted the sources so as to modify, if not to eliminate totally, any double standard in law and morality. To be sure, Jewish teaching did not attain universality in law and morality; social conditions failed to provide the necessary motivation for that: the Ghetto Jew naturally felt a far greater moral duty to his Jewish brethren than to members of the surrounding society. At the same time, Jews were certainly not taught to see their Christian neighbors as either the descendents or the representatives of those ancient peoples and sects to whom the tradition assigned a low legal and moral stature.

But precisely this was Eisenmenger's point. He wanted to demonstrate that everything derogatory or discriminatory that appeared in the Jewish tradition regarding any people whatsoever was seen by the Jew as applicable to his Christian contemporaries. The Christians are identified with the *minim* of whom it had been said, "Lowering down, but not raising up"; with Amalek, whose memory the Jews are commanded to blot out; and even with the seven nations whom the conquerors of Biblical Canaan were commanded to destroy. In the future, in the Messianic age, the commandment of destruction would apply to all mankind save the Jews. As the Jews awaited their redeemer every day, it stood to reason that they would carry out the commandment of destruction even in the present on those whom it was within their reach to injure and harm.[15]

Eisenmenger's point of departure was the belief that the Jews were habitually robbing and murdering their Christian neighbors. He believed the tales of ritual murder, of the desecration of the host and the like, regardless of whether they stemmed from folklore or from medieval chroniclers who failed to distinguish between fact and fancy. He supported his belief with Jewish texts saying that the Jews were commanded by their religion to commit the very crimes he accused them of. In his attempt to make this point, Eisenmenger drives his interpretation to the height of absurdity. In every case where he found such expressions as "deserves death"—for example, "a Gentile who observes the Sabbath deserves death," "a Gentile who studies the Torah deserves death," he explained them as requiring a death penalty to be imposed by human hands, while in Talmudic usage such language is no more than a severe condemnation. (It is said regarding the Jew, "Whosoever violates the words of the sages deserves death.") Jewish scholars would also interpret metaphors and figures of speech literally whenever the conclusions to be drawn from such interpretations corresponded to their views.[16] What is unique about Eisenmenger is not his exegetical technique, but rather the assumptions that served as his point of departure. To anyone who is knowledgeable in traditional Jewish literature, Eisenmenger's interpretations read like a parody of both the legal and homiletic literature. He would recognize the mortar and the bricks of which a familiar structure is built, but he would find the various parts of the structure arranged and connected to each other so arbitrarily as to defy identification. It is otherwise, of course, for the reader who is unfamiliar with that literature: he may fall for Eisenmenger's conclusions, not knowing that they are no more than the very assumptions that preceded the writer's examination of the material. He may accept the image of the Jews as a community of superstitious fools, hostile to those around them and despising whatever is holy to their neighbors. Completely unscrupulous in their behavior toward the stranger outside their community, therefore they cheat and wrong those who have business contacts with them, and this they do by command of their religion. If they are brought to court, their oaths are not to be trusted because they regard lying under oath of little consequence when their fellow litigant is a non-Jew. Their loyalty to the state is no more than lip service; and, in fact, they violate the law with impunity and are willing to betray their king and serve his enemies as spies and secret agents. The Jew cannot even be trusted in matters of life and death, and Christians who take treatment from a Jewish doctor endanger their lives. Eisenmenger fully believed the reports, in Christian chronicles and folk tales alike, that many a child had died at Jewish hands in order to satisfy ritual needs. Eisenmenger tried to gain the reader's confidence by quoting chapter and verse demonstrating that the absolutely unethical behavior of the Jew derived from that decadent source of his religion, the Talmud and Rabbinical literature.[17]

Considering the extremism of Eisenmenger's theses, his practical recommendations appear remarkably moderate. As mentioned above, he sought to restrict the Jews, but he demanded neither their expulsion from Christian countries nor their physical annihilation. Here, too, he is faithful to Christian tradition, which asserts that the Jews may live among the Christians as a degraded and inferior class so that the faithful Christian may observe the fate of those who are guilty of deicide and who stubbornly refuse to accept the true religion. However, the primary reason for Eisenmenger's relative tolerance is that one should not give up the hope that the Jews will one day see the truth and acknowledge the Christian religion. Eisenmenger's arguments about the worthlessness of the Jewish religion were meant to help the Jews to realize the true nature of their religion and abandon it. Eisenmenger wanted, in particular, to dissuade them of their vain hope to return to their former greatness when the Messiah comes. Indeed, one of the reasons that Eisenmenger sought to worsen the degradation and suppression of the Jews was to make them feel the burden of their lowly position and to see that they had no salvation from it but through Christianity.[18]

In essence, Eisenmenger did not deviate from the generally accepted Christian position on the fate of the Jews, the reasons for their exile, and the purpose of their future existence. The unique point about his book is that he painted his image of the contemporary Jew in a broad spectrum, the many colors of which he took from the Jewish tradition. As mentioned above, Eisenmenger neither forged his sources nor pulled his accusations out of thin air. There was a nucleus of truth in all his claims: the Jews lived in a world of legendary or mythical concepts, of ethical duality—following different standards of morality in their internal and external relation-ships—and they dreamed with imaginative speculation of their future in the time of the Messiah. Similar claims, however, could have been made against the Christian as well. One critic, a Christian theologian himself, said rightly that using Eisenmenger's method, an *Entdecktes Christenthum* could have easily been written.[19] The fact is, however, that no such book was ever produced, and the picture of horror drawn from Judaism in Eisenmenger's book has no Christian parallel. That a Christian *Entdecktes* was not published is hardly an accident. Christianity, the majority religion and the royal religion in Europe, enjoyed governmental protection, and no book like Eisenmenger's could have been published in condemnation of it. Judaism, on the contrary, was the religion of an ostracized and defenseless minority, whose only protection was granted by the grace of kings or bought by the influence of some court Jew. Such doubtful props gave sup-port in one place only to fail in another. Though Eisenmenger could not get his book published under the patronage of Vienna, his heirs succeeded in doing so under the patronage of Berlin. The shaky political and social position of the Jews is directly related to the abuse of their religion, much as poverty follows the poor. Consequently, more remarkable than the ac-cusations against the Jews themselves, is the fact that these accusations did not lead to their proscription and expulsion from Christian countries. This inconsistency can be explained by the usual gap between ideology and practice. The same Frederick I of Prussia who allowed the publication of Eisenmenger's book, and whose opinions of both the religion of the Jews and their character were distinctly negative, tolerated them in his land for reasons of economic interest.[20] And, in fact, the ideologists themselves did not extend their ideas to the logical limit, as we have seen in the case of Eisenmenger. They practiced the principle of intellectual self-restraint: they said that the Jews were imbued with superstition and were morally corrupt, and maintained that nevertheless they ought to be left alone, and given a chance to repent and mend their evil ways. If the Jews carried the most negative traits, their corruption was a product of their faith, and upon the return of the Jews to the true Christian faith they would experience a moral reform. The Christian expectation for the "return of the Jews"—that is, the acceptance of Christianity by the Jews in the end of days, is an essential part of traditional Christian teaching. This expectation served as a kind of antidote, neutralizing the poison that was mixed into Christian theory about Judaism. For the sake of the future, contemporary Jewry was allowed to continue despite the negative appraisal the Christians gave it.[21] The condition of the Jews—and with it the condition of the society that surrounded them—was not defined as static. If Eisenmenger and his like saw contemporary Jews as wicked, they did not imagine that they would necessarily be that way in the days to come. They left open a gate of hope for the future while practicing relative tolerance in the present.

2 | The Rationalist Reorientation

JOHANN EISENMENGER'S *Entdektes Judentum* expresses ideas rooted in the medieval world, in which theology dominated thought and in which the affairs of the Jews—their law, character, and actions—were judged in the light of theology. Consequently, Eisenmenger's work might be considered a kind of aftergrowth, obsolete even in its own time, and that is precisely how it was viewed by critics in the generations of enlightenment and rationalism. For at the very time that Eisenmenger wrote his book—in the last two decades of the seventeenth century—a new, rationalistic way of thinking was already developing, and one of its tendencies was to subvert the fundamentals of theological thought and reject the conclusions based on it. In the period 1680-1715 this new approach made its breakthrough.[1] The primary characteristic of the rationalistic approach is the spirit of criticism, the willingness and the ability to examine natural and historical phenomena with detached human understanding. The buds of such an approach had been appearing ever since the Renaissance, and now they gathered strength and blossomed in the thought of such intellectual and moral giants as Fénelon, Bayle, and Toland. If, until that time, rationalist ideas had appeared only at random and by implication, compromising with theology and even merging with it, from then on they gathered strength, appearing continuously and explicitly, becoming the dominant way of thinking. As mentioned, rationalism sought to explain natural phenomena, the essence of man, human society and its development. At the same time, it confronted the earlier view of the world that had dominated the minds of men and found it to be the product of imagination and delusion.

23

Background, 1700-1780

The rationalist approach did not restrict itself to theoretical matters; it also sought to direct man toward control of nature and improvement of the conditions of life through social reform or even by building an entirely new society. And indeed, the world of man in Europe underwent continuous change, his physical world of technology, economics, society, and politics no less than his spiritual world—his thought patterns, the fundamentals of his religious faith, and his philosophical outlook.

The emancipation of Jews in their lands of residence is one of the social changes that characterizes the modern period. Many factors, economic, social, and political, contributed to this change, which effected a crucial transformation in the lives of the Jews; but the influence of these factors depended on a parallel transformation in the theoretical sphere. Changing the Jews from residents tolerated on the margins of society to citizens with full political rights was impossible so long as the traditional Christian concept of Judaism and its influence on its adherents remained dominant. Rationalism, by subverting Christian tradition, undermined the authority of Christianity to judge its rival, Judaism. Rationalism engendered faith in the possibility of shaping the character of the individual and the community. Even those who found fault with the Jews as they actually were, or as they were reflected in popular opinion, could believe in their reform in the future. Above all, rationalism gave rise to the concept of the secular state. Such a state ignores, theoretically at least, the religious affiliations of its citizens and consequently eliminated the primary obstacle in the path of Jewish citizenship.[2]

The rise of rationalism was, then, to the benefit of the Jews. Without it, the process of emancipation is inconceivable. However, from the beginning, emancipation aroused opponents who fought to delay, obstruct, or limit it, relying only partially on the authority of ancient Christian doctrine. This doctrine in its literal sense—in which the Jew was disparaged because of his sin, his rejection of Jesus the saviour—was being discredited by the enlightened; and the opponents of emancipation could hardly rely on it. Criticism of Christianity and its sources was of the very essence of rationalism, and even if not all the rationalists could be portrayed as outright atheists, a certain repudiation of Church dogma, at times explicit and striking, characterized this entire movement. The rejection of Christian dogmas could have removed a great obstacle to the recognition of Jews as equals in state and society. And indeed, as already mentioned, the invalidation of Christian doctrine was one of the central factors leading to a change in determining the status of Jews in the modern age.

But the rise of rationalism, which produced criticism of Christianity, was a dialectic process, and its influence on the evaluation of the Jews and Judaism was hardly unequivocal. For, when religious criticism sought to

24

destroy Christian tradition, it struck at Judaism in the process. Judaism was also a target of rationalism for two reasons. First of all, it was one of the religions whose sources, Biblical and even some of the Rabbinic literature, were known to the enlightened and attracted the attention of the critical eye. Judaism served as an example of the system of beliefs and opinions, as well as ceremonies and rituals, that the rationalists presented as a meaningless product of the age of ignorance. Moreover, Judaism was made an object of criticism by virtue of its connection with Christianity. This connection was manifest and well known. Christianity, although repudiating Judaism, could not ignore it and had to acknowledge it as the ground from which it itself had sprung. The Pentateuch and the books of the Prophets, the Old Testament, by the definition of the Church were cast into the shadows by the Gospel, the New Testament; but their authority was not entirely discredited nor was their sanctity denied. Consequently, the criticism of Christianity implied a similar criticism of Judaism. Thus, even if the critics sought only to defame Christianity, Judaism was inevitably blemished as well. Criticism of Judaism was to lead to criticism of the bearers of the religion, the Jewish community, which existed in a unique social and political situation.

Not everyone who examined Judaism found it at fault, nor did all those who found it at fault draw similar conclusions regarding the contemporary Jewish community. Their affairs were not yet a public concern in the first half of the eighteenth century. However, after a few generations, when the Jewish question arose, the criticism of Judaism was to be a mighty tool in the hands of those opposed to a change in the status of Jews. The essence of their argument was that the adherents of such an inferior religion would be out of place in a respectable society and an exemplary state. Thus, we can observe the dialectic result of religious criticism in relation to the Jews: On the one hand, the criticism of Christianity removed the justification of discrimination against the Jews on the grounds of Christian doctrine; on the other hand, it provided new weapons to the opponents of the Jews by casting aspersions on their own religious heritage.[3]

So, religious criticism in general and Biblical criticism in particular played a significant role in the formation of opinion regarding the Jews and Judaism. A sharp historical cleavage divides the Biblical world from the European. Many things said in the Bible strike the European as foreign in terms of custom, good taste, or morality. That Abraham turned his wife over to Pharaoh and to Abimelekh has always puzzled readers of the Bible; likewise the moral sense is confounded by the command "Thou shalt not let a soul remain alive" (Deut.20:16), stated in connection with the peoples of Canaan, and many similar passages. However, so long as the

Background, 1700-1780

Bible was regarded the sacred product of Divine revelation, the uneasiness was expressed in the form of questions to be resolved—and indeed Christian exegetes strove no less than Jewish to eliminate such reprehensibilities through exegetical methods. The questions and objections themselves were insufficient to divest the Bible of its absolute religious and moral authority. This authority was deeply ingrained in the dominant beliefs of both Judaism and Christianity, creating a closed system consisting of the belief in revelation, the sanctity of the Bible, and the immunity of the Bible from destructive criticism.[4]

The various links of the system sustained and reinforced each other so long as they remained valid, but they all crumbled at once when the spirit of rationalist criticism began to gnaw at their roots. Explicitly since the days of Spinoza and implicitly even earlier, denial of revelation appeared together with historical criticism, that is, skepticism regarding the reliability of the facts the Bible relates. Once the denial of revelation and historical criticism became effective, free rein was given to doubt and ridicule of the world of values presented in the Bible.[5]

The loss of confidence in the reliability of Biblical tradition changed the basic attitude toward it. One could now dig into the books of the Bible, try to estimate the dates of their composition, to explain the development of Biblical laws and customs, and to pass moral judgment on Biblical personalities and their actions.[6] All this was done with naive audacity, with total confidence in the power of common sense—in short, without epistemological and methodological criticism of the criticism, which is fundamental to the scientific approach to history. Confidence in the powers of judgment of whoever dared to use logic is the outstanding trademark of early rationalism. The result of this self-confidence was that criticism did not spare the books of the Bible neither on account of their sanctity, which no longer existed so far as the critics were concerned, nor because of their age, which might have limited the critics' understanding and judgment of the world of generations long passed.

Not everyone who examined the Biblical world from a rationalist point of view arrived at a negative conclusion. On the contrary, some presented Biblical laws and teachings as an example that could guide later generations in shaping their world, offering guidance to both the individual and the society. In the sixteenth century, Jean Bodin, one of the first precursors of the rationalist movement, presented Judaism, that is, the law of the Old Testament, as religious legislation par excellence.[7] Spinoza took an ambivalent position. He saw the original Biblical legislation as the reason for the happiness of the people in its earlier period—until the interference of the Prophets who arrogated to themselves undeserved authority.[8] During the incipient stage of rationalism, John Toland expressed an unequivocally positive view of Judaism. Toland glorified ancient Judaism as a system of beliefs and a social and political way of life, clearly for the sake of deprecating its rival, Christianity.[9]

Toland was one of the writers and philosophers, known as Deists, who left their mark on the intellectual life of England and France during the seventeenth and eighteenth centuries. The name signifies the faith in God that these thinkers held and that they claimed was demanded by human reason and logic. On the basis of this positive article of faith, they launched an attack against Christian religious tradition for basing its principles, its ritual, and its institutions on the alleged revelation of God to mankind.[10] Those who shared this basic opinion were hardly in agreement regarding the conclusions to be derived from it. Some did not dismiss revelation altogether, but asserted that it could reveal nothing that could not be discovered eventually by the human intellect. Consequently, anything in religious tradition that did not agree with reason could not be the product of revelation, but only a human invention, the addition of priests in an age of ignorance long since passed. Others attributed the very concept of revelation and the testimony of it in the Bible to mendacious writers who did not distinguish between fantasy and reality.[11]

These ideas were new and daring, and the fact that they could be published testifies to the measure of tolerance in England. The Deists came from different elements of English society: John Toland was a wandering writer and political publicist; the earl of Shaftesbury, an active statesman of the upper aristocracy; Anthony Collins, a property owner and justice of the peace; Thomas Woolston, a cleric and fellow of a Cambridge college; Matthew Tindal, a lawyer; Thomas Chubb, a craftsman; Peter Annet, a schoolmaster; Henry St. John, Viscount Bolingbroke, a statesman and political thinker.[12] These did not constitute a united social movement and only a few of them even knew one another; they rarely referred to each other in their writings. What united them is the aggressively skeptical spirit revealed in their books, which in turn aroused the powerful reaction of the guardians of Christian tradition and the Church, occasionally to the point of penalizing those, such as Woolston and Annet, who held heretical opinions. Generally, however, the clash was only verbal, and the charges and countercharges were batted back and forth repeatedly by both sides.

The Deist writers called into question the details of Biblical and Christian tradition: their queries derived from the laws of nature that deny the possibility of miracles described in Scripture, from the contradictions in the narratives themselves, and from the demands of morality that would not countenance attributing to God commandments that could not be accepted by reason or setting up those who acted upon them as an example to be followed by later generations.[13] As already mentioned, these authors directed their criticism at the Christian tradition, and when Jews were mentioned, the reference was to Biblical Israel. Some Deists used the Jewish denial of Christian truth as a justification of their charges. Thomas Woolston puts the mockery of Jesus' miracles in the mouth of a Jewish rabbi, who, as it were, discusses these matters with him in a spirit of friendship and agreement.[14] Peter Annet used a similar literary device for a clear reason: the Jew had no obligation to the founder of Christianity and could make statements for which a Christian would undoubtedly have been penalized.[15] Still, on examining the history of Jewish tradition and ritual, the rationalists were able to conjure up a most unfavorable picture of Judaism.

Even in the Middle Ages, both Jewish and Christian scholars would inquire into the source of a custom, whether it was ancient, and whether it had been adopted from another people and had received the approval of the Divine Legislator ex post facto.[16] But the primary issue for medieval thinkers was to clarify the validity of the laws and to discover their meaning. As the sanctity of the Bible was eroded, the questions of validity and meaning were replaced by an interest in the historical background of the Bible, the origin of customs, and their similarity to the rituals of other peoples from whom the Jews learned, or conversely, whom they taught. The Deists tended to see the Jews as students of other peoples: both Shaftesbury and Collins claimed that Abraham learned circumcision from the Egyptians.[17] Thomas Morgan declared: "that this People, during their long stay in Egypt, for six or seven successive generations, had been perfectly Egyptianized."[18] Henceforth, the legislator could only treat them according to their intrinsic nature. They were by character Egyptian. Thus, the Israelites had been given laws and commandments that had their source in the customs of the ignorant Egyptians.[19]

These assertions were not originally intended to do more than reject the divine origins of the Jewish religion, but they inevitably aroused abuse for the adherents of that religion, the Jewish people. The Deist deliberations on morality, the source of man's aspirations to do good and his hatred of evil, cast a dark shadow over Biblical Judaism. Shaftesbury, the leading spokesman in this field, developed a theory of the innate moral sense that guides man in his relations with his fellow man.[20] Other Deists, although they did not accept Shaftesbury's theory, taught that man did not need religion in order to lead a moral life, that he could do right by virtue of his own reason and understanding. This basic assumption of man's ethical autonomy brought into question the entire religious tradition. For if man's morality does not depend on his adherence to religious dictates, the religious guise that Jewish and Christian tradition gives to moral imperatives is superfluous: it is, in fact, unsolicited religious interference. Moreover, the commandments found in religious tradition were now reexamined in the light of autonomous morality, and many of the details were found faulty. Joshua's war of annihilation against the peoples of Canaan—in accordance with a divine command to Moses—had been justified in Jewish and Christian traditions, both of which denied idolatrous peoples the right to exist. Joshua served as an example for Cromwell and his soldiers in the war against the Irish and for the white settlers in America in their struggle with the Indians. But Shaftesbury, on the basis of his theory of the innate moral sense of man, censured what was done in the name of a divine command:

> Notwithstanding the pious Endeavours which, as devout Christians, we may have us'd in order to separate ourselves from the Interests of mere *Heathens*, and *Infidels*; notwithstanding the true pains we may have taken, to arm our Hearts in behalf of a *chosen People*, against their neighbouring Nations, of a false Religion, and Worship; there will be still found such a Partiality remaining in us, towards Creatures of the same Make and Figure with our-selves, as will hinder us from viewing with Satisfaction the Punishments inflicted by human Hands on such *Aliens* and *Idolaters*.[21]

Likewise, the ethical sense would not accept the Israelites' despoiling of the Egyptians[22] or regard King David as God's chosen in disregard of his immoral actions.[23] David had already been the target of Pierre Bayle's harsh criticism, which evoked a polemic of its own.[24] This subject retained its attraction, and fifty years after Shaftesbury's critical remarks, in 1761, Peter Annet devoted an entire book to *The Life of David, the History of the Man after God's Own Heart*. An English writer, eulogizing King George II, had likened him to the Biblical king, and Annet claimed that it was offensive to compare the English king to one who took the wife of another man, sent the husband to die, and took vengeance on his enemies even after his death.[25]

Similar criticism appeared repeatedly in the writings of most Deists, and their purpose was to prove that the Bible could not be regarded as revelation because the morality found in it conflicted with the qualities of the beneficent God whose existence was required by human reason. Could God have commanded human sacrifice as Jephthah and even Abraham believed? Indeed, the latter did not in the end have to slaughter his son, but he did not rebel against such a commandment.[26] The conclusion is that the generations of the Bible were steeped in ignorance, and, far from serving as an example for the future, they should be pilloried and their influence should be removed.

Overtly, the struggle of the Deists was directed against Christianity, the tradition and ritual of which, at least as preached by its official representatives, repelled the Deists' spirit. Judaism came under attack simply because its lowest stratum, Biblical literature, was also the basis of Christianity. At the same time, while Christian tradition itself ascribed an inferior status to the Old Testament as opposed to the New, this discrimination was also adopted by the Deists. So long as the issue was one of accepting the literal sense of Scripture or the dogmatic traditions of the Church, the New Testament and the Old received the same judgment at the hands of the Deists: total rejection because of their irrationality. However, the Deists took the liberty of interpreting the sources independently, and the right to do so is one of the central issues of their struggle. Thomas Woolston, for example, sought to rescue Christianity by giving allegorical interpretations to stories, laws, and teachings which, if taken literally, contradicted the laws of nature or the rules of logic.[27] Matthew Tindal and Thomas Morgan made the distinction between essential and accidental, contending that there exists an uncontestable Christian doctrine, but that everything that opposed nature and reason was the product of external influence, Judaism being the first and foremost source of such external influence. Tindal granted Christianity preference over Judaism, even from the point of view of time, as suggested by the title of his book: *Christianity as Old as Creation*. Christianity was the religion implanted in the heart of man by nature, and Judaism a deviation toward superstition, enslavement to ritual, and submission to the yoke of priests who exploit the weak-mindedness of the believers.[28] Morgan's theory is also suggested in the title of his work, *The Moral Philosopher*, in which he identifies Christianity with the ethical dictates required by human nature. Biblical literature, its characters, teachings, and laws, appear to him totally to contradict true Christianity. The addition of the Old Testament to the New, even if the former is given an inferior status, is a distortion of Christian teaching which diverts Christianity from its original purity. Therefore, the link between the Old Testament and the New should be broken and the traces of Jewish influence on Christianity should be erased.[29]

Because of Morgan's consistent position on this question, some historians see him as a sort of spiritual descendant of Marcion, the second-century sage who also sought to separate Christianity thoroughly from Jewish tradition, and who was consequently regarded by Christians as a heretic.[30] However, Marcion, after eliminating Judaism, retained a revealed religion, while Morgan identified Christianity with natural religion, which he made the cornerstone of an autonomous morality. Morgan, like Tindal, wanted to adhere to natural religion without giving up the name of Christian. In a dialogue his own views are expressed by the "Christian Deist," and the opposing view by a "Jewish Christian."[31] This pattern serves as an example of the perpetuation of the Jewish-Christian conflict in the sphere of rationalism: all that is good and beautiful is attributed to

Christian origins and whatever is evil or ugly is attributed to Jewish origins. This tendency appears here in the context of an internal Christian polemic. The Jew described is an abstract creation, based on elements of literary tradition. There is no indication that Tindal or Morgan intended to ascribe their abusive descriptions of Judaism to contemporary Jews, who were not at all involved in the subject under discussion. The Deistic system did not influence Christian public opinion of Jews; its importance is that it revealed a possibility that was to come to fruition later, under circumstances different from those of mid-eighteenth-century England.

During this period, in 1753, the Jewish question became a public issue in England, but its treatment did not transcend traditional patterns. The arguments that surfaced in Deistic discourses and could have assisted the opponents of the Jews, were either unknown to them or ignored—as if they did not even exist.

Jews had begun to return to England—after their expulsion at the end of the thirteenth century—in the mid-seventeenth century. Approximately eight thousand lived there in the mid-eighteenth century, of whom some were immigrants from the continent and others were born in England. The latter were regarded as subjects of the king, but their religion prohibited them from serving in public office, which was open only to those who could take the Anglican "Oath of Allegiance." Foreign-born Jews suffered economic restrictions as well. They were allowed neither to buy land nor to be partners in the ownership of English vessels on which colonial trade depended. Wealthy Jewish merchants, some of whom were close to the Whig Prime Minister Henry Pelham, sought to correct this situation through the Naturalization Bill, which entitled a Jew to English citizenship by parliamentary decree. Obtaining such a decree—a separate act of legislation in each case—was a lengthy and expensive procedure from which only a few wealthy and influential Jews could benefit. Nevertheless, this step encountered fierce public opposition, and the government was compelled to reverse its position and repeal the law.[32]

Modern research has demonstrated that the outcry against the Naturalization Bill was not spontaneous. It occurred at the time of parliamentary elections when the Tory opposition was doing everything it could to smear the government and bring it down. Consequently, the conclusion has been drawn that the success of the opposition cannot be taken as proof of the existence of anti-Semitism in England. Thomas Whipple Perry takes this position in the detailed book in which he describes the affair with the skill of a competent political historian.[33] And indeed, if anti-Semitism is taken to mean active social hostility against the Jews, the events of 1753 do not prove its existence. But prejudice against Jews must have been widespread, since without it the political propaganda could

31

not have provoked the populace and terrified them with the threat of a Jewish takeover.

The question that must be asked is, What is the nature of the propaganda that found an echo in the hearts of the English public in 1753? Was it a remnant of medieval images or did it bear the marks of the ideas being developed in rationalist and Deist writings? The answer is unequivocal: anti-Jewish propaganda in 1753 was nourished by Christian tradition; only on the margins of the polemic, in remarks by a few participants, was there evidence of the Deistic criticism of Judaism.[34] Most of the critics of the Naturalization Bill upheld the theological concept that the Jews were doomed to degradation, to be a people wandering among the nations, and it was not fitting for the government of a Christian state to treat them kindly, increase their number, or extend their rights. Others warned against the losses that the Christian populace would incur from contact with Jewish merchants, who were regarded as faithless and dishonest.[35] But few of these critics relied on personal experience of having been deceived by Jews in business dealings.[36] Most of them gave no indication that they had ever known a Jew personally; they spoke on the basis of the patterns and stereotypes found in Christian anti-Jewish literature. Some foresaw or pretended to foresee a dismal prospect for England when the Jews would multiply, take over the country's institutions, and Judaize its inhabitants voluntarily or involuntarily.[37] This is much the same as the arguments set forth by Eisenmenger. His book was not known in England, but its content was no more than an expansion of the Christian accusations whose basic tenets were well known to anyone familiar with Christian tradition. Propagandists who held to this tradition did not lack arguments against the Jews, and they could expect a favorable response from the English public.

Traces of the Deistic trend can be found, as I said, only on the margins of the polemic literature of 1753. Some polemicists mention Deists and Jews in the same breath, regarding both as deniers of Jesus.[38] Others express the fear that the presence of Jews will only increase the number of Deists and atheists.[39] Still others scoff at both these arguments; one even states explicitly that among the opponents of the Jews there are Deists, who show no disdain for the Christian arguments heard in the general community.[40] Only one polemicist, the pseudonymous Philo Patriae, made use of a Deistic criticism of Judaism, and he was the most consistent and conscientious defender of the Jewish position and most probably himself a Jew.[41] In contrast to those critics who attributed the immorality of the Jews to their religion, Philo Patriae contended that one must admit that "the Jewish religion teaches a true system of morality, for it is inconsistent with the Deity to have given improper commands at any time."[42] And the writer concludes, "The denying of morality in the Jewish Religion is weakening the proofs of the Christian faith, and leaving room for triumph to the Deists."[43] This is an explicit reference to the rationalist way of thinking, used however, not to indict the Jews, but, on the contrary, to defend them.

G. M. Trevelyan expressed the hypothesis that the discontinuity of Jewish settlement in England as a result of the medieval expulsion prevented antagonism from developing against them in the period of decisive economic development. During the absence of the Jews from England, a culture of Bible-reading developed that mollified the religious hatred for the chosen people.[44] Herbert Schöffler went further, presenting the thesis that the absence of Jews from England made possible the absorption of the Old Testament into English culture in the sixteenth and seventeenth centuries. The figures of the Old Testament were not identified with contemporary Jews and thus there was nothing to prevent the English from identifying with them.[45] If this explanation is correct—and even if it cannot be directly substantiated, it has an appealing simplicity—it could shed light on the phenomenon we have encountered: even when times changed and the Old Testament became the object of Deist criticism, the critics did not feel that they were thereby criticizing the Jews of their time. It is a fact that criticism of the Bible by the Deists was not accompanied by hostile expressions toward the Jews and found no place in contemporary anti-Jewish propaganda. It had to be removed from its original context, given pungency, and directed toward a concrete target. The Deist doctrine underwent this process in the translation from the English version to the French; the primary translator and transformer was Voltaire, whose role in the development of modern anti-Semitism deserves a chapter unto itself.[46]

3|Voltaire

VOLTAIRE DID MORE than any other single man to shape the rationalistic trend that moved European society toward improving the status of the Jews.[1] Voltaire was, by his own definition, a Deist. He continued to develop the Deistic trend of thought where his English predecessors had left off. His vigorous effort to undermine the authority of the Church and to make tolerance prevail in matters of opinion and belief was nourished by his Deistic outlook; that effort began in the early 1750s, when the Deist movement in England was unmistakably declining. Until that time Voltaire had wished to excel only as a writer, philosopher, and historian. From then on, he saw his principal role in the public struggle for religious tolerance.[2] Voltaire lived in England from 1726 to 1731, and the contact he had with several Deist leaders reinforced his reservations about the teachings of the Church and Christianity. Voltaire had already developed a rationalistic world view,[3] although he did not arrive at his practical conclusions for social reforms based on rationalism until two decades later, when he was in his mid-fifties. Perversions of justice stemming from intolerance—the most famous being the death sentence on the Protestant Calas in Toulouse, who was suspected of murdering his son because the latter allegedly planned to convert to Roman Catholicism—roused Voltaire to depart from his passive course. He also felt that the Church's restriction on freedom of thought was too heavy a burden for the citizens of France to bear indefinitely, and that the time had come to take action. Therefore, Voltaire began to wage total war against what had been the founding principle of society and state—that is, the faith, ceremonies, and ritual of

Voltaire

Roman Catholicism. In articles, letters, and poetry, and in the *Encyclopédie* published from 1751 to 1772 by d'Alembert and Diderot, two of the leading rationalists of the time, Voltaire ridiculed the stories of the Bible and the Gospel. The customs of earlier generations seemed absurd to the enlightened mind of the eighteenth century. The religious commandments and laws were deemed meaningless, and even contrary to accepted morality. And worst of all were the miracles in which, according to dogma, the faithful had to believe literally.

This work of Voltaire's was not innovative in content. He quoted the English Deists extensively, not so much to give credit to the originators of an idea, as to give his arguments the added authority of such writers and thinkers as Toland, Shaftesbury, and Bolingbroke, who at that time were more highly respected than he.[4] Voltaire wanted to show that in England, which was regarded by many of the enlightened in France as the free state par excellence, anyone could criticize the accepted principles of faith without personal risk. In fact, Voltaire and the other French philosophes were more critical of Christianity than their English colleagues. Moreover, the French went further than the English in their social aspirations. There is no indication that the English sought to uproot the foundations of the Church. Their intentions leaned more to the theological: to achieve the right to interpret the Christian tradition in a radically rationalistic manner or to disregard it entirely and to base their ethical system on a secular footing. The French writers, and above all Voltaire, were militant thinkers raising their voices in a battle cry against a regime that was founded on principles of deceit. Voltaire's slogan "Ecraser l'infame," whatever its precise meaning,[5] is a call to the community of the enlightened to do away with prejudices and to uproot superstitions, and these terms included anything not consistent with common sense.

The French went further than the English in one more respect: they expanded the use of intellectual criticism. The rationalistic system of thought had made great strides during the first half of the eighteenth century, and the many trends of that development converged in Voltaire's brilliant mind. Others paved the way for him, but he is the one who gave historical writing a new basis.[6] Voltaire reached a new understanding of social dynamics and of the alternating ascent and descent of cultural creativity. This versatile writer is also regarded as one of the first ethnologists or anthropologists by virtue of his efforts to explain the cultural traits of tribes and peoples as natural phenomena that operate according to certain definable laws. Voltaire also took this anthropological approach in dealing with the history of nations, including that of Biblical Israel and the Jews of the Middle Ages and later generations. Christian historians looked at Jewish history from a theological point of view, with faith in the prov-

35

idential nature of the Jews, who had at first fulfilled a divine mission and ultimately suffered their punishment for rebellion and betrayal of their role. The criticism of the earliest Deists undermined this faith, thus destroying the basis for the theological explanation of the history of Israel and its destiny. For want of another explanation, writers who had abandoned the faith on which the traditional concepts were based continued to use the accepted clichés. This conglomeration of theological-religious language and rationalistic criticism is to be found even in the writings of Spinoza and recurs in the writings of most of the English Deists. Voltaire, however, uses the language of theologians only tongue-in-cheek, as will be demonstrated below. He himself is not in need of this crutch. He explains the phenomena of Jewish history, ancient or modern, in the same way that he explains human history in general: by inquiring into the nature of human societies and their variations. In Voltaire's teaching, rationalism became dialectic: with one hand, the rationalists erased the Christian tradition that had previously explained Jewish existence and given it the status of a divinely forsaken community; with the other they created a system of concepts suitable for characterizing Jews as despicable by their very nature.

Voltaire employed the same realistic terminology to reevaluate Judaism as he used in his general historiography. The nature, source, and significance of this terminology deserves consideration. The buds of a new study of human society, which we call ethnology or anthropology, first appeared during the Renaissance. With the discovery of America, the Far East, and Africa, the horizon of Europeans widened, as they were introduced to innumerable tribes and peoples that lived by cultural patterns totally different from those known in Europe until that time.[7] The variety of cultural patterns found in the world, as revealed by travelers and missionaries, aroused doubts as to whether all the peoples of the world had evolved from one source, as held by Biblical tradition. Furthermore, even had man derived from a common origin, he had become variegated under the influence of environment and time. When confidence in accepted explanations was undermined, new questions arose: What forces had shaped society and culture? What transformations had taken place? What factors were involved in such changes and transformations? The explanations given for these phenomena did not rest, of course, on scientific method, and for the most part they were no more than assumptions and guesses. The courage of writers and thinkers in using uninhibited speculations characterizes, for better or worse, the first generations of the Enlightenment.

The enterprise of describing the characteristics of societies and cultures in order to understand their formation reached its height in Voltaire's writings. His book *Essai sur les moeurs et l'esprit des nations* is an attempt to expose the basic characteristics of the European peoples by tracing their evolution while ignoring the details of their history. In this enterprise, as in his other historical works, Voltaire used various principles of analysis without methodically examining their nature and validity. He was aware that the results of earlier stages could be seen in subsequent stages, and thus when he describes the history of the peoples of Europe, he first turns backward and sketches the histories of China, India, Persia, and the Arab countries. Generalizing, he establishes that physical and moral causes influence the formation of the character of all peoples.[8] Simultaneously, he used such terms as *l'esprit des nations* and *l'esprit du temps* in order to demonstrate that the cultural patterns, laws, and customs of a particular period constitute an integrated, self-explanatory system. The common denominator of all these basic concepts is that they serve to explain historical phenomena naturally, without reference to the supernatural explanations of Christian tradition which were accepted at face value by previous generations, including that of Voltaire's youth. The new historical perception cast aside the idea of Providence; it rejected the assumption that the Jewish people were destined to play a special role in guiding mankind, which role the Catholic Church, in its theology, claimed to have taken over. Not only were these theological premises disqualified as tools for understanding history, but they also were conceived as outmoded fundamentals of the "spirit of the times" of past eras.[9] When Voltaire, in his militant years, fought to uproot dogma and subvert Church rule, one of his principal weapons was the new historical perception. Indeed, this perception was supposed to provide a natural explanation for what was considered until then the product of divine inspiration. The history of the Jewish people, the bearer of revelation until the coming of Jesus, and the history of the Church thereafter were presented as a part of human history—to be understood and explained by the same criteria as the general history of mankind. Jewish history, in any case, gained attention in Voltaire's descriptions as the history of a people of antiquity. However, the fact that the Jewish people were the source of the Christian faith that he despised heightened his interest in the history of Israel but diminished at the same time his ability to approach it calmly and objectively.

Outwardly, Voltaire pretended to adhere to the revealed nature of the Bible as required by the dominant Church. In the numerous articles he wrote about the Bible, expressing historical and moral criticism in the style of the Deists, he repeatedly declared, either at the beginning or end of each article, that as a Christian he was obliged to believe literally in the revealed writings.[10] He pretended to bow his head in reverence before the divine wisdom, which could alter the laws of nature or perform acts incredible by human criteria. However, as a historian, Voltaire declared his right to judge matter according to his own light: to verify the truth factually and to evaluate actions morally. In this way Voltaire saved himself from the accusation of heresy and saved his books from the omnipresent eye of the censor. At the same time, Voltaire gave a hint of his real opinion on the historical reliability of Biblical stories and the moral level that prevailed in the sacred book on which Church authority rested.

In fact, all of Voltaire's historical work is a polemic with Christianity, even when it deals with topics far removed from the Biblical world or from Jewish or ecclesiastical history. When he considers China and finds there only quiet, tranquility, and the highest morality, his critical stance is unmistakable: he wants to demonstrate that it represents a people of happy destiny because it built its worlds on belief in a supreme power—like that of the Deists—but without reference to irrational dogma or meaningless ritual.[11]

In Voltaire's day, modern historiography was still in its earliest stage: the crystallization of its basic categories and the development of its critical tools emerged alongside implicit philosophical and social trends. Voltaire's historical view of the world in general and his description of Judaism in particular are by-products of the philosophical and public controversy in which he was involved. The historiographer had only begun to forge the instruments of his craft; he had not yet reached a respectable degree of objectivity.

Voltaire reveals his subjectivity, in fact his arbitrariness, even in his evaluation of historical evidence, finding some sources reliable and others specious. On the issue of the formation of the Jewish people, he shows a preference for the testimony of Greek and Roman historians over the Biblical account of Jewish tradition. Originally, the Israelites were a nomadic Arab tribe living in the Sinai Desert; if they were in Egypt at all, they were expelled because of leprosy, as recorded by Apion, Tacitus, and others. The patriarchs, Abraham, Isaac, Jacob, and perhaps even Moses, never lived at all. Voltaire finds countless contradictions in the Biblical account of their history and abundant occasions to scoff at the deeds attributed to them. Many of the stories produce an ethical revulsion in the enlightened scholar. Abraham turns over his wife to the Pharaoh for money, acts cruelly towards his son Ishmael, and is willing to sacrifice his son Isaac like the barbaric peoples who practice human sacrifice. Moses orders the execution of a multitude because of the golden calf; there is the revolt of Korah and the affair of the Midianite women. The conquerers of Canaan perpetuated his cruelty: they also deceived the Gibeonites, much as their ancestor deceived his brother Esau, his own father Isaac, and his father-in-law Laban.[12]

Voltaire

The actions of Biblical characters, regardless of whether their historical existence is in doubt or not, were not considered by Voltaire for their own sake but in order to exemplify the low ethical level of the people whose imagination created them or among whom they lived. Voltaire was well-versed in the Biblical scholarship that had been developed in the generations before him, just as he knew Christian exegesis and theology. However, he lacked a precise method of research that might have enabled him to arrive at definite and well-founded conclusions. In fact, he took most of his statements and theories from his predecessors, especially the English Deists, without always trying to resolve differences between them. Occasionally, he even made contradictory statements in establishing facts or verifying hypotheses.[13] His primary interest was less in seeking factual truth than in describing the dominant morals and opinions of the Biblical period to represent the spirit of the Jewish nation. Having portrayed the spiritual image of the nation, he felt free to judge them by the rationalist ideas he advocated.

The evaluation was made on the basis of various criteria. The first was that of morality. On the surface, recognition of differing conducts and changing morals is part of Voltaire's historical method. Nonetheless, Voltaire did not fail to define an ethical norm binding for all generations; when he found historical figures who did not meet that norm, he judged them harshly. He finds the generations of the Bible guilty not only of cruelty and deceit, but also of sexual promiscuity, upon which he frowned sternly. He disapproved of the polygamy of the patriarchs and the kings, and even judged Ruth's conduct, in trying to ensure that Boaz would marry her as next-of-kin, by eighteenth-century standards "which may be no purer, but are at least more decent."[14]

The second criterion for evaluating the acts of past generations was reasonableness: Did those generations determine their way of life by reason or by superstition? To Voltaire, superstition applies to any ceremonial or ritual act that serves no clear purpose and is done only to appease God according to the anthropomorphic perception. God would not command man to perform meaningless acts. The very concept of a God that commands ritual acts, such as sacrifices, circumcision, and the Sabbath, and prescribes penalties as severe as capital punishment for their violation, is an offense and an abomination to the Deistic God, who was removed from the world of human action. Needless to say, by this criterion, Biblical figures appear to be sunk in the deepest depths of superstition. Voltaire heaps ridicule on Biblical commandments and pro-hibitions: the ritual of sacrifice, public ceremonies, and individual duties. The ritual acts that really are a part of the Jewish religion do not suffice: following Deistic scholars who preceded him, he includes human sacrifices, insisting that it was one of the rituals practiced in Biblical times.[15]

Voltaire's third criterion is scientific and cultural productivity. Just as Voltaire dismisses the value of practical religion in the life of a people, he attributes the highest value to art, literature, science, and technology, that is, to everything that gives man power over nature or improves his life by giving it an added aesthetic dimension, elegance, or beauty. He ranks the peoples of antiquity by their accomplishments in these areas. He praises the Chinese for the technical inventions that advanced agriculture, enabling the creation of great cities in their country. He celebrates the Greeks for their artistic creativity during the Golden Age. He glorifies the Hellenism of Alexandria for its advances in science and technology. In the history of the Jewish people, Voltaire finds almost no contributions of this kind; and when he does, he attributes them to the influence of surrounding peoples. The Israelites of the Biblical period were neither artists nor artisans. Did not Solomon rely on Hiram of Tyre to build the Temple? Does not the Book of Samuel record that those dwelling in the mountains lacked even the simplest iron implements with which to make a plow? The Israelites were no more than nomadic shepherds, or at best the most primitive of farmers. They showed no trace of scientific awareness of the laws of nature: instead, they believed in a divine source for phenomena like rain and the rainbow. The role of the doctor who is familiar with the body of man and the cause of his illness was filled by priest or prophet—those ready to take advantage of man's weakness to reinforce his faith in their own supernatural power.[16]

The final criterion by which Voltaire evaluated peoples and cultures was political: the ability to sustain a proper political system. Voltaire is not considered a systematic political thinker: he had only a secondary interest in the problems of state and government.[17] Nevertheless, he took note of the ability of peoples to create order by authority and law and to withstand external attacks on the commonwealth, and he regarded the absence of this capability as a defect in a nation's character. The exile of the Jews twice from their land was clear evidence that they lacked the qualities necessary for sustaining a state. The Jewish army was never well-organized or well-trained. The commanders knew little strategy, and the soldiers showed little courage. In essence, the Jews always leaned toward trade and money-lending, occupations that required far different qualities than those of the soldier or statesman.[18]

Voltaire seeks to prove the Jews' lack of political talent by reference to the beliefs of Biblical Judaism. He accepted the prevailing view of Christian scholars that the Old Testament knew nothing of immortality; and, much to our surprise, he regards that as a serious flaw. Hardly an avid believer in immortality himself, Voltaire did share the Deistic belief in God, but was agnostic toward the metaphysical principles of faith, finding them possibly true, possibly false, and certainly unprovable. The reasons for his zeal for the belief in immortality were practical rather than theoretical. According to Voltaire and most eighteenth-century thinkers, the only thing that keeps man within the bounds of morality is his belief in reward and punishment after death. Philosophers may doubt the truth of this belief and remain devoted to justice and right, but society as a whole needs the belief in divine retribution to supplement the deterrent effect of human institutions of law and order.[19] Indeed, Voltaire assumed he would find this principle of faith in the traditions of every ancient people except the Jews. Yet, they had had the opportunity to learn this important concept from the Egyptians, much as they had adopted other teachings and customs of no value.[20] The Jews, as Voltaire saw it, were impervious to that which was essential for political existence on a theoretical plane, in the same way that they were incapable of meeting the physical preconditions for the maintenance of the state.

The image of the Jews that arises from Voltaire's description of Biblical times is that of a people inferior from every point of view: culturally, religiously, ethically, socially, and politically. This venomous description, which recurs very frequently in the writings of a man considered the greatest of all rationalistic authors and philosophers of the eighteenth century, had a decisive influence on the attitudes of the enlightened toward the Jews and Judaism. Most of what Voltaire says about Judaism ostensibly relates to the people, religious rites, and customs of the Biblical era. However, he clearly does not focus just on that period. His historical illustrations describe the people and events of the Second Temple era and sporadically survey the history of the Jews in their wanderings, up to his own time.[21] His judgments, religious, cultural, and ethical, hardly distinguish one period from another. This attitude devolves primarily from the ethnographic tendency of his history, which saw as the purpose of historical research the discovery of the identifying characteristics of each people. Voltaire does not deny that changes do occur in the life, religion, and culture of nations. However, the guiding principle of his research is to discover the marked, abiding, and stable traits of every people rather than to trace their development (this, in fact, was an historical method created some generations after his time). Consequently, the people of Israel are conceived as one historical entity whose primary characteristics are permanent despite wanderings and dispersions throughout the ages.

Voltaire does not ignore the effect of time, and if his purpose demands it, he distinguishes between earlier generations and later ones. In an essay written in 1761 as a sermon on behalf of religious tolerance, condemning the Inquisition then active against Conversos in Portugal,

Voltaire has a Rabbi from Smyrna say: "Our enemies regard us as guilty of robbing the Egyptians, of slaughtering several small nations in the towns we besieged, of being base usurers, of offering human sacrifices, even eating of them as Ezekiel says. We were a barbaric people: but would it be just to burn the Pope and all the Monsignori of Rome because the first Roman kidnapped the Sabines and plundered the Samnites?"[22] In this case Voltaire absolves his contemporary Jews from the responsibility for sins attributed to their ancestors, as rationalistic ethics required. On other occasions, however, he ignores historical distinctions and treats the Jews of every generation as a single entity, as in the following example: "But what shall I say to my brother the Jew? Shall I give him dinner? Yes, provided that during the meal Balaam's ass does not take it into its head to bray; that Ezekiel does not mix his breakfast with our dinner; that a fish does not come to swallow one of the guests and keep him in his belly for three days; that a serpent does not mix into the conversation to seduce my wife; that a prophet does not take it into his head to sleep with her after dinner, as did that good fellow Hoseah for fifteen francs and a bushel of barley; above all that no Jew make a tour round my house sounding the trumpet, making the walls come down, killing me, my father, my mother, my wife, my children, my cat and my dog, in accord with the former usage of the Jews."[23] Facetious though this passage may be, it expresses Voltaire's opinion that the Jews of every generation are tainted by the same defects as their forefathers. To cite another example, Voltaire describes the Egyptian magicians who with their spells duplicated everything that Moses did. He concludes his description with the following caustic note: "It was only in the matter of lice that they were outdone; for that reason it has accurately been said that *the Jews know more than any other people about this profession.*"[24] Voltaire's emphasis bridges the periods, encouraging the reader not to distinguish between the slaves of the Exodus and the eighteenth-century Jews whom the author seeks to condemn. Regarding the prophecies of the Jews, Voltaire says: "The prophecies, which they understood only literally, prophesied on a hundred occasions that they would be the masters of the world: however, they never possessed more than a tiny corner of the Earth for a few years; today they haven't even one village of their own."[25] The distinction between past and present is entirely blurred.

Jewish history was also conceived as a single historical unit both by Jewish tradition and by Christianity, the latter, of course, regarding the appearance of Jesus as a decisive turning point. However, while the traditional concept, Jewish or Christian, was that the unity derived from a divine mission, Voltaire explained it in terms of permanent qualities deeply rooted in the spirit and character of the people. Evidence of these characteristics could be taken from any period in the history of the people: after all, periodization is essentially an external matter, and time creates no barriers between generations. Consequently, Voltaire's method allowed him to transfer his data from one period to the next and to attribute the basic characteristics of the Biblical people to later generations. Likewise, it is hardly surprising to find the converse: qualities discovered in later periods are attributed to Biblical Jews. That Jews are drawn to money and that they deal in business transactions and usury could be postulated in the light of their occupation in the Middle Ages and modern times, and Voltaire projects this stereotype back to the Biblical age.[26] For example, the Bible does not indicate explicitly any desire on the part of the Jewish people to rule over other nations, but in the Talmudic and medieval periods deluding images of the Messianic era did arise. These were the basis for the Christian polemic contending that the Jews sought world domination. Ex post facto, polemicists found supporting material for this view in the Bible as well; Voltaire accepted their Christian accusations and incorporated them in his rationalistic indictment.[27]

This last example elucidates the historical background of Voltaire's attitude toward the Jews. Without a doubt, Voltaire's primary aim was to combat the dominant religion by challenging the foundations of a Church built on the concept of Biblical revelation. He forged the intellectual tools for this project while developing his rationalistic historical method. However, in order to achieve this goal Voltaire had to reduce the stature of the Jewish people, denigrating their culture as of no value, ridiculing their character, and mocking their hopeless dreams and unfounded pride. Moreover, this deprecation applied not simply to a small group of people in antiquity, but to a community extant in eighteenth-century Europe, which Voltaire by no means ignored. Voltaire had contact with several typical Jews of his time: in London in 1726 he met a Jew by the name of Medina on whom he had a French bank-draft, but whom he found bankrupt. When in Potsdam, in the 1750s, he had some shady business dealings with one Hirschel from Berlin, against whom he got himself involved in an embarrassing lawsuit, this hardly increased his affection for his antagonist's co-religionists.[28] However, as Voltaire's biographical data bear out, his attitude toward the Jews is not to be attributed to such experiences. Voltaire's first evident derogation of the Jews precedes his incident with the banker Medina by four years. In 1722, he gave Cardinal Dubois information tending to arouse suspicion that Solomon Levy, a Jew from Metz, engaged in espionage for the Austrians. Voltaire spiced his report with notes having no bearing on the individual concerned, but defaming Jews as a whole. Voltaire speaks of "the Jew's talent for being accepted in and expelled from every place." "The Jew does not belong to

43

any place except that place in which he makes money: would he not just as easily betray the king on behalf of the emperor as he would the emperor for the king?"[29] In these early notes, Voltaire's gusto in listing the faults of the Jews—faults that relate not to the individual, but to the entire group and tribe—is glaring. Voltaire's image of the Jews was that harbored by the Christian mind for generations: a species alienated from the community, strange in language and customs, sunk in obscurantism and adhering to an anachronistic tradition, devoted to their brethren in the extreme but hostile to those around them, with whom they have no contact other than in business dealings, usury, and dishonest trade. Because of this image, Christians felt a sense of superiority, if not hatred, ridicule, and mockery, toward the Jews. Christian tradition appended to its image of the Jew the idea that the depravity of the Jewish community resulted from their great sin, thus justifying at the same time the Christian emotional attitude toward the Jew. Voltaire, like his fellow rationalists, omitted the theological explanation; he offered a characterological-historical one in its place. However, despite the change in reasoning, neither the general image nor its accompanying evaluation was modified. Voltaire, like a pious Christian, held that the Jews were a community of wretches and scoundrels; likewise, he remained faithful to the collective animosities that he inherited from his early Christian upbringing and from which he was never prompted to free himself.

Voltaire's adherence to remnants of the Christian tradition and to emotions it engendered could be seen as contradicting his position in general, which stressed severing these ties.[30] However, abandoning the dogmatic content of a tradition does not always assure liberation from the emotional attitudes related to it. Indeed, Voltaire was able to support his hostility to Judaism within his new value system. Antagonism toward Judaism throughout its history served brilliantly for the purpose of combating Christianity and the Church. Thus, Voltaire could, without conflict, at one and the same time abandon Christian tradition while maintaining a negative attitude toward Judaism.

Moreover, Voltaire hardly sought earthshaking changes in society and politics. He questioned neither monarchy nor the institution of nobility, nor even the privileged position of the wealthy bourgeoisie over the lower classes, the peasants and the masses. He fought the arbitrariness of the regime and the fanaticism of the Church, which often joined forces to abuse the individual unjustly. Voltaire devoted himself passionately to the defense of such individuals, as he did on behalf of the Calas family. His hope for the future was that as a result of the spread of knowledge by philosophers like himself, the abuses of the authorities would cease and the state would be governed by the enlightened principles of humanism and tolerance. In Voltaire's vocabulary, as in the terminology of his generation, a philosopher was not a thinker attempting to decipher the secrets of the universe and of man, but an enlightened man who acted according to reason, without relying on the dogmas, beliefs, or rituals of a positivist religion. He regarded all these as superstitions, the products of the weakness of men intellectually immature. Primitive man encountering the phenomena of nature—rain, thunder, and lightning—was awed by the wonder of life and death. He drew conclusions from his experience of the unknown and discovered the existence of a superior power who was the cause of the universe, nature, and man. But his anthropomorphic mind was not satiated by that conclusion; he also attributed the discovery of these phenomena and their details to the will of the Supreme Being and his providence. Consequently, he sought a way to influence that being—through prayers, sacrifice, or ingratiation—that he might make the rain fall, grant the supplicant long life, or give him prosperity and wealth. The desire to obtain God's favor was the source of the ritual that ornamented positivistic religion. It was nothing more than superstition, the product of ancient man's confused, anthropomorphic conception.[31] The advantage of the philosophers, a few of whom were to be found in every generation, but who in the eighteenth century constituted a whole community, was their liberation from superstition. The masses would continue to adhere to superstition forever.

In his social philosophy, Voltaire remained aristocratic; yet he placed enlightened philosophers capable of pure reason at the top of his social pyramid at the expense of the hereditary nobility. He did not foresee any developments that would ever change this situation. The enlightened philosophers would remain a minority, while most of the world would continue to wallow in the depths of ignorance and would never throw off the yoke of positivistic religion.[32] The Jews were lumped in this latter category by Voltaire, and he neither saw nor sought the possibility of their improvement, whether through education or through political or social emancipation.

It is important to take note of the period and to realize that in Voltaire's lifetime, the question of emancipating the Jews had not yet been raised. The precursors of that line of thought—in the works of Locke, Toland, and possibly Montesquieu[33]—were not known to many at the time, and certainly not to Voltaire. The enlightened writer had in fact encountered a new type of Jew who had acquired a European education and even contributed to European culture. Isaac Pinto, a philosophe, economist, and prolific author, attacked Voltaire for his defamatory remarks about the Jews in the *Encyclopedie*. Pinto pointed out that at least among Sephardic Jews there were educated and enlightened individuals who could compete with their Christian colleagues. Voltaire's answer was that if there were such, they were welcome to join the community of philosophers. However, such individuals, he claimed, were exceptions, while the majority of the Jewish community was no different from the ignorant masses. It was this majority, and not individual exceptions, whom he judged harshly.[34]

With this remark, Voltaire, as it were, opened up the way for a vision of the Jew's future in enlightened society. Hints of that vision appear in Voltaire's writings not because of a conscious search for a solution to the Jewish problem, but because of the internal logic of his new system of thought. The abandonment of Christian theology destroyed the justification for the existence of the Jewish nation as testimony to the truth of Christianity. Likewise, it eliminated the basis for the hope that the Jews would eventually recognize this truth and accept Christianity. A new solution to the problem of the future of the Jews had to replace the Christian expectation of their conversion. If the negative evaluation of the nature of the Jews was correct, but the ideological reason for their existence was no longer valid, they become a strange social phenomenon, harmful and lacking any justification. What then was to be done with this community, lacking in culture and human values from its inception, and now dispersed throughout the world, having become a paradigm and byword for its extreme ignorance and its asocial relation to its surroundings.

The alternative of naturalization presented itself to Voltaire when he witnessed the enactment of the "Jew Bill" in England in 1753. Voltaire recounted the episode in his history, but it is clear that he sided with the proponents of its repeal and doubtful whether it occurred to him that naturalization might be a general answer to the question of the Jewish entity.[35] He incidentally suggested the possibility of the return of the Jews to their own land; but this was little more than a light-hearted flash, hardly a proposal worthy of examination.[36]

In only one instance does Voltaire consider the question of the continued existence of the Jewish community among the peoples of Europe. In the supplements to the *Essai* that were first published in 1761, the question arises from the description of the fate of the Gypsies. What could testify better to Voltaire's view of the Jews' place on the social scale? He regarded the Gypsies as a remnant of Egyptian and Assyrian pagans, removed from their homes and carrying with them their faith and the beliefs of the sorcerer, the magician, and the witch doctor: "This race has begun to disappear from the face of the earth because recently men have become disenchanted with sorcery, talismans, augury, and possession by devils." The spread of the enlightenment had reduced the Gypsies' source of income and consequently they were disappearing. As a direct continuation to this assertion, Voltaire adds this about the Jews: "The same catastrophe can befall the Jews: when the society of man is perfected, when every people carries on its trade itself, no longer sharing the fruits of its work with these wandering brokers, the number of Jews will necessarily diminish. The rich among them are already beginning to detest their superstitions; there will be no more than the lot of a people without arts or laws, who, no longer able to enrich themselves through our negligence, will no longer be able to sustain a separate society, and who, no longer understanding their ancient corrupt jargon, a mixture of Hebrew and Syrian, ignorant even of their own books, will assimilate among the scum of the other peoples."[37]

In terms of scorn and mockery, this hardly differs from the way in which Voltaire generally speaks of the Jews. But in this case, the content is innovative. Voltaire approaches the sociological diagnosis of Marx and his followers. The Jews can exist so long as other nations need their services as merchants. When they stop fulfilling this function, they will lose the basis of their existence and disappear inevitably.[38] He is no longer talking in terms of the Christian concept of absorption of the Jews through conversion, but rather of gradual assimilation into the scum of mankind, the despised masses, to which they already belong and which will eventually swallow them up. This prediction occurred to Voltaire as an aside and was hardly the product of deep thought or the result of studied consideration. Nevertheless—and perhaps even consequently—it indicates the rise of a new concept of the place of Judaism and a new view of its future. All that was left of the traditional Christian concept was the stamp of aversion, mockery, and hatred. Lacking an ideology of justification, Jewry and Judaism were laid bare to crushing criticism and were judged totally worthless—lost remnants of ancient times that had no place in new circumstances. The prophecy seemed evident, and it held that they were destined and deservedly doomed to disappear from the world.

Part II: Germany, 1780-1819

4|Ideological Counterattack

JOHANN EISENMENGER AND VOLTAIRE were only separated by one generation. When Eisenmenger died in 1704, Voltaire was a boy of ten. Nevertheless the mental worlds they inhabited were as far apart as East and West. Eisenmenger was completely immersed in the theological world of the Middle Ages, while Voltaire was the harbinger of the modern age, the age of reason. The place of the Jews on the fringes of Christian society was permanently fixed in the concept of theological doctrine. The link of the Jew with Scripture, the validity and sanctity of which was acknowledged by the Christian also, assured him of a right to exist, albeit a relative and limited one. If the Jews were disparaged and accused by Christians, this was because the Jewish tradition confronted the parallel Christian one. Certainly it was the Jewish tradition—Talmudic Judaism in all its literary ramifications and moral and practical expressions—that served as the sole and almost indispensable authority for the arguments of Eisenmenger against Jews and Judaism. Scripture, which was to serve Voltaire for his scornful denigration of Judaism and its adherents, found no place in Eisenmenger's argumentation.[1]

Eisenmenger's and Voltaire's systems of thought appear to contradict and exclude each other not only by their cognitive contents but also by their social purposes. Eisenmenger intended only to strengthen the accepted attitude of the Christian world to the Jews and to justify their being kept in an inferior political and social situation. Voltaire's line of thought was associated with a drive for changes in the basic elements of society and particularly in the relation of Jews to society. As is well known, it was

51

change that triumphed; less than a generation after Voltaire's death in 1778, a fundamental shift took place in the status of Jews in France and other European countries: the process of naturalization had begun. This shift in the lot of the Jews was a direct result of a fundamental transformation that swept the countries of Europe and found expression and focus in the French Revolution. The change, in fact, was a mighty departure, not only from Eisenmenger's ideas but also from Voltaire's. Nevertheless, the ideas they had held were not consigned to limbo, for much theorizing and discussion, lively verbal battles and polemics, accompanied the enfranchisement of the Jews. The words of the accusers echoed throughout this polemic and shaped the modern anti-Semitism of later generations.

The first legal act granting the Jews living in a European state the right to regard themselves as permanent residents of the country was the Edict of Tolerance issued by the Austrian Emperor Joseph II in 1782. This royal decree affected the Jews of Vienna, lower Austria, Moravia, and Hungary. Contemporaries interpreted the edict as an expression of the emperor's will thenceforth to regard all the Jews of his lands as subjects for whose welfare he was responsible, just as he was responsible for subjects of other religions or classes. The emperor's contemporaries had not even contemplated full equal rights for all citizens; to Jews, the very fact that the emperor acknowledged their right to be permanent residents was revolutionary.

Joseph II's issuance of his Edict of Tolerance did not remain an isolated event. Two years later Louis XVI promulgated a law recognizing the Jews of Alsace as subjects of the king of France. Five years later, when the French Revolution eliminated classes and granted equality to all citizens, France had to choose between two alternatives: recognizing the Jews as equal citizens or expelling them. The latter possibility was raised only theoretically. In effect, the National Assembly's decision to recognize the Jews as citizens of the state was the only possible course. Moreover, legislation in all the countries that came under French hegemony between 1792 and 1814—Holland, the Rhineland in Germany, Westphalia, Switzerland and northern Italy—followed the pattern set by the French. Other countries like Baden, Württemberg, and Bavaria followed the Austrian pattern, recognizing the citizenship of the Jews, although restricting their rights to some degree. Prussia, still independent though defeated by Napoleon, resolved on internal reforms, the granting of citizenship to Jews being one of them. At any rate, by the end of the Napoleonic era all the Jews of western and central Europe had become citizens or subjects of the states in which they lived. Historians thus rightly include this era in the period of emancipation.[2]

These events do not indicate an anti-Jewish mood, rather, a desire to extricate the Jews from their isolation, place them on an equal footing with the other inhabitants, and integrate them among the elements constituting and sustained by the state. Indeed, practically speaking, that was the case. The situation of the Jews was drastically transformed, and their status incomparably improved. However, these economic, social, and political achievements did not prevent the eventual rise of extreme anti-Semitism. Quite the contrary: the progress of the Jews in achieving their goals in Gentile society served to spur the opposition of those who were scandalized by the very integration of the Jews into that society. The idea of naturalization and emancipation of the Jews was regarded by its supporters—in particular the intellectuals who struggled for it in public debate—as a lofty ideal, righting a grave wrong that had been committed by generations sunk in blindness and ignorance. However, their opponents defined it as a dangerous innovation, the perils of which had to be made clear in no uncertain terms. Since the belief in the unity of the human species was one of the widespread ideas of that era, the opponents of the Jews were compelled to adduce reasons why the Jews should be made an exception. In the course of their efforts to justify their stand, a heterogeneous collection of motives and arguments became manifest, old and new pretexts being produced to sustain the anti-Jewish polemic. The integration of these motives constituted a new chapter in the history of ideological anti-Semitism.

Chronologically speaking, the new-old argument against the Jews began as soon as the possibility of naturalization was raised. Before Joseph II's Edict of Tolerance had been promulgated, when word spread in Vienna and Prague that the emperor's council was considering extending the rights of the Jews, pamphlets appeared, some condemning and some defending the Jews. One of the anti-Jewish pamphlets carried the title "On the Uselessness and Harmfulness of the Jews in Bohemia and Moravia."[3] In Berlin, the public debate on the Jews was opened by a book written on their behalf, Christian Wilhelm Dohm's *Über die bürgerliche Verbesserung der Juden* ("On the Civic Betterment of the Jews"), which first raised the basic arguments for granting citizenship, and later equality, to the Jews. Dohm's book was followed by numerous other books, pamphlets, and articles, a majority of them in agreement with his opinion.[4] However, a few of them were critical, and some, principally those by Friedrich Traugott Hartmann and Johann Heinrich Schulz, were positively venomous.[5] A bitter controversy between supporters and detractors preceded the granting of citizenship to the Jews of France by the National Assembly. Hostile writers took part in the polemic, particularly in Alsace, where there was a long-standing and uninterrupted tradition of enmity toward the Jews. The polemic in France died down when Jews were granted citizenship in 1792, but it arose once again in 1806-1807 when Napoleon reexamined the Jewish question and their enemies saw an opportunity to drive the Jews from the status they had attained.

As we have seen, the French pattern of naturalization of the Jews was followed in other countries as well; everywhere, opponents expressed hostile opinions on Jews and Judaism. In the Dutch National Assembly, which finally granted equal rights to the Jews in 1796, there was no lack of critical voices and reservations. Likewise in the Rhine countries, Westphalia and Frankfurt, the granting of citizenship to the Jews was not achieved without opposition. In this respect Prussia was unique. There, the debate on changing the status of the Jews continued from the death of Frederick II in 1786 until the granting of citizenship in 1812.[6] Throughout that time the pros and cons were argued back and forth among the ministers and civil authorities. Moreover, the public had taken an interest in the Jewish question even earlier, as we have seen, and for a special reason. Indeed, in the capital, Berlin, Jews and Christians enjoyed social contact the like of which was not to be found elsewhere. Here one could find Moses Mendelssohn, friend and associate of the greatest Gentile thinkers and writers. Salons in Jewish homes were frequented by Christian intellectuals and people of standing. Consequently, strong social pressure was exerted to bring about equality in the political sphere as well. Yet the governmental apparatus operated slowly: sometimes the efforts for reform would seem to decline, and at other times they would be renewed. The intensity of the public polemic also varied. It would increase whenever ideas of reform seemed about to be realized, particularly in the period 1803-1805. The principal antagonists of the Jews were Karl Wilhelm Friedrich Grattenauer, Ernst Traugott von Kortum, and Christian Ludwig Paalzow. These were no more than occasional writers, who even in their own day carried little weight; but some of the great thinkers of the period also contributed to the debate on the Jews: Herder, Kant, and Fichte. Herder did so with a detached, though unfavorable, investigation; Kant with Christian aversion in a philosophic guise; and Fichte with a high degree of passion and deep hostility.[7]

Much of what was said against reform was in fact no more than a repetition of what had been said previously to justify the pariah position of the Jews. Despite the spread of rationalistic enlightenment, many still maintained the traditional Church view that the Jews were destined to dispersion, oppression, suffering, and degradation for the unatoned sin of having rejected Jesus. In 1785 the Academy of Sciences of Metz invited responses to the question whether there was a way to make the Jews of France, that is, of Alsace, more productive and happier. Most of the respondents replied that it depended entirely on the authorities. Only they could grant the Jews that citizenship that would inevitably lead to their betterment and happiness. However, one respondent, faithful to Christian dogma, held that if the Jews should achieve citizenship the Church would lose one of the proofs of its truth: the manifest victory of the Church over its rival, the despicable synagogue.[8] The theologian and scholar Jean André de Luc took a similar stand in the polemic over David Friedländer's open letter to Provost Teller in 1799, at the height of the struggle of Prussian Jewry for citizenship. Friedländer tried to circumvent the problem of naturalization. Making himself the spokesman of a group of wealthy Jews in Berlin, he proposed that they join the Protestant church, but without accepting its dogmas. De Luc was among those who rejected Friedländer's suggestion and accused him of trying to achieve the naturalization of the Jews by undermining the character of both the Christian and Jewish religions. De Luc could conceive of neither state nor society without a Christian foundation. Christianity granted the Jew the right to live under its protection, provided he believed in the Old Testament and the sanctity of its fundamental laws, such as the Ten Commandments. However, the Jew had no right to citizenship, to be included in Christian society, so long as he persisted in his ancestral refusal to recognize the "new order that God deigned to establish through the Redeemer that had been promised to mankind ever since Adam's sin."[9]

Only a minority of those opposed to Jewish enfranchisement based their opposition on simple Christian theological doctrine. The most vocal opponents were the enlightened, who had their reservations about the Christian tradition but were not, in practice, sundered from its influence. The anti-Jewish stereotypes and prejudices that had flourished against the dogmatic Christian background affected the views of the enlightened even when their attachment to Christianity was shaky or had even been broken off.

This situation applied primarily to the image of the Jew as a creature completely without moral restraint toward Christians. This image was rooted in the traditional Christian pattern of thought, as shown in the work of Eisenmenger. Nor did it cease to operate when Eisenmenger's theories lost their validity, at least for the enlightened. The opponents of Jewish enfranchisement or equality were in the toils of the frightening image of the Jew as a danger to his surroundings. Their argument ran roughly as follows: If the Jew had been a thorn in the flesh of the Christian when he existed only on the outer fringes of Christian society, how much greater would be his potential for harm were he to gain citizen status and live in the very midst of that society? This charge was expounded by Christian Ludwig Paalzow and his predecessors and followers. The moral impermeability of the Jew was an ancient Christian tradition; it was even widespread in places where the name of Eisenmenger was unknown as can be seen from the polemics over the "Jew Bill" in England in 1753. However, in Germany the argument was associated with Eisenmenger's name. His words were adduced in support and doubtless lent not a little weight to the charge.[10]

The negative image of the character of the Jew, especially from the moral aspect, was reinforced by the Deistic literature. Although this was not written in order to indict the Jews of that era, it was easy to turn it to the advantage of the polemic opposing the enfranchisement of the Jews. The contemporary Jews were presented in anti-Jewish literature as the descendants of the uncultured and immoral children of Israel whom the Mosaic legislation had separated from the rest of the peoples of the world. At the same time the Mosaic law had implanted the idea in the Jews that they were the chosen people, superior in status and rights to the rest of humanity. This was the source of the Jews' tendency to keep apart from their neighbors: not to eat with them, to shun them socially, and not to intermarry with them. This social isolation was also the source of the Jewish double standard of morality, which recognized no obligation to act with integrity and decency toward the non-Jew. Some claimed that the Jew was completely amoral, politics with him replacing morality, his sole interest being egoistical.[11]

The controversy between the advocates and opponents of Jewish enfranchisement revolved around the question whether the alleged negative characteristics of the Jews were a permanent part of the nature of the people or could change with time and circumstances. So long as Jews and Judaism were judged from the standpoint of simple Christian doctrine, moral improvement was believed to be dependent on the Jew changing his faith and embracing Christianity. When attention passed from religious differences to the Jews' distinctive cultural and moral attributes—according to the rationalistic and Deistic systems—then the question was whether Jewish propensities were immutably and permanently inrooted in the Jew. The tendency of the opponents of the Jews was naturally to assume this immutability. Karl Wilhelm Friedrich Grattenauer, in the title of one of the most venomous books of the era, *Concerning the Physical and Moral Characteristics of Contemporary Jews*, hinted at the inflexibility of the Jewish mentality, but he was also ambiguous. He spoke of Jews ridding themselves of their corrupt qualities, and he admitted that he himself knew Jews who did not possess the murderous characteristics of Jews in general. On the other hand, he held that a Jew remained a Jew even if he became a Christian. Christian preachers boasted in vain of their success in converting Jews; their baptism was as effective as "trying to wash a blackamoor white."[12] Friedrich Buchholz also refuted the efficacy of conversion as a means of purifying the Jew of his corrupt qualities: "The Jew will not renounce *Schacher* on account of baptism. If he should refrain from every other kind of bartering he will make the sacrament itself the object of commerce."[13] In contrast, Friedrich Traugott Hartmann saw conversion as the only way for the Jew to rid himself of his burdensome heritage. Not that Hartmann attributed any cleansing power or other religious significance to baptism. He added certain negative strokes of his own to the likeness of the Jew as it was portrayed in Deistic literature. The Jews celebrated their own festivals; they had their own jurisprudence and relied on concepts of justice and equity that differed from all those about them. Even more, the Jews gave great significance and religious force to all manifestations of the isolation of their community. Jewish isolation being religiously sanctioned, there was no hope that it would just disappear or be rooted out through internal reform or pressure or coercion from without. Hartmann saw no remedy for the Jew apart from his accepting Christianity, and even then not as an act of conversion—a genuine change in conviction and being born again, which is the traditional Christian concept—but as a declaration of accepting the laws of the state and society. "The matter does not depend on baptism but on the fact that the Jew in saying 'Baptize me!' says simultaneously: 'I obey the laws of the state, I undertake the duty of observing the rules laid down for the good of the state; I shall fulfil the duties incumbent upon me at all times.' "[14]

The young Fichte's view was much more extreme. He felt that the characteristics of the Jew were so anchored in his nature as to be beyond modification or eradication. Fichte found two faults in the Jewish mentality: adherence to a dual morality and belief in a misanthropic God. The first accusation is a central theme in Christian anti-Semitism, as we have seen in Eisenmenger's teaching; the second dates from ancient times and was revived by the English and French Deists. Fichte's question was: Can the Jew break through "the mighty obstacle before him—which looks insurmountable—in order to achieve love of justice, love of man and love of truth?" In answer, Fichte asserted that such an individual would be a "hero and a saint" and that he, Fichte, would not believe that such a man existed until he saw him with his own eyes. Because of their deeply rooted ideas, the Jews should be granted only elementary human rights and "the only way to give them citizenship would be to cut off their heads on the same night in order to replace them with those containing no Jewish ideas."[15] The shocking image of decapitation drew the ire of Fichte's critics. However, the import of this passage is not in the literal denotation of the language, but in the thought that it conveys. Fichte wants to say that the ideas in the head of the Jew are so essentially a part of him that they could only be changed by a physiological transformation.

57

The controversy over the ability of the Jew to free himself of his distinguishing characteristics affected the individual Jew, because in order to make the attempt he had to isolate himself from his community. Some Jews did isolate themselves, but the Jewish community in general evinced no signs of disintegrating, continuing to appear to the outside observer as a distinct and closely knit social group. Their cohesion was seen by the opponents of the Jews as an obstacle to their absorption into state and society. Hartmann included this internal Jewish cohesion among the phenomena that, since religiously based, would perpetuate their isolation.[16] Ernst Traugott von Kortum spoke of "the extraordinary unique esprit de corps which unites Jew with Jew, despite their dispersion." This writer dilates upon the reaction of Jewish communities whenever any one of their members suffered even a trivial injury—as though each and every cell in the national Jewish body felt the pain of every other. Underlying this caricature was the outstanding solidarity that distinguished the Jewish community before the process of disintegration began. One who saw these Jewish characteristics as immutable found it difficult to believe that the Jews could be integrated into another people or group. The conclusion was that Jews would still preserve their internal unity even if they came to stand on an equal plane with all other citizens; in brief the Jews constituted a "state within a state."[17]

The expression "a state within a state" came into vogue in the 1780s.[18] The first to make use of it in anti-Jewish attacks was Johann Heinrich Schulz. However, the expression was not first applied to the Jews. It reflected the desire of a modern state to achieve sovereignty, denying the right of any ethnic, religious, or social group to conduct its affairs autonomously. France conducted a genuine struggle against the Huguenots, who, until the repeal of the Edict of Nantes in 1685, not only enjoyed religious freedom but also occupied fortified towns in which they held political and military authority. The advocates of centralized monarchy saw in this situation a violation of the exclusive right of the central authorities to power within the borders of the kingdom. The expression "a state within a state" came to justify this position, saying that no group could be allowed to usurp authority that rightfully belonged to the state alone. In the course of the eighteenth century, power became so concentrated in the hands of the state authorities that the very existence of religious, professional, or social societies was considered a usurpation of the sovereign state. For this reason—at least in part—they disbanded the Jesuit order, made it difficult for the Freemasons to organize, and tried to eliminate the artisans' and traders' guilds. Each of these held a degree of authority over its members and was consequently termed "a state within a state."

The Jewish communities held an even greater degree of authority over their members than the societies did. Nevertheless, the critics of the Jews—Voltaire and others—initially made no use of this expression. The reason for this is abundantly clear. The expression "a state within a state" had a clear meaning at that time. Those who used it claimed that the religious, professional, and fraternal societies that demanded at least a part of their members' allegiance should disband and cease to separate the individual from the all-embracing state. The goal was a commonwealth in which the citizens would relate directly to the institution of the state. A parallel application of this expression to the Jews would have required disbanding of their communities and absorption as citizens. Such a thought was at that time far from the minds of the advocates of the Jews, not to mention their opponents. The Jews did not appear as a state within a state, but as a state barely sustaining itself on the margins of the state. This situation continued until the ideological, political, and social upheaval that affected every sphere of life, and, in the last third of the eighteenth century, even brought the accepted opinions regarding the Jews into question. Some thinkers saw them as entitled to human rights, at least, and potentially to citizenship; the proposal to change their political status and improve their social conditions resulted from this attitude. As soon as the reformers offered their proposal, the perspectives of the opponents changed. Jews were no longer conceived as standing on the margins of society and state, but as moving toward the center. The question that was raised was whether they would disperse among the general populace and take their places as individuals before the all-embracing state, as was expected of other elements of the population. The answer of the opponents of the Jews was negative; they denied the will or the ability of the Jews to free themselves of the bonds that tied them one to another by virtue of religion, tradition, and character. Their conclusion was that granting citizenship to the Jews would be in vain: it would not change their social cohesion or their characteristics. In short, they would not cease to constitute a separate social unit—a state within a state.

As mentioned, Johann Heinrich Schulz was the first, in 1784, to use this slogan in reference to Jewish exclusiveness; others followed suit, either owing to his influence or by their own initiative.[19] Those who first wrote of the Jews as a state within a state gave no indication that they were aware of the deeper significance of their arguments; perhaps they came to use the expression unwittingly, finding it a convenient way to express the opinion that the Jews constituted a separate religious-ethnic group, unable to be absorbed in society or state.[20] It was Fichte who employed the slogan pointedly and with full appreciation of its significance. Jewish affairs are introduced into Fichte's book incidentally; the central theme is a philosophical defense of the French Revolution. Fichte denies the right of

59

the state to regard its citizens as subject to it unconditionally and permanently. On the contrary, he describes to his readers the possibility that an ever-growing number of individuals will exclude themselves from the authority of the state and draw up a new civil contract founded on natural law. Immediately, the question arises, Will the existing state tolerate the formation of a new state within its borders? Surely that would be a state within a state in the full sense of the phrase. To defend his philosophical construction, he offers historical precedents: there is nothing new about the phenomenon of a state within a state; the existing state tolerates bodies that should be so classed and no one says a word. Here Fichte lists those groups that should be termed states within the state because of their cohesiveness: military officers, the nobility, the Church (the Protestant to a lesser degree, the Catholic to a greater degree), the guilds. But at the head of all these, Fichte places the Jews: "A mighty state stretches across almost all the countries of Europe, hostile in intent and engaged in constant strife with everyone else . . . This is Jewry."[21] Fichte's statements were not simply an eruption of hatred. They arose from the position he assumed in relation to a problem that was exercising the contemporary mind: What place could be set aside for the Jews in a state that was aiming at uniting its citizens, when their religion and culture would prevent them from full devotion to the state? With difficulty, Fichte was prepared to vouchsafe Jews "human rights," that is, the right to live in the country as aliens. Jews would only be fit for the right of citizenship if they were capable of changing their nature.

In a less hostile tone and without invoking the formulation of a state within a state, Herder defined the Jews in Europe as an alien Asiatic people. He expressed the hope that the day would come when "the question would no longer be asked in Europe whether one was a Jew or a Christian, because the Jew, too, would live according to European laws and contribute to the good of the state." He discerned the changes that had taken place in interfaith relations and noted that the Christians had ceased to work at converting Jews to Christianity. Nevertheless, the diminution in rivalry between the communities was no reason for the state to alter its attitude toward the Jews. The state was duty-bound to ask how much these members of an alien people, who gave themselves up to special employment, benefited the state in general; and under what conditions and supervision they should be placed. Their exclusive attachment to trade and finance was what had damaged the human nature of the Jews. Herder described the Jewish people as "a parasitic growth on the trunk of other peoples." It was an expression that was repeated often in anti-Semitic writings.[22]

The advocates of the Jews attributed the Jewish deficiencies to their social conditions, predicting that if the Jews were allowed to learn and practice every profession, they would adapt their behavior to that of the other citizens. The Jews' opponents scoffed at this prediction. Those who attributed the corrupt qualities of the Jew to his religious principles could not conceive how improving his political and economic circumstances could overcome the influence of his religion. Moreover, those who conceived of the Jew's qualities as inherent in his nature could not imagine any improvement as a result of merely external changes. And indeed, there was opposition on the grounds that the Jews might take advantage of freedom to exploit their neighbor.

However, some not only denied the possibility of improving the morality of the Jew by changing his economic life, but denied any possibility of change whatsoever. They claimed that the occupations of the Jews were not a result of legislation that restricted their economic activity. The precepts of Judaism, and perhaps even the inherent inclination of the Jews, prevented them from turning to crafts or agriculture, leaving them no occupation other than trade and finance. The severe prohibition against work on the Jewish Sabbath was in itself enough to keep the Jew from agriculture, which could not tolerate absolute breaks in work at predetermined periods. Moreover, there were indirect economic ramifications of Jewish exclusiveness. The fact that the Jew did not intermarry with his Christian neighbor, eat his foods, or engage in friendly intercourse with him prevented the creation of those relations of mutual cooperation without which neither the farmer in his village nor the craftsman in his quarter could exist.

Friedrich Traugott Hartmann had already made these points in response to Dohm's proposal for reforms.[23] After a few years, Ernst Traugott von Kortum tried to expand the economic analysis, demonstrating the harm that would derive from the professional narrowness of the Jews. The Jews took no part in hard jobs like those of farmer and craftsman "because the Jew is too lazy and too weak to choose an occupation that requires strength and perseverance, not to mention that he would lose one day a week as well as many holidays and festival days." The economic result of the absence of the Jews from the heavy labor force was an increase in the price of labor, because the Jews also needed the services of craftsmen, but did not contribute to the supply. On the surface, the Jew compensated for what he lacked in physical labor by fulfilling his unique function in the economy of the state—trade. However, Kortum tries to prove "that Jewish trade, *even if conducted with thorough honesty, can never mean anything but harm to civic society*" (italics in the original). For the benefit of the economy of the state, money had to be in perpetual circulation from hand to hand, so that every person disbursed

roughly what he took in. "Jewish commerce does not advance this circulation. The Hebrew always returns less than he receives. He is a swamp that
absorbs a great part of the water that passes through it." The Jew took an
interest in certain aspects of commerce and monopolized them for his
community. Indeed, the Jew never acted alone: "The Jew never trades as
a single individual, *but as a member of the most extensive trading company in the world.* His enterprises have a double purpose, that is, personal
profit and direct or indirect advantage to his people" (italics in the original).
The Jew did not disdain any business, small or great—"provided it does
not involve physical exertion"—and he transformed it into a source of
profit by virtue of the cooperation of other Jews upon whom he could rely.
"This singular unity of the Jews, their passion to advance the common
good of their people, is what equips them to undertake so much for which
others have neither talent nor taste. One thinks he sees one Jew working
and in effect all of Judaism is in operation." The non-Jewish trader was
distracted by his interest in political events, by a genuine or imagined sense
of honor, by the tendency to be wasteful and, above all, by the hope of attaining the ultimate success of being included in the ranks of the nobility.
The Jew was free from all that. He was notable for "standing apart from
the world, and for living a genuinely contemplative life" that prepared him
to examine what was happening around him from a purely businesslike
point of view. "The inevitable results of this are: accumulation of wealth in
cash by the Jews or a progressive increase of the commercial capital of this
group of the population and its decrease among Christian businessmen."[24]

Kortum's remarks reflect the reality of Jewish economic activity, with
an added tone of hostility and a negative evaluation based on a specious
theoretical conception. The agility with which Jews traded in every profitable venture, the close cooperation between Jews dispersed throughout
the world, and the economic advantages they derived from their detachment from other spheres of life—all are phenomena that could have contributed to a sympathetic examination of the life of the Jewish community.
However, Kortum's bias endows these phenomena with chimerical weight
and proportion. Kortum has no quarrel with merchants per se, but since he
sees the Jews as a foreign body in society, a state within the state, he treats
the capital concentrated in their hands as if it had left the state entirely.
Here, Kortum applies the central thesis of mercantilism, a theory about the
right trade relations between states, to the evaluation of the economic activity of the Jews within the state. In his estimation, even their economic
activity, which was "their only point of contact with the Christian citizens,"
remained outside the realm of the state.[25] The artificiality of the argument
is apparent, but its significance and ideological weight do not depend on its
internal logic, but on the motive that created it.

5|Philosophy the Heir of Theology

THOSE WHO ARGUED against the enfranchisement of the Jews believed that their arguments were based on characteristics of living Jews, individually or collectively. In fact, as our analysis has shown, their accusations stemmed, in content and form, from the ancient anti-Jewish tradition. The religious factor itself continued to operate: it did not disappear because of the rationalist revolution, but only cast off its old shape and assumed a new one.

It is a well-known fact that rationalist criticism did not always result in the abandonment of all the elements and concepts of religious tradition. Many critics, while rejecting religion in its latest historical guise or rejecting the institutionalized religion of the Church, justified its original form or character as they interpreted its true historical nature at the time of its appearance. Clearly, not all the rationalists declared themselves to be no longer Christians. On the contrary, many adhered to this designation and claimed the right to explain the true intentions of the founder of Christianity or the original significance of his teaching and the purpose of the movement associated with him. We have already encountered this type among the English—Matthew Tindal, for instance, was one of them—and shall encounter it repeatedly among the Germans. Many thinkers in Germany, among them the greatest minds of their time, interpreted Christian tradition so as to discover in it principles identical with their own teachings; but in treating Jewish tradition they forgot these skills of interpretation, and only the full intensity of rationalist criticism was applied.[1]

For the sake of historical truth one must note that afterward, when the

Jews produced philosophers, they repaid Christianity in kind. They, too, practiced a double standard, a harmonizing interpretation of Judaism alongside a strict criticism of Christianity.[2] However, in the late eighteenth and early nineteenth centuries, Judaism had no philosophical representative other than Moses Mendelssohn—and he guarded his tongue when he spoke of Christianity in public. This he did wisely: Mendelssohn was well aware of his status as the representative of a tolerated minority whose opinions on controversial matters were not judged by their intrinsic value alone.[3] The converse was true for the representatives of the Christian majority. Christian polemicists and thinkers, who gave Christianity a philosophical guise but laid Judaism bare, simply followed in the footsteps of theologians of ancient times. The diminution of the value of Judaism because of its being the religion of the "forsaken nation," in contrast to the religion of the ruling nations, relies on a long tradition going back to the beginning of the Middle Ages. The philosophical basis for this distinction seemed at this time, when the theological basis was crumbling, to be a convenient ideological tool for the perpetuation of the inferior social status of that remnant of the forsaken nation that was now seeking to uplift itself.

Analysis of the techniques of a few polemicists and thinkers of that time exemplifies the double standard. Johann Heinrich Schulz reiterated the rationalist criticism of the Biblical narratives and laws, not even sparing late Christianity the thrust of his critical remarks. However, the negative aspects that he saw in Christianity—its fanaticism, its exclusiveness, its focus on ritual—he attributed to Jewish influence. He regarded Moses as the source of all evils, ascribing to him the character of the shrewd and tyrannical priest who exploits the simplicity of his believers in order to enforce his will. By contrast, Jesus was judged spotless. Not only did Jesus seek to abolish Jewish ritual entirely, but he even arrived at the truth regarding the principles of faith: the truth of the rationalists that God is only the final cause, the sufficient cause, of the existence of the world, that there is no contact between him and man either through revelation and prophecy or by means of man's appeasement of him through either sacrifice or prayer. In short, Jesus was an enlightened philosopher who sought only to teach mankind the moral law that human understanding required. If Jesus is seen to act like a prophet under divine inspiration or to turn in prayer to his Father in heaven, one must know that he does these things only in order to make his teachings more palatable to the community he seeks to educate and lead. The converse is true of Moses, founder of the religion of the Jews. Even when giving laws that correspond to the requirements of morality, such as "Thou shalt not steal," he was only acting like the leader of a band of robbers who could not survive without police laws and behavior norms.[4]

Philosophy the Heir of Theology

Schulz's philosophizing is an extreme example of daring and naiveté in suiting the facts to the needs of a tendentious exegesis. His purpose is readily apparent. By making Jesus an eighteenth-century Deist philosopher, Johann Heinrich Schulz, who was engaged in a struggle to preserve his position as a Protestant minister despite his heretical views, could continue to call himself a Christian. At the same time, his acceptance of the Deistic criticism of the Law of Moses gave him the tools with which to fight his Jewish rival, Moses Mendelssohn, and to reject the demands of Mendelssohn's community for citizenship in the Christian state.[5]

Very close to Schulz in spirit and purpose is Friedrich Buchholz, whose *Moses und Jesus* is defined in a subtitle as "a historical-political essay." Buchholz also relies on Deistic sources in his assessment of the Biblical narratives, Moses, and his Law. He calls the legislator a "glory-seeking scoundrel" and his Law sterile "because legislation that makes fear the primary value shackles the spirit, preventing any free movement and stifling talent at birth." Buchholz's critique would seem to apply to every religion, including Christianity, except that he found justification and apology for his own faith by asserting that the fundamental principle of Christianity is morality. Jesus meant to destroy the whole ceremonial and ritual system so that "if religiosity should be lost in the process, morality would stand out all the more in contrast." In fact, Buchholz did not totally negate the value of religious ceremonies and even sought to preserve both baptism and holy communion. He understood them as eternally valid symbols. "Both must remain so long as we value the memory of the founder of Christianity; both will undoubtedly endure by virtue of their simplicity and the deep meaning they hold so long as Christianity, which is eternal, survives; since, without having recourse to dogmatics, there is no conceivable social condition under which it would not reveal its truth." Buchholz simply allowed Christianity the benefit of ethical and symbolic interpretation, but judged Judaism on the basis of its external manifestations and according to the prejudices associated with it.[6]

In the intellectual world of the period Schulz and Buchholz were no more than small fry. So it is surprising that, from a formal point of view, the thought of Immanuel Kant, the towering mind of the generation, is close to theirs. On the surface, Kant accepted the rationalists' and Deists' criticism of religion: ritual misleads the faithful, who think they fulfill their duty toward God and man by participating in ceremonies; the priests exploit the weakness of the masses for their own benefit. However, his reservations about religion in its historical manifestations did not bring him to negate it in principle. On the contrary, he used the concept of religion in order to establish morality, positing that man's recognition of his ethical duties brings him to acknowledge God, whom he defined as the absolute essence

65

of morality.[7] On the surface, Kant's religion is nothing but the religion of reason, a kind of rationalistic Deism, with the difference that the belief in God is here rooted in a deep philosophical system. Possibly, from a strictly philosophical point of view, he did not seek to approve of religion beyond these narrow limits. This seemed to be the case in his early works, such as the *Critique of Practical Reason*. But in 1791 Kant published his *Religion in the Limits of Reason Alone*, and here he revealed himself as one who strove to uphold the basic concepts, institutions, and rituals of Christianity: revelation, faith in the Trinity, the Church, baptism, communal worship, and the like. This is not to say that Kant accepted these fundamentals according to their simple, traditional meaning. He still condemned the supernatural concept of religion: that dogmas and ceremonies were a means of appeasement and atonement upon which man's success in this world or his salvation in the next depended. However, he claimed that this was a corrupt conception of the Christian religion that had gained wide acceptance as a result of man's psychological weakness and the influence of history. Christianity had to supplant concepts and customs that had been inherited from other religions—first and foremost, from Judaism—and it had not fully succeeded in this effort. The genuine, original Christianity was nothing but the detailed exposition of the religion of reason, which intended only to utilize a divine imperative to admonish man to fulfill his moral duty. The articles of faith, ritual, and ceremony came only to demonstrate to the faithful the principles of the religion of reason inherent in them.[8]

From praise of Christianity, Kant passes to condemnation of all other religions, first of all Judaism, the antithesis of Christianity in both history and character. Judaism did provide the background for the rise of Christianity—but the latter did not develop out of the former; rather, it arose in opposition to it. For Christianity is concerned only with the morality that devolves from man's recognition of his duties through the power of reason; its system of beliefs and practices serves only to urge the faithful to observe those duties. Judaism, on the other hand, knows only statutory laws, commandments that man must observe blindly as the will of God. The intention that accompanies the observance of the laws is of no consequence. Even when a law governs acts of an ethical nature, such as the prohibitions of murder and theft in the Ten Commandments, it is never more than a statutory law. The Jew who observes it does so not out of recognition of its rightness but because it is part of the yoke of commandments that he is obliged to accept.[9]

As already mentioned, there is some doubt as to whether Kant truly regarded all the Christian principles that he defended as being derived from philosophic premises. The strict censorship during the reign of

Philosophy the Heir of Theology

Frederick William II (1786-1797), who was bent on curbing rationalist criticism, had its influence on Kant's presentation of his opinions. But the fear of coming into conflict with the authorities affected at most his manner of expression. Indeed, his ambiguous expressions did not mislead his readers. It was immediately understood that he did not mean to defend the doctrine of the Church in terms of simple dogma. He meant to grant the fundamental concepts of Christianity symbolic significance as if they were only an offshoot of the religion of reason that critical thinking could accept. Consequently, Kant did not cease to be a thorn in the side of orthodox Christians; he was duly warned by the king of Prussia, who admonished him to publish no more opinions disruptive to the faith. At the same time Kant was a guide for those rationalists who, like himself, were forced to reject Church doctrine as a result of their own intellectual awareness, but remained attached to basic concepts and symbols that were cherished by them from youth. In this manner Kant paved the way for a compromise between the Enlightenment and Christianity, a compromise that involved the rejection of Judaism.[10]

In Kant's rejection of Judaism, traditional Christian motives merged with arguments taken from the rationalist criticism of religion. While Christianity enjoyed the defense of philosophical interpretation, Judaism was presented in its traditional, dogmatic character in phrases inherited from Spinoza through Deism and rationalism. Doubt was cast on the very right of Judaism to be called a religion in the full sense of the word, because its adherents constituted a public body whose members were subject to political laws, but not to a church whose role was to guide them to an ethical life. Therefore, the community that adhered to Judaism was inferior to the Christian community and should not be made equal to it in terms of political rights. Kant was aware of the developments that took place in the Jewish community as a result of the penetration of the Enlightenment into its ranks. Jews were among the first to comprehend his philosophical system. These he accepted as philosophers who had removed themselves from Judaism, its principles and commandments. He entertained the idea that should such Jews grow more numerous, they would ultimately accept the ethical teaching of Jesus—not necessarily in its Christian variation, but in the original form in which it was expressed to the Jewish people in the time of Jesus. In this way there would develop a Jewish church parallel to the Christian church, whose members would be worthy of equal citizenship in the state. Jews who retained the old style of Judaism, however, Kant found inferior and ineligible for citizenship. Kant expressed this conclusion explicitly, and the theme was taken up by other opponents of emancipation. It found an echo in the writings of Buchholz, and Ernst Traugott von Kortum relied on Kant's assessment of the amorality of Judaism in his arguments against the emancipation of the Jews.[11]

Kant's compromise between philosophy and Christianity aroused much attention in his time. Everyone, proponents and detractors of Christianity alike, understood that it marked a turning point, a cessation of hostilities between philosophy and religion and the creation of a synthesis out of them. That the same compromise could be highly significant for Judaism escaped most contemporary Jews. An exception was Saul Ascher, who understood that the revitalization of Christianity with a dose of philosophy—especially when combined with the disparagement of Judaism—would be a source of renewed strength for historical hatred of the Jews. It was clear to Ascher that the definition of Judaism as a religion lacking all concern for the morality of man would serve as a weapon against the Jews in their struggle to improve their lot. Immediately upon the appearance of Kant's book *Religion in the Limits of Reason Alone*, Ascher asserted the nature of the new opposition: "If heretofore the Jewish people had political and religious opponents, moral opponents now rise up." Ascher also expressed his suspicion of the imminent danger: "A totally new kind of adversary is developing before our eyes, armed with more awful weapons than his predecessors and whose principles are still in a germinating stage."[12]

At that time Ascher did not know that a third philosopher, Georg Wilhelm Friedrich von Hegel, was in the process of crystallizing his views and was, in effect, being drawn into the scheme of making Judaism inferior to Christianity.

Three stages are perceptible in Hegel's attitude toward Christianity; his treatment of Judaism evolved from this attitude at every stage. In the first fragments, composed in the years 1790-1800 more for the clarification of his own ideas than with the intention of future publication, Hegel assumed an outspoken stance against Christianity, both its doctrine as a religion of salvation and its organization into a full-fledged ecclesia. Christianity from its first inception forfeited its claim to be a popular religion such as had existed, in young Hegel's Graecophilic imagination, in ancient Greece. The inferiority of Christianity in comparison to Greek religion was already evident in the differing character of the leading figures of the two cultures—Socrates and Jesus. Socrates was a teacher and master, and the exemplary conduct and excellence of his reason could become a source of inspiration to anyone who came into contact with him. Jesus, on the other hand, chose twelve apostles who alone became the emissaries of his message. In addition, the efficacy of the Christian message was made contingent upon a ritualistic act—baptism—a condition that impaired the moral quality of the message. Thus the sectarian character of the movement initiated by Jesus was manifest from its very beginning, and it was only consistent with this tendency that the apostles should have taken Jesus' requirement of faith to mean not only faith in general but faith in Jesus as a precondition of salvation.[13]

Although these first philosophical exercises concerned the relative inferiority of Christianity vis-à-vis Greek religion, Judaism almost inadvertently became subject to similar criticism, because the initial defects of the apostles, which disqualified them from realizing the Christian ideal—not to mention the Greek—were attributed to their Jewish origins: "How little were they able to forsake their vision and longings for a Jewish Messiah who was the founder of a kingdom in which high offices and dignities would be apportioned, so that they would abandon that egoism which puts self first in order to crave only to be a member of the kingdom of God." This denunciation of Jewish messianism, based as it was on its materialistic political objectives as well as the notion that the Jewish character was incapable of concern for others, is a traditional Christian stereotype which is here carried over into the anti-Christian matrix as a matter of course. While the anti-Christian attitude of Hegel changed—though the extent to which it did is contested—the negative evaluation of Judaism persisted.[14]

The first shift in Hegel's attitude occurred very early in his career. "The Life of Jesus," completed in 1795, is the first indication. This lengthy retelling of the Gospel story has been dismissed by Hegel scholars as insignificant because of the lack of philosophical originality. Indeed, as far as the ideas are concerned, this piece does not contain anything but an exposition of Kantian ethics put into the mouth of Jesus. The episodes in Jesus' life, his admonitions, his parables, his symbolic acts—including his tragic death—are intended to convey only one tenet: that virtue prompted by the spontaneous recognition of moral law through reason is the only real value in life. Those who follow this teaching—and they alone—will inherit the kingdom of God. This teaching, not unlike the original version of the Gospel, is proved demonstratively by Jesus' encounters with the Pharisees as well as with the common Jews. These latter are portrayed as impervious to such lofty ideas, blinded as they are by Jewish prejudices, "their lack of sense for anything higher." Jews could neither surrender the notion of a political messiah who would restore their national independence, nor extricate themselves from the yoke of the law imposed upon them externally—that is, move toward an acceptance of the Kantian ethic of autonomy instead of a religious, moral heteronomy.[15]

The treatises under consideration so far had as their subject Christianity, either by itself or in contradistinction to folk religion. Judaism, therefore, came in only for indirect, almost inadvertent observation. In "The Spirit of Christianity and its Destiny," written in 1796, Christianity is depicted as emerging out of the matrix of Jewish history, and thus Judaism serves as the clearly defined background to the character of Christianity. The scene is thus set for a studied evaluation of Judaism, resulting in one of the most inimical descriptions of Judaism extant in literature. Hegel seems to have absorbed all the prejudices and misrepresentations of Judaism promulgated by Christian as well as rationalistic sources, and to have woven them into the texture of his philosophical concepts. To be sure, Hegel by this time had evolved the tendency of abstraction—the immense capacity of endowing physical facts as well as historical phenomena with spiritual, if not metaphysical, significance. Thus his negative characterization of Judaism, basically the same, familiar old stereotype, appears substantiated by the philosophical conceptualization that lends it an air of metaphysical truth.

The essence of Judaism, its nature, character, and destiny, is predetermined from the very outset: "With Abraham the true progenitor of the Jews, the history of this people begins: i.e., his spirit is the unity, the soul, regulating the entire fate of his posterity." This opening sentence of the treatise sets its tone, indicating that the historical characteristics of Jewish existence can be derived logically from its essence. Hegel offers us a definition of the Jewish essence: it is the keeping of a distance, an aloofness and possibly an estrangement from the world, physically as well as socially. Abraham "was a stranger on earth, a stranger to the soil, and to men alike." This separateness is not restricted to the domain of the tangible world; it is projected into the sphere of metaphysics: "Abraham regarded the whole world as simply his opposite . . . he looked at it as sustained by a God who was alien to it." The alienation between God and nature on the one hand, and between the Jew and the world on the other, accounts for the exclusive relationship claimed between the Jew and his God. "Since its [God's] divinity was rooted in his contempt for the whole world, he [Abraham] remained its only favorite . . . In the jealous God of Abraham and his posterity there lay the horrible claim that He alone was God and that this nation was the only one to have a God." Judaism in its totality, as well as in its details, is found to be inadequate and despicable. Even when the overt function of Jewish law seems to be humanly or socially beneficial, the philosophical interpretation of it turns it into something objectionable. Indeed, in Hegel's description, Judaism appears as an unnatural, inhuman, petrified social system, the product of a peculiar metaphysical bent of the human spirit. The highly negative overtones accompanying the description clearly served the purpose of emphasizing the contrast to Christianity, or rather to the original teaching of Jesus. Jesus' teachings found followers among men of other nations. As far as the Jews were concerned, the effort of Jesus to liberate them from their self-imposed limitations was to no avail. The hitch lay in the Jewish resistance to change simply in response to the appeal of love. "Even his sublime effort to overcome the whole of the Jewish fate must therefore have failed with his people."[16]

Hegel clearly conceived of the Jewish people as being entangled in the web of their original concepts and predilections, which were there from the very beginning and had persisted ever since: "The subsequent condition of the Jewish people which continues up to the mean, abject, wretched circumstances in which they still find themselves today is all simply consequences and elaborations of their original fate. By this fate—an infinite power which they set over against themselves and have never conquered—they have been maltreated and will be maltreated continually until they appease it by the spirit of beauty and so annul it by reconciliation." Divested of its philosophical trappings, this sentence shows that Hegel attributed the abject circumstances and pariah status of the Jewish community to its adherence to its religion, and saw no prospect of its being extricated without transcending its spiritual commitments. Moreover, the tribulations inflicted upon the Jews in the past and to be expected in the future had to be understood as a direct result of their self-chosen aloofness, excluding them from the rest of humanity.[17]

This anti-Jewish theory, not uncommon at the time, here received a philosophical justification. At the same time, it implied a certain stand on the issue of Jewish citizenship: Jews should be prevented from receiving it as long as they cleave to their present religious position. This was, as we remember, also the conviction of Kant. Hegel, it is true, later changed his mind and in his *Philosophy of Right* (1820) categorically recommended the inclusion of Jews in the body politic on equal footing with others.[18] This shift in his position did not result from a reconsideration of the merits of the Jewish religion. It was, rather, a corollary of Hegel's theory of the state as it evolved in his mature philosophy. The secular political institution, formally defined, could not take cognizance of a citizen's religious convictions. However, on the plane of philosophical interpretation and evaluation, Hegel continued to be vitally interested in the role that religion in general, and Judaism and Christianity in particular, played in the course of human history. The theories outlined above were only his first attempts to come to grips with this problem. Later, as he proceeded to develop his full-scale system, he expounded, deepened, and redefined his themes. Thus Judaism and Christianity came in for repeated reconsideration. It would be beyond the scope of this analysis to follow in detail the development and shifts in Hegel's thought. What is of importance is the fact that however the essence of the two religions, Judaism and Christianity, was redefined, the order of precedence remained always the same: Judaism occupied a lower rank, representing a more primitive stage in the evolution of the human—or absolute—spirit. The thesis of the inferiority of Judaism to Christianity is integral to Hegel's doctrine at all stages.[19]

The fact that this scheme of placing Judaism below and Christianity above continually recurs in the systems of various independent and profound thinkers—and that it remains a fixed element in their thinking even though their ideas may change from one extreme to another—leads one to believe that they were either incapable or uninterested in freeing themselves from it. Many instances of this will be adduced later, but only one additional example will be explored here: the view of Arthur Schopenhauer, the severest critic and opponent of Hegel.[20]

There are many facets to Schopenhauer's criticism of Hegel and the whole idealistic philosophy. One point of opposition is traditional religion. Schopenhauer despises the attempts to achieve a compromise between religion and philosophy; on the contrary, he emphasizes and stresses the tension between them. The philosopher examines the different religions from the standpoint of the Weltanschauung expressed in their teachings to determine whether they lean toward optimism or pessimism. There are two basic metaphysical positions that seemed to him to be characteristic of entirely separate cultures. The archetype of pessimism—the metaphysical principle of his philosophy—he found in the religions of the East, especially in Buddhism, and its clear antithesis, unlimited optimism, in the Judaism of the Old Testament. Schopenhauer made a distinction in Christianity between the kernel and the shell. The kernel was the doctrine of Original Sin, the view of the world as a vale of tribulation that demands asceticism, which is the essence of the pessimist outlook. In the view of the philosopher, this atoned for other, optimistic aspects of Christianity. The tale of the sin of Adam in the Garden of Eden, which Schopenhauer understood in its Christian meaning as the Original Sin, had its source of course in the Old Testament. However, Schopenhauer thought it out of place there, because it contradicted the dominant spirit of the Scripture. He concluded that the story had come into the Scripture by accident from some other place—an arbitrary philological method that would correspondingly open other parts of the Bible to unrestrained assaults. In fact, the tales in the Bible and its figures were, for the philosopher, targets for scorn and ridicule in the best Voltairian tradition, with which he consciously associated himself.[21]

Schopenhauer's historical-philosophical interpretation was mingled with a profound investigation of cultures on the one hand and a yielding to traditional stereotypes on the other. The pessimist's opposition to

Judaism, which does attach value to man's activity on earth, was understandable. However, his philosophical ideas could have been expressed without the barbs of dismissal and contempt that are dispersed through the length and breadth of his argument. Schopenhauer's attitude to Judaism has been rightly defined as "metaphysical anti-Semitism."[22] But this is not to say that by elevating the discussion to the metaphysical sphere, he did away with anti-Semitism at the social level. Rather, the attitude of dismissal and contempt that was the lot of the Jew socially now penetrated the lofty sphere of philosophical consideration and historical discussion.

In his personal contacts Schopenhauer was not averse to Jews. He associated with some individually in his youth, and in the later period of his life, when he had gained fame and praise, Jews were among the standard-bearers of his system and his personal supporters. In this he was no different from Kant and Hegel.[23] Their negative attitude toward Jews in general did not prevent them from regarding some Jews as exceptional and capable of throwing off the negative Jewish characteristics. Like Kant in his time, Schopenhauer, too, saw a way to liberate Jews from their Judaism in the future: his way was intermarriage. But for the time being, the philosopher saw the Jews carrying the burden of their people's heritage—a heritage that aroused both disgust and amazement, not only because of its marvelous persistence but also because of its ability to join Jews together despite their dispersion all over the globe, where they were nowhere at home and nowhere strangers. "Moreover, it asserts its nationality with unprecedented obstinacy; it would also like to set foot somewhere and take root in order to arrive once more at a country, without which, of course, a people is like a ball floating in air. Till then, it lives parasitically on other nations and their soil; but yet it is inspired with the liveliest patriotism for its own nation. This is seen in the very firm way in which Jews stick together, on the principle of each for all and all for each, so that this patriotism *sine patria* inspires greater enthusiasm than does any other. The rest of the Jews are the fatherland of the Jew."[24] This hymn to Jewish solidarity contained a thorn. In its time and place, it served as an obstacle to Jewish emancipation. When it was written, in the 1840s, the Jews already enjoyed rights of general citizenship; the question was whether Jews should be able to fill posts in the state administration. Schopenhauer, like others who held the conservative view, was against this. His description of the Jews as a separate, closely knit people was an argument for denying this right.

6 | Nationalism and Romanticism

WITH THE DEPARTURE of Napoleon from the European political scene, a new situation was created, not only in the relations between states, but also in their internal affairs: there were changes in the character of the regimes, in social tensions, in the ties between religion and the state, and in the intellectual atmosphere, literature, and the arts. All this affected, directly or indirectly, the lives of the Jews, both in those countries where they had already achieved civic equality and in those where the question of equality was still pending. In France, the decisions of the National Assembly of 1790-1791 remained in effect. Napoleon's order, the "Infamous Decree" of 1808, affected the status and even the honor of the Jews, for it restricted the Alsatian Jews in their freedom of movement and choice of vocation, and it impugned their trustworthiness before the courts. The order was due to expire in 1818, but opponents of the Jews attempted to extend it. Public opinion in Alsace—and perhaps outside it—did not yet regard the equality of the Jews as a matter of course, and there were some propagandists who demanded the abolition of Jewish emancipation.[1]

In Germany, the position of the Jews was repeatedly reconsidered, both in legislative and governmental debates and in literary controversies. Attempts to examine the situation of the Jews for the purpose of improving it were made in Germany even before the French Revolution, but substantial steps toward civil equality were taken only under the pressure of the French conquerors or under the influence of their dominating example. Jews achieved civic rights in most German states in the years 1806-1808, and in Prussia in 1812. When French hegemony was abolished, a revisionist mood—an aspiration to obliterate the traces of the occupation and the surrender to French influence—took hold in Germany. Doubt was cast on the right of the Jews to retain what they had achieved in the wake of French influence, and their opponents rallied their forces for a struggle to abolish the citizenship of the Jews or to limit its significance in practice.

The primary arena of the political struggle was the Congress of Vienna, where government representatives decided questions affecting the relations between states, and an effort was also made to restore, as far as possible, the prerevolutionary status quo—hence, the aspiration to reestablish a political framework uniting all the German states that had belonged to the German-Austrian Empire before the Napoleonic era. This framework was the Germanic Confederation, consisting of thirty states which preserved their political independence but established a kind of political forum, the Bundestag, or council of the confederation, which was to meet at Frankfurt and adopt decisions on matters affecting all the states. These countries accepted at Vienna common principles of government, such as equal status for members of the various Christian churches: Catholics, Protestants, and Calvinists.[2]

Thus, the question of the Jews also appeared on the agenda, for everyone admitted in principle that it was desirable to arrive at a uniform arrangement that would apply throughout Germany. They could not agree, however, on the nature of the arrangement. The differences of opinion between those who favored granting citizenship to the Jews on the Prussian model and those who wanted to relegate them to the position they had occupied before the French Revolution were unbridgeable. The discussions were concluded by a compromise formula, the practical significance of which was quite obscure. It was decided that a uniform arrangement would be established at Frankfurt by the council of the confederation, and until then the Jews would enjoy the rights they had been granted by the various states. In the first draft of the decision, "in the states" appeared instead of "by the states"—meaning that they would continue to enjoy the rights they had been granted by the governments during the Napoleonic era. The final version, however, was interpreted as confirming the rights that had been granted *by* the states, namely, the local authorities that had been in control before the time of Napoleon and had regained their place and power. afterward.[3]

It is not clear whether those at the congress who insisted on the final version of the decision, including the phrase "by the states," foresaw what the implications of the change from "in" to "by" would be. Actually, it was not the wording agreed upon by the statesmen at Vienna that decided the fate of the Jews in the various states of Germany. Before the final decision was taken at Vienna, the municipal authorities of Frankfurt, Bremen, Lübeck, and Hamburg had withdrawn the rights granted to Jews during the French occupation, and even later, when Jewish affairs were discussed at various forums, little more than lip service was paid to the Vienna formula. The decisions were taken by the local factors in possession of political power.[4] In any case, the political decisions needed ideological justification for abolishing the rights the Jews had won during the period of French hegemony.

An entire literature was written on the Jewish problem during the years that followed the fall of Napoleon and, unlike the publications of the revolutionary and Napoleonic periods, the great bulk of it was anti-Semitic. Supporters of Jewish claims now appeared to be following in the wake of out-of-date ideas, while their opponents could take advantage of the dominant mood. This trend was well expressed by the chief spokesman of the anti-Jewish controversialists, the historian Friedrich Rühs of Berlin, who wrote *On the Claims of the Jews to Civil Rights in Germany*—a claim he denied unambiguously and categorically.[5]

Rühs admitted that previously, during the years of French occupation, he too had believed in the humanitarian ideas that led to the Jews being granted civil rights in various countries. He ascribed his change of opinion to his study of Jewish history, to which he had come in the course of his work on the history of the Middle Ages.[6] It seems more likely, however, that he was caught up in the mood that dominated Germany in the years of preparation for the War of Liberation and thereafter. The principal manifestation of this mood was the deepening of national consciousness, admiration for everything rooted in German culture and history, and the rejection of anything regarded as the fruit of foreign influence. These feelings of exclusivity were deepened and strengthened through the experience of suffering and struggle that united the fighters for independence. The Jews of the Germanic countries who had already attained citizenship, notably those of Prussia, tried to become a part of the unifying experience. Many of them served in the armies of the countries that fought Napoleon, and there were some who volunteered with the deliberate purpose of promoting the removal of the barriers between the Jewish community and the surrounding nations. This hope, however, was not realized.[7]

Among the characteristics of the new German nationalism was a devotion to the Christian faith. The Jews, therefore, found themselves outside the national pale so long as they did not join the Christian religion, even if they were capable of taking on the other qualities that were regarded as characteristics of the German nation. Rühs developed his argument in this declaration: "Christianity has always opened to the Jews its sacred circle, in which the true salvation of the human race arose in *one faith and in one love*" (italics in the original). This was the timeless, theological, dogmatic basis of the Christian appeal to the Jew to adopt Christianity; in the context of the time, the appeal was presented to the Jew as a condition for his integration into the German nation and absorption into one of its states: "A people cannot become a single whole [*in ein Ganzes*] except through the internal coalescence [*inniges Zusammenwachsen*] of all the traits of its character, by a uniform manner of their manifestations: by thought, language, faith, by devotion to its constitution."[8] This is the essential definition of nationalism in the romantic conception, which expected to find collective traits of character revealed in the cultural, religious and political traditions of a people. These characteristics are inherited, but later generations must develop them and bring to the point of completeness. A foreigner, such as a Jew, may be capable of adopting, if not for himself then for his children, the characteristics of the nation if, when joining it, he removes the barriers that separate him from it. The significance of this condition for the Jew is that in order to become a member of the German nation, he must first accept the faith that is characteristic of the German: namely, Christianity.

Let us remember that even in the period of rationalism, writers and thinkers appealed to the Jew to become converted not so much through sincere conviction of the religious truth of Christianity, but as an expression of his desire to adopt the laws of the state and the manners of the society to which he wished to belong. Rühs' outlook is a continuation of this line of thought, but his devotion to Christianity is deeper and more comprehensive than that of the rationalist thinkers and writers. The latter appreciated only the ethical teachings of Christianity and called themselves Christians only because of their support for Christian morality; but with the rise of romanticism, which played a part in the creation of the new nationalism, there emerged a readiness to accept Christianity together with its symbols and rituals, its didactic content, and the experiences associated with its tradition. The individual Christian was absolved of the need to confront the question of the truth of the Christian dogmas and the beliefs and opinions contained in its teachings. Moreover, Christianity was presented as an integral part of German nationalism, and Christian truth was acquired, almost automatically, together with it. The demand that the Jew should become a Christian as a condition for joining the German nation, therefore, assumed a new significance. Neither recognition of Christian truth nor admission of the superiority of the ethics of the Gospel was the question. Christianity was presented as one of the elements of German national culture, and a Jew who acquired German culture also acquired Christianity as one of its parts.

Rühs did not conceal his opinion that "It would have been better if they [the Jews] had not settled in our midst." Now that they had done so, their numbers should be kept down by preventing immigration and, especially, by paving the way for the adoption of Christianity "as a first and essential condition by which they can become German." He visualized the possibility that "in this way it will be possible in the course of time to achieve the disappearance of the Jewish people" and the problem would be solved once and for all. Until that time, however—and Rühs did not think it was within sight—the Jews were defined as an alien people that the German nation was unfortunately compelled to tolerate. The Jews were alien, first of all, because they did not participate in German culture, of which the Christian faith constituted an essential and fundamental element. Moreover, the Jews were distinguished by characteristic traits of their own. They pursued profit "even where they were not in need of it: where all roads to a livelihood were open to them the Jews sought to penetrate into business which gave them the opportunity for the largest possible profits without consideration for the welfare of others, hence the explanation for the hatred that pursued them even in ancient times." To confirm this thesis, Rühs mobilized "facts" from Jewish history in Spain and Poland, which allegedly proved that even in places where the Jews achieved the status of free citizens they did not abandon their devotion to commerce, peddling, and finance. He believed he had found proofs of this even in the last generation. For forty years, attention had been paid to the reform of the civic status of the Jews and much had been done for them—"but has this people as a whole taken a single step in the course of this time for its own reform?" The Jewish faith taught the Jews to believe that all physical labor was a punishment, while the accumulation of capital by trade, usury, and the like was "an immediate proof of God's protection for his chosen people." In describing the characteristics of the Jews, their pursuit of gain, their tendency to usury, and the like, Rühs followed the prerationalist Christian tradition, and Eisenmenger served as a major source for his quotations. But the aim of the description was not merely to denigrate the Jews. Rühs wanted not so much to defame the Jewish character as to show that there was a collective Jewish mentality that separated the Jew from his German environment. This mentality was the outcome of the Jew's devotion to his faith, and so long as he adhered to it he was not entitled to claim equal rights with Christian citizens. "So long as the Jews want to remain Jews, they proclaim themselves a separate and distinct nation. They proclaim that they do not want to become merged into a single whole with the people in whose midst they live."[9]

The definition of the Jews as a separate people, alien to the German nation, destroyed, in Rühs' view, the basis of their claim for civic rights in a

German-Christian state. This claim had been made in the time of the rationalists, when attention was concentrated only on the ability of the citizen to contribute to the material wealth of the state, because the state was regarded merely as the framework of an apparatus that operated mechanically to supply the needs of society. Hence, an increase in the number of citizens was regarded as beneficial, irrespective of their attitude to spiritual matters. The truth, in Rühs' eyes, was that a state existed only thanks to the inner unity of its citizens by virtue of their common faith and their readiness to sacrifice ephemeral assets for the sake of eternal and sacred values. Rühs saw a close inner bond between the nature of the state and the character of the nation that maintained it, thus expressing an idea that became dominant in the minds of his contemporaries.[10]

In accordance with this concept, it was easy to find a reason, or an excuse, for the exclusion of the Jews from the community of citizens. "The Jews are in the nature of a nation; they have compatriots [*Landsleute*] throughout the world, with whom they are bound by origin, outlook, duty, faith, language, and inclination. Together with them they constitute a single unity, and they are necessarily obliged to be closer and more devoted to them than to the nation in whose midst they live and which will remain alien to them forever." Furthermore, according to Rühs, the Jews constitute not only a nation, but even a state: "The basic laws of the Jewish faith are at the same time the basic laws of their state." This sentence, with only one word changed—Rühs wrote *Grundgesetze* instead of *Grundsätze*—is taken from the memoirs of Solomon Maimon, who used it to begin his summary of Moses Mendelssohn's theory about the character of Judaism. Mendelssohn and Maimon, however, referred to the laws of Judaism at the time when a Jewish state actually existed; insofar as their own time was concerned, they taught that obedience to the principles of the laws of Judaism depended on the will and conscience of each individual. According to Mendelssohn, therefore, there was nothing in the devotion of the Jews to their faith and laws that prevented them from belonging to the state within whose boundaries they lived. Rühs, on the other hand, ascribed to the sentence in question a contemporary significance, as if the Jews in his day were subordinate to a statute-book of Jewish tradition.[11]

Rühs was aware, of course, that a considerable minority among the Jews had already discarded the customs of the Jewish faith without going over to Christianity, but he included them, too, in the Jewish nation that was supposed to be bound by the laws of its state. Here, the stereotype that Rühs required to support his argument overpowered his perception of things as they were. The entire Jewish community was portrayed as an alien nation living its life in obedience to laws that were not the laws of the state under whose protection they lived. Hence, the conclusion seemed obvious: this community was not entitled to claim the rights of citizenship in the state: "No man can serve two masters, and indeed it is only a strange contradiction that a citizen of the Jewish state or kingdom should seek to be at the same time a citizen of a Christian state."[12]

The question that arose in the light of this conclusion was, of course, What should be done with these alien residents until they became citizens in the wake of their hoped-for conversion to Christianity? Rühs' reply was that citizens' rights were not identical with human rights, and although the Jews were not entitled to the former, they should not be deprived of the latter. It was the duty of governments to protect the Jews against injustice and injury, and not to give any excuse for the propagation of hatred against them. In practice, Rühs proposed to relegate the Jews to the position they had held before the period of reform and revolution, to restrict their numbers, as Frederick the Great had done in Prussia, and to compel them to wear a sign on their garments, as had been the custom throughout the Middle Ages. The body tax should be abolished, because of the degradation it involved, but the Jewish tax (*Judensteuer*), which the German Jews had paid the emperor in medieval times, should be reimposed for the benefit of the German Confederation. Among themselves, Jews were entitled to be judged before their own judges, but in the state, they should, of course, hold no office, power, or honor, and they should not have the privilege of serving in the army. The scope of vocations that the Jews could practice might be expanded insofar as was compatible with "the rights of the German people and the Christian residents."[13]

Rühs' attitude, which took shape with the rise of romanticism and nationalism, is a clear expression of the dialectical process in the history of anti-Semitism. If, during the stage that preceded this period, Christian and rationalist motifs were intermingled in the arguments against the Jews, there are no traces of the second type in Rühs' system. He rejected the rationalist concept of the state because he was against the entire system of rationalism, and he consistently refrained from reliance on anti-Jewish arguments that had grown on rationalist soil. It was only in the identification of the precepts of the Jewish faith as the laws of a Jewish state that the rationalist motif infiltrated his arguments, without his knowing, presumably, that the idea had been handed down from Spinoza to Mendelssohn and from him to Solomon Maimon, from whom he took it.[14] The other features of his portrait of the Jew and Judaism he took from the anti-Jewish Christian tradition. This tradition, however, was now operating in a different situation than in previous generations. The state, which Rühs defined as Christian, was entitled to that name because of its ties with the symbols and tradition of the Christian faith, but in fact its ties with the institutions of the Church had long been weakened. The state had ceased to be the secular arm of the Church, imposing its customs and principles on the citizens, and even Rühs did not aspire to restore the ancient glories. The same applied to the Jewish community, which no longer held sway over its members. Both Jews and Christians were capable of severing connections with their religious institutions, or of limiting them to an almost negligible formal minimum. The secularization of society, which had started in the eighteenth century, did not lose momentum even when the rationalist world outlook began to lose its hold.

It is against this background that Rühs' view of the social and political distinction between Jews and Christians should be seen. According to Rühs, the abyss between the two faiths also differentiated between the two communities, but unlike similar theories in medieval times, when social and political differentiation was a solid fact, Rühs' theory was not designed to explain and justify an existing situation, but to decide a question that was on the national agenda. The question was whether the Jews should be regarded as belonging to a separate sociopolitical group irrespective of whether or not they continued to be attached to their religion. A social and political struggle over this question had been waged for more than a generation, and polemicists like Rühs wanted to tilt the scales by means of anti-Jewish ideologies. In the service of this aim, they created the stereotype of a Jewish people that clung to its laws with a kind of metaphysical attachment that could not be severed except through baptism. Any social or cultural adaptation by the Jew would, according to this conception, be no more than superficial, and in fact he would remain, in all his metamorphoses, the same eternal Jew. His characteristics—his obduracy and materialism, his utter devotion to his coreligionists and his callous indifference to anyone who was not of their number—were unalterable in the eyes of Christian tradition and the collective consciousness of most of the European peoples.

Rühs' theory was based on a system of thought that was flourishing throughout Germany at the time. Ruhs found support from the philosopher Jakob Friedrich Fries of Heidelberg University, who devoted a long essay to Rühs' book in the *Heidelbergische Jahbücher der Literatur* and later published it as a separate brochure.[15] Fries summed up his colleague's thesis in brief and effective formulas. He used the term "caste," which Rühs had only mentioned by the way, as a definition of the nature of the Jewish community. The expression "a state within a state" also appears in Fries' essay to define the status of the Jewish community. The Jewish community was seen as a separate social unit, hostile to its environment, and it was out of the question to grant its members citizenship unless they completely transformed their nature. The personal liberty of the Jews had to be restricted: they must not be allowed to settle wherever they wished, to establish a family without restrictions, or to move about without an external mark of identity.[16]

All this is no more than a summary of Rühs' doctrines, but on one fundamental subject the philosopher from Heidelberg took a different view from the historian from Berlin. Fries also regarded the restrictions to be imposed on Jews as interim measures: he, too, envisioned the end of Jewry in the absorption of the Jews among the German people. In his opinion, however, this absorption need not come about through conversion to Christianity. The Jews had to emancipate themselves from their traditions, laws, and rituals, and from the inferior morality contained in them. This could be achieved by deliberate cultural adaptation: the children of the Jews would be educated in the Christian public schools, while their rabbis would study at the universities and publicly proclaim their abandonment of the Talmud, which they would exchange for "a wise morality of love of the homeland and universal love of mankind." In short, the grant of citizenship should be conditional not on the acceptance of Christianity, but on the reform—one might say the sterilization—of Judaism.[17]

The divergence between Fries and Rühs over this central point is due to the differences between them in the evaluation of religion, and especially in the relationship between church and state. The Heidelberg philosopher contended that to make the granting of citizenship to Jews conditional on their adoption of Christianity made sense only if "the German people is regarded as a Christian people and Christianity is made the state religion." But this assumption was incompatible with his liberal attitude and heritage of the rationalist tradition, to which he adhered despite his identification with the new national trend. This is also apparent in his arguments against the Jews. Rühs found the source of their moral corruption in the prescriptions of the Talmud, as exemplified in Eisenmenger's book. Fries added that the tendency to corruption, cunning, and exploitation were already apparent in the scriptural stories: "Where is there another people of a similar level of development which has such vile sacred tales, lacking any poetical sense, and interwoven everywhere with glorified acts of thievery." Their father Jacob steals his brother's birthright and deceives his father-in-law. His sons sell their brother into slavery in Egypt, and that pious man dispossesses the Egyptian people of its property. Moses, their great teacher, steals vessels of silver and gold from Egypt. And so forth. This is the style of argument known from the books of the Deists, which a Christian, devoted to the Holy Scripture, would not permit himself to repeat.[18]

In contrast to Rühs, who represents the Christian shade of the national romantic attitude, Fries stands for total nationalism, which does not enter into partnership with Christianity, but takes over its assets in order to take its place. Fries abandoned the Christian dogmas and rejected the church's claim to a dominant position in the state, even denouncing the attempts of the romanticists, like the philosopher Schelling, to refurbish the edifice of the church with the patchy plaster of mystifying symbolistic interpretation. He himself based religion—no doubt in the wake of Kant—on inner faith and its emotional element, which led to the urge to ethical action, such action consisting mainly of activity for the sake of the public interest, which elevated the individual above his personal interests and aspirations. During the years of French hegemony, Fries denounced his compatriots for lacking a unifying and liberating public goal. When they fought for liberation from Napoleon, he found in the national awakening that accompanied this fight the public goal to which he aspired, and he identified it with the content and significance of religion, namely Christianity, as he understood and defined it. In his appeals to German youth to play their part in the struggle and, later, in the realization of the national aims—the unification and social regeneration of Germany—he ascribed to the national goals the sublime and sacred epithets of the Christian faith.[19]

Fries' objections to religious dogma and ritual did not prevent him, therefore, from incorporating Christian emotionalism and rhetoric in the new nationalism. Even if this was no more than a verbal and emotional element, it was enough to exclude the Jews from the German nation. In practice, this watered-down Christianity was more detrimental to the Jews than were the remnants of faith and dogma in the nationalist theories of others. This is an example of a phenomenon to which we have already drawn attention: namely, that anti-Semitism devoid of any real Christian element may go further than Christian anti-Semitism. And indeed, Fries' anti-Jewish attitudes are more virulent than those of his predecessor, whose views served as his point of departure. Rühs, the Christian, looks forward with comparative confidence and tolerance to the days when the Jews will adopt the faith of Jesus, but Fries, the secularist, shows impatience at the obstinate refusal of the Jews to abandon their religion. Sometimes, his words sound like a threat of pogroms or of the general expulsion of the Jews from the country. He paints a shocking picture of the exploitation of the German people by the Jews and concludes: "This scandal will not come to an end without dreadful acts of violence, if our governments do not halt the evil quickly and with great force." On another occasion, he sums up his thesis thus: "If our Jews do not wean themselves completely from the abomination of their ceremonies, rituals and rabbinate, and do not adopt, in theory and in practice, ways of understanding and honesty to such an extent as to be able to merge with the Christians in one civil society, then it would be right to announce their loss of all civic

83

rights among us, to withdraw protection from them, as in those days in Spain, and to expel them from the country."[20] Even if the philosopher's words are not to be interpreted as a recommendation to punish or expel the Jews, these thoughts testify to the atmosphere that enveloped them in those years in Germany. Doubt was cast on the Jew's right to exist so long as he was a Jew, and the doubts received variegated ideological support from intellectuals of weight and authority.

There is much evidence of widespread hostility to Jews in Germany at this time. Anti-Semitism was promoted especially in places where the status of the Jews was being actively reconsidered, namely, in the districts and cities where the Jews had attained, during the period of French occupation, positions from which efforts were now being made to evict them. The city of Frankfurt is an outstanding example. Frankfurt had previously been an imperial city, governed by a senate elected by its privileged citizens. Jews had been living in the city since the twelfth century, being regarded as protégés of the emperor alone. As the power of the separate countries and the cities grew, in comparison with the authority of the emperor, especially after the sixteenth century, the Jews became protégés of the Senate, which laid down the conditions for the existence of the community and took most of their protection money; about one-third of these payments went to the imperial treasury, as a relic of the previous attachment of the Jews to the central government. When the French occupied the city in 1806, all these obligations were canceled. The city and its environs became a separate state, and its government was entrusted to Karl von Dalberg, one of Napoleon's supporters in Germany. Under the new regime in Frankfurt, the inferior status of the Jews was still maintained, but after great effort and many representations to the authorities—and in return for a payment of 440,000 guldens, a sum equivalent to twenty times the annual payment from which the Jews were now to be exempt—the Jews were proclaimed in 1811 to be citizens with full rights. After Napoleon's defeat by the allied forces in 1813, however, Prince Karl left Frankfurt and the government was restored to the members of the Senate, who categorically refused to recognize the rights granted to the Jews under Karl's rule.

The Jews of Frankfurt sought support in their conflict with the Senate: the representatives of the Jewish community appealed first to the acting governor on behalf of the Allies, Freiherr von Stein, and later to the representatives of the states assembled at the Congress of Vienna. When these entrusted the problems of the Jews to the Germanic Confederation, this institution was regarded as the appropriate body, especially since from 1816 onward it held its meetings in Frankfurt. While the Jews went on presenting their case to various bodies, they saw to it that their protest against the action of the Senate should be given wide publicity. A considerable number of articles and pamphlets in defense of the Jewish case were published during the years 1814-1817. To counteract these publications, various writers tried to explain the Senate's attitude in order to influence the public and, indirectly, the individuals and bodies who had the power to take decisions on the problem of the Jews. The argument was mainly concerned with historical, political, and juridical questions: whether the Jewish community had previously been under the authority of the emperor or of the Senate; whether Prince Karl's government had been a legal government and whether the agreement he had made with the Jewish representatives was valid; and if it was valid, whether it was binding on the authority that had succeeded him, namely, the Senate. The two sides tried to present their claims objectively. Legal opinions were obtained from three faculties of law, two by the Senate and one by the Jewish community—as if the question could have been decided by the ratiocination of a judge trying to be fair to each of two litigants. Actually, this was a political struggle, in which both sides used any means available: pressuring the bodies that had to decide, persuading anyone involved, influencing public opinion by praising themselves and denigrating their opponents.[21]

Behind the technical arguments, there were two opposing conceptions of the Jews: one that regarded them as ordinary men and favored their inclusion among the citizens of the state, and a second that clung to the ancient idea that the Jews were a separate people, without roots in the countries where they lived and unattached to their social environment. Doubt had been cast on the second conception long ago, but its devotees tried to restore its validity by both new and old ideological arguments. Even if this conception was not systematically presented in the arguments of the opponents of the Jews in Frankfurt, it emerged everywhere between the lines.

The anxiety and concern of the citizens of Frankfurt about the admission of Jews to their society were sincere and comprehensible. Since the Jews had won civic rights, many of them had taken up residence in streets where, under the previous regime, they had been forbidden to live. In 1817, a spokesman for the Senate argued that 48 houses and plots and 382 houses or shops had been rented by Jews outside the Judengasse. Jewish merchants had started to enter areas of commerce that had previously been closed to them, and their competition was undoubtedly irksome to their Christian counterparts. But the complaints of the Christians were not confined to the immediate, visible damage; they launched into prophecies of what would happen in the future: "Within a few years, most of the Christian residents will become beggars," one of them warned. The city of Frankfurt would become a Jewish city and "the offspring of the

Christian merchants will be happy if the Jewish merchants employ them as caretakers in their warehouses." The Jews in any case were in control of extensive funds, and if they achieved citizenship, they could increase their capital at the expense of others. For the Jews, moral considerations that might control their lust for money did not exist: "Their own advantage is the only motive and also the only purpose of all their actions." Under the prince's rule, they had been given the opportunity to choose the vocations they wished, but, as ever, they had rejected handicrafts and used the freedom only for "the expansion of their traffic [*Schacher*] and unrestrained usury." Furthermore, they "strove for wealth, honor, power and political influence." The end of this process would be that "we shall get Jewish lawyers, Jewish judges, Jewish tax collectors [*Einnehmer*], Jewish teachers, and finally Jewish ministers and perhaps even some kind of Jewish dynasty of rulers." This picture of the future was calculated to frighten the reader, who was accustomed to see the Jew as belonging to the lowest stratum of society—and now he was portrayed as liable to become his superior and rule over him.[22]

The reason why the Jew had to remain forever in an inferior position was derived from the Christian character of the European countries in general and the city of Frankfurt in particular. Support for this could be found in the terms in which the states of the Holy Alliance defined themselves. "If the Jews of Frankfurt claim that they now hold these civic rights, then they are subjectively comparing themselves with the Catholic and Calvinist citizens, and thus also with the Lutheran Christians." This comparison seemed absurd to Georg Friedrich Karl Robert, who came out in defense of the Senate's position: "a state that presents itself as a Christian state, being a state of the Germanic Confederation, and also because the principle has been established of equality of rights for the Christian citizens . . . and (this state) cannot comprise citizens, namely residents with equal rights, from other world religions."[23] The Christian character of the state excluded the Jews from the ranks of its citizens.

Sometimes, however, the argument for a Christian state is not expressly stated, but is implied in the argument from German nationalism, in which the Jews could have no part. The Jews claimed citizenship on the basis of the decision of the ruler during the time of the French occupation, "as if no more were needed for the grant of the national right, for acceptance in the national community, but the capricious wording of a decision, as if nothing were needed for entry into the family of a great nation—a community established over thousands of years by destiny, faith, tradition, law, and customs, an inestimable heritage acquired by struggle and effort—than the opening of the gates that lead to these shrines."[24] Religion here is only one factor determining the character of the nation. The Jews had no part in the German cultural heritage in any of its aspects. They were nothing but aliens.

The alienness of the Jews is a recurrent theme in anti-Jewish polemics. The definition of the Jews as aliens was one of the reasons given by Prince Karl at the beginning of his reign, in 1807, for refusing to grant them citizenship. The opponents of the Jews never wearied of quoting him and pointing to the contradictions in his attitude. They wanted to prove that the prince had granted the Jews citizenship only under the compulsion of capital or the pressure of circumstances: "The Jewish nation, which was flung by fate and a series of accidents into the midst of the European nations and is still alien in its ritual, manners, customs, habits, and prejudices—so long as it continues to remain alien, that is, so long as it does not merge with the majority of the people by abandoning them and accepting the manners, customs, and habits of the country, as well as by giving up its prejudices against close integration with the Christians, the main obstacle to any rapprochement—until then it is impossible, and in our view it would also be unjust, to allow them equal rights with the Christian inhabitants." The same point is made repeatedly: "The Jew does not truly belong to the country in which he lives, for as the Jew from Poland is not a Pole, the Jew from England is not an Englishman, and the Jew from Sweden is not a Swede, so the Jew from Germany cannot be a German and the Jew from Prussia a Prussian." "The Jews are an alien people, they are nothing but guests in the lands of their dispersion . . . So long as they remain Jews, their integration with the Christian peoples of Europe is impossible, both because of their different nationality and, especially, because of their different faith and ritual." Here, the religious factor was the decisive one as it was for most of those opposed to the Jews. For those who based the uniqueness of the German people on their exclusive national tradition, the denial of rights to Jews was based on their having un-Germanic traits of character with which they were imbued irrespective of their religion: "And indeed, from all the facts clearly revealed beyond a doubt by history and unshaken by a few exceptions, it is plain that the Jews are a great and very widespread hereditary band of merchants closely welded by faith, political principles, and strange and outlandish customs who have inevitably found themselves in this position by virtue of inner necessity since its members have lived among other nations. Since they separate themselves by clinging to their strange character and deliberately inhibiting any participation in any local national association, the latter has also been compelled by virtue of national character to close itself up against them."[25]

Both trends in the rejection of the Jews, the one founded on the idea of the Christian state, as developed by Rühs, and the second based mainly on the new nationalism and represented by Fries, are revealed in the Frankfurt controversy, and the words of the two writers are quoted here and there. The main principles of the ideology of rejection, however, did not have to be drawn by the Frankfurt polemicists from the works of the two scholars. The intellectual atmosphere of the generation was imbued with them, with little variation in idioms and with stereotyped formulas. The first anti-Jewish work, the anonymous *Was soll bei der neuen Verfassung aus den Juden werden*, was written before the appearance of Rühs' book and foreshadowed Rühs' views that the Jews had remained "in all parts of the world for eighteen centuries a closed nation, attached only to itself, a state within a state."[26]

The separateness of the Jews was emphasized by their opponents, who pointed to it as the main obstacle to their integration. One of the disputants arguing on behalf of the Senate accused the Jews of inconsistency, for while in theory they were fighting for integration among citizens, in practice they were making themselves a separate group by the very fact of their collective struggle: "This means that, in contradiction to the rule that this is a matter for individuals as limbs in the entire body [*Glied des Ganzen*], they seek to see themselves (and their characteristics leave no room for any other way) as a body within the body [*Ganzes im Ganzen*]." Furthermore, the spokesman for the citizens of Frankfurt complained that "it may be concluded from certain indications that the Jews of the whole of Germany regard [the interests of the Jews of Frankfurt] as their common interests and act accordingly."[27]

The fact that the Jews of various places, and even of distant countries, could be seen to constitute one social unit was regarded as an obstacle to their citizenship, and their enemies in Frankfurt did not weary of pointing this out: "In our days a great cry has been raised about political groups, but apparently it has not occurred to anyone that you can hardly find a more dangerous group than the group of the Jewish people so long as it remains in its present constitution [*Verfassung*]." "Where are the conditions of a political group to be found in a more complete form than here—money, secret ties in all parts of the world, ease and reliability in the transfer of information are the external means, and equal egoistic interests, religious fanaticism, hatred due to acts of oppression and anger which will be revealed in irresistible strength?" Radicalist secret societies, which aroused fear in that generation, served here as a model and example to intensify repulsion from the Jews, by virtue of the syllogism that if the secret societies are dangerous, even more so is the Jewish community, known and unknown. One writer declared simply: "Even now there is a secret Jewish alliance throughout Europe." Fichte had complained that the Jews, scattered over the whole of Europe, constituted a single political unit. Now this accusation was accompanied by the charge that they acted in secret, behind the scenes. We have here an outstanding example of the tendency to identify the Jew with the most objectionable and threatening phenomenon of a particular time. The downfall of Napoleon had involved the repression of social and political aspirations, which were not satisfied under the new regime. Consequently, fears arose of the creation of an underground of secret societies, which would endanger the survival of the recently restored regime. As soon as the fears arose, frightening epithets were attached to the Jews, on the principle of blaming a known criminal for a new crime. The "criminal" in this case was a minority community of an inferior status, to whom it was permissible and even reasonable, in view of its lack of status, prestige, and presumption of good character, to ascribe undesirable qualities, even those that had not been revealed in it.[28]

The inferior status of the Jews, which left them open to baseless accusations, was manifested in the opprobrious terms that were casually embodied in the writings of their opponents. Ostensibly, the writers were dealing with the legal or political aspects of the question of the right of the Jews to citizenship by virtue of Prince Karl's declaration, or on the basis of the agreement signed between him and them—but by the way, as an introduction to the rejection of a certain argument of the Jews, the writer might say: "However, how far Jewish cunning and pretense can go . . ." The spokesman of the Senate speaks of the cunning fabrications of the Jews and another writer called one of the Jewish claims "Jew-lies" (*Judenlüge*), implying that lying is in keeping with the essential nature of the Jew. Expressions of this kind, when interspersed with ostensibly objective arguments, reveal their authors' feelings of superiority over their Jewish rivals. It is hinted—and even more than hinted—that the position of the Jews in the quarrel is fundamentally unsound because of their moral character—actually, because of their inferior social status. Sometimes this is expressly stated: "An astonishing phenomenon is the fact . . . that the local Jewry ventured to intervene in discussions on the constitution of the city . . . and to set itself up against it as a party." One of the writers, describing the historical and legal development of the argument until it reached the institutions of the Germanic Confederation, finally rebukes the Jews for their impudence in taking up the time of this distinguished German institution with their affairs: "The Jewish community ought to be ashamed of trying to steal the valuable time of the Council of the Germanic Confederation, which has a different function and has to fulfill much higher aims than to defer even for a single day the determination of the noble aims of the German people because of the claims and arguments of Jews like these." Similarly, another writer criticizes the faculty of law at Giessen, which had given an opinion in favor of the Jews, not only for "lack of understanding of all juridical principles," but because the faculty "sinned at the same time against the honor of the German nation" by granting to "the remnants of an oriental people scattered all over the world" civic rights in a city which was once the city of the election and coronation of the German emperors.[29]

The Jews' claims were rejected not only on the basis of the arguments that could be adduced against them, but also because they were regarded as unworthy of litigating with the defendants. The Jews continued to be considered by their opponents as a community of wretches and outcasts, whose very right to reside in Frankfurt was doubtful—much less their right to citizenship. The Jews' opponents never wearied of pointing out that the Jews had come from a far-off country and had only been admitted to the city by the grace of the authorities and under the conditions those authorities had laid down. Some writers even suggested that the problem of the Jews would be solved by their departure from the city. One of those who saw the solution in the conversion of the Jews concluded the presentation of his case by expressing the wish that the Frankfurt Senate had at its disposal "free stretches of land on which it could settle, like the Tsar of Russia, the largest possible number of Israelite Christians who are really such in colonies of peace." Another writer suggested, in the course of discussing the Jews of Frankfurt, how it would be possible "to put an end to the unfortunate Jewish presence in the whole of Europe": the rulers of the powers "will start negotiations with the Turks in order to restore to the scattered Palestinians their ancient promised land where they could once again become the true chosen people of God." These were not practical proposals, but simply wishes cherished by their authors, who regarded the discussion of the affairs of the Jews as a burden. If only it had been possible, they would have got rid of them and their troubles at one stroke.[30]

The atmosphere that reigned in Germany during and after the Congress of Vienna is clearly demonstrated by the reaction of the public to the play *Unser Verkehr*, which caricatured Jewish characters. The hero of the play is a young Jew, Jacob, whose father tells him to go out into the world and do what a Jewish father expects of his son, according to the current stereotype, namely, to make money—by whatever means possible. "If you go and do not return ninety-nine times as heavy, I will spit in your face. Go, let people trample on you, throw you out of the room, bring you to trial, put you in jail, shackle you with ropes and chains, let them beat you and torture you to the point of death, but you must get rich." But the young man has different views. Jacob accepts the goal put before him by his father, but he believes that he can attain it by different methods. He regards himself as a talented intellectual, a genius: "I was not born for trade." "A merchant trades in commodities, a genius with his talents."

90

Jacob represents the spurious intellectual who wants to escape from the bonds of his community and deludes himself that he does not show the marks of his Jewishness. He proclaims his aim in the Yiddish language, which demonstrates the contradiction between his self-image and his nature. The development of the plot is meant to hint that the aspiration for enrichment without effort is rooted in the Jew and is the most important thing in his life. Jacob falls in love with the daughter of a wealthy Jew, who was his childhood playmate in the Jewish quarter, but has now gone further than he in the abandonment of Judaism and goes to church accompanied by the Christian choirmaster. At the beginning, father and daughter reject the lovesick youth with contempt, but suddenly the news arrives that Jacob has won the big lottery prize, and immediately he becomes a welcome suitor and is admired as the hero of the day by all the Jews assembled at the announcement of the great tidings. It transpires, however, that the news was false. It was not Jacob who won the prize but another Jew, and poor Jacob returns to his lowly position. He finds that he has no other way to wealth except trade, and he appeals to the audience: "Gentlemen, which of you has any merchandise to trade with?"[31]

This play, by the unimportant writer Karl Borromaus Alexander Sessa, whatever its artistic merit, presents the image of the Jew exactly as it is reflected in the polemical literature opposing the grant of civic rights to the Jews, and the play, as well as others like it, delighted the German public during the years when political decisions were being made on the fate of the Jews. Julius Voss, who sometimes defended the Jews, followed the fashion in those days and in some of his plays presented the Jewish stereotype with all its negative aspects. In a play that tried to see the other side of the coin—how writers and actors tried to extort money from the Jews by threatening to depict their ugly side—he reveals the reason for the enthusiasm for the subject of the Jew: "Thieves' kitchens and Jews are still the rage." The Jew had become the subject in which everyone was interested, for good or—in the great majority of cases—for worse.[32]

7 | Incitement and Riot

THERE IS NO DOUBT that public interest in the subject of Jews was fed by the political factor: the awareness that the questions of Jewish citizenship, rights, status, and perhaps even permission for Jews to live in a specific city or street were still not finally decided. This accounts for the plethora of publications of various kinds at this period. In 1816, the historian Heinrich Luden, editor of the important magazine *Nemesis* in Weimar, stated that he had recently received no less than eight articles about Jews and matters relating to them. He decided to print only three. From him we also know the trend of those writings: "On the question posed whether Jews in the German states should be given, without precautions and limitations, the citizen rights they are seeking, there is not one article in favor out of all those submitted." Citizenship was the issue around which all the arguments revolved.[1]

Ludolf Holst, in 1818, published anonymously a work entitled *Über das Verhältniss der Juden zu den Christen in den deutschen Handelsstädten*. He represented this work as "historically authentic," a personal evaluation that was taken seriously by Jewish historians, who cited it as testimony on the status of Jews, their activities and economic dealings. In truth it was a propaganda tract, which was most probably commissioned by interested parties in one of the powerful industrial cities, apparently Holst's own birthplace Hamburg, where the Jewish question was very much alive. The book was dedicated to "every politician throughout the Fatherland for serious consideration." Clearly missing in the book is any material drawn from direct observation. The author deals exclusively in anti-Jewish generalities disguised as facts. The Jews corrupt commerce by hawking, dealing in secondhand clothes, and the like. They debase the currency by clipping coins, trading in "paper," and performing fictitious banking transactions. They import shoddy cloth from England and other wares and luxury items from abroad; they thus undermine the livelihood of the merchants who are dependent on local products. Holst's method is quite simple: he enumerates the troubles and hardships that are the subject of contemporary complaint and blames them on the Jews. Spiraling prices, unemployed artisans, even the pursuit of luxuries, the decline in morality, and the increase in the number of children's asylums as a result of people being unable to sustain a family, are all the fault of the Jews. Naturally, no proof is offered for all this; but since the hardships are tangible and painful, the imputation falls upon ready ears.[2]

Furthermore, while the author draws these detailed accusations out of thin air, it is a fact that his depiction of the Jewish situation in general is not completely sundered from reality. It is certainly true that, by comparison with conditions a generation or two earlier, the Jews' lot had improved perceptibly. The Jews themselves looked upon what had taken place in most parts of Germany in the years following the fall of Napoleon as a setback from what had been gained in his time and during the French Revolution. Their disappointment was all the sharper in view of the expectations that had been aroused by the idea of equality that had emerged from the Enlightenment and the tenets of the Revolution. Despite this, the Gentiles, almost without exception, compared the position of Jews in their own time with the situation in which they had existed before the Revolution. Thus, they measured the extent of Jewish progress against that of other classes in the state and found that the Jewish situation had improved immeasurably by any criterion. This claim appears repeatedly in Holst's writings, suggesting that he was expounding current opinion. How did the Jews fare fifty years previously, it was asked, and what is it like for them today? In those days they were shut up inside their narrow streets, never emerging except to do business. Now one finds them in places where Christians assemble, at public gatherings and places of entertainment. The Jews have bought fine houses in the most splendid parts of the town, where they dared not show their faces hitherto. Formerly, Jews were hard put to find a common Gentile to extinguish their Sabbath lamp. Today, for the most part, they employ Christian servants over whom they lord it directly and indirectly. While the other classes are progressively losing out, the Jews are advancing apace.

Holst employs the misery of the general population, resulting from wars, unstable governments, and economic ills, as background for depicting the advantages that he alleges the Jews to have extracted from the suffering of others. Thus, it was easy for Holst to confront his readers with the horrifying prediction that, if the Jews were not stopped, they would take over from the Christians all the sources of their livelihood. They would go on to realize their messianic dream of "getting rid of all the Christians at one fell swoop . . . and turning Germany into a second Canaan."[3] In order to offset this development, Holst offers the draft plan prepared by the opponents of the Jews for settling the Jewish issue: *"The Jew must remain completely within specific limits which will be drawn with intelligent caution and will be based on right and justice [Recht und Gerechtsame]."*—Holst's italics. This abstract formulation possessed a concrete significance for Holst's generation. They took it to mean that Jews should not stand on the same level as other citizens nor enjoy any rights other than those bestowed on them by the city or state rulers. The principle by which the Jew's rights would be determined was thus expounded by Holst: The welfare (*Wohlfahrt*) of the Jews would be dependent on that of the Christians, and obviously, in the event of any contradiction between the two, that of the Christians, the citizens and lords of the state, would take precedence over that of the alien Jews. Holst held that it would be in the Jews' interest to strive for such a compromise. They should recall what befell them previously when the populace of the lands where they dwelled rose up against them to free themselves from their subjection. This phenomenon could happen again in Germany. Holst points to signs of unrest directed against the Jewish domination. What was the dizzy progress of the Jews worth when they would ultimately "pitch down into nothingness from the high estate they had conquered, this being the miserable consequence of their deluded megalomania and unbridled arrogance."[4]

Holst's book is the most comprehensive work of its genre, but its general motivations occur repeatedly in other contemporary publications. In his book *Uber Deutschland, wie ich es nach einer zehnjährigen Entfernung wiederfand*, published in 1818, Garlieb Helwig Merkel has a chapter on the Jews. Among the changes he found in Germany after being away for ten years was a change in the condition of the Jews. While the "German peoples had, in many years of political disaster lost their precious political rights and had diminished in stature, they [Jews] had increased their wealth [*Wohlstand*] at a terrifying rate. They knew how to gain equality with the Christians everywhere and they zealously set about developing this equality into further privileges."[5] This statement of Merkel has some truth in it; Jews had exploited, economically and socially the new status they had achieved in the past generation. Previously, Berlin Jews had only been permitted to live "on the other side of the river Spree opposite the Palace"; now the Jews bought up every house offered for sale in the main streets and filled the city with their shops. The Jews had long dominated in financial deals and trade in bills. Now they lead in occupations such as the book trade, which had previously been closed to them. Almost all the country homes (*Landhäuser*) on both sides of the Tiergarten, the Berliners' only place of recreation, had passed into Jewish hands. "So, there these mobs of aliens sit on the lovely summer evenings in the doors of their homes watching the citizens walking in sand and slush."[6]

The Jews had made their gains at the expense of the other citizens. The proliferation of Jewish shops had forced rent up intolerably; the penetration of Jews into the book trade had downgraded this occupation through the flooding of the market with books printed without a license. If, just then, the Jews seemed to be treading hard on the heels of the Christians, the outlook for the future was that they would dominate them completely. The Jews were trying to buy up the estates of the nobility (*Rittergüter*). "If they are allowed to do this, thanks to the vast sums of ready money at their disposal, then, lo and behold, the debilitated nobility will be uprooted in a few decades time, while the citizens of the state, the tillers of the soil, will become subjected to these aliens and in certain areas will be their serfs."[7]

The familiar mixture once again: a smattering of facts—the Jews reach positions of economic and social advantage as a consequence of their improved political condition—combined with exaggeration in presenting the facts and blaming the sufferings of others on the achievements of the Jews. Then, the last step, ballooning the future consequences of Jewish progress. Merkel had been forced to leave Germany because of anti-French activity in 1806 and lived in Riga until 1816. It is possible that his absence from Germany in the decisive years sharpened his view of the changes that had occurred in the status of the Jews, in Prussia particularly. The Edict of 1812 had given them freedom of residence, occupation, and business. But it was not just the status of the Jews that had changed, but the views of the beholder. At the beginning of the century, when public opinion was concerned with the Jewish question, Merkel had adopted the typical enlightened attitude. In his book *Letters on Hamburg and Lübeck*, written in 1801, he had lauded the Hamburg authorities for their understanding in granting Jews a firm legal status that would enable their ability and wealth to be fully utilized for the benefit of the city. He also censured, by contrast, the mass of the people and those citizens who clung to Christian prejudices and rejected social intercourse with Jews.[8] Now, nothing remained of this attitude of enlightened tolerance. He invoked ideological arguments against bestowing civic rights upon the Jews: "The European countries are Christian." The justification of this definition was

95

that "giving recognition to the sanctity of the faith and moral teachings of Christianity had been made the basis of social righteousness [*Rechtlichkeit*] and political loyalty." This clumsy argumentation patently indicates that Christianity was not being taken to mean submission to the dogmas and church rituals in the ordinary sense. Christianity was expressed, rather, through the linkage of society and state to symbols and a complex of ideological concepts of Christian origin. This kind of Christianity was now prevalent in the public life of Europe, and even committed members of the Enlightenment like Merkel came to terms with it, not because they confessed it as a faith but because they recognized its utility. With reference to the Jewish issue, this recognition led to an unequivocal conclusion. The Jews were not adapted to integrate into a society or state whose basis for existence they did not acknowledge. The Jews "who, even without this, are separated off from the Christians by their nationality and way of life [*Sitten*] do not recognize the sanctity of the faith and teachings of Christian morality"; therefore, they could not be permitted to become partners in the life of their Christian neighbors. They remained aliens in Christian society and state and were entitled to concessions (*Freiheiten*), but not to rights.[9]

We have already heard this tune before. Its echoes now reverberated throughout Germany and served as a sop to the humanistic consciences of men of the Enlightenment. Merkel also vents his disappointment with the highest political authority in Germany—the confederation council in Frankfurt. The Jews of the mercantile cities of Frankfurt and Lübeck had complained to this body about those cities which had deprived them of the rights granted during the French regime. It is a sign of the times that the Jews dared lodge a complaint against the authorities in whose jurisdiction they resided, and that the council took up their complaint and did not reject them lock, stock, and barrel.[10]

Like other writers who polemized against the Jews, Merkel sets himself up as the guardian of the German people. He comes to the conclusion that if the citizens and masses of the people will not obtain the necessary protection against the Jews from the authorities, they should take the law into their own hands and act for themselves. Merkel goes far beyond his predecessors in the vehemence of his language and the confidence with which he predicts what will happen. He recalls Fries' warning of a bloody uprising against the Jews if they did not call a halt. There were those who had censured Fries for this, but Merkel was surprised that anyone could have disagreed, for all past analogies from history showed how correct he was: "There are very few countries in Europe where the Jews have not attained excessive power which they used for ill purposes and thus brought persecution upon themselves." At one time the persecutors depended on accusations of desecrating the host or murdering

Christian children. Such accusations were no longer made, "But much more reasonable charges will doubtless be found whose effectiveness will be far more terrible."[11]

As has been stated, these warnings of popular indignation against the Jews were intended to goad the authorities into taking action to restrain Jewish progress, to refrain from enlarging their rights, and to annul those rights they already possessed. However, insofar as these warnings were heard in public, they caused, in the first instance, a hostile reaction to the Jews, and thus they could have been interpreted as incitement. In the first months of 1819, two contemporaries, one a Jew, the other a liberal Christian, expressed their apprehension that if the atmosphere continued to worsen, Jews would not escape injury to their persons and their fortunes.[12] Rachel Varnhagen said, after the riots broke out, that for years she had been claiming that the continuous incitement would end in violence against Jews.[13] Most Jews lacked a sense of security in those years, and this is emphasized by an episode in Breslau in 1818. A sort of minor revolution took place there. Local inhabitants who had been called up for military reserve duty rebelled against the order to leave their own city while alien soldiers were billeted in their homes. The army crushed the uprising, and order was restored at the cost of some casualties among the citizens. An eyewitness, Wolfgang Menzel, concluded his account with this observation: "The very next morning the people were laughing again, especially at the corpulent police chief and the Jews who had gone into hiding during the riots. This was because, despite the fact that 2,000 Jews regularly resided in Breslau at that time and disturbed the people with their open ostentatious appearance in the city streets, on August 23rd (the day it all happened), they all hid away. Not one showed his face. Their fear was certainly well-founded, because the Hep Hep which swept throughout Germany the following year, proves how detested this people is."[14] Menzel was referring to the riots that broke out against the Jews in the summer of 1819. The slogan the rioters used, "Hep! Hep!" gave its name to the movement.

The Hep Hep riots began in the city of Wurzburg, Bavaria, on August 2, 1819.[15] All the factors that created the hostile attitude toward Jews were present there in an intensive degree. The change in regime that occurred in Napoleon's time resulted in profound transformations in the government of the city and its political and social affairs. Until 1803, Wurzburg had been the capital of the bishopric, and Jewish residence had been forbidden there since the expulsion in 1567. In 1803, following the abolition of the Catholic duchies in Germany (known as secularization), the bishopric and country were annexed to Bavaria. Three years later, the country became a secular principality under a ruler of the Austrian Hapsburg house, but at the time of the Congress of Vienna it was again annexed to Bavaria. Decisive changes took place in Wurzburg during the Austrian principality, one of them being that Jews were permitted to reside in the city. Jews in the area took advantage of the opportunity. In 1813, some thirteen families were living there. Among them were the brothers Jacob and Solomon Hirsch, the former being the court banker at Munich. The number of Jews grew steadily in the following years, despite the indignation of the merchants and other interested elements and a general spirit of prejudice. The bitterness found expression in propagandistic writings produced in anticipation of the session of the Assembly of the Estates at Munich in February 1819. This assembly had been convened by virtue of a parliamentary statute that King Maximilian Joseph I had enacted under the influence of liberal elements in the state. Citizens were looking forward expectantly to the assembly, as each group hoped it would enact measures for its benefit and the improvement of its position. Lively propaganda was going on, and the Jewish question too was widely discussed. The Jews looked forward to an improvement in their legal status that would raise them to the same level as other citizens, and their hopes were sustained by writers and certain public figures. Their opponents pressed the Assembly of the Estates to restrict the freedom of the Jews, especially their right to dispose of their wares by hawking. In the assembly, the views of their opponents were forcibly presented; but those who defended the Jews did not spare them criticism. The foremost spokesmen in their defense was Professor Josef Behr, the delegate of the University of Wurzburg. His was the stance typical of liberal critics. In principle, he wanted to see Jews placed on an equal footing with other citizens. In practice he made their inclusion conditional on changes in their way of doing business and on reforms in their education and religion.

Echoes of the debate in Munich were obviously heard at Wurzburg, where heated literary activity took place on both sides. A memorandum was composed on the Jewish side claiming full citizenship rights; it was published in the name of Solomon Hirsch. A Christian lawyer, Theodor A. Scheuring, came out with a fierce attack on this pamphlet, bringing about one of the sharpest polemics in Germany during that period.[16] Scheuring linked up the anti-Jewish arguments from all quarters. He infused them with the Christian and rationalist ideology formulated in the books of Rühs and Fries and added the local complaints emanating from the fanaticism and jealousies of the inhabitants of Wurzburg and surrounding areas. He stated that daily experience proved that "those districts which the spirit of Jewish violence and corruption have not reached are the happiest," and one should compare their happiness with the tragedy of those afflicted by the presence of Jews. On July 10, 1819, Scheuring an-

Incitement and Riot

)unced the appearance of his book in the *Intelligenzblatt*, giving a short
immary of its contents. Scheuring's words did not remain unanswered.
rofessor Sebald Brendel of the law faculty of the University of Wurzburg,
:acted in the same newspaper on July 15 and 21. Brendel had a more
onsistent liberal approach than his colleague Josef Behr. He attacked
scheuring severely for intolerance, inhumanity, and even non-Christianity
1 his views. He accused him of ignorance of the sources of Judaism and
)ther related subjects. Scheuring had arrogated to himself authority on the
)asis of citations whose meaning he had not grasped, in order to decide an
.ssue that was beyond his understanding. Brendel announced that he was
about to publish a book refuting Scheuring's views and establishing the
position that the Jewish question could only be resolved by granting full
citizenship rights to the Jews, immediately and without any reservations.
This announcement elicited an abrasive and insulting reply from Scheuring. It was printed on Thursday, July 29, in the above-mentioned Wurzburg newspaper. On the following Monday evening, August 2, harass-
ment of the Jews began in the city. They were forced to flee public places
to cries of "Hep! Hep!", a rallying cry for the attackers. The argument between Brendel and Scheuring raised the temperature of unrest against the
Jews to the boiling point, while their intemperate language ultimately produced acts of violence.[17]

On August 3, Behr returned from Munich. His colleagues and
students went to meet him in a procession, and it is quite likely that this additional traffic increased the unrest in the city. It is a fact that on that day
the disturbances reached a fever pitch. Jews were removed from the city
streets, the rioters attacked their houses, smashed windows, broke doors,
and tore down signs over Jewish firms. The house of Jacob Hirsch was
among those damaged. Jews who defended themselves were beaten up.
The police were unable to impose restraint, and the security authorities
had to invoke the assistance of the army. Despite this, the rioting continued until August 4. There were two fatal casualties during the riots: a
citizen and soldier were killed by shooting. There were no fatalities among
the Jews, but many fled screaming from the city or hid away inside their
homes until the storm subsided. Ultimately, army reinforcements restored
order. The leaders of the riots were arrested and brought to trial. Despite
this, the anti-Jewish incitement continued through anonymous an-
nouncements demanding the removal of Jews from the city or limitations
on their commercial activity. The anger of the attackers was turned against
Brendel, who was accused of having been bribed to defend the Jews. The
anti-Jewish ferment went on throughout August and the beginning of
September. Meanwhile, the disturbances spread to other cities. In Bavaria,
Bamberg and Bayreuth were hit, and serious riots occurred in several

99

villages. In one of them the synagogue was razed and the Scroll of the Law and sacred objects were vandalized.[18]

The outbreaks were followed with growing concern by the central government in Munich. King Maximilian Joseph and other observers of the situation viewed them not just as attacks upon Jews but as the beginning of an insurrection against the regime, and even, perhaps, a conspiracy directed by hidden revolutionaries. The king reacted very strongly. He ordered military force used to suppress the disturbances. He held the city councils responsible for the riot damage. The latter eagerly proclaimed their loyalty and placed the responsibility on radical classless elements over whom they had no control. Nevertheless, there were hints that the authorities should learn a lesson from the riots and put the Jews in their place. The initial cause of what had happened was evident: The riots originated because the Jews had been permitted to live in places where they had hitherto been forbidden and to enter into occupations previously closed to them. The protesters found ideological support in intellectual circles, while their complaints and slogans stirred the masses to hatred and destruction. Thus matters erupted in violence.[19]

The happenings in Wurzburg served as a pattern for other places in Germany even beyond Bavaria. Disturbances broke out in Frankfurt on August 10, 1819 and continued for three days. Some thirty other cities were also affected, the most important being Heidelberg, Karlsruhe, and Hamburg. The wave of riots reached Copenhagen and other places in Denmark. All the riots resembled the Wurzburg disorders, with some local nuances arising out of special local circumstances. In Frankfurt, the seat of the Germanic Confederation Council, deputies of the states demanded that the Senate take care of law and order. Because Frankfurt was such a vital center, the riots there aroused reactions much further afield. The riots influenced the representatives of the German governments who were sitting in Carlsbad at that time drawing up preventive measures to be taken against revolutionary movements that were threatening the regime and the peace of society. During the course of the discussions, the chairman of the assembly, Prince Metternich, issued an order that the confederation's military forces at Mainz should be placed at the disposal of the Frankfurt Senate to put down the riots. Although the Bavarian force quartered at Mainz was placed on a state of alert, the Senate managed to quiet the city without recourse to outside help. In Heidelberg the rioters exploited a holiday, Prince Ludwig's Feast, when the police were occupied elsewhere, to descend upon Jewish homes and wreak havoc in a manner reminiscent of the Russian pogroms of a later era (tearing open pillows and counterpanes, throwing furniture into the street). The outrages were brought to an end by the intervention of students and professors who defended the victims of the attack. These academics were lauded by the authorities and denounced by civilian and university elements. Those who participated in rescuing the Jews declared that it was not their intention to side with the Jews. They had just been fulfilling a humanitarian obligation toward the weak and assaulted.[20]

The disorders continued in Hamburg from August 20 to 26. They began with the pestering of Jewish passers-by in the Jungfernstieg, the main promenade. Jews were driven out of the coffee houses, and stones were thrown at Jewish houses. However, the young Jews did not pack up, but actively counterattacked to the extent that the rioters could claim they were the aggressors. The Senate warned the populace to observe law and order and ordered the police to fire on anyone found in the street after a fixed time in the evening. The Senate's warning was first directed to the rioters, but following protests from the citizens, the Jews were included in those who were warned that no disturbances would be permitted. Although the disorders in Hamburg persisted longer than in other places, they did not assume as serious dimensions as those in Wurzburg and Heidelberg. Nevertheless many Jews left the city and sought refuge in Altona, which, though adjacent, was under Danish rule and had remained quiet.

The Hep Hep riots lasted only two months, but had extensive repercussions. Despite prior warnings, the outbreaks nevertheless took by surprise all those concerned—Jews, propagandists, and authorities. Immediately after the disturbances began, the question was raised: Who was responsible? The authorities at Munich, as we have seen, worked on the assumption that the riots against the Jews might be the beginning of an uprising against the regime. This view was widely accepted by those who supported the existing regime. In March 1819, the writer August Kotzebue was killed in Mannheim by Karl Ludwig Sand. The victim was a supporter of the reactionary regime, while his assassin was a member of an extremist student organization at the University of Jena. He had intended his act as a violent protest against the regime and as a call to his comrades to follow in his footsteps. In June that year there had been a similar attack on a minister of Nassau. Tension increased between those responsible for the existing regime and those seeking to change it. At that time, the debate was still continuing in the southern states whether to increase the freedom of the citizens by the grant of a constitution and the creation of a parliamentary regime. The tangible threat of violence by the revolutionaries strengthened the conservatives. Prince Metternich, the architect of the conservative regime created at the Congress of Vienna, now sought to consolidate his system. He assembled the German states at Carlsbad with the aim of deciding on joint measures to restrain the fermenting

101

elements—introducing severe police control, imposing censorship, and so forth. News of the riots at Wurzburg and Frankfurt reached Carlsbad while the consultations were in progress. The reports helped Metternich and his associates to demonstrate that a subversive movement against the regime existed and the time for a strong hand had arrived. It is possible that Metternich and his associates deliberately exaggerated the danger revealed by the attacks on the Jews, although they certainly believed the danger did exist and did view the attacks on the Jews as part of the ferment against the regime. In this view they were not alone. Several propagandists, one apparently a Jew, claimed that "men seeking to turn everything into anarchy" caused the anti-Jewish riots. Voices warned against seeing the riots as actually anti-Jewish. "Those who today plunder and destroy the house of a rich Jewish merchant will, with the same motives and pleasure, do the same tomorrow to the house of a Christian merchant."[21]

The thesis that the anti-Jewish riots derived from general social unrest has gained a place in modern historical research. It finds expression in Eleonore Streling's statement that the anti-Jewish disturbances were no more than a diverted social protest really directed against the harsh and oppressive regime, but finding an outlet in the depressed and weak Jewish group.[22] However, this theory is refuted by the facts: The participants in the anti-Jewish riots were not those who held the ideals of national unity and social revolution and who formed those underground cells that so terrified the existing regime. These cells were made up principally of university students who did not participate in the anti-Jewish riots. We have clear testimony from Wurzburg of the absence of students from the area of disturbances. There were no universities in Frankfurt and Hamburg, while in Heidelberg the students went to the rescue of the Jews. The ground for the riots was prepared by prolonged anti-Jewish propaganda whose purpose was to tilt the balance against the Jews on the question of full citizenship. The disturbances were concentrated in places where the question of citizenship was still open—in Wurzburg, Frankfurt, and Hamburg. The stimulus for the opposition came from those who saw themselves harmed by the entry of Jews into their occupations, namely, merchants who had previously enjoyed a monopolist position within the civic commerce. A brooding apprehension, perhaps even fear and terror, over infiltration of society by residents of the ghetto, who were held to be a dangerous element, was aroused in the population even when there was no actual, direct competition. A physical attack on Jews was imminent. However, until the riots actually broke out, the political leaders closed their eyes to the problem. In every other aspect of life they closely scrutinized every conceivable threat to the peace of the community and existence of the regime. Had any hostility been aroused against any group other than the

Jews there is no doubt that the state would have taken steps to restrain it. With regard to the Jews, they allowed matters to ferment until they actually resulted in violent outbreaks.[23]

It is evident that the improvement in the status of the Jews from the time they left the ghetto was only a formal achievement. It did not gain them social immunity: derogatory statements, aspersions on their character, and insults to their religious beliefs were still permissible. The relationship between the Jewish community and non-Jewish society was still strained by a heavy historical burden and social tension. This strain by itself can suffice to explain the outbreaks of hostility; one need not seek an explanation in the general unrest prevailing in society. Despite the fact that they now were a part of the general social framework, having been recognized as citizens of the state—albeit in an inferior class—the Jews were still a discernible and separate group and a problem to themselves and their environment. The disturbances of 1819, which were directed against the Jews alone, prominently highlighted this separation. Although only certain elements of society actually participated, the riots did demonstrate in a very clear manner the isolation of the Jews, their status as a group distinct from German society. It is true that at that time the authorities hastened to help the Jews and that, here and there, individual Gentiles publicly condemned what had happened. However, the majority of the public, while not actually justifying the violence, did draw the conclusion that the very presence of the Jews in German society was fraught with danger. About a year after the riots, the historian Georg Sartorius reviewed the situation in Germany to see whether there was a foreseeable danger of the revolution that writers and politicians had been foretelling for some years. Sartorius analyzed the political and social conditions of the German states, one by one, and reached the conclusion that the fears of revolution had been exaggerated in previous years and that careful and intelligent action could prevent the danger in the future. Sartorius saw the anti-Jewish riots of the previous year as an exceptional happening flowing from the tension existing between the Jews and their surroundings as a consequence of their growth and their entry into the occupations of their rivals. He looked on the steps taken by the governments to crush the disturbances as a legitimate necessity and recommended a policy of firmness in the future should the occasion require it: "For no matter what type of uprising there be, no matter what its causes may be, what causes anxiety at this time is that we cannot calculate where it may lead and how the flames may spread."[24] The advice he tendered the regimes was not to wait for disturbances to break out but to take measures to preempt them, and to remove the causes that were likely to lead to a recrudescence. The regimes should prevent the further spread of the Jews and stop their infiltration into locations and occupations where they had not hitherto been found; in brief, they should stop the emancipation process and possibly even reverse it. Sartorius was convinced that the Jewish problem was not derived from the other problems that were troubling German society, but was an expression of the difficulties that the Jews had encountered—in his view for good and logical reasons—in their attempt to gain acceptance as members of equal standing in German society. Although the conclusion that Sartorius derived from his diagnosis did not remain valid for very long—the process of emancipation was not halted but for a short period—his diagnosis was the fruit of his realistic consideration of his own time and is confirmed by us in hindsight also in the historical perspective.

Part III: France, 1780-1880

8 | The Revolutionary Promise and the Catholic Reaction

THE PERSISTENCE OF anti-Jewish sentiments in modern Germany, even before the outbreak of political anti-Semitism in the last decades of the nineteenth century, is often attributed to the slow process of political emancipation in that country. Indeed, most of the public debates on the Jewish problem were occasioned by some measure taken, or proposed, by one or another political institution—a fact that kept the Jewish question very much alive.[1] Even the anti-Jewish expositions of philosophers like Kant and Schopenhauer, though woven into their systems, were related, as we have seen, to the issue of Jewish political status.[2] The recurring discussions left behind a residue, even after the issue was finally and positively resolved, which was again to come to the forefront with the emergence of the anti-Semitic movement proper.

The protracted wrangling over the Jewish question in Germany undoubtedly contributed to the store of anti-Jewish arguments and reflections. Yet to attribute to it the ultimate outbreak of overt anti-Semitism is to ignore what happened in other countries—Austria, Hungary, and especially France—where there was no such wrangling. Nonetheless, the ground there was well-prepared for emulating the German example.

The most striking difference between Germany and France is certainly the fact that in France, owing to the Revolution, Jewish emancipation was granted, as it were, at a stroke.[3] The nature of Jewish social existence had been thoroughly discussed both inside and outside the National Assembly, in speeches and in pamphlets. From these it is easy to discover the sentiments that prevailed toward Jews and how these were ideologically propounded. After the Revolution, however, the cause of the Jews was rarely a subject of public interest. A notable exception was when Napoleon, in revising the revolutionary legislation concerning the Jews, convened the Assembly of Notables and the grand Sanhedrin in 1806-1807.[4] The literature on Jews in French, favorable or unfavorable, of the first two-thirds of the nineteenth century is exceedingly dull especially in comparison with its German sequel. It is only through occasional direct or indirect references that one can discover how Jews were looked upon by the French in these first generations of their common citizenship.

For a correct appraisal of the French situation, it is equally important to keep in mind the smallness of the Jewish community and its restriction to certain districts. At the time of the Revolution the entire Jewish population of France was less than 50,000, of whom some 8,000, the former Marranos of Portuguese extraction, lived in the south—in Bordeaux, Bayonne, and Marseilles. The bulk of the community, the Ashkenazim, were concentrated in the two eastern departments of Alsace and Lorraine, and a few thousand, arrivals from the south and the east, were settled in Paris.[5] It was the Ashkenazi Jewry of the eastern districts that posed a problem, owing to their social cohesion, their foreign culture, and, particularly, their one-sided economic function—moneylending and retail trade—which was deeply resented by the local population. It was the claim of the Alsatian Jews to citizenship that elicited the discussion in the National Assembly, while the complaints against them stirred Napoleon to action. In both these cases, this caused the local problem of Alsace-Lorraine to become a nationwide issue. The stereotype of the Jew that impressed itself on the public mind was decidedly formed on the model of the Jews of eastern France. Then, with the growing migration after the Revolution, the Jew became a conspicuous type elsewhere as well, especially in the capital. Thus, the Jewish problem in France became a national issue.

The hostility toward Jews in Alsace had found literary expression before the political aspiration for emancipation, and it was unaffected by the rationalists' criticism of Judaism. It is well represented by a pamphlet of 1779 which was occasioned by the legal struggle of Jewish creditors to secure payments due to them in the face of forged receipts produced by their debtors. Francois Hell, who was himself implicated in the forgery, resorted to the literary weapon in an attempt to defame the Jewish community collectively. Hell presented the forgery as a justifiable counter-measure of the Alsatian farmers against their Jewish oppressors, the merciless usurers and eternal enemies of Christianity.[6]

Hell's pamphlet breathes that popular animosity against Jews, the tone and verbiage of which are deeply rooted in Christian tradition. It is only in the application of the phrase "state-within-a-state" that he seemingly transcends the scope of the Christian arguments.[7] This slogan, as will be remembered, was intended to indict groups that arrogated to themselves that authority over their members that was the prerogative of the state. Later, it became directed against Jewry for retaining its statelike cohesion in spite of having accepted inclusion in a non-Jewish commonwealth. Hell, however, though using the formula, had not implied in it an appeal to Jews to accelerate the process of their integration into state and society. For him, the Jews being a state-within-a-state meant that they were an absolutely foreign and harmful element that was not to be tolerated. His practical recommendation was that they be expelled.

The possible expulsion of Jews from France had been mentioned in the National Assembly debate, but not as a real possibility. Rather it had been raised as the unreasonable and unthinkable alternative to the obvious solution, the radical integration of Jews into the newly created body politic. The representatives of Alsace-Lorraine imparted into the debate their local image of the Jew. His firm attachment to his group, his economically parasitic occupations, and his moral insensibility toward aliens made him incapable of being absorbed and unworthy of being accepted into state and society. The phrase "nation within a nation" recurs in the petition of the burghers of Strasbourg and Colmar to the National Assembly warning against the plan to enfranchise the Alsatian Jews as French citizens. The deputy of Colmar summed up his objection to the admission of Jews to French citizenship as follows: "In no way have they mixed with the inhabitants of the place where they are settled for many generations. This is why it can be stated uncontestably that even in the smallest village they unite as a nationally distinct group. This political existence of a nation within another nation can certainly have consequences as dangerous as its principles are anti-social."[8]

The designation "nation within a nation," though unfriendly in intention, is factually not incorrect. It was not, in fact, even contested by defenders of the Jewish cause, the most eloquent among them being the deputy from Paris, Count Stanislas de Clermont-Tonnerre. He accepted it as a premise, though he drew from it a contrary conclusion: "But it will be argued, the Jews have their own judges and particular laws. But, I answer, this is your fault and you should not permit it. Jews, as individuals, deserve everything; Jews as a nation nothing. One has to disavow their judges, they should have none, other than ours. The legal protection for the maintenance of their pretended statutory Jewish corporations must be removed. Within the state there can be neither a separate political body nor an order. There can only be the individual citizen. It is being argued that they themselves refuse to become citizens. Let them say that and they would be expelled; because it is inconceivable that there should be in the state a society of non-citizens, a nation within the nation."[9]

The concept of the Jewish community as a closed corporation was also held by the party that opposed the Jews in the Assembly. Clermont-Tonnerre resorts to the same expression of "nation within the nation." He objects to that state of affairs, however, not because of the alleged harmfulness of the Jewish minority to the Gentile society, but because the existence of such a closed corporation is incompatible with the basic idea of the state as it was conceived by the promoters of the Revolution. This state related directly to its individual members, its sovereignty postulating that no order, guild, or corporation be interposed between the citizens and the agencies of the state. That is why all such units among them, including the Jewish community of the old type, had to disappear.

The representative of Colmar, whose expostulation was quoted above, concurred in this postulate. Yet the consequence of it, the inclusion of Jews among other citizens, he wished to postpone until such time as the Alsatian Jews would adapt themselves to the model set by the Gentile society—a method followed, as we have seen, by most German states.[10] The revolutionary assembly, however, was reluctant to adopt such half-measures. Because of its highly optimistic view of the plasticity of human nature and its trust in the redeeming influence of the Revolution, it believed Jews and Gentiles were capable of making an absolutely new beginning in their relationship. This sanguine confidence has been succinctly expressed by M. de Bourge, another deputy from Paris: "If they have any foundation, the moral and political objections against the Jews do not mean anything but that Jews like Christians will have to regenerate themselves through the Constitution."[11] This speaker conceded that Christians and Jews alike were in need of mending their ways and suggested that the Constitution, the blueprint for the revolutionary world, ought to be the instrument of their common regeneration. In the climate of revolutionary expectations, the hope of regeneration may indeed have been applied to society at large. In the course of time, however, as we shall see later, the appeal to regenerate became a specific Jewish concern—Gentile critics demanded it from Jews and Jews themselves saw it as a goal to which they should aspire.

The expectation of an easy adaptation of the Jewish social structure and mentality to the pattern of society at large facilitated the decision of the Assembly in favor of the Jewish cause, but it led to a backlash within the lifetime of a single generation. Napoleon's revision of the revolutionary legislation concerning the Jews, together with the curtailment of legal equality of Alsatian Jewry for at least the next ten years, were prompted by the disappointment at the Jews' failure to adapt as expected. The revision had been prompted by the complaints of local agencies in Alsace about unsavory Jewish business practices, which, they argued, had continued and even increased since the grant of greater liberties to the Jews. It is difficult to ascertain whether these complaints conformed to the facts.[12] There is no doubt, however, that no major change had taken place in the professional distribution of the Jewish population. Nor had a cultural metamorphosis transmuted the average type of the Alsatian Jew. Hence, the glaring discrepancy between the high hopes of the Revolution and the reality of fifteen years later. The disappointment is reflected in the literature on the question, which, as usual, trailed behind the political and legislative transactions.

The preparation of the Napoleonic revision, as well as the convocation of the Notables' Assembly and the Sanhedrin, served as an occasion for the Jewish problem to be discussed in the press and in pamphlets. Though the problem concerned only the eastern departments of Alsace-Lorraine, because the events took place in Paris the discussion once again gained national significance and visibility.

The tendency to transmute the local problems of Alsatian Jewry into an issue of broad significance is evident in the approach of Napoleon himself. In seeking to have his reforms approved by an authoritative Jewish body, the Sanhedrin, Napoleon wished to take the lead in solving the Jewish problem posed in the postfeudal and, in many respects, post-Christian state and society.[13] The underlying intention of the practical measures taken by the emperor is overtly stated by the two intellectuals, Poujol and Louis Gabriel M. de Bonald, who wished to guide and possibly did influence Napoleon's thinking.

Poujol wrote his pamphlet *Quelques observations concernant les Juifs en général et plus particulièrement ceux d'Alsace*[14] in 1806 when it became obvious that Napoleon, following his sojourn in Strasbourg in January of that year, was about to take some action to meet the complaints of the Gentile population in Alsace. Poujol set out to survey the situation in Alsace against the background of the historical experiences of the Christian states during the time they had tolerated the presence of Jews within their borders.

As to conditions in Alsace, Poujol simply repeated the accusations of Jews being engaged in doubtful practices—usury, receiving stolen property, contraband, forgery, and the like—these being absolutely detrimental to the welfare of the population.[15] To this description of Alsatian conditions in general, he adds the devastating indictment that, in spite of the freedom granted the Jews after the Revolution, no Jew had ever availed himself of the opportunity to become a farmer, an artisan, or a soldier—abandoning their highly objectionable transactions in favor of some useful employment. Nor had Alsatian Jews relented from their cultural isolation; if they had, they would not have continued giving their children the same education, based upon the Talmudic tradition, in which they had been brought

111

up.[16] It was a widely held view among the critics of Judaism, including Poujol, that this system of education was the main source of the deplorable moral situation of the Jews. Indeed, the whole national segregation of the Jews was attributed to their attachment to the Talmudic interpretation of the Bible. The repudiation of this tradition thus emerged as an indispensable condition for remedying their situation.[17]

Obviously, in his diagnosis of the Jewish predicament, Poujol followed the lines of the traditional Christian evaluation of Judaism. Indeed, he repeatedly refers to authorities with a Christian background to support his argument, among them Johan Andreas Eisenmenger.[18] In his therapy, however, he adopts the point of view of what could be called a revelational Deism. We have already encountered something similar, though on a higher level, in German thinkers such as Immanuel Kant. Jews, according to his view, are in possession of a wholesome tradition that could guarantee their morality, the ultimate objective of all religions. This tradition is contained in the original teachings of Moses, to which they have to return while cleansing it from all later Talmudic accretions.

Poujol, in a curiously unsophisticated attempt to enlighten his Jewish contemporaries, spelled out in detail those Jewish religious practices that were obsolete: circumcision, the dietary laws, the retention of the Hebrew language in the religious service, and the Jews having their own Sabbath and festival days. All these mistakenly hallowed customs were incompatible with the ordinary conduct of a citizen in a free state. Therefore, they should be abolished in a sweeping reform of the Jewish religion. Such a reform was the only way to regenerate the Jewish people, the ultimate objective of all the measures to be taken in their interest. As, however, Jews had revealed no inclination to carry out such reforms on their own initiative, it was the duty of the imperial government to encourage them to do so.[19] This conception conformed to the objectives of the Sanhedrin, though with a program less ambitious in detail than that designed by Napoleon and his advisers.

De Bonald's expectations of how Napoleon would handle the Jewish question went far beyond those of Poujol. De Bonald, who was among the consistent opponents of the Revolution, was permitted to return to France from his emigration to Germany only after the rise of Napoleon.[20] Rejecting the philosophy that prompted the National Assembly to its revolutionary measures, de Bonald claimed that the admission of the Jews to citizenship was the result of religious indifference or possibly even the deliberate degradation of Christianity. De Bonald regarded Voltaire's animosity toward Jews as a combination of anti-Jewish and anti-Christian idiosyncrasy, which diverged from the mainstream of the rationalistic philosophy that paved the way for the Revolution and was operating in the favor of Judaism to the detriment of Christianity.[21] This is implied in de Bonald's whole line of argument that, when Napoleon brought the Revolution to a halt, the situation would be redressed.

De Bonald ventured the suggestion that the naturalization of the Alsatian Jews by the National Assembly was able to pass unprotested by the population because it concerned only a "half-German province situated at the extreme end of the kingdom." What was going on in that province even before the Revolution ought to have warned the French of what would be in store for them when Jews were allowed to multiply and ascend to all positions open to every citizen. De Bonald cites the 1779 pamphlet of François Hell and accepts his indictments against the Jews, especially since the complaints of the Alsatians were corroborated by the experience of other Christian nations past and present. Fearing the Jews' economic and social predominance, German governments, though abolishing the defamatory body-tax, at the same time took measures against the expansion of the Jewish population. Those apprehensions materialized in Alsace because, in the wake of the Revolution, the farmers who had been liberated from the feudalism of their seigneurs became subjected to the "feudality" of Jewish money. Indeed, in view of the limited living space of the European countries and the extraordinary fertility of Jewish families, Jews could be allowed unrestricted freedom to multiply only at the expense of other families. Their national propensities would prompt Jews to take advantage of the situation, as would obedience to their religious tradition.[22]

De Bonald depicted the severe consequences to be feared from Jewish emancipation. But his basic objection to it stemmed rather from its contradiction of certain theological assumptions. "I think that a government that has the honor of ruling Christians and the good fortune to be Christian itself, should not deliver its subjects to the domination of a religion which is hostile to Christianity and is indeed subservient to it. Christians may be cheated by Jews but they ought not be governed by them. Such subordination offends their dignity even more than the cupidity of the Jews harms their interests."[23] Jews were denied the right to rule because their exile was part and parcel of the Christian doctrine concerning them. Granting Jews a share in the governing of Christians was therefore an abhorrently intolerable idea.

In view of his theologically based condemnation of the Jews, de Boland could not be expected to share Poujol's optimism for the beneficial effects of a possible reform of Judaism. As de Bonald correctly surmised, the expectation that the Jews could be improved through their integration into society was the product of a rationalistic interpretation of their situation: their suppression had led to their degeneration, so their liberation would lead to their regeneration. Those who defended this view "voluntarily closed their eyes to the light in order not to see anything supernatural in the destiny of the Jews." Those who asserted the contrary were convinced that the degradation of the Jews, their suffering and exile, was a punishment and atonement for their sin, as well as a result of the curse that rested upon them. The sin had to be atoned before there could be any change in their political condition. "To put the matter clearly: The meaning is that the Jews cannot be citizens under Christianity. *Even if they should be made citizens, they will not really become such* unless they first become Christians."[24] The emphasis added by de Bonald indicates that he was aware of the crucial significance of his conclusion, which reflected the state of mind of all those who confronted the postrevolutionary situation of the Jews on the basis of dogmatic Christianity. Having denied the legitimacy of the Revolution, they consistently rejected its consequences with regard to the Jews. De Bonald must have expected from Napoleon more far-reaching decisions than even the emperor contemplated, namely the revocation of the emancipation of all Jews and for all time. But even if he realized that emancipation was there to stay, he continued to put forward his arguments against it. For in his view, the actions of statesmen and their institutions could not have the last word on this matter. Even if Jewish citizenship was granted by the states, it remained unwarranted because it was denied by a higher authority, that of the Christian tradition. De Bonald's assertion that even if made citizens by the state, Jews would never legitimately become such, reflects the kind of mental reservations that the uncompromising Christian held toward the actions of the state. The everlasting political degradation of the Jew becomes here a metaphysical postulate not to be altered by the secular agency of the state.

The reflections of Poujol and de Bonald are guided by two different visions of the ultimate destiny of Jews in Christian countries, the same two we encountered in our survey of the German scene. The one expected the Jews to remain Jewish but to shed all the particular traits that differentiated them from their Gentile environment, while the other looked forward to the complete absorption of the Jews through their conversion to Christianity. In Germany, these opposing views evolved in the course of the debate on Jewish emancipation, and it is probably no coincidence that in France, too, they were articulated when, owing to Napoleon's revisions, emancipation once again became an open question. The formal equality of French Jewry was reestablished—the Napoleonic restrictions lasted only a decade—but the expectation persisted that in the future French Jewry should conform to the image conceived for them.

In the first decades of the Restoration, the more radical Christian vision loomed large. Reacting against the upheavals of the Revolution,

The Revolutionary Promise and the Catholic Reaction

French society rediscovered its Catholic past and derived from it important ingredients for the construction of a world view for the present. Social thinkers of no little importance, like Joseph de Maistre, Louis de Bonald, Felicité de Lamennais, and others, all of whom infused Christian elements in their philosophy, commanded the attention of their contemporaries. These thinkers, though they knowingly compromised with those consequences of the Revolution that were irrevocable, retained their mental reservations toward them.[25] Jewish emancipation, though one of the revolutionary acts that seemed to be irreversible, was not willingly accepted, but rather deplored and resented.

De Bonald's reflections on the doctrinal impediments to Jewish emancipation, which he revealed on the occasion of the Napoleonic revision, can serve as an example of the prevailing sentiments in the ensuing decades. In his larger sociophilosophical treatise, de Bonald himself supplied the broader theological conception that warranted his anti-Jewish verdict. Ancient Israel was the original depository of the divine revelation embodied in the Mosaic Law—a system that in its hierarchical structure could be taken as a guide for all nations for all eternity. This positive interpretation of the Mosaic Law—not too common among Christian theologians—provided a welcome prop for the conservative sociopolitical structure recommended by de Bonald. Though in possession of an ideal constitution, the Jewish people, because of its thoughtless and erratic nature, failed to live up to the lofty ideals involved in it. That is why it had been chastened by God even when still living in its own country.

When Christ appeared and Jews proved incapable of recognizing him as their saviour, they finally incurred the loss of divine grace and, being left to their own resources, degenerated utterly. The natural consequence was the dissolution of their commonwealth and the destruction of the Temple. "Since his last catastrophe, the Jew has been dispersed throughout the whole world . . . Intermingled with all the nations he cannot combine with any of them . . . He always remains alone, always a stranger . . . a nation without territory, a people without *power* . . . . His error became his crime and he cherishes it; he killed his liberator and he waits for him."[26] Conceived of in this way, Jews could scarcely be lifted from their degradation by the secular act of political emancipation. Their only hope of regeneration was to recognize their fatal mistake by accepting Jesus as the Messiah.

Felicité de Lamennais, the outstanding intellect among the Catholic theologians of the time, came to a similar conclusion.[27] He diverged from the traditional exposition of Catholicism into a liberal and even revolutionary interpretation that brought him into conflict with the pope. These deviations were an effort to adapt Christian doctrine to the exigencies of modern social conditions; however, his evaluation of Jews and Judaism

115

remained unaffected by them. It was based on the acceptance of Jewish emancipation as a fait accompli without granting it any spiritual significance whatsoever. Lamennais, in his *Essai sur l'indifference en matiere de religion* (1823)[28] and elsewhere, repeats the traditional doctrine of the Church concerning the spiritual blindness of the Jews and the political and social consequences of that blindness, using language that testifies beyond doubt to his personal identification with the doctrine. The whole existence of the Jew after the appearance of Christ is a prolonged miracle "that manifests until the end of days the inexorable justice and the sanctity of God whom this people dared to deny. It will live without an apparent principle of life; nothing can destroy it, neither captivity nor the sword nor time itself. Isolated among the nations which repulse it, it finds nowhere a place of rest . . . It carries in its hands a torch that enlightens the whole world while itself remaining in darkness . . . Suppressed everywhere it is everywhere . . . All the nations see it passing by, all are seized by horror at the sight of it, it is marked by a sign more terrible than that of Cain. On its forehead a hand of iron has written: 'Deicide'."[29]

Such anathemas, reiterated by thinkers who wished to give Christianity a new lease on life through philosophical reinterpretations, could not but strengthen the odious and even sinister notion that clung to the very name of Jew. For the pious Catholic in France, the foremost connotation may have been the idea of the killing of Jesus, as shown in the phrase *juif deicide*, which has no parallel in any other European language.[30] The phrase had been widely used, as we know, and Lamennais, in associating the word "deicide" with Jewry as its main characteristic, was only voicing a common sentiment. The accusation of deicide, more than any other, was apt to put the Jew outside the human pale. One who would commit this crime was capable of any other crime—cheating, forgery, or treason. The theological condemnation of the Jew prepared the ground for his moral defamation.

The notion of the divinely disgraced Jew was impressed on the minds of people through teaching and sermonizing, the time-honored channels for the dissemination of Christian doctrine, as well as through the Catholic press. From the time of the Restoration the Church had tried to regain a hold on the population with newspapers and periodicals, which had become a powerful agency of Catholic education and propaganda. Inevitably they included derogatory concepts of Jews and Judaism, which continued to represent an integral ingredient of Catholic doctrine.[31]

The anti-Jewish front received unexpected reinforcement from a type of Jewish convert peculiar to the first decades of postrevolutionary France. Germany is usually regarded as the classic example of Jewish defection during the first generations, which still labored under the pressure of political and social discrimination. Yet it is not at all clear whether there were not more converts proportionally in France than in Germany. What is certain is that France produced a type of convert conspicuously absent in Germany, one who himself became active in propagating Christianity and assailing his former coreligionists, his "brethren in the flesh." The emancipated Jew in France had, seemingly, no reason for changing his religion. But paradoxically it is in France that we meet a whole category of converts who demonstrated their conviction by becoming active in missionary work and joining hands with other detractors of Jews and Judaism.[32]

The first and perhaps the best-known such case is that of David Drach, a learned rabbi of Alsatian origin, the son-in-law of the chief rabbi of France and himself a probable candidate for that post. Drach converted to Catholicism in 1823, causing a special scandal through his successful attempt to take his three children with him against the will of his rejected wife. After taking holy orders, he became professor at the Sorbonne and active, not entirely unsuccessfully, in evangelizing Jews.[33]

Great interest was also aroused by the conversion of the brothers Theodore and Alphonse Ratisbonne, the first in 1827 and the second in 1842.[34] The Ratisbonne family was one of the most distinguished in Alsace. The mother was a daughter of Naftali Cerfberr, a pioneer in the struggle for equal rights at the time of the Revolution. The father had been head of the *consistoire* at Strasbourg. The children had received a modern education with but slight Jewish content. Theodore, from early youth, felt alienated from Judaism and religion in general. However, at the age of twenty-one, when a law student at Strasbourg University, he fell under the influence of Louis Bautain, a Catholic theologian with original ideas. Bautain demanded full identification with the Catholic tradition, not on any rational basis, but as an act of faith, by the method of fideism. The fiery theologian succeeded in awakening dormant religious feelings in young Ratisbonne and two other Jewish students of similar bent. He convinced them that Christianity alone, with its symbols and mysteries, could satisfy the religious craving of man. Judaism, even in its original shape of the Law of Moses, was no more than a first step in the progress towards true religious experience, and its subsequent Talmudic embodiment was a perverted and corrupted product. This theory fitted in well with the attitude of these young Jews, who had become estranged from Judaism as they had known it. Thus it justified for them their apostasy. All three entered Catholic priesthood.[35] Theodore Ratisbonne tried to draw his widely ramified family after him. His brother, Alphonse, twelve years his junior, followed in his train, though not through his direct influence. Without previous preparation and with no transitional period, Alphonse was overwhelmed by a vision he had while visiting a church in Rome and became a devout believer. The brothers established an institute in Paris, and later in Jerusalem, dedicated to winning souls from Judaism to Christianity.[36]

Like similar apostates, the Ratisbonne brothers were convinced that the emancipation of the Jews was not enough to lift them out of their degradation. The feeling of social inferiority no doubt contributed to the sense of malaise from which they hoped to escape by conversion. In his correspondence with the three candidates for conversion, Louis Bautain adduced not only the argument of the inferiority of Judaism to the Christian faith, but he pointed to the low social situation of the Jews and represented conversion as the royal road to deliverance from both. "The Jew today is as he was in the time of Titus and Vespasian. He has his distinct character, habits and physiognomy. He persists as a peculiar anomaly, a pariah among the family of Christian peoples."[37] This no less than forty years after emancipation!

In their appeals to the Jews the apostates mixed up the social and spiritual arguments. Alphonse Cerfberr de Medelsheim, Ratisbonne's cousin and himself an apostate, though not a cleric, published in 1842 a description of French Jewry in all its divisions and social components.[38] Although he knew Sephardic Jews, to whom he attributes positive characteristics, he takes the ordinary Alsatian Jew as his exemplar: "He is crafty, rapacious, avaricious for money, without faith and legal scruple, though possessed of a fanatical dedication so long as he is in the lower ranks of his people."[39] Apparently the reference is to the Jews of the villages and hamlets of Alsace who still clung to their own way of life and their own traditional methods of making a living. In effect, Cerfberr also applied the traditional stereotype to those Jews who had succeeded in freeing themselves from their former condition.

Two years after writing this article, Cerfberr reprinted it in a separate work in which he answered critics who had attacked his findings. Although a less fanatical Christian than the Ratisbonnes, Cerfberr nevertheless did accept that Christian doctrine which denies the right of a Jewish community to exist inside Christian society. In his original article, Cerfberr described the efforts of the Jews to regenerate themselves by their own forces, but concluded the picture with this ambiguous sentence: "We respect the ancient faith of our fathers too much not to hope to see Israel newly born in the true faith, raising himself up before God and man and in her own eyes."[40] In the new edition of the essay, he enlarged upon the subject and his clarifications leave no doubt as to the aim of his social criticism. His intention was to prove that there was no room in French society for the Jew who would not abandon Judaism in favor of Christianity.

9 | The Socialist Indictment

ALTHOUGH THE TERM *anti-Semitism* only emerged in the late 1870s, it can be aptly applied to earlier phenomena, for example, to the religious and theological anti-Semitism described in Chapter 8. Important elements of the propaganda employed in the anti-Semitic movement of the last decades of the nineteenth century were already in evidence in the anti-Jewish criticism of the neo-Catholic thinkers and Jewish apostates.

The same is true of what came to be called socialist anti-Semitism, which emerged contemporaneously with the Christian trend. Charles Fourier, Alphonse Toussenel, Pierre-Joseph Proudhon, and others, the social critics of capitalism in France, implicated the Jews in their criticism of the money-based system. These were conceived of as supporting, representing or symbolizing this system, especially its negative aspects.

The Catholic and socialist anti-Semites both extrapolated the Jewish problem from its local confines in Alsace to the country at large, and especially to Paris. The problem of Alsatian Jewry had reached Paris at the time of the Revolution and the Empire, but only on the level of public discussion and legislative transaction. In the ensuing decades, however, the concrete object of the problem, the Jewish population, transplanted itself to Paris. For if emancipation had failed to bring about the dispersion of the Jewish population all over France and their absorption into the Gentile environment, as was expected by some sanguine observers, a significant shift in the demographic distribution did take place through a substantial migration to Paris of Jews from Alsace, from the south, and also from abroad. While at the time of the Revolution, Paris had harbored no more

119

than 500 Jews, by 1840 the number had grown to nearly 10,000 and by 1860 to some 23,000. At the same time, the overall Jewish population of France had jumped from 40,000 to 90,000 because of a substantial immigration from neighboring countries, especially from Germany.[1]

The socioeconomic structure of the Jewish community of Paris, and particularly its cultural make-up, was altogether different from that of Alsatian Jewry. Along with craftsmen, petty traders, and the destitute, Paris Jewry comprised notables of the business world, writers, artists, and scholars, as well as the most important branch of the family of Rothschild, whose fame and financial power reached its peak about this time.[2]

This newly created Paris Jewry drew the attention of friend and foe, but its image could not fail to be influenced by its connection with those Alsatian Jewish communities whence the great majority of Parisian Jews originated. We have already observed how the neo-Catholic critics transferred traditional prejudices from the Alsatian Jews, who served as a prototype, to the newly emerging Jewry of Paris. A similar process of transference and generalization in the evaluation of Jews was carried out by the exponents of early socialism. We shall find Charles Fourier's attention fixed to the image of the Alsatian Jew. Alphonse Toussenel's attacks, on the other hand, were already directed against the new type of Jew, though the substance of his charges was basically unchanged.

Fourier was one of the first social thinkers to react to the dissolution of the semi-feudal system of the ancient regime, and he did so by evolving a new scheme of things, a previously unheard-of pattern of social organization. The scheme depended on certain assumptions about human nature and has been described as utopian. The kernel of his suggestion was the organizing of society into social units called phalansteries. Within these units people would, in their work as well as in their personal lives, follow their spontaneous and genuine impulses. Under the existing social order these had been suppressed and adulterated.[3]

Fourier's theory thus contains a severe criticism of the prevailing conditions of man and society and a projected solution of all their problems—provided people were prepared to implement the reorganization of their life according to the vision of the socialist prophet. It was a highly speculative vision, owing very little to external, literary, or other influences. On the other hand, it was stimulated by the observation of the social evils that were arising out of the disfunctioning of social agencies in the incipient stage of capitalism.

Born in 1772, Fourier was the son of a wealthy merchant but, lacking the ability or the inclination to succeed in this or in any other profession, he became a civil servant in Lyon. There he wrote his books in his spare time until 1816, when, thanks to an inherited income, he became independent.

The Socialist Indictment

In 1823 he settled in Paris and there awaited the appearance of the adherents who would be willing to try out his proposed social experiment, especially the rich man who would provide the means for financing it in its initial phase.[4]

Fourier's social diagnosis, as well as his utopia, were replete with deep reservations and even resentment against commerce and business transactions of any kind and those who engaged in them for their livelihood. He believed the worst possible offenders were Jewish hucksters and moneylenders. Fourier's phalansteries were supposed to be economically self-sufficient, thus excluding the need for, or the possibility of, trade or business activity, which, in his diagnosis, was one of the main sources of the failure of capitalistic society. A contempt for Jewish businessmen—Fourier had in mind, particularly, Alsatian Jews—was a part of this theory. Fourier spoke about the "hordes of Jews and vagabonds" who had invaded Alsace; a few hundred of them had even reached Lyon, where Fourier could encounter them in the flesh.[5]

There is, however, no reason to suppose that Fourier's notion of Jewish character was influenced by his own experience. His statements, judgments, and condemnation simply reflect the stereotypes current in society at that time: Jews were "unproductive and deceitful", they practiced usury and fraudulent bankruptcy and were bent upon the economic destruction of French farmers and businessmen. Fourier accepted the Christian verdict of the Jews' lack of moral scruples towards non-Jews and attributed their financial success to their unparalleled social cohesion.[6]

Fourier does make a somewhat original contribution to anti-Jewish theorizing in his differentiation between the *esprit corporatif* and the *esprit patriarcal*. The first, revealed by Christians in adversity, produced "noble passions"; the second, shown by Jews under similar circumstances, become "the root of ignoble passions which debased them even in their heyday."[7] The actual difference between the *esprit corporatif* and the *esprit patriarcal* remains obscure, and one is entitled to conclude that the good and bad marks attached to them stem from their association with Jews and Christians, respectively.

Though pinning his hope for a major social breakthrough on the establishment of the phalansteries, Fourier also passed judgment on political and social measures within the existing world. Thus, Jewish emancipation was deemed by him to be premature, to say the least. He termed it "the most shameful of all recent vices of society," to be explained by the overconfidence of philosophers in their abstract principles. Religious tolerance ought to have been disregarded with regard to Jews until such a time as they mended their ways and abandoned their unsocial professions and unsavory practices. As they would scarcely do this voluntarily, the

121

state would be obliged to take an active part in the re-education of Jews. "In order to make this nation honorable it must be given a collective education and, first of all, forced to engage in productive work, agriculture and industry."[8]

This was exactly the program evolved by some would-be reformers of Jewish society in Germany, and Fourier regretted that France had adopted instead the granting of citizenship at one stroke. By premature admission of Jews to citizenship, French society risked the danger of being infected by the Jewish vices and in the long run of being compromised in its vital interests. "Leave the Jews in France for a century and they will organize their sect in each town; they will cooperate only among themselves. They will become in France what they are in Poland and will eventually snatch commercial vocations from citizens who thus far have carried on quite smoothly without the Jews."[9]

Fourier's thinking moved on two different levels: the existing reality and his utopian scheme of social reconstruction. This may explain the curious fact that in his last publication before his death he ascribed to the Jews a pioneering role in carrying through the Fourierian social program. As Edmund Silberner surmises, Fourier must have heard something of a plan to resettle Jews in Palestine with the assistance of the House of Rothschild. Thus, disappointed as he was that to date no man of substance had volunteered to give his plan a try, he caught at this last straw. If it were true that the Jews were about to create a new society, they would need a blueprint for its construction. What better plan could they have than the ready-made scheme of the phalanstery?[10] Desirous to implement his long-cherished idea, he was ready to close his eyes to the much lamented vices of the Jewish people, whom he despised and slandered but did not think to be incorrigible. Either through compulsory re-education or through the medium of the phalanstery, Jews might well find their way to humanity. Whatever his animosity toward Jews, Fourier did not hold that their faults were predetermined by their race. Like most critics of Jews and Judaism in the first part of the nineteenth century, Fourier maintained some hope of the Jews' future regeneration. However, the picture of the Jews that appears in his work is that of one of the most despicable and harmful species of human beings.

Though Fourier failed to see in his lifetime the realization of his social utopia, in the decades to come, some followers tried to establish settlements on the lines suggested by the master's teachings. His ideas were disseminated by his disciples, who represented a school of social thought, not a political coterie. The Fourierists were certainly not a homogeneous group. With respect to the Jewish issue, some of them followed in the footsteps of the master, others seem to have regarded his anti-Jewish bias as irrelevant or perhaps even contradictory to the basic tenets of the school. The former trend is best represented by Alphonse Toussenel's *Les Juifs rois de l'époque, histoire de la féodalité financière*, the first French book from outside Alsace to announce its anti-Jewish tendency in its title. The basic thesis of the book, as indicated by the subtitle, concerns the all-pervading role of money in the life of modern society, owing to which fact the capitalists gain control over the rest of the population. To substantiate his point, Toussenel describes in detail, and with the passion of a radical social reformer, the capitalists' involvement in and their impact upon all walks of life. His arguments then lead up to an appeal to the victims of financial feudalism to make common cause with the state—represented by the king—in order to crush it. The functions usurped by the bankers and capitalists ought to be taken over by the agencies and institutions of the state.[11]

In assailing what he terms the "féodalité financière," Toussenel is attacking Gentile capitalists as well as Jews. Some of them, notably the Protestant bankers of Geneva, come in for repeated criticism. Why then does he single out the Jews and use their name in the title to cover the whole phenomenon? Toussenel's answer was that he simply followed the common usage of the word.

To the sentence in the preface that anticipates the central thesis of the book, "Les juifs règne et gouverne en France," he adds the note: "I am forewarning the reader that the word [*juif*] is taken here in general in its popular meaning: *juif, banquier, marchand d'espèce*." Then, in a studied attempt to countervail the affront implied, he enlarges on the "superior character of the Jewish nation," the immense role the Jewish people have played in human history, and the outstanding capacities revealed by Jews in all provinces of creativity. Then this excessive praise is once again neutralized through the observation that "all the readers of the Bible . . . Jews, Genevans, English or Americans" believe that God granted them the right to exploit the world's riches for their exclusive benefit—thus ascribing the rapacity of all the mercantile nations to the influence of the Hebrew Bible. The note that began by lauding the Jews concludes with the startling sentence: "That is why I understand the persecution that the Romans, the Christians and the Moslems made the Jews suffer. The prolonged universal repulsion inspired by the Jew is nothing but just punishment for his implacable haughtiness; and our contempt is a legitimate retribution for the hatred which he seems to bear towards the rest of humanity."[12]

Instead of proving the author's fair-mindedness, the apologetic note could only strengthen the suspicion of anti-Jewish bias raised by the title of the book. No wonder that the editor of the book, published under the auspices of the Fourierists' Library, felt constrained to disavow the anti-Jewish tendency thus displayed. The reviewer of the *Archives Israélites* protested the book's anti-Jewish implications, and he was certainly not the only one to react to it in this way. At any rate, the author felt obliged to return to the subject in the preface to the second edition, published in 1847.[13] Having in the meantime severed his connection with the other Fourierists and obviously angered by the censure of his former editor, Toussenel emphatically restated his case for substituting Jew for capitalist: "It does not depend upon the whim of the writer to alter the sense [*valeur*] of the expression as sanctioned by usage and I do not find in my national language a better name than that of *juif* to designate what I wish to condemn." The responsibility for the identification of the vices of commerce with the noun "Jew" rested with the national linguistic tradition.[14]

This had been the basis of his defense in the first edition, but this time he made no effort to conceal his intention to capitalize on the national tradition to propagate his own views on Jews and Judaism. The praiseworthiness of the Jewish nation, adduced in the first edition to balance its defects, is now summarily dismissed: "I am told that I ought to have treated with more respect a people that did such great things, a people in the bosom of which God has for so long been pleased to choose his elect." Toussenel's answer to this criticism is a complete denial that any merit could be attributed to Jews past or present: "I don't know the great things that the Jewish people has done, never having read about their history, but in one book where there is no talk about anything but adultery, incest, carnage and savage war . . . where every great fortune invariably begins with fraud and reason; where the kings who are called saints have husbands assassinated in order to steal their wives; where women who are called saints enter into bed of the enemy's generals in order to cut off their heads."[15] And so it goes, in obvious indebtedness to Voltaire, whose direct influence on French anti-Semitism of the nineteenth century here comes to the fore for the first time.

However, Voltaire's spirit is not here preserved in its original purity. Voltaire combined his anti-Jewish sallies, based on derision of the Old Testament, with attacks on Christianity—a combination that perforce neutralized its effect for people who remained attached to Christianity. No loyal Christian could possibly accept Voltaire's defamation of the Jewish people, based, as it was, on the Old Testament. Religious anti-Semitism drew its ideological weapons, as we have seen in the previous chapter, from the perennial Jewish-Christian antagonism that continued unaffected by the newly evolved rationalist indictments. Toussenel, however, wished to have it both ways. He repeated all the Voltairian charges in their most vitriolic fashion and at the same time harped on the Christian resentment against Jews. He was not ashamed to refer to the Jewish deicide: "I do not call the people of God the people that put to death mercilessly all the prophets inspired by the Holy Spirit, that crucified the Redeemer of men and insulted him on the Cross." This Christological incrimination is then linked up with the alleged unsocial behavior of contemporary Jews: "If the Jewish people had truly been the people of God they would not have put to death the son of God; they would not continue exploiting through parasitism and usury all the workers whom Christ wanted to redeem and who are the militia of God"—a frightening example of anti-Jewish invective of the lowest and most deceitful kind.[16]

In using the word *juif* to denounce financial feudality, Toussenel could have pleaded that *juif* was just a synonym for banker, trader, and the like; however, by using it to denote these categories in the context of a critical survey, he was attempting to besmirch them with the negative associations attached to *juif*. He wanted to condemn all those associated with financial feudality and *juif* was a useful pejorative epithet.

But then Toussenel also applied to the financiers other expressions that pertain exclusively to Jews, such as "Israel," "Judah," and "Maccabees." In addition, Toussenel's invective was often directed against individual Jews: the Foulds, the Rothschilds, and others, whose ethnic origin was emphatically stressed. Toussenel made much of the role these Jewish capitalists played in the building of the railways. According to him the railways were turned over to them through the cooperation of leading statesmen and with the acclamation of the greater part of the corrupt press. The two capitalists were presented as: "M. Rothschild, de la tribu de Juda" and "M. Fould de tribu de Benjamin," and the press had cried "gloire aux juifs!"[17]

In other instances Jews are explicitly lumped by Toussenel with other carriers of the financial feudality: Protestant bankers from Geneva, Amsterdam, and London. To be thus classified did not alleviate the charge from the standpoint of French Jewry. It must, on the contrary, have made it more hurtful. To be listed with capitalists of foreign countries meant not to be acknowledged as belonging to the French nation and the French state. But this is exactly what Toussenel wished to convey, as epitomized in the following sentence: "One Fatherland—the merchants have none: *Ubi aurum, ibi patria*. The industrial feudalism is personified in the cosmopolitan Jew."[18]

If, in the original text of the book, such anti-Jewish quips and observations surface only occasionally, and, in view of their marginality to the general argument, lose their edge, in the introduction to the second edition they appear concentrated, accentuated and pursued to their ultimate logical conclusion. Quoting his master Fourier on the deplorable mistake

125

France made in granting the Jews citizenship, Toussenel acclaims the Russian and Prussian governments for acting more circumspectly. Russian Jews, it is true, are more easily recognized as a group apart owing to their cultural traits, which are evident even in their clothing. The outward adaptation of French Jews to the culture of their environment does not alter their nature. Like the Russian Jews they too remain "a nation within the nation."[19]

Toussenel was obviously bent on making the second edition more explicitly anti-Jewish than the first had been. A full-length chapter added to the new edition is tellingly entitled *Saint Simon et Juda*. The author sets out here to demonstrate that the school of the Saint-Simonists—at loggerheads with the Fourierists—provided the *féodalité financière*, until then a mere growth of circumstances, with an ideological superstructure. The affinity between Saint-Simonism and the budding capitalism is then simply put down to the Jewish participation in both the philosophical school and the economic activity. "This alliance is the more natural as the Saint-Simonist church counts among its faithful a good number of circumcised." In the course of his exposition Toussenel dwells as often as possible on the Jewish origin of the Saint-Simonists who were engaged in evolving the school's theory or were active in putting it into practice—though Enfantin, the leader of the group and the main target of Toussenel's attack, was not Jewish. This notwithstanding, at the end of his observations Toussenel concluded that there was nothing surprising in finding the disciples of Saint-Simon in both camps. "These were Jews; there had to be gold and treason at the bottom of these people's thoughts."[20]

To affix the name Jewish to a movement because of some Jewish participation in it later became a common practice with anti-Semites. Toussenel anticipated it in his attack on Saint-Simonism in the second edition of his *Les Juifs rois de l'epoque*. This book can rightly be called an anti-Semitic classic, foreshadowing as it does important trends that later developed. However, there are no traces of overt racism in Toussenel's book. He uses the term "race," but without attributing to it a determining force. He regarded himself as a Christian and declared that "there is no possible alliance between that race and us, the Christians." At the same time, he noted with satisfaction that "the greater part of distinguished Jews of our time abjure Judaism." He certainly had no reservation against absorbing Jews in the Gentile environment, but did not expect it to happen on a scale that would ensure the solution of the Jewish problem altogether.[21]

What lends Toussenel's arguments their special weight is the combination of the Christian resentment against Jews as Jews with the protest against the economic-social role they came to play in post-emancipatory society. Unlike Fourier, his attention is not focused on the small fry of Alsatian traders but on the big capitalists of Paris, to whom he attributes the traits ascribed by anti-Jewish prejudice: "The children of Lorraine are convinced that Jews would never part without asking each other: How much have you stolen today from the Christian? Indeed that is what two Jews could say to each other today in leaving the Bourse." In this quip, appearing only in the second edition, we have epitomized the transfer of anti-Jewish prejudices from the marketplace of the Alsatian town to the scene of the economic transactions in Paris.[22]

That this transference did indeed take place, and not without the influence of Toussenel's book, is borne out by a number of instances. The Rothschilds and the other big bankers were repeatedly attacked not only as capitalists but also as Jews, and since the appearance of Toussenel's book these attacks were clearly colored by the ideology evolved by him down to the very vocabulary. Rothschild is dubbed *roi des Juifs* in the title of a pamphlet published by G. Dairnvaell a year after Toussenel's publication. Dairnvaell then wrote a second pamphlet in defense of the first, concluding it with an epilogue, a quasi apology *aux Israelites* for employing *juif* where *vendeurs brocanteurs d'argent* was meant. This apology is as double-edged as Toussenel's comments on the same subject. Referring to the accepted usage of the word *juif* as a synonym for "financier," he pays his homage to the Jewish people, who occupy such a glorious place in the history of mankind and have produced such a number of brilliant individuals. Then comes the inevitable anticlimax: "Unfortunately they believe that God granted them the monopoly of exploitation and they have displayed a kind of fanaticism in the art of ransacking the human species." This type of Jew had not shown himself worthy of the rights he had been accorded, Dairnvaell argued in a version of the differential anti-Semitism with which we are well acquainted.[23]

The propagandistic potential latent in the phrase *les juif roi de l'epoque* is further demonstrated by its being chosen by another writer, Pierre Leroux, for a treatise on the Jewish problem. A social critic with a mystical bent, Leroux found fault with the prevailing socioeconomic system and epitomized his objections by expounding on the preponderance of the Jewish spirit over the Christian notions of recent times. Jewish spirit was tantamount to materialism, the relentless pursuit of economic gain irrespective of moral considerations and the like. That these were not exclusively Jewish propensities, and that their preponderance was not to be attributed to Jewish influence alone, was conceded by Leroux. Yet, following Toussenel's reliance on linguistic tradition, he had no hesitation in employing *juif* to designate all the negative elements to be condemned in contemporary society.[24]

If, in adopting the slogan *les juifs le roi de l'epoque*, Leroux followed in the footsteps of Toussenel, in the combination of the Christian aversion for Jews with the condemnation of modern social evils, he needed no external stimulus. Toussenel resorted to such combination only in the second edition of his book in 1847, a year after Leroux's treatise appeared in print. The latter was indeed better disposed to follow such a course, given his inclination to theologically oriented speculations. Indeed, his account of the alleged deterioration of Jewish character and its subsequent impact on the moral standard of humanity at large has an irrational if not mystifying ring. In rejecting Jesus as the Messiah, Jews tainted themselves with a kind of metaphysical evil. Once it had contaminated one segment of humanity, this evil could not help but affect other segments as well.[25]

Leroux was perhaps less severe than Toussenel in his judgments about the actual behavior of Jews. He indeed argued that the deterioration of the Jews had been intensified by the treatment they had suffered through the ages at the hands of Christians. Still, in placing the original source of all social evil in the sinning Jew's rejection of Jesus, Leroux exemplified the easy confluence of religious and social resentment against Jews in one ideological complex.

The wedding of anti-Jewish sentiments with socialist teachings and theories is a widespread phenomenon, not restricted to authors who announce their anti-Jewish beliefs in the titles of their books. Pierre-Joseph Proudhon did not concentrate his views on Jews and Judaism into a single work, but his many publications are replete with references to Jews that are consistently negative. In assailing capitalism, Proudhon encounters the group that, owing to its economic role, seems to stand in its very center and, accordingly, incurs the reprobation of the social critic. This convergence of socialism and anti-Semitism became quite common in France during the mid-nineteenth century. The socialist literature and its propagating agency, the *presse rouge*, thus became an important vehicle for disseminating one version of anti-Semitism—in the same way as the *presse noire* became an instrument for spreading other versions.[26]

10|The Liberal Ambiguity

THE CHRISTIANIZING TREND that was on the ascent in French society during the Bourbon Restoration was opposed by the adherents of the Enlightenment and the Revolution. While in the first generation after the fall of Napoleon, under the rule of Louis Philippe, this opposition was subdued and remained almost silent, they later recovered their force and became as vocal as their antagonists. French history in the decades following the July Revolution in 1830 is characterized by the struggle between the partisans of the Christianizing trend—the "clericals" or "clericalists" as they were called by their opponents—and the liberals, the advocates of a secularized state and society, called the "anticlericalists."

This dichotomy paralleled the division between those who took the inclusion of emancipated Jewry into French society for granted and those who maintained their reservations against it. That this division was not absolute is obvious from the socialists' criticism of Jews, described in the previous chapter. The socialists were on the left wing of the liberal camp, but nonetheless some of them espoused anti-Jewish sentiments and ideologies. They did so, in part because, criticizing the capitalist foundations of society, they could easily include the Jews as capitalists in their critiques; the liberals lacked this simplistic identification. But the economic role of the Jews was only one factor sustaining the anti-Jewish bias of some socialists. Other incentives of a more traditional kind were at work, and these were strong enough at times to affect liberals, who were generally immune from the socialists' anticapitalist antagonism.

The historian Jules Michelet, at least in the second half of his career, can be seen as a typical representative of consistent liberalism. Born in 1798, Michelet was brought up in the tradition of eighteenth-century rationalism, but during his formative years, which coincided with the revival of Christianity in France, he evolved a historical conception that granted Christianity a unique role in the guidance of humanity. What is known about his approach to Judaism at this time seems to indicate that he was not negatively disposed to it; on the contrary, he presented it as fulfilling an important task in the providential course of human history.[1] Then in the 1840s, in the wake of crucial personal experiences but certainly not unconnected with the growing conflict between the clerical and the progressive elements in French society, Michelet joined the latter and became one of their most radical spokesmen. His commitment to the cause of anticlerical liberalism was reflected afterwards in all his historical writings, which he unhesitatingly put at the service of the contemporary struggle.[2]

Michelet's views are most outspokenly presented in his *Bible de l'humanité* (1866), an exposition of the religious development of the human race, allotting every known civilization its position in the historical process. As indicated in the title of the book, his avowed intention is to displace the Judeo-Christian Scripture from its unique position and substitute for it a summary of the religious creativity of all ages and all civilizations that have a claim to share the past and guide the future.[3]

Michelet discussed the religions of Persia, Greece, and Egypt, as well as ancient Judaism. Although the appraisal of Judaism is simply a part of his survey of ancient civilizations and religions, it is clear from the tone and tenor of his remarks that they bear directly on contemporary problems in which Michelet was passionately involved. In positing the election of Israel as a gratuitous choice of God, not based on the worthiness of its object, Michelet argues that Judaism established the principle of divine grace—the most obnoxious tenet of Christianity in his eyes. Since divine grace is bestowed regardless of the worthiness of its recipient, it contradicts the principle of justice and the demands of morality and reason on which human society ought to be based. Michelet is aware of the fact that the Law, undoubtedly the legitimate expression of Judaism, is deeply committed to the idea of justice. "Yes, but that Law itself, given exclusively to one *favored* people, to one that Moses himself declared to be *unworthy*, this Law is built on a foundation of unjust preference." The prophets Jeremiah and Ezekiel, Michelet concedes, proclaimed the idea of absolute justice and denied the possibility of retribution unless it conformed to the measure of the vice and virtue of the individual. Therein the prophets attained, according to Michelet, the standard of equity central to the teaching of Socrates. The prophets, however, only reached this height through the bitter experience of captivity, which shook the very foundations of Jewish national existence. Thus, Michelet discounts the moral achievement of these expatriates as an intrinsic feature of Judaism.[4]

This example is typical of Michelet's selective treatment of the sources in his evaluation of Judaism. While in connection with the idea of Justice, later developments are dismissed as not genuinely Jewish, in another context what emerged at a later stage is projected back to earlier periods of national existence. Propensity for trade is seen as an integral part of the original Jewish national character. "The Jew is from his origin a man of peace, a man of business [homme d'affaires]. His ideal is neither the warrior nor the laborer nor the farmer. Formerly a nomadic shepherd, he later returned to his nomadic life as a hawker, as banker or huckster [brocanteur]." "The true Jew the patriarch" was not a simple shepherd, he was "berger speculateur who knew how to augment his flock through intelligent care, acquisition and calculation." If Mosaic Law, in referring to agricultural feasts and the like, seems to reflect rural peasant life, Michelet explained this away as an attempt on the part of the lawgiver to accustom the Israelites to a sedentary life, an attempt that could not have succeeded, given the Jewish proclivity to nomadism.[5]

In his characterization of Jews as the eternal agents of business transactions, Michelet, while supposedly descending into the depths of the remote past, is clearly enmeshed in the web of contemporary Jewish images. In adopting this attitude he was probably influenced by Alphonse de Toussenel, who once served as his secretary and whose book on the Jews could not have remained unknown to him. There are also unmistakable vestiges of Voltairian ideas in Michelet's appraisal of Jews and Judaism. He follows him in maintaining that it was the Jews who invented the bill of exchange as the best instrument (even better than the gold to which Jews had been traditionally addicted) for securing the wealth of wandering traders. Of Voltairian origin also is Michelet's evaluation of the Jews as a culturally sterile people, as well as his curious judgment on the Jewish Bible, which he describes as extremely arid even though the authors of Genesis, Ruth, and the Book of Kings did possess "true narrative genius."[6]

Michelet was prepared to absorb strictures on Jews and Judaism from different quarters with little attempt to harmonize them or to square them with his own observations and perceptions. Thus, on the one hand, Jews are accused of being caught up in "the narrow formulation of the Mosaic prescriptions," while on the other hand they are taken to task for engaging in the mystic lore of the cabala, which Michelet learned from Adolph Franck's book, La Kabbala où la philosophie religieuse des Hébreux. He concludes, however, that this mystical inclination failed to find an outlet in "the effusion of the heart; it fell into the strange accentuation of a cult of grammar, the adoration of the language and the religion of the alphabet."[7]

In spite of this eclecticism, Michelet's evaluation of the Jewish role in history does not lack originality. Besides his thesis that Judaism is the source of the idea of divine grace, he contended that the main characteristic of the Jewish belief system is an outgrowth of the Jewish situation: that of the emigrating outcast, addicted to ritual, the manifestations of the exclusive bond between the chosen people and its God. The projection of a better future inherent in the idea of Messianism is a compensation for the outcast's present predicament.[8]

This interpretation of Jewish history, indicated in the chapter title "Le Juif—l'Esclave" is strongly reminiscent of the conception of the Jews as a pariah people evolved some generations later by Max Weber. Yet, while the great sociologist succeeded in keeping his exposition within the bounds of scholarly analysis, Michelet's presentation assumes a moralistic and discriminating tone: "The great and true glory of the Jews, which is due to their misery, is that they alone among the peoples have given voice, a penetrating eternal voice to the groan of the slave." What is first called an eternal glory is later described as its opposite. The enslaved situation of the Jew has engendered in him a resentment of the whole world; it also had led him to total acquiescence, a readiness to accommodate himself to every situation and serve whoever is able and willing to protect him: "The Jew will have the kings. There is no better slave, more docile, more intelligent." The Jew is capable of enduring his situation because, in developing an internal dimension of his own, expressed in the strict observance of the Law, and by cherishing the hope of redemption and revenge in the future, he remains untouched by his external predicament. "In keeping his Law within himself [en lui] he believes he cannot be degraded internally. In praxis [this is] a delicate and difficult distinction: to be internally a saint, externally the supple instrument of every tyranny of the world."[9]

Although this characterization of the Jewish mentality is given within the context of the ancient world, there is no doubt that it refers to the contemporary world as well. The historian himself, sensing that the censures contained in his exposition might offend Jewish sensibility, wrote an explanatory note at the end of this chapter. It was only with great reluctance, he noted, that he had expressed himself on this subject. He admired the Jews of the past because of their martyrdom and those of the present because of their domestic virtues and the manifold talents they deployed. The Jewish virtues, however, were outweighed by present faults and historical liabilities. Biblical Judaism was serving, even then, as a paradigm for the slaveholders in the United States, and the Jewish Bible, along with the Christian one, was the source of authority for despotism over all of Europe. Jews continued to serve tyranny all over the world and were well disposed to do so because of their "religious sentiments that allow them to bear easily the servitude and the disgrace" of such service.[10]

The Liberal Ambiguity

Michelet's complaints are obviously prompted by his resentment against his Jewish contemporaries—typical of many radical social thinkers in the nineteenth century—for not joining him in his struggle for a better world. Such resentments disposed those who harbored them to absorb time-honored anti-Jewish prejudices in spite of their otherwise liberal and universalistic world view. We can see, by the example of Michelet, that this type was not limited to Germany, where we shall encounter it later. French liberalism as well as French socialism produced, along with the philo-Semitism more concordant with its basic nature, disharmonious preludes to anti-Semitism as well.

A historian whose whole lifework touched upon the image of the Jew, past and present, is Ernest Renan. Educated as a theologian, Renan, after experiencing a religious crisis, turned to philosophy and history. Besides his scholarly contributions to the history of language and religion, Renan was regarded as a legitimate reinterpreter of Christianity and, by the same token, as a competent judge of Judaism. Some of Renan's most extensive works, notably *Histoire du peuple d'Israel*, were written after the ascendance of the anti-Semitic movement in the early eighties. In presenting Renan's view I shall rely, at this stage, only upon his writings that preceded this period and could possibly have influenced it.[11]

Renan's impact upon the evaluation of Jews and Judaism in modern France is primarily the result of his reinterpretation of the essence of Christianity. Having lost his faith, Renan nonetheless viewed Christianity as the religion representing the highest possible religious development of the human spirit. "Jesus founded the eternal religion of humanity, the religion of the spirit liberated from all priesthood, from all cult, from all observance, accessible to all races, superior to castes, in one word absolute." This formulation is, of course, the same as that conceived by the liberal German Protestant thinkers and theologians who greatly influenced Renan's thinking. Concomitant to this concept of Christianity as pure spirituality, Renan saw Judaism—the historical backdrop for, and conceptual contrast to, the credo promulgated by Jesus—in a negative light: "Judaism contained the principle of a narrow formalism, of exclusive fanaticism disdainful of strangers; this is the Pharisaic spirit, which later became the Talmudic spirit." This unnecessary reference to the Talmudic period is indicative of Renan's tendency to expand his judgment on Judaism beyond the historical time of the emergence of Christianity.[12]

What is hinted at in his lecture of 1862 ("De la part de peuples Sémitiques dans l'histoire de la civilisation"), from which the above quotations are taken, is more explicitly stated in Renan's most famous book, *Vie de Jésus*. Contrasting the allegedly more lenient Judaism in Galilee, Jesus' homeland, to that of Jerusalem, Renan continues: "The North alone created Christianity, Jerusalem on the contrary was the true homeland of obstinate Judaism founded by the Pharisees, fixed by the Talmud, and transmitted during the Middle Ages until our day." Even assuming that Renan indeed believed that he had reconstructed the original spiritual creed of Christianity—and not simply created an ideal type that appealed to him—he was of course aware of the historical reality that Christianity very soon became a ritualistic and institutionally organized religion. There is good reason to believe, as has been suggested by Renan's critics, that in depicting Jesus as the revolutionary prophet intent on destroying the Jerusalem religious establishment he projected into the remote past his own role—and that of his anticlerical companions—in his struggle against the prerogatives of the Catholic church. What is beyond doubt is that Renan, in portraying Jesus as the herald of unritualistic, inwardly directed religion, offered his liberal contemporaries the option of retaining the Christian identity while rejecting the authority of the Church and its claim to superior spiritual guidance. On the other hand, Renan's exposition of Judaism as ritualism alone denied Jews similar options with respect to Judaism. Thus, while he salvaged Christianity for modern man through reinterpretation, Judaism was declared absolutely obsolete—a discriminating attitude which parallels that of many liberals in Germany as well.[13]

The definition of Judaism as absolute ritualism harkens back, of course, to the eighteenth-century enlightenment to which nineteenth-century liberalism owes some of its major intellectual impulses. The reduction of Christianity to its alleged spiritual components itself conforms to the credo of the rationalist—with a difference. Most rationalists, self-proclaimed as Deists, forwent the label of Christianity, while Renan, dressing Christianity in a new garb, was obviously bent on retaining it. The formal attachment to Christianity then finds its expression in the relationship of Christianity to Judaism: Judaism is rejected in terms of the time-honored Christian-Jewish antagonism as if Christianity still contained its traditional conceptions.[14]

The Pharisees, representing the Jewish nation as a whole, are portrayed in Renan's work on the life of Jesus as narrow-minded hypocrites who were as culpable for Jesus' death as in any traditional record of the gospel. Renan does doubt the historic validity of the Christian tradition of the Jews having spoken the terrible words: "His blood be on us and on our children"; however, he adds "But they are the expression of a deep historical truth." While Jews as individuals can disclaim responsibility for what happened in Jerusalem eighteen centuries ago, "Yet nations have their responsibility like individuals. If ever there was a crime of a nation it was the death of Jesus." He rationalizes this statement by the claim that the religious intolerance inherent in Biblical Judaism led to the death of Jesus, and the Jews as a nation are accountable for what they have willingly accepted as their religious legacy. More than that, Jews are at least historically responsible for any intolerance to be found in Christianity—"for intolerance is essentially not a Christian fact. It is a Jewish fact" even if at times Jews themselves became the victims of it.[15]

Renan's reinterpretation of Christianity thus failed to clear Jews of the traditional charges against them. What it did accomplish was that it transplanted the old charges, including that of deicide, from the historical to the symbolic plane. Important as the denunciation of dogmatic Christianity may have been in other respects, it made very little difference to the defamatory function of the anti-Jewish charges. The divine curse that Jews had borne for generations was simply replaced by a cultural or racial propensity that now marked the descendants of the Pharisees of Jerusalem for all eternity.

The context in which Renan refers to the national responsibility of Jews for religious intolerance seems to indicate that, in positing this permanent Jewish characteristic, he had in mind a cultural predilection rather than a biological determination. On the other hand, Renan used the term *race* quite liberally and was, in fact, the first writer to give it free currency as an explanatory concept of historical phenomena. Unaware of its fateful historical consequences, he introduced the notion of race in the Jewish context.

The term *race* had been used quite freely by Europeans since the seventeenth century to denote the multiple variety of the human species that were being encountered in newly discovered parts of the world. In the early decades of the nineteenth century, the term was used as a conceptual tool to interpret certain aspects of European history, such as the stratification of medieval society, its division between aristocracy and commoners. According to this theory, the different social castes originally belonged to different races, the commoners being the autochthonous population, the aristocracy the descendants of foreign conquerors. Another important application of the term was in connection with linguistic theory. Having detected the common roots of what became known as the Indo-European tongue, linguists developed a theory that all the peoples who spoke the language were of the same origin, the race of the Aryans. The other large group of people whose language had common roots were the Semites, who were regarded as a separate race. The culmination of this kind of racial theory was reached by Count Gobineau, one of Renan's contemporaries, in his *Essai sur l'inégalité des races humaines*. Gobineau attempted the interpretation of all human history, the ascendance of empires, cultures, and civilizations, through the operation and cooperation of the three races—the white, the black, and the yellow.[16]

Ernest Renan played an important part in linking racial theory to anti-Jewish thought and as such contributed to the development of modern anti-Semitism. Renan had published his major treatise based on the concept of race in 1848, five years before the appearance of Gobineau's famous treatise. His acquaintance with Gobineau and his work may have reinforced his confidence in the intellectual efficacy of racial theory. Renan posited a basic contradistinction between the two races, the Aryan and the Semitic, the first endowed with boundless natural gifts, the second totally devoid of any positive qualities whatsoever. Renan later took pride in having been the first to recognize the superiority of the Aryans over the Semites. His claim to have originated this idea was directed not against Gobineau, who made no such distinction, but against a German linguist, Christoph Lassen, who almost simultaneously came forward with an identical suggestion.[17]

Despite inconsistencies and contradictions in details, the asserted dichotomy between the two races and the distribution of qualities between them is a central theme in all Renan's linguistic and historical writings after 1848, including his last work, *Histoire du peuple d'Israel*. An analysis of one of his early statements on the subject, *Histoire générale et système comparé des langues sémitiques* of 1858, will suffice to illustrate the theme. Here Renan enumerates the alleged qualities of the two races: "The semitic conscience is clear but little expanded; it conceives marvelously the unity, it does not grasp the multiplicity. Monotheism sums up and explains all its character." As is evident from tone and context, monotheism is conceived of as an inferior stage of the religious consciousness of man. "This [Semitic] race has never conceived the government of the universe other than as an absolute monarchy; its theodicy has never progressed since the book of Job; the grandeur and the aberration of the polytheism always remained strange to it." Why, and in what sense, aberrations can be counted as praiseworthy is not made clear; it is possible they are considered so simply because they are characteristic of polytheism, which is extolled above its contrary, monotheism. Polytheism is to be preferred to monotheism because of the religious intolerance inherent in the latter and the broadmindedness of the former—a charge against monotheism we have already encountered in the purely Jewish context of the life story of Jesus. Before their conversion to Christianity, the Indo-European peoples did not regard their religion as "an absolute truth . . . and that is why one finds only with these peoples the liberty to think, the spirit of inquiry and individual research."[18]

This whole passage on polytheism seems to suggest an unqualified preference for it—a strange attitude on the part of someone who, as we have seen, declared Christianity to be the eternal religion of humanity.

The Liberal Ambiguity

That Renan was not unaware of this disharmony is evident in the obviously futile attempt he made to overcome it in the closing sentence of this passage: "No doubt, the tolerance of Indo-Europeans derives from a more devoted sentiment of the human destiny and from a grand broadness of mind; but who would dare to say that in revealing the divine unity and in suppressing the local religions the Semitic race has not laid the foundation stone for the unity and the progress of humanity." There is no doubt where the author's sympathies lie, but his formal attachment to a diluted Christianity forced this evaluation of the Semitic concept of divine and human unity.[19]

In evaluating the respective contributions of Aryans and Semites to human culture, Renan's judgment is unequivocal: "The absence of philosophical and scientific culture is due, it seems to me, to the lack of extension, of variety and consequently of analytical spirit which distinguishes them." "The Semitic people almost entirely lack curiosity." As for the arts, music, because of its subjective nature, is the only art that the Semites became acquainted with. The Semitic mind has shown itself insensible to all others.[20]

The same dullness is revealed by the Semites in connection with "civic and political life . . . one does not find in their midst either great empires or commerce or public spirit . . . The true Semitic society is that of the tent and the tribe." The negative image of the Semites culminates in his evaluation of their moral capacity: "The Semite knows almost no duties except for himself . . . to ask him to keep his word, to do justice in a disinterested position is to ask something impossible."[21]

Reading these passages, one is compelled to think of Voltaire and his Deistic predecessors, who in speaking of Biblical Israel passed judgment similar to that of Renan in talking about the Semitic race. In fact Renan, despite occasional references to the Koran and other non-Jewish sources, directs his attention primarily to the Jewish Bible. For example, on the crucial issue of morality, while Mohammed is cited as having "obeyed his passion more than his duty," an alleged Semitic characteristic, this is the only instance of a non-Biblical quotation. Beside the Moslem prophet there is a whole series of Biblical figures—David, Solomon, Samuel, Eli—in sum "almost all the prophets of the old school eluded [echappent] . . . all our rules of moral criticism."[22]

Renan's shift from Biblical Israel to the Semitic race is no more than a generalization of the Deistic condemnation of the former. Renan, in trying to determine the common denominators of larger ethnic units, followed the general trend of linguistic and historical studies. At first sight this expanding of the negative judgment to include the whole race blunted its anti-Jewish edge. Jews, though included in the Semitic race, were not singled out. The notion of race in Renan's conception has not yet assumed the meaning of biological determinism. The much debated question whether the different races are of independent or of common origin—a point not unrelated to the issue of the basic equality of man—he left undecided. But whatever their origin, he allowed for thorough variations influenced by environmental circumstances. This most important qualification of the idea of race was stated in connection with contemporary Jewry: " . . . the Israelites of our days who descended in direct line from the ancient inhabitants of Palestine have nothing of the Semitic character and are no more than modern men, assimilated through that great force superior to races and destructive of local originalities which we call the civilization." Subjectively, Renan could have not intended his theories to be used as anti-Semitic weapons. Objectively, however, the theories contained elements that could easily be employed for this purpose. The negative characterization of ancient Judaism connected with the name of modern Jewry was too obvious in his work to be overlooked. The notion of race, once promulgated as a quasi-scientific principle, was to undergo significant changes in preparation for discrimination and defamation.[23]

11 | Jews and Freemasons

THOUGH LIBERALS as well as socialists evolved their own particular anti-Jewish attitudes, it was the Catholics who maintained the strongest reservations against Jewish integration in France. Catholics had learned how to come to terms with life within the secular state, but they could not be compelled to discard their mental reservation against its laws and institutions, indeed against its very foundations. Jewish membership and equality in state and society ran counter to the orthodox Christian conception; they had come about only under the impact of the revolutionary forces and could therefore only be accepted by Catholics as stubborn facts lacking internal ideological or spiritual justification. Most Catholics more or less consciously resented these developments.

There was no anti-Jewish treatise of the magnitude of Eisenmenger's *Entdecktes Judenthum* at the disposal of French writers. Nevertheless, the basic elements of the medieval Christian conception of the Jew had been transmitted through various channels. The Jewish convert David Drach presented the Church's doctrine in a series of books stressing Christianity's superiority over Judaism and disparaging at the same time Jewish theological concepts and moral teachings.[1] *Theorie du judaisme*, by Luigi A. Chiarini, published in Paris in 1830, could pass for a shorter version of Eisenmenger's *Entdecktes Judenthum*. The author was an Italian cleric serving as professor of Oriental languages at Warsaw University. The book had been occasioned by the Russian government's attempts to define the Jews' position within the Russian state. Chiarini belonged to the school that recommended rapprochement with the Jews, hoping for their ultimate conversion to Christianity. Since the Talmud was regarded as the main source of Jewish exclusiveness, Chiarini's denunciation of it was regarded as a timely enterprise.[2] At any rate the book, written in French and printed in Paris, served as a welcome source for attacks on Judaism when the occasion for them arose. Such an occasion was the famous Mortara case in 1858 that scandalized liberal public opinion all over Europe.

A six-year-old child of the Mortaras, a Jewish family of Bologna, had been abducted by the papal police because, when dangerously ill as a one-year-old baby, it had been secretly baptized by a Christian domestic servant. According to canon law such baptism was valid, and the papal authorities upheld their claim to educate the child as a Catholic in the face of the parents' protest and in spite of the worldwide scandal caused by their decision.[3]

The Church found, of course, its apologists among the believers. In France it was the clerical *L'Univers*, edited by Louis Veuillot, which went out of its way to convince its readers that in securing for the baptized child a Christian education, the Holy Father had done nothing but his Christian duty. Otherwise the Christian child would have been brought up by his parents in the despicable Jewish faith.[4] To prove the despicability of Judaism, the militant Veuillot exploited all the sources at his disposal. He knew no Hebrew or Aramaic and seems to have been unable to read Eisenmenger's *Entdecktes Judenthum*. Yet being a convinced and dogmatic Catholic, he took the doctrinal inferiority and moral insufficiency of Judaism for granted and was satisfied with what he could cite from Drach and Chiarini.[5] Veuillot was considered the outstanding intellectual among the Catholics and was a gifted writer and polemicist. His sharp pen caused the most deprecating accusations against Jews and Judaism, including the charge-of-the-blood libel, to be propagated in broad circles of Catholic France.

The anti-Jewish campaign caused by the Mortara affair was joined by the theologian Louis Rupert with his *L'Église et la synagogue* (1859).[6] The gist of Rupert's retort to critics of the Church was that not Christianity but Judaism had been since time immemorial the symbol of intolerance, immorality, and hatred. Though relying on the data of the past, Rupert's conclusion clearly referred to the present: "Has this nation given up its habits and prejudices?" This was obviously a rhetorical question, and the negative reply was self-evident: "Is it any wonder that the Jewish people always remains separate, a state within a state despite its mingling with other peoples . . . Its morality cannot be considered in the same context as that of the Gospels. Its politics are not subject to the same standards of those of other peoples. The principle of the honor of citizen status is concealed by the Jewish demand for world domination. In vain are they granted citizen's rights. In vain are they vouchsafed honors and positions of dignity. These have not prevented them from holding on to their own views and principles, nor has it weakened their tendency to act according to these views and principles. This is because these are so deeply embedded in them that no power can uproot them. The principles and way of Judaism remain as they were in every place and for all time." Rupert too included the blood libel in the category of Jewish crimes; To verify this accusation he garnered evidence from the recent and remote past, the latest allegation being the 1840 Damascus blood libel, which he claimed set the matter beyond any possible doubt.[7]

As Jews appeared unchanged, the shift in their favor by the modern state was altogether unwarranted. It could have derived, according to Rupert's interpretation of history, only from sources inimical to the foundations of Christianity. Jewish emancipation was the work of modern philosophy intent on negating the unique position of Christianity among the world's religions. To achieve the humiliation of the Christian church it became necessary "to place the divinely rejected Synagogue on a par with all the other denominations."[8]

The incidental origin of Rupert's attack, its connection with the Mortara case, in no way reduces its significance, which lies in its demonstration of the continuing influence of the Christian concept of the Jew—his spiritual status, his posited pariah status, and his moral evaluation. The fact of Jewish emancipation failed to secure a respectable status for contemporary Jewry. In the eyes of Rupert and his like, the Jews still reflected in their status and mentality the image of the Pharisees of the Gospels and the Ghetto dwellers of bygone centuries.

In truth, the gap between the theological perception and Jewish reality was widening as time went on. In the 1860s and 1870s French Jewry seemed to be integrating into some of the more important segments of French society, occupying positions in business and finance, the professions, and the press, as well as in academics.[9] Since, however, Jews remained concentrated professionally and closely connected in many other ways, they did not cease to be regarded as a separate social unit. As such, they were resented by all those who wished to see France unified as a Christian nation. The outstanding success of Jews in fulfilling their allotted tasks in state and society, instead of atoning for their Jewishness, was apt to magnify their guilt. While in the 1820s theologians referred to the social inferiority of Jews as a proof of their divine forsakenness, now they had to come to terms with the fact of Jewish social advancement. Theodore Ratisbonne in his youth saw in the Jews' destitution evidence of their being forsaken; now he declared their wealth and fortune a sign of their moral degeneration: "Jews are not Jews anymore; neither are they Christians, they hover between past and future. How could such a thing happen to the descendants of Abraham the father of all believers . . . Skillful and ingenious by nature and possessed by instinct for domination, the Jews gradually monopolized all avenues which lead to richness, dignities and power; their spirit gradually infiltrated modern civilization; they dominate the bourse, the press, the theater, literature, the administration, the great routes of communication on earth and sea; and thanks to their fortune and genius they keep the whole Christian society ensnared as in a net."[10]

The social ascendance of Jewry gave the lie to the Christian expectation that Jews would be kept in a state of deprivation until they joined Christianity at the end of days. Still, theologians were not at a loss to explain away the disturbing facts. A world order cast in disarray, where those below were now above and vice versa, was interpreted by theologians as a portent of the end of days when all the expectations, including the conversion of Israel to the true faith, would be fulfilled![11] Whether this interpretation could have seemed plausible to nontheologians may well be doubted, but the inimical characterization of Jewish reality that served as its starting point certainly left its mark.

The tendency represented by Rupert and Ratisbonne was expanded upon on a grand scale by Gougenot des Mousseaux in his *Le Juif, le judaisme et la judaisation des peuples chrétiens* (1869). An officer in a religious order, des Mousseaux wrote in an involved and sectarian fashion not likely to have a broad appeal or gain a large circulation. As we shall see later, the significance of his book is in the use made by propagandists of the ideas of this esoteric ponderer.[12]

Des Mousseaux's starting point is the traditional doctrine of the divine rejection of the post-Christian Jew, whom he burdens with both the traditional as well as the modern condemnation. Adherence to the Talmudic tradition is the source of both Jewish immorality and irreligion. Even orthodox Judaism lacks the crucial ingredient of a true religion: the institution of sacerdotalism, the priest as the bearer of authority entitled to impart consolation and forgiveness. Rabbis, like the scribes of evangelical times, are doctors of religious lore but beyond that are just laymen like other members of the community. Accordingly, it was a scandalous act when the Jewish community in France was granted not only citizenship but even an overall "imperial organization of the Jewish religion"—the *consistoire* established by Napoleon the First—thus elevating the mortal enemy of the Church of Christ to equal status. That many of the emancipated Jews drifted away from Jewish orthodoxy in thought and conduct left des Mousseaux's conception unaffected. For the deviation from religious thought and observance did not entail a change in morality. Nor did the religious schism in Judaism destroy the basic unity of the Jewish nation.

Jews and Freemasons

The divided parties in Jewry were united in their common aspiration to strive to dominate the world. The force behind this drive was a national instinct common to all members of the community. The division between Orthodox and Reform Jews seemed almost a predetermined strategy in dealing with the Gentile world. The Orthodox, who blindly followed the Talmudic way of life, represented "the undestructable nucleus of the nation," while the nonobservant free thinkers, unrestrained by any religious or moral inhibitions, were at work in the Gentile world, undermining the foundations of Christianity and infecting their surroundings with moral disease. This was what was meant by the "Judaisation of the Christian Nations" hinted at in the title of the book.[13]

Des Mousseaux's argumentation followed in the footsteps of Christian tradition, but also drew ideas from contemporary anti-Jewish literature. Indeed, his book is replete with quotations not only from Catholic writers such as de Bonald, Rupert, and Ratisbonne, but also the hated adversaries of the Church, the liberals Michelet and Renan. These could not be suspected of anti-Jewish bias because of their religious stance and could be cited as objective witnesses. Toussenel's book, on the other hand, was exploited to substantiate the charge of Jewish predominance in the economy and finances.[14] Never doubting the truth of anti-Jewish charges from whatever quarter they emanated, des Mousseaux was satisfied that they bore out his view of the Jewish determination to realize the messianic hope of world domination.

The conspiratorial dimension of the Jews' drive for domination is explicitly referred to by des Mousseaux in connection with what turned out to be his most consequential contribution to anti-Semitic theory and propaganda: the combination with, and partial identification of, Jews with Freemasons. At the time the antagonism between Catholics and Freemasons was already of long standing. As early as 1738, fifteen years after the inception of Freemasonry in England, the Masons were excommunicated by Pope Clement XII. Ever since, they had been regarded as the carriers of heretical teachings, the enemies of Christianity and especially of the Catholic church. Because of the exclusive and secretive character of the lodges' activity, they became for the popular imagination the target of suspicion and wild speculation. There is no conspiratorial design that has not been at one time or other attributed to the Masons. In postrevolutionary France there was a popular theory—evolved by the Jesuit August Barruel in 1797-98—that the great upheaval was nothing but the work of a Masonic conspiracy.[15]

Catholic hostility against Freemasonry ran parallel to that against Judaism, and occasionally the two were combined by anti-Jewish writers in Austria and Germany. They hinted at the possible cooperation between the two groups to the detriment of their common contestant, the Church and Christian society. In Germany, where Jews had great difficulty in being accepted by the Freemasons even at the height of the liberal era, the insinuation had no chance of gaining ready acceptance. After the Revolution in France, the Masonic lodges were, on principle at least, open to Jews and some of the leading figures of French Jewry, Adolph Cremieux for instance, were known to have a central role in Freemasonry.[16]

The idea of Jewish-Masonic cooperation seemed thus to be confirmed by tangible facts and became easily credible for anyone for whom the culpability of both groups was a foregone conclusion. Des Mousseaux stands out among those, for he not only enlarged upon the theme but collected all the facts that could be cited in support of it. Did not Jews flock to the Masonic lodges, ascending in them to the highest grades—like Adolph Cremieux, the president of the Alliance Israélite Universelle, who at the same time was the grand master of one of the branches of the Freemasonry, the Scottish rite. And did not the Masons pursue the same aims as the Jews in combating Christianity and the Church? Was it not obvious that their common interest would unite them in common action?[17]

Because of his esoteric style, des Mousseaux's expositions had little impact outside of the circles of the like-minded. On these, however, his efforts were not lost. The idea of Jewish-Masonic identity gained ground, and, at the end of a decade, it was taken up by E. N. Chabauty, who devoted to it an even more voluminous and cumbersome volume. Chabauty believed he had detected the signs of the impending apocalyptical destruction of the world—foreshadowed in the deterioration of the Christian faith and morality. Jews and Freemasons were identified as the two emissaries of evil, operating for the decay and degradation of Christianity. Since decay was their appropriate element, both groups throve in the waste they had created, to the sorrow and despondency of the believers.[18]

Chabauty's book was even more bigoted and sectarian than des Mousseaux's and was a step forward in publicizing his main thesis, as epitomized in Chabauty's title: *Francs-Maçons et Juifs, sixième age de l'Eglise d'après l'Apocalypse.* The association of Freemasons and Jews in the title conjured up the idea of a conspiracy of the two uncanny enemies. This idea, as well as the other anti-Jewish charges implied in the treatises of des Mousseaux and Chabauty, were at this juncture still considered by most people to be a part of their rigmarole of absurd notions and fantasies. Later, we shall see how these anti-Semitic insinuations became detached from their original settings to gain an impetus that carried their destructive power to unexpected heights.[19]

Part IV: Germany, 1830-1873

12 | The German Liberals' Image of the Jew

THE DECADE FOLLOWING the Hep Hep upheaval of 1819 is often described by historians as an era of stagnation, retrogression, and disappointment for Jews—rightly so if measured by the expectations of the proponents of Jewish emancipation. Objectively, however, the improvement in the Jewish position far outweighed the retrogression. It is true that in Prussia, where the Edict of 1812 granted the Jews almost full citizenship, save for the restriction denying them the right to be employed in the service of the state, this disability was extended rather than removed. Similarly, in Bavaria, no steps were taken to implement the much-discussed social, economic, and educational reforms that ought to have led to civil equality. But in Frankfurt, where the Jews were struggling against the curtailment of their acquired rights by the Senate—and feeding, by their struggle, the nationwide public controversy—their adversaries were compelled to compromise. In 1824, except for participation in the political conduct of the municipality, Jews regained all the prerogatives of a free citizen—free choice of residence, occupation, and acquisition of property. In Hamburg, too, the Hep Hep uproar may have retarded the process of political advancement and social integration, but it did not block participation by Jewish tradesmen and bankers in the economic development of the city. Nor were the Wurzburg burghers able to remove the Jews from the town. In Wurzburg the result of the uproar was stricter control over the residential rights of individual Jews. Those who lived in Wurzburg legitimately could remain there, and they succeeded in strengthening their communal organization.[1]

147

At any rate, the overall situation of the Jews was far better than what had been proposed by Rühs and Fries: that they be thrown back once again into the ghettos, wear a Jewish badge, and pay the special Jewish tax. As far as their practical program was concerned, these Jew-baiters were revealed as reactionaries attempting to implement measures that ran counter to the trend of the times. For, in spite of the harkening-back to the remote past that characterized the newly emerging nationalism and the concomitant movement of romanticism, state and society were moving away from the corporate structure that had led to the ghetto exclusion of the Jews. The increasing importance of industry, as well as other aspects of the money-based economy, operated in favor of a greater mobility, rather than the assignment of a fixed status to individuals according to their ethnic or religious origins. In addition, Jews played a conspicuous role in the management of the ever-expanding money market and thus had acquired a marked degree of influence. Indeed, the Rothschilds, by now very powerful indeed, played an active role in securing Jewish rights in their native town of Frankfurt. The connections between other Jewish financiers and those in political power operated in the same direction.[2]

That the Jewish community was moving out of the ghetto was also evident in the intellectual sphere. The seclusion of the Jews in their linguistically and culturally distinct world had been broken by Moses Mendelssohn's entrance into the circle of the Berlin intellectuals in the late eighteenth century. This could have been interpreted as an exceptional individual achievement; by the 1820s and 1830s, however, the number of Jewish writers, poets, scholars, and publicists was far too great and their contribution far too conspicuous to be dismissed as an ephemeral phenomenon. Among the reading public and theater audience, too, Jews were conspicuous and contributed more than their share. Goethe, no great friend of Jews and Judaism, found the keen interest of Jewish readers in his work remarkable.[3]

The notion of a Jewish return to the ghetto under these circumstances seemed to be absurd; the idea was in conflict with the prevailing liberal outlook. Nevertheless, rejection of a return to the past did not answer the question of what the fate of the Jews might be in the future. The liberals imagined a society characterized by rationally motivated individuals with unlimited mobility; laissez faire economics that would secure the well-conceived interest of all concerned; freedom of association on the basis of common religious conviction, with the churches denied any compulsory power. Jews could hope to be integrated into this society if they behaved according to its rules and standards. Whether or not they were capable of doing so was the big question, but, even if the answer was affirmative, it was conditioned on a most radical change in Jewish mores, religious character, and mentality. It was in order to assess the measure of the change required—or to prove its impossibility—that critical views of Jewish life were presented in the writings of these liberals. From the standpoint of our subject—the transmission of the negative image of the Jew from generation to generation—it makes little difference whether a writer's conclusions tended to be optimistic or pessimistic, or whether he did or did not believe in the ability of the Jew to reform himself. The fact of the negative representation of Jews and Judaism, whatever the conclusions were, constituted a link in the perpetuation of the Jewish stereotype.

C. H. Pfaff was a man of high intellectual standards and genuine liberal convictions. Pfaff was a scientist—a kind of polyhistor combining work in physics, chemistry, and medicine with a propensity for popularization,—who at times felt called upon to take a stand on questions of public interest.[4] The occasion for his essay on the Jewish question—printed in the *Kieler Blätter*, an annual of liberal professors—was the translation of two treatises on the same subject by the Danish scholar and statesman C. F. Schmidt-Phiseldeck. The latter wished to answer the question: What position ought the state to assign the Jews so long as they retained their constitution as a socially distinct group engaged exclusively in trade and finance and separated from the bulk of the population by the prescription of their ancient religion? Schmidt-Phiseldeck's answer conformed to that of many of the German opponents of Jewish citizenship: Jews could not claim more than protection of persons and property—the universal human rights granted by the state to anyone who wished to dwell in the country without joining the body of the autochthonous population, the original incumbents of citizenship. To justify his stand, Schmidt-Phiseldeck drew a picture of the Jew as an eternal stranger who, owing to his religion, his faith in the special nature of his descent (seed of Abraham), his commitment to his brethren wherever they lived, and his hope for ultimate restoration to his ancient homeland, would forever remain apart and separated from the nation within which he happened to sojourn.[5]

Pfaff echoed Schmidt-Phiseldeck in his proposition as well as in his argument, but, while the Danish scholar presented his thesis with studied detachment and coolness, his German colleague spoke in a fiery and passionate manner. Stagnation—like a swamp of filthy water along the permanently moving stream of the nations—was the characteristic of Jewish life through the ages. The main aspect of the Jewish character was a quality by which they paradoxically gained a supremacy over the Christians: "their natural versatility and vivacity, their bent for speculation [*Spekulationsgeist*], the concentration of all their mental forces on gain."[6] The combination of ethnic exclusiveness and the professional concentration on trade and finance evoked the term "caste" by which Schmidt-Phiseldeck designated the Jewish community, a term fully approved by Pfaff who, as usual, only sharpened his predecessor's definition: Jews were "a caste of tradesmen and hawkers who shun every serious and strenuous work, agriculture and handicraft."[7] The members of the caste were closely united with each other; by the same token, they were radically alienated from state and society at large, indeed scarcely accepting any ethical obligation toward them. This double morality was aggravated, according to Schmidt-Phiseldeck and Pfaff, by the economic development of the previous generation. The enhanced role of private credit, the creation of public funds and state securities, opened the way for agiotage and speculation, offering Jews, the eternal traders and bankers, the chance of concentrating in their hands the wealth of the nation. Since the Jews were to all intents and purposes conceived of as a foreign power, the possibility of their economic dominance conjured up some frightful images: The Jews were like "a rapidly growing parasitic plant that winds round the still healthy tree to suck up the life juice until the trunk, emaciated and eaten up from within, falls moldering into decay."[8]

Similar images of Judaism are propounded by other authors of similar background. We are acquainted with Ludolph Holst from his inciting statements that preceded the Hep Hep riots in Hamburg. He persistently warned about Jewish domination of the inhabitants of the city, before and after the riots. In the book he published in 1821 that dealt with the Jewish question—purportedly "from the standpoint of political science"—he depicted the image of the Jew as poisonous in every respect.[9] He attributed Jewish survival, in all its manifestations, to a unique human spirit active in the deformation of the social environment in which Jews happened to be.

Alexander Lips wrote that the petrification of Jewish life, the result of their harkening-back to the past, excluded the Jew from the human ideal of perfectability.[10] The self-exclusion from the common ideals of mankind led to social aloofness and this, in its turn, to an ethical indifference toward the rest of society. Lips's Jew, too, preferred trade, exercised with cunning and subtlety, to any other productive engagement. Thus, understandably, he too resorts to the term "caste" to characterize the Jew's position in society. "The Jew appears . . . as. a distortion, a shadow, and the dark side of human nature."[11]

J. B. Graser, a Bavarian liberal like Lips, writing at the end of the 1820s, echoes Lips's charges and even aggravates them. He stresses the inaccessibility of Jews to change, their tenacious adherence to the painless but profitable profession of trade, and adds a most contemptible description of the Jewish religion, the supposed origin and mainspring of all this evil. Judged by their practical proposals for the future status and position of the Jews, Lips and Graser were not at all inimical to them. Lips's book was, in fact, hailed by Jewish intellectuals, among them Jomtov Lippman Zunz, for its effective advocacy of Jewish rights. Correctly so, for Lips's book recommended unrestricted citizenship for Jews, although this went along with a compulsory system of re-education, as an act of just and reasonable statesmanship. Similarly, Graser, a noted educator in active service with the Bavarian government, wished to lead the Jews to citizenship through the reform of their religious and educational institutions.[12]

Schmidt-Phiseldeck, Pfaff, Holst, Graser, and Lips, differing as they did in their practical attitudes toward the Jewish issue, carried with them a very similar image of Judaism as well as of the common type of Jew. The negative image of Judaism appears against the background of an idealized notion of Christianity. None of these authors was a Christian in any ecclesiastical sense, but all of them believed they possessed in Christianity a source of inspiration for liberal ideas and attitudes that was lacking in Judaism. Schmidt-Phiseldeck saw in Christianity "an internal mark [Gepräge] of universal validity . . . applicable to all nations under all forms of constitution or in all civic conditions." Judaism, in contrast, had "a definite tendency toward isolation." "The divine founder of Christianity" attempted to divert Judaism from its particularism, to no avail.[13] Pfaff echoed these sentiments with his usual eloquence: "Christianity is the religion of love that embraces the whole of mankind, the joyful message of a loving Father before whom all men are equal . . . a religion the adherents of which honor and celebrate in its founder a divine friend and benefactor of man [Menschenfreund] only because he announced these simple and spirit-liberating truths in their purity and innocence and sealed them by the deeds of his life and through his death."[14] This is the prelude to the crashing denunciation of Judaism presented above. Lips, too, declares the Christian religion ("not because it is ours but because it is the truth") to be "full of love and tolerance . . . imbued with the spirit of humanity and morality . . . molded to the needs of another, higher epoch," leaving Judaism, from which it originated, far behind.[15] Graser compares Judaism with Christianity on the plane of their institutional practices. The Christian priest or pastor supervises the education of children and adults, admonishes his congregation to lead a moral life, "visits the sick, tenders consolation and brings tranquility to the dying." None of this is included in the duties of a rabbi. Graser purported to have studied Judaism through direct inspection of Jewish life, but was incapable of judging it except by the Christian yardstick. His prejudice in favor of his own religion is most strikingly demonstrated when he takes the Jews to task for their failure to appreciate the wiseness and nobility of Jesus as revealed by his deeds and his teachings. These characteristics of Jesus are the ground of the liberal-minded educator's own adherence to Christianity, and they ought to be apparent to Jews also.[16]

The only liberal critic who tries to avoid a direct confrontation between Judaism and Christianity is Holst. The negative features of Judaism, according to Holst, are absolute; they revealed themselves in the contact of Jews with non-Christian nations—the Persians, the Greeks, the Romans. This would seem to suggest a secular justification of anti-Jewishness along Voltairian lines. Holst, however, was far from disavowing Christianity; he strongly approved of it because of its universalism, as against Jewish particularism. The direct source for Holst's depiction of Judaism was Eisenmenger. Holst confessed his indebtedness to Eisenmenger and other authors from whose writings he derived the accusation that Jews were morally insensible to non-Jews, perjury, robbing, and killing allegedly being permitted. He did not share Eisenmenger's theological premises, approaching the Jewish issue instead from an entirely different angle—that of the political scientist. Nonetheless, Eisenmenger served as a welcome source for moral condemnation of Jews.[17]

This readiness to retain elements of the Christian objections and absorb them into the context of a basically secular criticism of Judaism is a prevailing tendency of other liberals. Schmidt-Phiseldeck, too, shares the suspicion of Jewish moral unreliability; a Jew's oath, he argues, cannot be trusted, because of the alleged general absolution granted by the Kol-Nidre ceremony on Yom Kippur. Schmidt-Phiseldeck quotes Eisenmenger elsewhere, so we can assume that the *Entdecktes Judenthum* was the source of this piece of information also. Pfaff simply echoes Schmidt-Phiseldeck. Lips's portrait of Judaism does not contain any details that can be traced to Eisenmenger, but his overall evaluation of Jewish morality as a consequence of the inferiority of Jewish religion conforms to Eisenmenger's pattern. No wonder, for Eisenmenger appears at the head of the list of Lips's reading on Judaism. J. B. Graser contended he had studied Judaism by firsthand observation. He quotes a whole list of Hebrew sources in support of his lethal judgment of Jewish religion and moral sentiment; close study, however, reveals that all these quotations are copied from Eisenmenger, and Graser's firsthand observations turn out to be at least strongly colored by perennial prejudices of Christian provenance.[18]

The liberal observers of Judaism transcended, no doubt, the traditional Christian concept of Judaism. They no longer judged it mainly from the standpoint of the doctrinal differences between the two religions. They became interested in the economic, social, and political role Jews played in the past and might play in the future. It was primarily through the evaluation of this role that they either recommended the granting of greater freedom to the Jews or advocated the status quo of semi-citizenship. Still, they were far from adopting a purely secular sociological, political, or economic viewpoint. Behind these considerations, the negative image of Judaism as transmitted from past generations loomed large. The yardstick for measuring Judaism's worthiness vis-à-vis Christianity was, to be sure, not its theological truth. Rather, it was the fitness of each religion to be a guide to a moral, useful, and beautiful life. On all these counts, Judaism was found lacking. Religious inadequacy was now cited in support of the social, ethical, and political deficiencies of Judaism, and thus secular and religious anti-Jewishness complemented each other; indeed, they blended into a single ideological concept. The traditional stereotyped image of the Jew continued to be reinforced by the Jewish reality: differentiated by his language, his attire, his Talmudic culture, his lopsided occupational structure, the Jewish type as it existed in the first decades of the nineteenth century seemed to approximate the traditional stereotype. Those who wished to see Jews as a separate social entity had ample reason for doing so.[19]

Still, Jewish society could no longer be said to be homogeneous. Side by side with the class that, outwardly at least, conformed to the old stereotype, there now appeared a new specimen of Jew who seemed to have shed all the characteristics of his group. This enlightened Jew, educated in modern schools and universities, was in full command of the common language; he adopted the current patterns of social behavior and was religiously as far from traditional Judaism as any liberal Christian was from medieval Christianity. The emergence of this new type was quite apparent and could not escape the attention of the ideologue who wished to locate the Jew in the framework of the evolving society. Indeed, all the liberal critics refer to the existence of this new type of Jew, usually implying in their reference an answer to the question of how the existence of this new Jew squared with the Jewish stereotype. Schmidt-Phiseldeck characterized the "majority" of the Jews, whether they were small businessmen or big bosses, as harmful hagglers, but then he added in parentheses, "however, this description is not applicable to the enlightened, truthful, honestly industrious who are to the glory of mankind, not rarely to be found also in this nation." The author clearly admits then that there is a substantial minority of Jews who do not fit the stereotype. However, this minority is separated from the bulk of the community. The expression "to the glory of mankind" even implies that these good Jews are to be seen, first of all, as human beings, not as Jews. At the end of the book Schmidt-Phiseldeck does refer to a class among the Jews who by education and enlightenment diverge from the common type. Yet this variation does not appear to him a change for the better. The enlighten-

153

ment is, in most cases, no more than a veneer barely covering "complete indifference and cool insensibility towards everything." Only a minority of this new class is in possession of the "true religious enlightenment and genuine culture" that makes them "a glory and a pillar to their nation."[20] The presence of these does not warrant a revision of the Jewish stereotype.

Pfaff simply records Schmidt-Phiseldeck's characterization of the Jewish stereotype, and Lips and Graser evolve a similar attitude on their own. There are "worthy exceptions among them who are engaged in ordinary trade, useful to society at large [Gesammtheit], or who joined the world and united themselves intimately through cultivation of their heart, refinement of their mind, through human and cosmopolitan sentiments, through adaptation of all forms of better and social life, through all kinds of nobility of the soul [Seelenadel]." This excessive praise for the newly evolved minority nevertheless failed to dissolve the negative image of the average Jew; it might, on the contrary, have strengthened it by the inevitable comparison. Graser too conjures up, in contrast to the stereotype, the educated and morally blameless Jew, stating that the figure of Nathan the Wise was to be found not only on the stage but also in the arena of the world. But it cost the Jew a tremendous effort "to shed the tastelessness that clings to him from his youth," and the same is presumably true of his achievement in the field of ethics. At any rate, these Jews are exceptions, and indeed they are often "only Jews in name alone."[21]

The problem of the exceptional Jew is treated most explicitly by Holst. Holst observed in Hamburg the deviation of some of the Jews from the traditional way of life: the stockbroker who appears in the stock exchange on the Sabbath, "the new believers who like to be called the enlightened." Holst was also aware of the attempts of the Reform community and their leaders in Hamburg to divert Judaism from its traditional rabbinical foundations and put it on a new basis. Although rabbinical doctrines were regarded by Holst as the main source of the moral inferiority of the Jews, he was reluctant to accept the repudiation of rabbinism by the Reform Jews as the beginning of a true moral rehabilitation. The tendencies expressed in the rabbinical teachings were, according to Holst, too deeply ingrained in Jewish mentality to be eradicated through a simple disavowal by the exceptional few. "What are the few men of better sentiment [besser denkende] in comparison with the overall mass of Jewry; and how one becomes everywhere aware in what irresistible way the spirit of Judaism springs forth [hervordrängt] from the bosom of even the best Jew."[22]

Ludwig Börne, who wrote a deadly critique of Holst's book, interpreted the Hep Hep riots and the polemics that preceded and followed them as the last flutterings of medieval hatred: "The flame of enmity flared up clearly once again to be extinguished forevermore."[23] Borne awaited the realization of the principles of liberalism which he thought would bridge the gap between Jews and non-Jews. Certainly an important step in the progress of liberalism was the 1830 revolution, which caused many German regimes to introduce a parliamentary system into their countries. In the wake of the success of the revolution, Jews made a claim for equal rights, or "emancipation" as it was universally called.[24] The justice of the claim, which was loftily presented by Gabriel Riesser, a great Jewish protagonist, was considered self-evident, but the belief that the detractors of the Jews would no longer raise their voices was disappointed. Riesser's demand was answered by the renewal of the anti-Jewish argument by an extreme liberal, the Heidelberg theologian, Heinrich Eberhard G. Paulus.[25]

Paulus was a full-fledged theologian, albeit of a very peculiar kind, a deeply convinced rationalist who succeeded in retaining his Christianity by limiting its obligatory tenets to a minimum and lending even to them an absolute, rationalistic interpretation. Jesus continued to be celebrated as the Messiah, for his life and death signified a radical turn in the destiny of mankind through the proclamation of a new religious principle. The quintessence of this principle was "the adoration of the universal God through convinced loyal [überzeugungstreue] rectitude." This was the revelation to be disseminated by Jesus' disciples, and its implementation was to bring about the Kingdom of God. In emphasizing the unique role of Christianity in world history, Paulus resorted to theological terms but divested them of their original meaning. The theological phraseology served simply as a cover for a kind of Kantian morality: the demand for consistency in one's ethical commitments. Still, as this pseudotheology had a distinctly Christian coloring, it carried with it the traditional contrast to Judaism. If Christianity stood for rectitude deriving from personal conviction, Judaism knew only a very contrary attitude: the mechanical execution of rites and ceremonies. The basic notion of true religion, it is true, had already been conceived by Abraham. This Paulus conceded in following a well-trodden path of Christian tradition. However, Abraham's anticipation of Christianity had been forsaken by his descendants when they subjected themselves to the Mosaic Law. Moses may have had the good intention of transmitting the Abrahamic tradition of true religion, but at the same time he also wished to shield his people from foreign influences and secure for them "a long and happy life within the boundaries of the land." To this end, he imposed upon his people an involved system of legislation, many details of which, the dietary laws for instance, are clearly intended to keep the Jewish people apart. In posterity, the Abrahamic faith and the Mosaic Law became interlinked, with the Law gaining preponderance over faith. Ultimately, it became the universally accepted conviction still upheld by the greatest part of Jewry "that one cannot become a true adherent of the Jewish faith unless one adds the Mosaic Laws to the religious teachings." Mosaic legislation was the constitution of the nation in possession of her state and living in her country. Only as long as this situation lasted could the Law be fully implemented. That is why the messianic expectation is an integral part of the Jewish faith: it represents the natural wish to restore the conditions necessary for the full functioning of the constitution. Paulus takes pains to emphasize the difference between Christian and Jewish messianism. For the Christian, messianism is a universalistic idea; for the Jew, a national expectation. Jewish messianism provides irrefutable evidence that Jews retained the nature of a nation—the conclusion Paulus is intent on reaching. Ideally, Jews belong to the land for which they long, Palestine, and they cannot simultaneously belong to any other country, Germany, for instance. In Germany, they are foreigners, a state within a state. As foreigners, they are protected by the law but cannot expect to be integrated into the local population. One who separates himself from the nation through laws and customs cannot claim more than the protection of the foreigner who becomes a resident, the "protected subject." The cry for emancipation is, then, an absurdity.[26]

By defining Jewry as a nation, Paulus offered a cognitive justification for a deep-felt aversion against the possible ascent of Jews to an equal position with Christians. That this was indeed the case he naively reveals in a remarkable passage: "Why should Jews come into positions and circumstances in which they could become superior to the non-Jewish members of the state, when wherever Jews reside, there is a general, obscure aversion towards them?" This obscure, dim, and "enigmatic" aversion Paulus wished to elucidate and justify through his historic theological analysis.[27]

The intention to sanction ideologically a widespread prejudice is even more obvious in Paulus' observations on the economic role of the Jews. He wanted the path to the service of the state to be continuously barred to Jews. He would have countenanced a transition of Jews to agriculture and handicraft, to which Jewish youth had indeed been directed, especially in Baden, by governmental as well as Jewish communal agencies.[28] That these attempts, in spite of some success, still left the Jews economically one-sided was a fact. Paulus cited instances of Jews who were trained as artisans but later returned to brokerage (Macklerei), but he lacked either the insight or the will to elicit the deeper sociological reasons for this phenomenon. Instead, he resorted to a historical-theological explanation, maintaining that Jews had acquired an incorrigible addiction to trade ever since they had begun to live among other nations, beginning in Babylonia. Hoping to return to their own country, they refrained from committing themselves to the more steady occupation of agriculture, foreseen by the Mosaic constitution as valid for their own lands, an observation not entirely baseless. Paulus attempted to lend his theory a greater plausibility by referring to the Hebrew origin of the German word *Schacher* ("haggling"), and he argued that Jews never engaged in trade proper but only in useless and non-risky mediating: "Not trade where one sells one's own merchandise with a profit proportionate to the risk and the toil is imputed to Jewry, but this mongering [*zwischentragn*] . . . mostly with other people's goods and now especially also with other people's money . . . bearing profit through all kinds of cunning and fraud, despoiling rich and poor, princes and people . . . the latest version of the situation is the paper securities. This has been inflated to the extreme only since it fell into the hands of the separated nation." Once again Paulus observed an aspect of social reality and slanted it with his prejudiced and distorting interpretation. It was not that the Jews had been found to be exclusively absorbed by *Schacher*, rather, that anything the Jews were engaged in drew upon itself this derogatory epithet.[29]

In general, Paulus applied his pejorative description to all Jews without qualification. Yet now and then he felt constrained to concede that there were exceptions to the rule. Some rich Jews did contrive "to disassociate themselves permanently from Judaism." Similarly, the messianic expectation was "being now tacitly pushed aside by the more thoughtless as something impossible by the standards of the present situation in the world, but seldom out of a more thorough insight." Still, Paulus offered two reasons why such a departure from the traditional pattern of Jewish thought would not exclude these individuals from membership in the Jewish nation, any more than would the neglect of Jewish observances. First, the deviation was neither resolute nor consistent. Nonobservant Jews looked for sophistical excuses to explain their negligence, rather than for a principle to justify it. The messianic expectation was not dismissed as absurd but only deferred as impractical. Then, these dissenters regarded their divergence from the accepted as a kind of privilege for themselves or their groups, but did not wish to turn them into a norm for the whole nation. No doubt, Paulus had encountered the escapees from the ghetto so common in the first generations of emancipation. He had observed their struggle for cultural accommodation but doubted their success. At any rate, they were not to be taken as representative of the whole. Individual accommodation was excluded as a possible solution to the Jewish problem, while there were no signs of a collective determination to enter the path of assimilation.[30]

The religious tolerance this liberal theologian so loudly professed is revealed as tenuous, if not fictitious. He makes acceptance of the Jews dependent on their shedding all the characteristic rites and symbols of their religion, including circumcision ("an indecent operation appropriate only to the gross old times"). At the same time he sees fit to defend most emphatically the rite of baptism as "a purification symbol inoffensive in every respect." The freedom of the Jew to retain his religion if it be cleansed of its legalistic outgrowth is granted by Paulus only as a formal concession. What concept Paulus entertained of the Jewish religion as a moral force becomes clear in his conclusion, where he once again summarizes the quintessence of Judaism, this time in truly Voltairian terms: Someone who considers that as a part of his religion "he may borrow from the Egyptians silver and gold and take it with him, that the Canaanites must cede their land to him, etc.," one who believes "that God chose his people over other peoples and at the end He would raise it through the Messiah over all others," to such a man "to be sure a liberal would not forbid his faith but neither would he grant him a share in offices where he could in advance . . . train himself at our expense for his privileged world domination."[31] One can justify denying Jews the rights of full citizenship by reference to the alleged teachings of Judaism. The Jew who wishes to become a citizen must renounce not only his religious practice but also the doctrinal tradition of his faith; empty-handed, he has only one way out of his predicament: to join the community of the real religion, that of Christianity. This indeed was what, according to Paulus, ought to happen. His occasional reservations about pressuring Jews to convert are given the lie by his attack on Gabriel Riesser, who had expressed his contempt for those who joined the Christian church without being convinced of its religious message. Paulus argued that it is sufficient for the Jewish convert to recognize that in passing from Judaism to Christianity he has opted for the better and the truer. Occasionally, Paulus was ready to condone the transition to Christianity without the slightest identification of the convert with his new religion. Although the converted Jew was perhaps no better, and might be worse, than the loyal ones who remained within Jewry, the former had renounced the national separation which those latter continued to maintain. For this reason only, and not because "he abjures certain dogmas and embraces others," the convert could be accepted. He will then at least make his children equal to the other citizens of the country through a similar kind of education." Political and cultural considerations are a sufficient justification for conversion.[32]

Paulus transforms Christianity into a pallid rationalist theory. What is startling and instructive about him and his teaching is that such a tenuous attachment to Christianity should have sufficed to bring in its train such a fanatical resentment of its rival, Judaism. The liberal interpretation of Christianity was not geared to toleration of Judaism and could even convert it into a source of greater fanaticism.

13 | The Radicals: Feuerbach, Bauer, Marx

THE ANTI-JEWISH LIBERALS described in the preceding chapter all evinced the semblance of a positive attitude toward Christianity. Although they may not have been orthodox by the canons of any Christian church or sect, they nevertheless considered themselves Christians by their own concept of what Christianity essentially was and what it represented. Indeed, as Christianity became more diluted, it often came to represent a more extreme contradiction to Judaism. Of course, adherence to Christianity did not necessarily induce an anti-Jewish position; many who were wholeheartedly devoted to Christianity supported the struggle of the Jews for emancipation and equality. Nevertheless, Christians who evinced opposition to Jews for whatever reason were inclined, on the ideological level, to connect that opposition with their link with Christianity.

On the other hand, we have learned from the case of Voltaire that anti-Jewish feelings and notions can coexist with a frontal attack upon Christianity. In such cases, the rational justification for the anti-Jewish ideology could not be derived from Christianity and had to be sought elsewhere.

The frontal attack on Christianity was also manifested in Germany, albeit a few generations after Voltaire, and was based on philosophical premises that differed from his. In the 1830s, a group of young Hegelian intellectuals appeared: David Friedrich Strauss, Ludwig Feuerbach, and Bruno Bauer. They entered the public arena as extremist critics of Christianity and as protagonists of the political and social doctrines that flowed from this criticism. The combination of a radical criticism of Christianity

159

with the development of a whole social doctrine found its outstanding expression in the teachings of Karl Marx.

It is not surprising that Judaism was caught up in this criticism of religion and that, at times, conclusions should be drawn as to the political and social status of the Jews, a question still unresolved. Some of the young Hegelians, like Strauss and Feuerbach, were apparently quite devoid of any hostility toward Jews; Friedrich Wilhelm Carové and Karl Grün were among the unequivocal supporters of emancipation. Marx and Arnold Ruge, on the other hand, included a lack of sympathy toward Jews in their criticism of Judaism and this found expression in attacks upon them when the occasion arose.[1] Bruno Bauer's hatred of Judaism was deeply rooted intellectually and emotionally; it pursued him throughout his philosophical peregrinations after he had abandoned the Young Hegelian position.[2]

The radical thinkers can be divided into two categories: the Young Hegelians and the socialists. The two groups had in common an almost unlimited faith in the efficacy of theory, the possibility of understanding historical and social reality, and the laws that governed them, to such an extent that the future could be predicted. This orientation toward the future is typical of Young Hegelians and Marxists, all of whom try to guess what is in store for mankind even if they are not prepared to engage in action for the practical realization of their conclusions.

The Jewish question, as the problem of emancipation had been dubbed, asked: What should happen to this seminaturalized group, conspicuous by its occupational narrowness and its religious nonconformity? This question could hardly be ignored by anybody who examined existing social conditions and tried to look into the future.[3] It had arisen from the dissolution of the ghetto, a sequel to the breakup of the old order in general. One would have expected all those who had evolved the idea of a thoroughly changed and liberated society to include the integration of the Jews in their vision of the future. And indeed some did, but not all by far. The pressing burden of the past and the singularity of the Jews made themselves felt even in the reaction of radical thinkers who boasted of having left behind all the residues of bygone times.

The radical thinkers' general inclination to fuse their perception of the past with their forecast of the future shaped their attitude toward Jews and Judaism. This is exemplified by the early work of the historian Heinrich Leo (later to become a staunch conservative), who set out to reconstruct critically the history of ancient Judaism and derive from its analysis a valid description of the permanent features of the Jewish national character.[4] A man of great erudition and original mind but, at the same time—in 1828—still under the influence of the living master, Hegel, Leo defined the essence of Judaism in terms strongly reminiscent of the Hegelian vocabulary: "The Jewish nation stands out conspicuously among all other nations of this world in that it possesses a truly corroding and decomposing [*zerfressenden und auflösenden*] mind. In the same way as there exist some fountains that would transmute every object thrown into them into stone, thus the Jews, from the very beginning until this very day, have transmuted everything that fell into the orbit of their spiritual activity into an abstract generality [*ein abstract Allgemeines*]."[5] The historian then goes on to explain that this propensity for abstraction accounts for the Jewish success in commerce. For it is the capacity for abstraction that enables the businessman to conceive of every object in terms of what it represents and thus assess its value.

Leo concedes that, at the time of the patriarchs, conditions were not yet ripe for these characteristics to reveal themselves: "That cutting egoism that later so markedly singles out the Jew in history emerges in the oldest stories; but only in isolated instances: Jacob's fraud and Joseph's vainglorious dreams." The term "egoism," which was later to become a central concept in the theories of Ludwig Feuerbach and Karl Marx concerning Judaism, creeps in here almost inadvertently. At any rate, if the historian had some hesitation in ascribing such characteristics to the earliest periods of Jewish history, they did not prevent him from generalizations that took Jewish history of all ages in stride: "The Jew in our time especially distinguishes himself in that he always considers and compares all objects from the standpoint of their common money value. He is also wont to make the center of his life this value which is simultaneously both so general and so abstract. In the same way, already in ancient times, he was seeking out, even in all spiritual circumstances and relations, only an abstract generality. It is this peculiarity which is responsible for the fact that Jews were the first and most tenacious in maintaining the unity of the divine Being."[6]

The tendency to combine the basic tenets of Judaism with the economic role fulfilled by the Jewish community is here patently obvious. Thereby, as we shall see later, Leo anticipated Karl Marx. In other respects Leo adopted the anti-Jewish stereotype current in the liberal school. Christianity in its original shape is seen as the very opposite of Judaism, while in its later deterioration it appears as its imitation. The Catholic hierarchy is nothing but a reproduction of the Mosaic legislation as it developed under the guidance of priests and prophets. Yet, while the Catholic hierarchy consists of the officers of a church, the Jewish hierarchy embraced the whole nation. The details of the constitution, the festivals and religious ceremonies, especially circumcision and the dietary laws, were intended to preserve the nation in its separation. As documented by the whole of

161

Jewish history—for the tragic course of which Leo the historian, though ambivalent, does not lack some sympathy—the constitution achieved its objective. The Jew survived in spite of the most adverse circumstances, at a price, "reminded by his religious constitution daily and hourly that he does not belong to those other nations but to the nation of God"; he retained his national pride and avoided blending culturally or socially with other nations. In return for this aloofness he incurred the contempt of his environment, and Jews "became the hated nation that they were in general in antiquity."[7]

Leo regarded the basic constitution of the Jewish community as unchanged since the days of antiquity. On one occasion he compared the circumstances of the Jews of his day with those of the first exiles in Babylonia: "Influence, wealth, culture [*Bildung*], comfortable life—the Judeans could have all that in their exile, if they had force and skill. *They stood then in approximately the same relation as they do now with us*" (italics in the original). This optimistic assessment of the Jews' position meant, however, only that the liberal age offered the Jews the opportunity to exploit circumstances to their advantage. It did not imply that Jewish self-separation and the concomitant hostile reaction to it by the surrounding Gentiles were approaching their end. The way Leo described the Jewish national characteristics clearly reveals his belief that these were permanent qualities not expected to be influenced through external circumstances.[8]

Leo was an exception among the Hegelians in having written on Jewish history while addressing himself directly to the problems of Jewish quality and continuity. The other Hegelians commented on Jews and Judaism only in connection with Christianity, the role of which concerned them. Ludwig Feuerbach's *The Essence of Christianity* contains a chapter on Judaism, and occasional observations on Jews appear throughout his philosophical writings.[9] As is well known, Feuerbach began as a loyal disciple of Hegel only to turn, in time, into perhaps the most severe critic of the master and his system. The pupil accused the master of having identified religion with philosophy, falsifying the essence of both. The critic wished to separate the two, granting philosophy the whole realm of cognition and reducing religion to a mere psychological agency. Religion is, according to this view, no more than the projection of human failures and frailties into the image of a God, who possesses all that human beings sorrowfully lack. Man then looks for consolation and help to the divine being he created in his own image. Religion proper—contrary to theology and, for that matter, the philosophy of religion, which are of secondary nature, products of reflection—derives from deeply seated emotional needs of man and fulfills, as such, a basic function in human life.[10]

The Radicals: Feuerbach, Bauer, Marx

In spite of this anthropological concept—thus designated by Feuerbach himself—the phenomenon of religion was not conceived to have been continuously uniform during the whole of human history. Following Hegel in this respect, Feuerbach accepted a development in three stages: polytheism, Judaism, and Christianity. The main purpose of the book being the exposition of the essential features of Christianity, the characteristics of the two other religions served the author as a mere foil to his central objective. His interpretation was as fraught with subjectivism as that of the philosophers of religion whose method Feuerbach described as lacking factual foundation in history and anthropology. It is, therefore, almost unnecessary for us to follow Feuerbach's explanations in detail. Suffice it to say that, of the three religions, Judaism gets the least favorable marks. It is not only inferior to the other two, but insufficient and unsavory in itself.

Judaism is, according to Feuerbach, inferior even to polytheism. The polytheist approaches nature as it reveals itself to the senses and conceives of it as an object of aesthetic admiration as well as of scientific observation and inquiry. The Jew, on the other hand, in his conception of nature transcends its immediate appearance and projects behind it its creator. As the initiator of the creation, the creator is the master of the universe; he is capable of manipulating it at will, changing the course of nature through what appears to the onlooker as miraculous events. "The sea is divided . . . the dust turns into life, the staff into a serpent, the river into blood, the rock into water . . . And all these unnatural events occur for the benefit of Israel purely at the command of the Jewish God, who does not concern himself with anything but Israel and who is nothing but the personified selfishness of the Israelite people to the exclusion of all other peoples, the absolute intolerance—the secret of monotheism." While Feuerbach derived the basic essence of religion from the fundamental predicament of man, he found the special features of each religion reflected in the state of mind of the people that evolved it. The special qualities of the Jewish religion, he believed, lay in two peculiarities of the Jewish mind: utilism (*Utilismus*) and egoism. "Utilism, profit [*Nutzen*] is the supreme principle of Judaism," he writes, and elsewhere: "Their [the Jews'] principle, their God, is the most practical principle in the world—egoism, and that egoism takes the form of religion."[11]

Feuerbach thought he had deduced these principles from Jewish religious doctrines—the dogma of creation and the concomitant belief in the specific providence bestowed by God upon his chosen people—and had then discovered a correspondence between these principles and the collective qualities of the Jewish religious community. But it is likely that the characteristics allegedly distilled through the analysis of the ancient

163

literature of the Jews were present in the mind of the analyst in advance. They may have been derived from the current prejudices about Jews, in general, and influenced in their formulation by Heinrich Leo's history. The congruency between the principles expressed in the religious tenets of the Bible and the alleged unflattering qualities of the Jews of his time turns out to be an ideological underpinning of current prejudices. Feuerbach failed to heed his own repeated warning to his colleagues to be on their guard against their propensity for speculative thinking.

Feuerbach's fame rests on his devastating critique of speculative philosophy. This had a lasting catalytic effect. He achieved this in spite of the loose thinking evident in his vocabulary and the marshaling of his argument—shortcomings that are patently obvious in his thoughts on Judaism. The inferiority of Judaism, as against polytheism and Christianity, is simply taken for granted. This is obvious in one of his censures of Judaism that was never used by anyone else. Speaking about the artistic and scientific creativity of the Greek, he says, "The Greek occupied himself with humanities, the liberal arts, philosophy; the Israelite did not rise above the exploitation of the study of theology in order to earn his bread [*Brotstudium der Theologie*]."[12] To say about Judaism that it did not know study for study's sake could occur only to someone entirely ignorant of Jewish life and history. Feuerbach seems to have assumed that for anything positive in the life of Greeks and Christians there must be something comparably negative in Judaism.

There is no information available on Ludwig Feuerbach's personal attitude toward Jews or his position on the Jewish question. In his youth he studied Hebrew with Rabbi Wasserman in Ansbach and became friendly with the rabbi's son, later a leading figure in the Reform movement and rabbi of Stuttgart. Feuerbach may have retained his friendly attitude toward Jews and, as a convinced democrat, must have voted for Jewish emancipation in the Frankfurt parliament of 1849, of which he was a member.[13] But, such a positive attitude toward individual Jews, as well as toward the possible absorption of the Jewish community into the non-Jewish state and society, could go along comfortably with the most condemnatory judgments about Judaism in general. Often the two were even complementary. Condemning Judaism as a force operating in the past paved the way for assuming a liberal stance concerning the future. Jews would be acceptable on condition that they, too, repudiate all that had been supposedly implied in their religious tradition. Thus, liberal and even radical thinkers helped sustain the sinister image of historical Judaism, involuntarily assisting those who shaped this image into a weapon to be used in the political fight against Jews.

Bruno Bauer, too, began his career as loyal disciple of Hegel.[14] Establishing himself as a privatdozent for Protestant theology at Berlin University, he revealed in his first publications an unmistakable tendency to harmonize orthodoxy with Hegelian thought. In an article on "The Principles of the Mosaic Legal and Religious Constitution," published in 1837 in the *Zeitschrift für spekulative Theologie*, edited by himself, he spelled out the rules by which an inquiry into the nature of the Old Testament's world had to be guided. Taking issue with the Deistic interpretation that attributed the Mosaic laws and institutions to the inventiveness of cunning priests, he committed himself to a method described as genetic and speculative, meaning that the laws and institutions were to be interpreted as the expression of the people's spirit and its religious consciousness, the last term being obviously a substitute for revelation. Thus, Biblical institutions, as well as Biblical history, having been conceived of in a certain sense, at least, as divine, retained much of the dignity and incontestability conferred upon them in Christian tradition.[15]

This tendency is clearly evident in Bauer's *Die Religion das Alten Testaments* (1838), a book of two volumes in which Bauer implemented the principles laid down in his programmatic article. Obviously, his mind was bent on shielding the Jewish Bible from moral criticism, and he achieved this purpose through a sophisticated philosophical reinterpretation. The conquest of Canaan by Joshua, a divine assignment according to the Bible, could not, because of the atrocious circumstances involved—the extermination of the local inhabitants—possibly be conceived of as such by later generations: the Gnostics of the old Church, the English Deists, or modern theologians. It would have contradicted the very idea of the divine will. Subjectively, Bauer explains to us, the Israelites, as God's people, felt entitled to disinherit the Canaanites by whatever means at their disposal in order to possess the country needed for their purpose. What they did was no more than the retribution decreed by the Law for the Canaanites' pagan existence. On the objective, historical-philosophical level, Bauer finds a justification of a higher order for the execution of the decree. The universal spirit can be realized only through the replacement of one nation's state by that of another, presuming that the former represents a lower rank of values than the latter. The Israelites manifested at that time the "highest stature of the universal spirit." For, while the other nations acted only out of their own consciousness, unaware of the fact that they were a stage in the evolution of the universal spirit, in the "self-consciousness of the Hebrews was the idea of their nationality as the limited consciousness of the people and the idea of the universal objective of History bound together in one unit."[16]

Human sacrifice, as documented by the story of Jephthah's daughter, was a major object of criticism of the Old Testament by its detractors.

Though it was defined by Bauer as an aberration of the religious consciousness, it is nonetheless found to have had a positive aspect. It depends on who is practicing this horrible ritual. In the service of Baal and Ashtoret, where it is linked with debauchery, both the sensual pleasure and the sacrifice of one's beloved are surrenders to the enticement of nature. Human sacrifice for the sake of the Biblical God entails "an ethical contrast between the strict master and the finite subject" and as such it still "retains a ring of the gravity of the Law."[17]

In these deliberations Bauer clearly reveals his commitment to the Hegelian way of thinking, as well as a conservative protective attitude toward the Jewish Bible. It is most improbable that at the same time he could have harbored a grudge or resentment against Jews and Judaism, as such. He regarded Judaism as the precursor of Christianity; imperfect, of course, but still valid and justified in its time.

But in the ensuing years Bruno Bauer experienced a mental revolution that uprooted his attachment to the system of Hegel, severed his ties to Christianity, and prepared him for his severe criticism of historical as well as contemporary Judaism.[18] The external circumstances of this metamorphosis are linked with Bauer's transfer from the University of Berlin to that of Bonn. He was imposed upon the Bonn faculty by the Berlin authorities, and he found himself boycotted and thwarted by his colleagues. In the course of a two-year period (1839-1841), he shed his entire Weltanschauung, replacing the Hegelian-tinged orthodoxy with a summary rejection of Christianity and assuming a most critical stance against the established order, based as it was on the cooperation between state and Church.

In the course of his transformation, Bauer poured out a stream of learned treatises attempting to disprove the authenticity of the evangelical tradition; meanwhile, in his publications on topical subjects, he attacked the major institutions of society. His formerly protective attitude toward the Old Testament now turned into an extreme condemnation reminiscent of that of the English Deists, whom he had combatted in his earlier period.

There is one key word that governs Bauer's expositions in both the scholarly and the topical field—it is criticism. Bauer believed that in rejecting the methods of speculation by which the Hegelian school erected its systems, he gained a firm ground for establishing historical facts as well as for diagnosing the present state of society and prescribing the course of action for the future.

The problem of Jewish emancipation was a much debated subject at that time, extensively discussed by the correspondents of the *Rheinische Zeitung*, the organ of the radicals and socialists like Karl Marx.[19] In a letter to his friend Arnold Ruge, the editor of *Deutsche Jahrbücher*, Bauer wrote

166

that in the summer of 1842 he had read all that had been written on the subject since the time of Dohm and Mirabeau. Dismissing all that, including what had been published in the paper of the socialists, he formed his own opinion and was confident to have found "the only solution of the problem on which so much has been written, but not one true word." The confidence in his capacity to transcend those who preceded him was due to his trust in the efficacy of the newly evolved method of criticism. "All the Jew-helpmate [*Judenfreunde*] and the Jews did until now was as if no criticism existed." He was resolved to show the world what the core of the problem was, expecting and even anticipating the scandal his unexpected interference with the ongoing debate would raise.[20]

The result of his inquiry into the problem was his *Judenfrage*, published first in the *Deutsche Jahrbücher* in 1842 and then in 1843 as a separate pamphlet. The ultimate conclusion of Bauer's reasoning was, indeed, novel, unprecedented by anyone else who had addressed the problem. Bauer has often been classed by historians with the opponents of emancipation, and his Jewish contemporaries had reacted to him as such. This is, however, a misrepresentation of his position. Bauer did not deny the possibility or desirability of Jews being granted social and political equality with other citizens, but did declare that the conditions under which this was feasible were altogether different from what had been suggested by the proponents of the idea. The latter held that religious differences should not be allowed to influence anyone's rights in the state or position in society: every right given to Christians must also be granted to Jews. Now, the very fact that Jews aspired to equal standing with Christians meant that both religions would also retain in the future their hold on their followers—a prospect that stood in glowing contradiction to what Bauer prescribed for the future development of society, namely, the abolition of all dogmatic religions. It was his almost limitless self-confidence, bordering on megalomania, that deluded Bauer to believe that just as he, through his criticism, had uprooted the historical foundations of Christian orthodoxy, society would follow suit. What was left of the religious tradition would be discarded, and the state would establish itself as an association of free men.[21]

Bauer felt his criticism to be in accordance with the general trend of the time: "It is impossible that the deeds of the newest criticism and the universal clamor for emancipation and liberation from tutelage should remain even for the most proximate future without an effect." It was not the Jews alone who had to be emancipated, but society at large: "The issue of emancipation is a general one, the unqualified issue of our time." If this should be accomplished, Jewish emancipation would be taken in its stride. But then, Jews would cease to be Jews as much as Christians would cease to be Christians. "The emancipation of the Jew in a thorough, successful, and secure fashion is only possible if they will be emancipated not as Jews, that is, as beings who must remain forever alien to Christians, but if they will make themselves human beings who will not be separated from their fellow creatures through some barriers falsely deemed to be essential."[22] Bauer repeated this prognosis at the end of his article on "The Ability of the Jews and Christians of Today to Become Free," with which he thought to conclude the debate that arose in the wake of his *Judenfrage*. "The historical movement that would acknowledge the dissolution of Christianity and of religion in general as an established fact [*vollendete Tatsache*] and secure the victory over religion for mankind, cannot delay for any length of time, because the awareness of freedom stands in total contradiction to the prevailing circumstances." No doubt Bauer regarded himself as a pioneer of a movement that would usher in an era of the absolute liberation of man from the burden of his past.[23]

Though the ultimate objective of Bauer's polemical thrust was to wipe out the differences between Jews and non-Jews in the wake of the disappearance of religion, the major part of his reasoning concerned the reverse side of the proposition, namely, that as long as the two religions remain effective in any sense of the word, emancipation of the Jews was inconceivable. To substantiate this contention, Bauer assembled all the wonted arguments of the opponents of Jewish emancipation, sharpening them with his caustic style and lending them, through the application of an abstract phraseology, a quasi-philosophical relevance. A congenial critic like Karl Grün nevertheless grasped correctly Bauer's ultimate intention. The average reader of the *Judenfrage*, however, must have received the impression of a severe attack on the cause of the Jews, rather than the opening up of a new vista for their future.[24]

Bauer accepted the definition of Biblical and Talmudic Judaism as a religion of absolute exclusiveness, regardless of some attempts through the ages by prophets and reformers to lend it a universalistic tinge—attempts that never stood the test of practical implementation. It was this Jewish exclusiveness, evolved since early antiquity, that brought upon the community all the suffering they chose to attribute to their adversaries. It was the alleged barrenness of Jewish existence that vexed Bauer most of all. The rejection of Christianity at its inception meant a negation of historical progress, and ever since Jews and Judaism had kept out of the mainstream of historical development: "No one Jew can be named. Spinoza was not a Jew anymore when he created his system." Jews as Jews had failed to contribute to the evolution of the modern world founded on science, philosophy, and art. Similarly, when a decisive turn in history was being prepared by the criticism of Bruno Bauer and his like,

Jews once again were sitting back: "How did they behave toward the criticism that the Christians directed toward religion in general in order to liberate mankind from the most dangerous self-deception, from the arch-error." What did they do in the way of assisting those who were engaged in this fight for a better world? The answer is, nothing. They were apathetic and insensible; they acted as if the whole matter did not concern them. Instead of pulling down the edifices of the old order so as to pave the way for human freedom, they tried to secure for themselves a niche in the structure of that established system. The emancipation they longed for was not synonymous with liberation, but with a privilege—the permission to continue to live within the exclusive mentality of Judaism. Nor was it true that the struggle for Jewish emancipation had a stimulating effect on the general drive for freedom. The Jewish aspiration was nothing but an epiphenomenon of the general trend, and not the other way around.[25]

With regard to the future, Bauer was equally impatient toward Judaism and Christianity. If he agreed with the radical and liberal demand that Jews should give up circumcision, he also declared baptism, as well as the other Christian sacraments, to be obsolete rituals. It was when he evaluated the two religions and their adherents in the past that he evinced discrimination. From the historical point of view, he showed appreciation of the faith that he had abandoned. The basic historical merit of Christianity—in its Protestant formulation—was that criticism, in the manner of Bruno Bauer, stemmed from it and not from Judaism. This was not simply fortuitous: basically, Judaism was concerned with external observances. Therefore, it followed automatically that the criticism that developed within Judaism only touched the externals of religion: rituals, institutions, and the like. By its intrinsic power, Protestantism overcame the religion of deeds and based it on faith, which, in the pure spiritual field, is illusion. When this illusion was dispelled, there emerged the total criticism of religion that uprooted it completely.[26]

Observations of this kind, penetrating as they may be, are, of course, of a subjective nature and carry with them overtones of discrimination against Judaism. They represent a striking example of the transfusion of the partisan evaluation of Judaism into a post-Christian, even anti-Christian, context. In the history of anti-Semitism, this is the basic significance of Bauer's ideas. At the same time, Bauer carries the denial of Judaism to unheard-of extremes. He expects Jews to eradicate Judaism altogether without embracing Christianity. Reforming or reinterpreting Judaism would not do. The Reform Jew, "while renouncing the Law, still wishes to acknowledge Moses as the herald of truth, the founder of a new—even the highest—ethical principle," and thus he still remains a Jew. Nor is the reshaping of the messianic idea by the modernists of any avail:

169

"For the state, freedom, and humanity, it is of no consequence whether an actual messiah would in fact establish the Jewish world kingdom or whether it is only the idea of such a kingdom that alienates Jews from the world, history, or the human interest." Since baptism is excluded as a possible way of escape there is no solution for the Jew except to join the revolution through criticism as it shaped itself in the imagination of Bruno Bauer.[27]

The reasoning of Bauer is, at this stage of his development, characterized by highly abstract and airy concepts. His description of the Jew relies on the current stereotype and owes very little to actual observation. Bauer may have encountered the Jew who tried to retain his Judaism and keep the Law while escaping its consequences—the broker who attended the bourse on the Sabbath but refrained from doing business personally, or the employer who attended the Synagogue on such a day and left his business in the care of his Gentile employees. This type of Jew was especially common in the generation of transition from the ghetto. Bauer poured his derision on such behavior. It scandalized him, as it did some of his enlightened Jewish contemporaries.[28] Bauer also had only contempt for his Jewish opponents who, intrigued by the many paradoxical statements of the *Judenfrage*, responded defensively to the disparagement of Judaism in the past and present rather than turn their attention to the dimly conceived image of the future.[29] Still, the whole polemic of Bauer moves on a highly abstract level and lacks the air of acrimony that results from intense personal involvement. This involvement we shall find in the continuation of the polemic by Karl Marx and by Bruno Bauer himself, once he sheds his radical stance and integrates his anti-Jewish arguments into a newly won conservative Weltanshauung.

Bauer's criticism elicited a whole series of rejoinders, mostly by Jewish apologists wishing to refute his anti-Jewish charges and prejudices.[30] The most impressive and, in the long run, most influential reaction to Bauer's thesis, however, came from his own camp, from the pen of his former student and friend Karl Marx.[31] The controversy between the two turned on Bauer's diagnosis of the driving force in the development of state and society. Rather than soften Bauer's evaluations of Judaism and the Jewish character, Marx appears to sharpen them. Still, the personal attitude of Marx toward Jews and Judaism poses a problem complicated by two disparate facts—Marx's Jewish origin and his application of anti-Jewish terminology in evolving one of his basic tenets, the theory of historical materialism.

Marx was a descendant of old rabbinical families. His father's ancestors included some of the most famous sixteenth-century Talmudists in Italy and Poland.[32] Aware of this fact, some of his biographers have

The Radicals: Feuerbach, Bauer, Marx

thought to find in Marx's thinking patterns characteristic of Talmudic argumentation.[33] But Karl's father, Heinrich Marx, though the son of a rabbi of Trier, converted to Christianity around the date of Karl's birth, in 1818; Karl, together with his six brothers and sisters, was baptized by him six years later, in 1824. The children's mother, the daughter of the rabbi of Nijmegen in Holland, followed them a year later, after the death of her mother. Whatever Jewish cultural traits Heinrich Marx might have acquired in his youth, he no doubt made an effort to shed before his conversion. In a memorandum to the governor of the Rhien province, by then annexed to Prussia, he appealed in 1815, on behalf of the Jewish community, for the annulment of the restrictions on Jewish rights—a relic of the Napoleonic regime that heavily impaired the emancipation of the Ashkenazi Jews of France and the occupied territories. Heinrich Marx, in his memorandum, denied the existence of any Jewish peculiarity that would warrant a special status, his arguments reminiscent of the ideology of the radical assimilationists. The Prussian authorities, however, did not agree; they were just about to reexamine the details of their own 1812 edict of emancipation, with the outspoken intent of limiting its scope. Jews would not be admitted to any position of official status, a restriction pertinent to Heinrich Marx since it would have prevented him from exercising his profession as a lawyer.[34]

Faced with the risk of losing his livelihood, Heinrich Marx preferred to be baptized—a step that, owing to his rationalistic outlook, could on the intellectual level easily be justified, but which socially must have represented a considerable burden. It meant joining a new community while severing his ties with kith and kin who lived nearby. One of Heinrich's brothers was the local rabbi; the post was a long-standing privilege of the Marx family. In taking the step of an insincere conversion, Heinrich Marx had to overcome some hesitancies and inhibitions. This is indicated by the fact that he let his family follow him only in the course of time. Once embarked upon, this course had to be followed through to its logical conclusion—at the price of repressing some scruples and avoiding some embarrassing situations.[35] There were sure signs, in the correspondence of Heinrich Marx with his son Karl, as well as in the behavior of the latter during his whole life, that the family adopted an ostrich policy, shutting their eyes to the fact of their Jewish origin, never mentioning it, and overreacting whenever reminded of the unpleasant fact.[36]

Culturally, no doubt, the father and, even more, the sons had been absorbed by their German environment. Christianity had been brought to bear upon the mind of Karl through his education in the humanistic but still religiously oriented *Gymnasium*. If this did not turn him into an ardent Christian, it integrated him intellectually into the world of Christian ideas.

Among the elements he absorbed in this way was the negative image of Jews and Judaism—and this ingredient of his intellectual make-up, together with the awareness of his link to the despised race, goes a long way toward explaining his attitude to Jews and their problems. In Marx's rejection of Judaism we encounter a special type of anti-Semitism, burdened by personal involvement and a kind of self-hatred.[37]

Since the problem of Jews and Judaism played such a conspicuous role in the thinking of Marx's predecessors, Hegel, Feuerbach, and Bruno Bauer, it was inevitable that he, too, would be compelled to formulate a position on it. Bauer's contention, especially, though presented on a highly abstract level, involved the practical problem of Jewish emancipation. The problem was on the agenda of the legislative bodies, the Landtag in Prussia, for instance; it was also discussed by the Rheinische Zeitung, of which Marx had been editor since 1842.[38] In a letter to Arnold Ruge in 1843, Marx said he had been approached by the head of the Jewish community in Cologne to support the Jews' bid for full emancipation. Though Marx could not help expressing his utter contempt for the object of this appeal, he found it politically expedient and possibly also judicious to concede to it: "Repulsive as the Jewish faith may be to me, nonetheless Bauer's view seems to be too abstract." By defining Bauer's view as too abstract, he meant to say that the issue had to be decided on the basis of existing circumstances. Bauer's accusation that the Jews had failed to assist the rest of humanity in transcending the present stage of development was no justification for the semisecularized, semiliberal state to withhold equal rights from Jews. Even if revolutionary philosophers thought the existing state to be transient, they should not lose the opportunity to assail it for its inconsistency. The emancipation of the Jews was an opportunity for such an assault, and Bauer had missed it by sticking to his poorly conceived theoretical considerations.

For, on the abstract philosophical level, Marx thought Bauer's ideas were not far-reaching enough.[39] Bauer expected society to be purged of the curse of religion, Christian and Jewish alike, and thus a state of free citizens would be established—free in the spiritual as well as the political sense of the word. The state would continue to function. Its right to exist was never doubted by Bauer, but emphatically rejected by Marx. Marx denied man's ability to free himself from religion simply through the removal of state protection from the institutions of religion. He held that religion was rooted in the economic activity of bourgeois society, each man being driven by his own egotistical motives, yet failing to derive from his activity an appropriate satisfaction. These individuals were associated only through the monetary exchange of their products and services, a situation Marx categorized as a condition of alienation—that is, the removal of the destined conditions of man's existence according to his true nature. Because of its unnaturalness, bourgeois society was not adapted to operate without the help of two tools: the state and religion. The state ensured the functioning of society through the use of its power of coercion, while religion compensated man with its illusions for what he was deprived of by his alienation. Religion and state were destined to wither away when society itself returned to a condition that accorded with the true nature of man, following the abolition of the alienation in all its manifestations, together with its practical and spiritual corollaries. Marx imagined that with this new metamorphosis in the life of humanity the individuals would function spontaneously as complementary parts of a harmonious apparatus. The divisions between different religions and classes would then disappear; the distinctions between Jews and Gentiles would fade away. The solution of the Jewish question was thus relegated to this future utopia. But meanwhile, this utopia served as a starting point for a lethal criticism of the irredeemable reality of bourgeois society; one of the main lines of the critique was the identification of that society with the character of Judaism.

It is purely accidental that Marx should have initially presented his historical diagnosis, which became the kernel of his socialist doctrine, as a sequel to a polemic on the Jewish question. This mingling of the two issues contributed nothing to the clarification of his stand on either. Certainly anyone interested in the development of Marx's socialist doctrine can dispense with his linkage of it with the Jewish question. Indeed, many of his exponents did just that, viewing his statements on this issue an empty and dispensable shell.[40] However, from the biographical standpoint, and certainly in relation to our own subject—the transmission of the negative image of Jews and Judaism from generation to generation—the combination of the two subjects is not irrelevant. Even if it was an accident that the views of Marx on the two issues were intertwined, how he related the two tells us something. What happened to Marx is what happened to Toussenel, who wrote his book two years later without being influenced by Marx. When Marx came to indict the capitalist society, he applied the widespread negative image of Judaism, forcing it on the society of which the Jews were a part:[41]

> What is the worldly basis of Judaism? *Practical* need, *self-interest*.
> What is the worldly cult of the Jew? *Haggling*.
> What is his worldly god? *Money*. Very well! Emancipation from haggling and money, that is from the practical and tangible Judaism, might well be the self emancipation of our age.[42]

These sentences illustrate the two aspects, the anti-capitalistic and the anti-Jewish, of Marx's thesis on the Jewish question. The bourgeois society is flawed because of its dependence upon commerce—the exchange of the goods and labor of one person for those of his neighbor. Here trade is not called by its general name, but by the pejorative term *Schacher*, which, as we observed previously, is customarily applied to the contemptible dealings of Jews. Another fault of bourgeois society is that individuals work only out of self-interest, with the egoistic principle dominating all. But this principle is not presented here as a general human failing, but as an essentially Jewish characteristic. If Marx, in identifying commerce with *Schacher*, was following the popular anti-Jewish linguistic tradition, his making the quality of egoism dependent on Judaism follows in the footsteps of Ludwig Feuerbach, his predecessor in the development of the philosophical criticism. The terms *Schacher* and *egoism*, which are bound up with Judaism, were used ostensibly to illustrate the nature of bourgeois society, but they are at the same time a reflection of the essence of Judaism. This essence is expressed in the economic and social function fulfilled by members of the Jewish religion, but that religion itself is only an ideological reflection of this socioeconomic actuality. This thesis, hinted at in the repetitious use of the word "worldly" in the three questions stated above, was explained in the sentence with which Marx preceded the question: "We must not seek for the secret of the Jew in his religion, but must seek for the secret of religion in the actual Jew." The idea implied in this formulation was applied by Marx to all religions, in fact, to the whole spiritual apparatus of man immersed in the unredeemed conditions of bourgeois society. However, the debasement of religion and its degradation to the level of man's self-deception are exemplified by the application to the Jewish religion.[43] A clear anti-Semitic tenor runs through the lines of Marx's brilliant essay.[44] This aroused less attention from Jews than the work of Bruno Bauer that preceded it. However, in the course of time, Marx's essay proved more influential. From it socialist thinkers like Lenin learned to regard Judaism as the flesh and blood of capitalism, to find justification for encouraging its disappearance and even actively hastening its demise.

14 The Scandal of the Jewish Artist: Richard Wagner

THOUGH FED BY historical sources of the remote past, the anti-Jewish movement of the late eighteenth and early nineteenth centuries received its main impetus from what was occurring in the present: the striving of the Jewish community to enter state and society on an equal basis with other groups and denominations. The resistance to and resentment of this striving defined the social and political goals of the anti-Jewish attacks and lent them their ideological coloring.

In the 1830s a new source of animosity to Jews arose. About this time the first group of Jewish intellectuals, writers, and artists made their appearance in public life, demanding to be recognized. Previously, there had been exceptional individuals, like Moses Mendelssohn and Saul Ascher, who by virtue of personal effort and outstanding talent had succeeded in participating in German intellectual life. Although their appearance at times had elicited inimical anti-Jewish reactions, being exceptional, they did not have more than marginal significance.[1] In the 1830s, however, a generation arose that had benefited from early childhood from the cultural rapprochement between Jew and Gentile. They had attended modern Jewish or German schools and universities or enjoyed private tutoring, as was the custom of well-to-do families in German society. To be sure, modern education of this sort was enjoyed only by a minority of Jews, but this minority was large enough to produce a substantial number of gifted intellectuals and artists whose appearance in German public life could not be overlooked. Among them were some whose impact was great enough to be remembered by posterity: Heinrich Heine and Ludwig Börne among

175

the writers, Felix Mendelssohn and Giocomo Meyerbeer among the composers. Others, by now forgotten, were important enough to contribute to the perception of significant Jewish participation in literature, journalism, and music, among them, the writers Moritz Gottlieb Saphir and Berthold Auerbach, and the composer Ferdinand Hiller.[2]

Although many of these men, approximately two-thirds, converted to Christianity, they seldom did so out of conviction. Most of them made their decision on the grounds of cold rational calculation, after a period of estrangement from their Jewish origins and a concomitant acculturation to the non-Jewish environment. But conversion failed to transform these new Christians spiritually or integrate them socially; they continued to be counted as Jews, at least to the extent that their work was labeled Jewish by those who looked upon the infusion of the Jewish element into German culture with suspicion and disfavor.

The antagonism to Jews as participants in cultural life elicited a different kind of argument than did the Jewish aspiration to political and social equality. The opponents of Jewish citizenship concentrated upon the alleged inadequacies of the Jewish character, the inability of the observant Jew to serve his country as a soldier, his economic unproductivity, his unreliability in social contact, his unreserved solidarity with his own group, and his moral indifference toward strangers. Given these alleged character traits, the continuation of Jewish social and political separateness could well be defended. The Jewish intellectuals and artists, on the other hand, working as individuals, seemed to have circumvented the obstacles that blocked the Jews' approach to society.

It is in the nature of modern society that cultural functions—the writing and publishing of books, the producing of plays and music—are not attached to institutions of closed character; the creations and performances are produced for an open market of the culturally interested, in contrast to the semifeudal period, when all these depended upon the aid and protection of kings and princes. It was the free marketing of cultural productions that opened culture, along with other areas where a more or less free competition was the rule, to Jewish participation. At the same time, free competition required free criticism, and free criticism served as the vehicle for the opponents of Jewish participation in cultural life to make their voices heard.

While cultural performances were exposed to free criticism, the critiques functioned to direct public taste, the final arbiter of the competition. This competition provided the Jews with the opportunity to show their mettle and to be judged objectively on the basis of individual achievement. On the whole, no doubt, the cultural and artistic activity turned out to be beneficial for the Jews. Some Jewish authors, composers, and actors sprang into prominence, holding the attention of the public and commanding the respect of the critics. Their Jewishness was overlooked or ignored by their admirers, and those who took exception to their performances based their judgment on objective criteria.

This rule, however, had significant exceptions. Some of those who found fault with the Jews' performances ascribed their shortcomings to the Jewish origins of their creators. This happened most conspicuously in connection with the appearance of the group of writers who chose to be designated by the name Das Junge Deutschland. Headed by Karl Gutzkow and Heinrich Laube, Young Germany included two of the outstanding Jewish writers of the time, Heinrich Heine and Ludwig Börne, both baptized, but still regarded as Jews by themselves and others.[3]

As indicated by their very name, the members of the group regarded themselves as an avant-garde heralding the rejuvenation of Germany. The hoped-for process of restoration pertained mainly to two aspects of life, the political and the intellectual. Politically, Young Germany advocated the institution of a radical democracy to supersede the authoritarian rule of kings and princes. Intellectually, they cherished the vision of a free life—which they imagined to have existed in ancient Greece—liberated from the burden of Christian dogma and taboo, the emancipation of the flesh.

Naturally, those radical ideas elicited loud and vehement protest from the traditional-minded. The counterattack assumed at times a personal note, as the Junge Deutschlanders were accused of wanting to undermine the material and moral strength of German society. Characteristically, the attack, especially when it was directed against one of the Jewish members of the group, almost inevitably drew Judaism and Jews in general into the orbit of criticism.

Dr. Eduard Meyer of Hamburg took issue with Ludwig Börne on the occasion of the latter's publication of his *Letters from Paris*.[4] From his more or less voluntary exile in Paris, Börne hurled his missiles against the bulwark of German society, castigating German political backwardness, which was in his opinion a reflection of the sluggish character of the German Philistines. The sarcastic sallies of Börne no doubt infuriated many Germans, and, in venting his indignation, Meyer, a teacher at a gymnasium in Hamburg, could well feel that he was speaking the mind of his compatriots.

Meyer's pamphlet, though entitled "Against L. Börne, the Letter Writer Oblivious of Truth, Right, and Honor," dealt in fact not with Börne alone. Heinrich Heine's *Reisebilder*, which had appeared two or three years earlier, also aroused Meyer's wrath, probably because of its pleasantries at the expense of Christian religious symbols. Börne had the audacity to defile "the most beloved venerable poet [Goethe], the pride and crown of our nation," removing him from his pedestal and replacing him with two Jews, Heine and Moritz Saphir. Saphir, baptized but of a strong Jewish background, is now forgotten, but was in his own time (1795-1858) a most successful wit. Still, to mention him in the same breath as Goethe could have been viewed as an aberration of taste. Meyer's objection, however, was not aesthetic or literary. Meyer took exception to Börne's political ideas, protested the tone in which they were presented, and the passion of his rejection was nourished by his conviction that Börne and his like had no right to meddle in the affairs of German society. Börne was calling himself a German: "But we beg to decline him this honor in all courtesy for not the place where one happened to be born makes one a German but primarily German sentiments [*Gesinnung*] and love of the fatherland." This sounds as if Meyer is denying Börne's right to be called a German because of his personal behavior. But in quoting Börne's unpatriotic arrogance, Meyer decries what otherwise

> would be better to have been suppressed. Börne is a Jew like Heine, like Saphir. Baptized or not, it is all the same; for it is inappropriate to use the name [Jew] in contradistinction to Christian. It designates not only the religion but a whole nationality . . . We do not hate the faith of the Jews as they would like us to believe, but rather [we hate] the many ugly peculiarities of these Asiatics which cannot be laid aside so easily through baptism: the often recurring shamelessness and arrogance among them, the indecency and frivolity, their noisy demeanor [*vorlautes Wesen*] and their often mean basic disposition.[5]

Börne was rejected not because of his demeanor, or at least not because of it alone. His behavior only afforded an opportunity for depicting the hateful traits shared by all who belong to his nationality. Meyer hastens to add that this judgment on Jews in general does not preclude the possibility of their being some "nobler individualities among them." He himself knew such Jews, and would be glad to know more. The exception, however, did not invalidate the judgment on the collective.[6]

In the case of Börne and Heine, Meyer finds additional aggravating circumstances for which to condemn them. Not only did they slander the German people to which they pretended to belong, but they showed utter contempt for their own brethren, the Jews. Estranged from both the Germans and the Jews, "they became unsavory interlopers [*Mitteldingern*] . . . they dissolve absolutely all the bonds of piety. They do not belong to any people, to any state, to any community, they lack a definite sphere of activity, they roam about in the world like adventurers, they snuff about everywhere in order to make themselves interesting through repeated changes of residence where they find as much as possible to grumble about."[7] This is a somewhat inimical but not entirely incorrect description

178

of the uprooted Jewish intellectual, for whom the dissolution of traditional Jewish society had a profound effect. Meyer, at any rate, was fully aware of the position of men like Börne and Heine, who were socially distant from both the community of their aspiration and that of their origin. Still, discounting their social predicament as well as their individual traits of character, Meyer attributed all that he found objectionable in their behavior to their Jewish background.

Meyer's criticism was aimed at Jewish intellectuals as such. Worse was to come when the activities of writers like Börne and Heine became linked in the popular mind with the "obnoxious" Young Germany. That the pronouncements of the new school, inveighing as it did against the whole system of prevailing values, would outrage the more conservative elements in German society was to be expected. Nor is it surprising that these elements would do whatever was in their power to discredit Young Germany. What is strange is that in spite of its Gentile leadership and membership, Young Germany came to be labeled as a Jewish contrivance. That this was the case is testified to by one of the most authoritative figures of the day, Wolfgang Menzel.[8]

Menzel was a forceful literary critic who had been deeply dedicated to national ideals since he had participated, in his youth, in the patriotic activities of the gymnasts and of the students in the Burschenschaften in the aftermath of the war of liberation (the gymnasts aimed at national education through bodily exercise, the Burschenschaften through companionship within the student unions). Nevertheless, Menzel combined his patriotism with an upright defense of progressive causes in state and society. He ridiculed the opponents of Jewish emancipation in a spirited rebuttal of Paulus's contention that the Jews were incapable of joining non-Jewish society. Menzel in 1835, speaking about the affinity of Young Germany with the spiritual aspirations of Heinrich Heine, startled his Jewish admirers by asking, "I should like to know what Jewry anticipates from such literary inadequacy in view of the rather delicate issue of their emancipation, since one cannot avoid being told that the so-called Young Germany is, properly speaking, a Young Palestine and because public opinion credits all that is loathsome . . . in the Frankfurt propaganda to Judaism." This last sentence refers to the agitation of some radical republicans in the vicinity of Frankfurt. In an attempt to justify his bluntness, Menzel reminded his readers of his unreserved intervention on behalf of Jewish emancipation, a cause that was being compromised by the Jews' association with objectionable ideologies.[9]

Menzel failed to adduce any justification for his identification of Young Germany with the Jews, but others did, some under the direct influence of Menzel. Two anonymous pamphlets appeared in 1836 taking issue with the hated movement. The "Votum uber das junge Deutschland" first focused on Karl Gutzkow, the radical critic of Christianity, accusing him of resuscitating the obsolete ideas of radical eighteenth-century rationalists, then drifted into another vein of thought to account for the anti-Christian tendencies of Young Germany. Is it not the "children of Israel" to whom these young cosmopolitans show "so much sympathy and congeniality [*Wahlverwandlschaft*]?" Gutzkow went out of his way to quote Jewish authors in his "Letters from Berlin," wrote a drama on Uriel Acosta, became the biographer of the Rothschilds, and assailed Wolfgang Menzel because of his anti-Jewish sallies. When speaking of Jesus, Gutzkow adopted a negative tone as if he were a Jewish apostate. The author of the pamphlet argues that Gutzkow's mentality reveals the borrowed traits of Jewish character. It is "the corroding and consuming [*ätzende und fressende*] intellect which is, according to Leo, a characteristic mark of Judaism."[10] Forced as this ascription of Jewish propensities to a non-Jewish author may be—or perhaps just because of that—it is telling evidence of the tendency to detect Jewish influences in what was deemed decadent and inconsistent with German mentality.

This tendency found a much more consistent and at the same time more poignant expression in the second pamphlet, "Die Jeune Allemagne in Deutschland," attributed to Samuel Gottlieb Liesching. As indicated in its title, the whole movement of Young Germany is presented here as the transference of French ideas and attitudes to Germany. This tract is permeated with overt animosity toward the French and unqualified glorification of the Germans. The former are superficial, frivolous, void of "religiosity by which all that is of higher value [*alles Bessere*] is generated"; the latter, the very contrary, are "a nation that through its deep religiosity would find a firm anchor for its external as well as internal bearing, for its history, its politics, for its national singularity." Thus, one must be prepared to judge the German nation according to its potentiality. As far as actual conditions are concerned, Liesching does observe in his own country as well signs of "cowardice inflated through the lowest kind of egoism, through money and pleasure . . . a market of empty heads and full-fed senses." But while such phenomena are considered inherent in the French national character, for the Germans they are ascribed to the unfortunate cultivation of foreign habits. Liesching speaks of "moral stagnation . . . French spirit and French manners" that are being infused into German public life through journalism, theater, and literature.[11]

The question naturally arises, Who are the agents infusing this "gallic poison"? It could not be the Germans; their sense of shame and conscience would militate against it. The French, on the other hand, are too unfamiliar with German language and literature to be able to use it as a tool. There exists, however, a third party of men who, for duty and humanity's sake, have been granted civil rights, and whose "perseverance steeled through bitter fortunes, their ingenuity refined through numberless struggles, their lurking dexterity and a talent of a thousand colors made everything possible except what is enjoined upon them by the painfully acquired emancipation—to denationalize themselves, no longer to be what their history, their religion, their internal nature, their future demands—that is, the Jews." The transplantation of the French spirit to Germany is the work of Jews, who are well disposed to such a task because of the affinity between French and Jewish mentality. The outstanding feature of the Jewish character is its proclivity to negation—possibly the result of the persecution the Jews had suffered at the hands of Christians, a concession Liesching is prepared to make on behalf of the culprit. In seeking out other characteristics, Liesching resorts to an expression of Heinrich Leo's, "the corroding intellect." It is the tool of the Jewish conquests, one of the last of these being the "magic endowment to create gold from paper," an allusion to transactions with bonds and securities. The Jewish conquest is at the same time achieved through "the contraband of a grandiose moral deception," exemplified through the Jew's capacity for accepting other nationalities in name but not in essence.[12]

What emerges as this author's basic thesis is the idea that the Jews, having been integrated into society at large, found it possible to apply their destructive abilities to an extent unprecedented in earlier generations. Applying the most emotive metaphors, Liesching refers to the medieval fiction of the Jews poisoning the wells and causing the Great Plague. At the time it was told, the story was a figment of popular imagination; but "the lie is destined to become reality," because perverting the budding German nationality is tantamount to poisoning the fountains of "all that is beautiful and wholesome in life, art, and literature."[13] Though the Young Germany movement was regarded as French in origin, Liesching ultimately blamed it on the Jews. Liesching apparently found it unnecessary to mention the Jewish participants in the movement by name; he simply identified the prevailing spirit as Jewish. Since this spirit was conceived of as immoral and destructive, it was absolutely at variance with the idealized image of the German character. Since it could have become effective in German society only through external influences, Jews, operating as they were within the orbit of German society, were the obvious vehicle of such evil.

This stylistically clumsy literary production might have passed unnoticed had it not been reviewed and praised by Wolfgang Menzel in his *Literaturblatt*. Menzel seems to have known the author, for he refers to him as the representative of a new generation. Menzel also explains that he blames the Jews for the pronouncements of Young Germany, because of the organization's great admiration for Heine, a Jew by birth: "Young Germany does not swear by anything more exalted than Heine." Menzel concedes that Heine had no intention of becoming a political or, for that matter, a spiritual leader. It was only his admirers who depicted him as such and outdid him in their extreme radicalism. "Thus has Heine been transformed without his knowledge, from the poet that he is into a great philosopher and reformer of the whole present world view, at least by Wienbarg." Wienbarg was one of the ideologues of Young Germany.[14]

Because of the prestige of Wolfgang Menzel, his attack was particularly painful to the Jewish intellectuals who felt their basic convictions under assault from the pamphleteers. Their sentiments were voiced by Berthold Auerbach and Jacob Weil in their responses to the pamphlets of 1836. The earlier attacks of Eduard Meyer in Hamburg were answered by Gabriel Riesser.[15] These protagonists of Jewish social and political emancipation pinned their hopes on the acceptance of Judaism as a mere religious confession. They accordingly protested against the identification of Jewry with individuals who converted to another creed. Adhering to the basic principles of liberalism and knowing individual responsibility to be one of them, the Jewish respondents could easily castigate the pamphleteers for their attempts to lay the faults of a few essayists at the door of a whole community. These defenders of the Jewish cause felt that they were in full harmony with the dominant trend of the times—we shall later see why their answers were beside the point and therefore of no avail. The arguments of the adversaries were not, as one might have surmised, mere residual reflections of past prejudices. They were frequently repeated, and instead of disappearing they culminated in the theory proposed by Richard Wagner after the revolution of 1848, the event that signified the close of the liberal period in his life as well as in the lives of many of his contemporaries.

Indicative of the tenacity of the anti-Jewish mood that grew out of the polemics against Young Germany is the fact that one of the former leaders of the movement, Heinrich Laube, joined the chorus of adversaries a year before the revolution. In the introduction to his drama *Struensee*, Laube tells the story of his conflict with Giacomo Meyerbeer over a drama by the same title written by the late brother of the composer, Michel Beer. When Laube conveyed to Meyerbeer his intention to produce a sequel to the brother's production, the composer did all that was in his power—and in view of his standing among artists and his excellent social connections, this was regarded as immense—to prevent Laube's play from being produced by any theater. Laube calls this intervention of the zealous brother "Kaufmannskonkurrenz," that is, business competition entirely at variance with "the good manners prevailing among German poets." Of course

182

The Scandal of the Jewish Artist: Wagner

Meyerbeer was an unconverted Jew, and in addition he was accustomed to the competitive practices of the world of Paris opera.[16]

How much truth there is in Laube's report is impossible to say. What is of interest for us is Laube's closing observation: "In recent time a foreign element has penetrated everywhere in our midst, and into literature as well. This is the Jewish element. I call it foreign with emphasis; for the Jews are an Oriental nation as totally different from us today as they were two thousand years ago." Laube then assures the reader that he is not, nor was he ever, an opponent of Jewish emancipation. "As fellow men, the Jews have the claim to human, that is, to civil rights." Radical emancipation is indeed the only chance for removing what is repulsive in the Jewish character: "Either we have to become barbarians and expel the Jews to the last man or we have to incorporate them." Yet his trust in the suggested remedy was not strong enough to allay his attitude toward what he deemed to be repulsive in Jewish behavior. Berlin Jewry serves as an example for Laube of what is unsavory in the Jewish character in general. Life in Berlin lacks the quality of being organically whole; even spiritual exercise there is the product of mechanical forces rather than an indigenous natural growth. Jewry found this an adequate atmosphere in which to thrive, for "Judaism, even at its best . . . would never have an organic German character."[17]

From this rather clumsy attempt to reveal the Jewish essence, Laube jumps to the real objective of his deliberation: the moral discrimination of his opponent. "From this element of Judaism, and Berlin Judaism in particular, derives the methods of Herr Meyerbeer, which he introduces into our literary world and which we reject as strange and repulsive to us." Envy was not unknown among German artists either; nevertheless, if this "ugly inheritance of human nature . . . cannot be conquered it can at least be kept down." This was what German artists were wont to do. What was entirely contrary to German style was "the overt chaffering [Schacher] with the objects of art and scholarship"—the methods of Meyerbeer and his Jewish consorts. The pejorative term Schacher, which as we have had the opportunity to observe, clung to the business transactions of the Jews, now became affixed to Jewish art as well.[18]

Still, Laube seems to have had some twinges of conscience about the moral justification of his generalization. At any rate, he concludes his remarks with the qualification that he does not consider the Jewish mentality absolutely incorrigible. There is a way of "turning off the Jewish impulse in literature. The way is exemplified by Berthold Auerbach, who absolutely conquered in himself the impulse that is repugnant to us." Auerbach achieved this objective by avoiding the atmosphere of the coffee

183

houses and the bourse, retreating instead into the "chaste solitude of country life." Another example is Gabriel Riesser. How Riesser succeeded in this moral metamorphosis is not stated. Still, he, Auerbach and their like have shown "that nationalization for the Jew is generally possible as far as the thoroughly cultivated Jewish types [*Naturen*] are concerned."[19]

Shallow and confused as Laube's argument may be, it is nonetheless telling evidence of the tendency among intellectuals to attribute the real or alleged failures of their Jewish competitors to their Jewishness. Laube declared that "by now every writer could easily point to the penetration of Jewish maxims in his province."[20] He meant to say that his experience with Meyerbeer could be replicated by that of other non-Jewish intellectuals in their contact with Jews. Of course, with the growing number of Jews active in artistic and literary life, the chances of conflict between them and their non-Jewish fellows must have increased as well. Since the moral inferiority of the Jew was a current stereotype, it was very tempting for the non-Jewish party to the conflict to apply the charge to his opponent. It saved him possible self-examination and even the trouble of probing the individual characteristics or the particular motivation of the other party. This is what happened with Heinrich Laube and later, on a much higher level and with more far-reaching consequences, to Richard Wagner.

The life of Richard Wagner can be divided into two parts, with the turning point in the aftermath of the 1848 revolution—a turning point in his musical creation as well as in his political and social attitudes. The political shift is reflected in his first outburst of anti-Jewish sentiments, documented in "Das Judenthum in der Musik," published anonymously in *Neue Zeitschrift fur Musik* in September 1850.[21] Up to this time there is no evidence of anti-Jewish activity or even utterances by Wagner. He had contact with many Jewish contemporaries, baptized and unbaptized: Heinrich Heine and Berthold Auerbach among the writers, Felix Mendelssohn, Giacomo Meyerbeer, and Ferdinand Hiller among the composers. There were some otherwise unknown Jewish admirers to whom Wagner would turn for financial support as uninhibitedly as to anybody else among his acquaintances. To Meyerbeer, Wagner owed much needed professional assistance and moral support in his first endeavor to be recognized as a musician of rank, and we know from contemporary historical sources that this debt was at that time openly and genuinely acknowledged.[22]

In the case of Heine, Wagner on one occasion came out in defense of the much-maligned poet. In an article published in the *Abend-Zeitung* of Dresden, Wagner chided his contemporaries for chasing away from his home "a talent the like of which Germany has only a few."[23] In his "Judaism in Music," Wagner also refers to his own participation in the struggle for Jewish emancipation, but there is no proof of his having participated in any practical sense of the word. Speaking in the plural, "at that time we contended for the emancipation of the Jews," he was probably simply including himself in the group of liberals who did support emancipation, and with whose political and social aspirations he at that time identified himself.[24]

That Wagner concerned himself with the Jewish problem and was puzzled by the phenomenon of Judaism is evident from his arguments in his "Judaism in Music," as we shall see later. His intimate association with Berthold Auerbach in the Dresden years (1845-1846) gave him an opportunity to become acquainted with the Jewish problem as seen by somebody who lived it from within. In his autobiography *Mein Leben*, dictated in the mid-1860s, Wagner remembered Auerbach as the only Jew among his acquaintances who was prepared and even eager to discuss Jewish matters without being embarrassed. Preoccupied with Judaism to an extent that seemed to Wagner to be obsessive, Auerbach must have become an important source of information on the subject.[25]

The turnabout of Wagner in relation to Jews and Judaism coincided with his alienation from liberalism, or, rather, has to be seen as an integral part of it. It is linked up with his involuntary exile in Switzerland after the defeat of the revolution, which had crushed Wagner's hopes of realizing his artistic schemes and ambitions in the wake of a newly established social order. The radical break with his whole past, imposed by external circumstances, led him to take stock and project his hopes into the future. His ideas on this subject are summed up in his essays "Art and Revolution" and "Art: Work of the Future," which belong to the very first months of his exile in 1849.[26] These essays contain a devastating criticism of the musical and theatrical productions of the time. The essay "Judaism in Music" a year later linked this criticism to the involvement of Jews in the artistic life of recent generations, an event that coincided with its general deterioration. On the personal level, the essay culminates in a venomous attack on Meyerbeer who, though unnamed, was pilloried as the cause of the degeneration of artistic taste and the beneficiary of that degeneration.

"Judaism in Music" is, like most of Wagner's writings, a complicated piece of reasoning. Indeed, only through sifting its components can one arrive at an understanding of its central logic.

The basic element of this anti-Jewish explosion is an emotional revulsion to the physical characteristics of the Jew of the old type, whom Wagner no doubt encountered, and the negative stereotype he had opportunity enough to absorb through literary channels. What provoked the reaction of Wagner the musician was, first of all, the Jewish way of expression in language and song. "To begin with . . . the manner of Jewish

185

speaking strikes our ears as absolutely foreign and unpleasant." In order to demonstrate this unpleasantness Wagner employs four onomatopoetic verbs, *zischend, schrillend, summsend, murksend*—some of them quite uncommon in German. Similarly Wagner reproduces the sensual impression one would receive of the religious service of the popular synagogue (*Volks-Synagoge*), clearly indicating that he speaks on the basis of personal experience. And once again, the musician resorts to discordant expressions, *Gegurgel, Geyodel, Gepplapper*, to demonstrate the atmosphere of the synagogue and ridicule it at the same time. It is well to remember that this aesthetic revulsion against inherited forms of Jewish popular culture was also shared by contemporary Jewish intellectuals. If Wagner happened to discuss the matter with his friend Auerbach, he no doubt found him in sympathy with his aesthetic judgment. According to his own testimony, in his liberal period Wagner closed his eyes to the realities of Jews and Judaism and defended the Jewish cause as a matter of principle. Now, with the dissipation of his abstract principles, the original repulsion at Jewishness was reasserting itself. This "irresistible" (*unwillkürlich*) or "instinctive" revulsion, as Wagner was inclined to call it, demanded a rational explanation. Having been estranged from Christianity since his early youth, Wagner was reluctant to accept the original cleavage between Jews and Christians as the reason for the continuing gulf between them. Yet Wagner did not succeed in substituting another theory for the Christian one. "The Jew, as it is well known, has a God all to himself"; the hint of the almost metaphysical singularity of the Jew is reminiscent of the doctrine of Bruno Bauer. Wagner probably picked up such expressions directly or indirectly from Bauer, but avoided combining them into a consistent theory. He was content with the repeated assurance that the Jewish existence would universally elicit repulsion.[27]

Wagner's interest was not in historical or philosophical understanding of the Jewish phenomenon, but rather in the exploration of its present function. In passing, he paid some attention to the economic ascendancy of the Jew. In view of this ascendancy, the impetuous clamor for political emancipation revealed itself as an obvious hypocrisy: "The Jew is, in view of the present state of affairs of this world, already more than emancipated." He was not merely emancipated, he ruled—a clear adaptation of Bauer, right down to the words employed.[28]

The main concern of Wagner is, however, the penetration of Jews into European, and especially German, culture. It is in this respect that his "Judaism in Music" has to be seen as the consummation of the anti-Jewish trend described earlier in this chapter. His exposition is epitomized in the catch phrase *Verjudung der modernen Kunst*, the "Judaization of the modern art," *Verjudung* being a neologism used here most probably for the very first time. Wagner's wish was to impress the importance of his theme upon his contemporaries. More pressing and consequential than the alleviation of Jewish preponderance in other domains, "the emancipation from the pressure of Judaism" in the field of culture was most important, and it was for this "war of liberation" that forces had to be marshaled.[29]

The diagnosis of the "Judaization" of modern music rested on two disparate observations: the first was the involvement of Jews and people of Jewish descent in the composition and performance of music. As we shall see later, according to Wagner, baptism did not make any difference. Wagner specifically mentioned Felix Mendelssohn, who had died three years previously, and hinted, in a manner that made his identity quite obvious to any contemporary reader, at Giacomo Meyerbeer. The latter, once much admired by Wagner as an artist and appreciated as a benevolent mentor, was now dismissed as a mere eclecticist who owed his unheard-of success to the deteriorated taste of the public and his skill—assisted by his inherited wealth—at putting himself and his works at the center of public attention. This judgment, by the way, was shared by Heinrich Heine. On the other hand, Mendelssohn was regarded by Wagner as a most gifted musician whose artistic achievement, however, was unsatisfactory. This puzzling contradiction was taken by Wagner as evidence for his remarkable theory of the insufficiency of Jewish cultural creation.[30]

The nucleus of Wagner's theory is that individual capacity is no guarantee of artistic creation. To fully exploit his potential, it is imperative that the artist be inspired by the artistic tradition of the national group to which he belongs. It is only through contact with the popular musical or poetical culture that the composer or the poet can be stimulated to create his own more complicated works. According to Wagner, the misfortune of the modern Jewish artist is the want of such a popular culture to fall back upon. The Jewish composer or poet plays his role as an artist in society at large, but the way to the popular stratum of this society, whence the adequate inspiration should be derived, is barred to him. This for a double reason: his lack of insight into what is foreign to him and the refusal of this stratum of the population to share with him its basic experiences. It is only among the richer classes that the reluctance to associate with Jews is "weakened or broken through calculation of the advantages and the attention to certain common interest." But this sector of society will never serve as a medium of inspiration to the artist.[31]

Wagner reveals himself here as a keen observer and trenchant critic of Jewish assimilation: "The educated Jew made the inconceivable effort to shed all the observable [auffällig] characteristics of his lower coreligionists:

in many cases he deemed it even useful to aim at effacing all traces of his descent through Christian baptism. This zeal of the educated Jew, however, never made him gain the hoped-for fruits: it only resulted in his being absolutely isolated."[32] This is not an incorrect perception of what happened to some radically assimilated Jews. But to these observations Wagner added contentions and evaluations that were clearly distortions of facts and unfounded conjectures.

Because the common Jew spoke his Yiddish dialect, Wagner asserted that no Jew would ever be able to regard any of the European languages as his own: "The Jew speaks the language of the nation within which he lives generation after generation, but he speaks it always as a foreigner." Of course this assertion is not the result of observation, but an inference from the accepted premise of the eternal strangeness of the Jew among the nations. "A language, its expression and evolution is not the work of individuals, but of a historical community [Gemeinsamkeit]: only one who grew up unconsciously in this community takes part in the creation." Wagner is here probably indebted to the theory of Fichte, who posited an essential identity between the historical spirit of the nation and its original national language—an identity said to have been attained by the Germans, but not by the French who, though of Teutonic stock, did in one stage of their history adopt a Latin tongue. Wagner applied the theory to the case of the individual Jew who, because of his non-German origin, would never become a genuine member of the German-speaking community. What was true of the language was also true of the other elements of popular culture. As a Jew was incapable of being inspired by that culture, he was also unable to contribute to the cultural creation on a higher level.[33]

The natural source of inspiration for the Jewish composer was the musical tradition of the synagogue. Wagner does not exclude the possibility of the Jewish religious service having been "in its original purity . . . noble and sublime." What is certain, however, is that the tradition reached us "only in this most repugnant turbidity." Nor has the original healthy kernel of this tradition become productive in the course of time: "Nothing further out of the fullness of life developed here for thousands of years but everything, as in Judaism in general, remained rigidly fixed in content as well as in form." Here, once again, is one of the stereotypes possibly transmitted to Wagner through Bruno Bauer. Wagner was not unaware of the attempts of the modern synagogue to reform the religious service to recover what was surmised to have been its original purity. Yet he had no difficulty in dismissing this as the work of the "mentally inbred Jewish intelligentsia," which was no substitute for the inspiration that ought to and indeed does come from "the real source of the people's life."[34] It was the popular type of religious service, with all its dissonant musical atmosphere, that had made its impact on the Jewish composers. In the same way as he believed he had observed the traces of the Jewish dialect in the language of the modern Jew, he similarly claimed to have detected the influence of the despicable Jewish music in the compositions of men like Mendelssohn and Meyerbeer. Indeed, whatever signs of inferiority he found in their creations, he attributed to this source of inspiration and not to any possible shortcomings of the individual composer.

Having designated the inferior music of Mendelssohn and Meyerbeer as Jewish, Wagner faced the problem of how these products of the foreign Jewish spirit could have found such favor with the German public. The answer to this question was anticipated by Wagner's severe criticism of the prevailing standards of musical life. As German music of the last generation deteriorated, musical taste, he claimed, had become adulterated and the sense of judgment blunted. The way had been paved for the absorption of Jewish music by the public. "As long as the peculiar art of music contained genuine organic drive [*Lebensbedürfniss*], up to the time of Mozart and Beethoven there was no Jewish composer to be found anywhere; it was impossible for an element absolutely foreign to this living organism to participate in the formation of this life." In elaborating this idea of the immunity of German culture, in its pristine state, to Jewish influence, Wagner resorted to an analogy of the biological process in a living body, in contrast to that in a corpse. The living organism would not suffer the entrance of a foreign element. Once it was dead, the external elements gained the upper hand. "Then the flesh of the body would dissolve into the multiplication [*Viellebigkeit*] of worms: Yet, in view of these, who would regard the body itself as being still alive?" The application of such a repulsive metaphor is indicative of Wagner's disgust at contemporary musical life.[35]

It is only fair to state that Wagner did not attribute the decline of German music to Jewish influence. On the contrary, he explained the predominance of the Jewish element as the result of the deterioration. Still his diagnosis of the whole situation implied a devastating judgment on Jewish creativity. For, while the German deficiency had been conceived of as a temporary one, to be remedied through revitalization, the Jewish inferiority was presented as inherent in the Jewish essence.[36] By association, at least, the Jews shared the guilt for the lamentable state of musical affairs at that time. For they were quick to use the opportunity offered them through the temporary weakness of the German spirit. Wagner heaped scorn and ridicule on the Jewish contribution to music, by hinting at the purely businesslike interest the Jewish artist took in his profession. The fruits of the work of the ancient and medieval world were turned into money by the modern Jew, who similarly transmuted the artistic creation of two thousand years into wares to be paid for in bills and bonds [*Kunstwarenwecksel*].[37]

The adulterated German music was, in essence, Jewish music. Germans who were prepared to defend and even glorify it revealed themselves as having turned Jewish in spirit. Those who were insensitive to this diagnosis or reluctant to act upon it "we do include in the category of Jewry in music."[38]

Music was the central theme of Wagner's deliberations. However, he also talked of poetry, which, according to him, had suffered the same fate as music at the hands of the Jews. In the closing paragraph of his essay the author addressed himself directly to the subject, maintaining that the role of Mendelssohn and Meyerbeer in the field of music had been filled in poetry by Heinrich Heine. At the time of Goethe and Schiller, no Jew could have found a place in German literature. When the true poetry of the classics was replaced by simulated creativity, it was once again a Jew, the most gifted but negative Heine, who exposed the pretentiousness of his contemporaries as well as his own poetical poverty.[39]

These remarks on Heine were not Wagner's last words on the subject. As if moved by association of ideas, he opened the last paragraph with the sentence: "We have still another Jew to mention who has come forward among us as a writer." The man was Ludwig Börne.[40] What Wagner had to say of Börne can be seen as a paradoxical reversion of the central thesis of the pamphlet, or at least an incisive qualification of his argument. Börne entered German public life "to seek redemption among us." He did not find what he was after, but he surely became aware that his chance to find it was linked up with "our own redemption as genuine human beings." Wagner meant to say that Börne was striving for the establishment of a better world, so that man could transcend his own imperfect nature. In the course of such transmutation, a Jew, too, could reach the status of purified manhood. Surely for the Jew it would mean leaving behind all that had adhered to him in his previous existence. At any rate, it could be only achieved at the price of "sweat, want, anguish, the fullness of suffering and sorrow"—shared with other human beings. Wagner drifted here in a quasi-religious terminology with a Christian coloration. On the other hand, he spoke about the "curse burdening the Jew" and on the other about the "regenerative work of redemption." In using these terms he certainly did not have simply conversion to Christianity in mind. The transmutation to be experienced by the Jew was much more far-reaching. It amounted to the "self-extinction," the complete disappearance. The redemption of Ahasver (the wandering Jew) was his *Untergang*—his self-annihilation.[41]

Why Wagner should have chosen Börne as the qualifying counterpoise of his theory is not difficult to guess. In his youth Wagner was prob-

ably among the admirers of Börne, owing to the latter's intrepid champion-
ship of the democratic principle. In his early life he also thought highly of
Heine, as we have seen, but with the growing bias against Jewish intellectuals he became critical of him—an attitude that may have been
strengthened through personal acquaintance with the poet in Wagner's
Paris years, 1839-1840. Börne was no longer living at that time; he had
died in 1835, years before Wagner assumed his anti-Jewish stance, thus
leaving his image unimpaired in his memory.[42]

Yet, whatever the reason, the very fact of his having conceded the
possible union of a Jew in common humanity with others was telling
evidence of the conceptual foundations of Wagner's world view. Radical
and venomous as his rejection of the Jew may have been, it was not based
on racial notions. It was only for a fleeting moment that he entertained the
idea of a physiological origin for the Jewish peculiarity in the use of
language.[43] This explanation was very soon supplemented by considerations of what might be called cultural addiction and, on another level, a
metaphysical predisposition of the Jew. This clearly was a secularized version of the Christian concept of the Jew's nature, which consistently admitted the possibility that the Jew could be redeemed through a self-sacrificing
transmutation.[44]

Indeed, Wagner adhered to the nonracial concept of Judaism when
in 1869 he republished "Das Judenthum in der Musik" under his own
name. In a lengthy appendix, written in the form of a letter to one of his
aristocratic admirers, he tells the story of his struggle for recognition in the
face of a hostile press and other resistance to appreciation of his music.
Wagner attributed all this to the machinations of Jews who, knowing his
responsibility for "Judaism in Music" in spite of its anonymity, would not
forgive him his audacity. In fact, Jews no less than Gentiles were at that
time deeply divided on the artistic merits of Wagner's music; some Jews
were among his most ardent supporters, and Wagner had no hesitation in
accepting their assistance. In reaffirming his theory about the devastating
Jewish influence on music, Wagner somehow had to accommodate the
fact of this Jewish support, which he did by allowing that a Jew might get
rid of his Jewishness by psychological effort. Indeed, Wagner maintained
that exceptional Jews—particularly those who saw the light with regard to
the superiority of Wagnerian music—were the first to suffer because of
Jewish inferiority. At any rate, their existence hinted at a possible solution
of the Jewish problem: absolute and unreserved assimilation. It was in the
service of this solution that Wagner claimed to have offered his analysis in
writing his pamphlet: "Should this element be assimilated to us in a way
that it may mature in common with us into the higher development of our
more noble human abilities, then it is obvious that, not the concealment of

the difficulties concerning this assimilation, but only its open disclosure could be conducive to it." Forced and sanctimonious as this self-interpretation might have been, it could not well be presented in the context of a racially oriented Weltanshauung. Obviously, Wagner was not yet possessed of that Weltanshauung even in the late 1860s, some two decades after the publication of "Judaism in Music."[45]

What is true of Wagner is also true of his predecessors, from Eduard Meyer to Heinrich Laube, who like him found Jewish cultural activity foreign, inferior, and noxious, but did so without reference to a racially oriented doctrine. No hint of such a tenet is to be found in even their most defamatory arguments. The truth is that the adversaries of the Jews lacked a consistent theory by which to interpret their own dislike of Jews. The main polemical tool at their disposal was an emphasis on the strangeness of the Jew, which excluded him from the community of other nations.

The question to be asked is whether this was a mere prejudice, or whether there was something in Jewish reality that gave it credibility. Did those who decried the intrusion of Jewish elements into German culture indeed perceive traits in the poetry and music of Jewish artists that struck them as peculiarly Jewish, or did they simply associate the idea of strangeness and inferiority that clung to the name Jew with the productions of these artists?

Naturally, no entirely conclusive answer to this question can be offered. In some cases, especially that of Heine, typically Jewish traits have been surmised in his style, his wit, and even in his ideas and imagery, not only by antagonists but also by detached observers. A Jewish contemporary, no admirer of Heine, said that "after reading even only a few lines of Heine there was no Jew who would not know at once that Heine was of Jewish descent."[46] But the attempts of this observer to spell out the indices by which the poet's Jewishness was to be recognized was as vague as vague could be. Gustav Pfizer, a Christian critic, wondered and could not decide whether Heine "had inherited certain traits in his essence and character from the peculiarities of his people, as for instance the wit and audacity." Pfizer also made a general remark about the "increasing Judaization in literature," but on how to characterize the recognizable qualities of Jewishness in literature, Pfizer was clearly at a loss. What he had to say was that it carried with it a characteristic smack (*Beigeschmack*) of Jewishness and that it revealed "a polemic squint-eyed sullenness." This is no more than we can gather from Richard Wagner's observations of Heine's allegedly notable Jewish characteristics.[47]

Wagner was not more successful in spelling out the Jewish characteristics of the music of Mendelssohn and Meyerbeer, with which he attempted to exemplify and solidify his theory. There is no conceptual link

The Scandal of the Jewish Artist: Wagner

between what Wagner had to say about traditional Jewish music and his diagnosis of the insufficiency of the compositions of modern Jewish composers. In fact, the epithet "Jewish" does not occur in the course of his criticism, and only in the last sentence of the long passage on Meyerbeer does Wagner revert to it, when he claims that the discrepancy between will and capacity, and his self-deception concerning this discrepancy, makes Meyerbeer a tragicomic figure—qualities that are attributed to Judaism.[48] We cannot escape the conclusion that, contrary to what the critics maintained, namely, that they detected inferior traits typical of Jews in the productions of these artists, their inference actually worked the other way: because they knew that the producers were Jewish, the real or imaginary shortcomings of their productions were attributed to their having a Jewish origin. This is not to say that there is not a Jewish mentality that has left its mark on some creations of Jewish artists. What is sure is that the verification of this influence was not a precondition for classifying works as Jewish. It was sufficient that a work be known as the product of a Jew to be classified as Jewish, with all the derogatory connotations that went with this name.

The reversed sequence of causation in the judgment of what is Jewish is strikingly parallel to what we have found in the field of economics. There, no doubt, some typical features could be found in the ways the Jews transacted their business in banking, petty trading, and hawking, but these were scarcely ever judged on their merit. Whatever Jews were engaged in was associated with the disreputable characteristics of Jewish trading—schachermacher and the like.[49]

The comparison between attitudes toward Jewish economic, artistic, and intellectual activities has still another revealing aspect. The suspicion of the non-Jewish tradesmen against their Jewish competitors was nourished by the fact of Jews conspicuously cooperating with each other, owing to their social cohesion, which transcended purely businesslike connections. This most plausible phenomenon, sociologically, could easily be interpreted by the opponents as a conspiracy harmful to the population at large and especially to Gentile competitors of the Jews. When Jews became conspicuous in art, literature, journalism, and the like, a similar aspersion was cast upon them: a Jew would support a Jew despite his real merits, and do the reverse for a Gentile.

The first signs of this attitude was already evident in the 1830s. Eduard Meyer accused Börne of being biased in favor of Heine: "Of course Heine is being extolled by Börne, his consort in faith and aspiration." Pfizer contended that Jewish solidarity also embraced baptized Jews like Heine, and these accordingly shared the responsibility for his antireligious audacities. True, at times Heine poked fun at the Jews, and he was overtly denied by them because of his conversion to Christianity: "But still a part of them and especially those who are the hardest in clamoring for emancipation have not ceased to regard him secretly as belonging to them." A tacit cooperation among Jews active in public life is here assumed as a fact and decried as a breach of the unwritten terms on which they had been accepted in society at large. This reproach is then most forcefully accentuated by Richard Wagner who, as we have seen, conceived of an actual Jewish conspiracy at work to frustrate his well-deserved success.[50]

The similarity between attitudes toward Jews in economics and in art is evident also in the pejorative application of the word "Jewish" to the activities of non-Jews. Critics of society, especially conservatives in matters of art and economics, regarded much of what emerged in their lifetime as coarse, vulgar, and uncalled-for innovation. As Jews by now had access to these fields of activity, they too participated, sometimes even conspicuously, in these modernizations, with the result that they became identified with them. For those who were startled and frightened by the hated novelties, the combination of the objectionable phenomena with the despised name of the Jew was a welcome cause for rejecting both. The term *Verjudung*, "Judaization," which was applied to novelties of allegedly Jewish provenance or character, in art as well as in economics, was an unmistakable indication that the same tendency was at work in the two disparate domains of society.

15│The Christian State

THE RADICALIZATION OF theological, political, and social thought by men like David Friedrich Strauss, Ludwig Feuerbach, Bruno Bauer, Karl Marx, and others was the greatest innovation in the 1840s in the intellectual life of Germany, if not of all Europe. It is not surprising that such thinking has attracted the attention of historians, diverting them from the conservative trends that were prevalent in German society at that time. In regard to the "Jewish question," the radical thinkers might appear to have opened up some unheard-of vistas of lasting and far-reaching influence. However, the less conspicuous trends of that time may have had a greater contemporary impact.

It was in the years 1842-1844 that the term "Christian state" first appeared in the titles of pamphlets (or their chapter headings) that dealt with the position of the Jew in Gentile society at that time or in the future. The first use of it was in Wolfgang Bernhard Fränkel's *Die Unmöglichkeit der Emancipation der Juden im christlichen Staat* ("The Impossibility of the Emancipation of Jews in the Christian State"); the second, H. E. Marcard, *Über die Möglichkeit der Juden-Emancipation im christlich-germanischen Staat* ("On the Possibility of Jewish Emancipation in the Christian-Germanic State"); the third, Constantin Frantz, *Ahasverus oder die Judenfrage*, chapter 3 of which is entitled "Ueber das Verhaltniss der Juden in dem christlichen Staat" ("On the Relation of the Jews to the Christian State"). For the sake of our analysis we can also add two books of Philip Ludwig Wolfart, which, though avoiding the use of the term in their titles, apply the argumentation implied in it.[1]

Germany, 1830-1873

The attribution of the adjective "Christian" to the state in the context of the Jewish problem is, of course, not new. In the title to his book, discussed earlier, Schmidt-Phiseldeck used the words "christlicher Bürgerverein" ("Christian association of citizens")—*Bürgerverein* being identical in meaning with the term *state*.[2] In 1833 the Prussian privy councilor Karl Streckfuss entitled his treatise on the issue of Jewish emancipation "Über das Verhältniss der Juden in den christlichen Staaten" ("On the Relation of the Jew to the Christian States") and he applied the same title to a second book ten years later. In the first he was still reluctant to recommend a universal emancipation because of the alleged moral and civil deficiencies of the common type of Jew; in the second he waived his objections.[3] Streckfuss, Schmidt-Phiseldeck, and others discussed the question of Jewish emancipation as a matter of propriety and feasibility, mainly in view of the moral and mental disparity between Jews and Gentiles. The term "Christian" is applied only to convey the objective fact that the population was of this religion. It is not without significance that while Streckfuss speaks about the Christian states in the plural, Frantz, though otherwise adopting the exact wording of Streckfuss's title, changed "states" from the plural to the singular. "Christian state" in the singular is an abstraction and conveys the idea that the state as such possesses the qualities of Christianity, excluding Jews by its very nature. This conclusion is either explicitly stated or indirectly implied by the exponents of the idea. Wolfart starts off with the observation that the inquiry into the problem of Jewish emancipation has to take its cue not from the Jews' condition but from an understanding of what is the essence of the state. As the Prussian state is a "pure Evangelic-Christian monarchy," Jews are automatically excluded from fulfilling a role in its institutions. The most they can expect is to be tolerated as passive subjects of the sovereign. For Fränkel there is "an organic bond between state and church"; according to Frantz, "the complete moral community [of the state] presupposes a common faith of its members"; and in the view of Marcard, the "Christian-Germanic state emerging as it did from a Christian-Germanic folk has a Christian-Germanic personality"—definitions that lead to similar, though not always identical, decisions.[4]

The deliberations of these polemicists turned on the issue of the political and civic status of the Jew in the Christian state. Our interest is to see how their argumentation kept alive, engendered, or variegated the anti-Jewish sentiments and their concomitant ideologies.

Ideologically, the theories of the Christian state reflect the ideas of Friedrich Rühs, the leading anti-Jewish propagandist in the preliberal era. In the opening paragraph of his long treatise, H. E. Marcard openly admits his debt to Rühs, which is further revealed in his reasoning and in his use of the term "Christian-Germanic" in the title of his book. Like Rühs, Marcard combined an emphatically nationalistic—*völkisch*—conception with a Christian commitment, the obvious result of which would be to debar the Jew from the community of Germans because of his religion, his foreign descent, and the lack of common historical memories. The upholding of the Christian principle implied at the same time that the Jews would be absorbed through their ultimate conversion to Christianity.[5]

This paradoxical attitude required a good measure of intellectual acrobatics to allow Marcard to marshal the traditional Christian stereotypes—Jewish stiff-neckedness, abandonment by God, and the like—while riding at the same time on the inherent or acquired characteristics of the Jews, be they cultural, intellectual or moral. Therein, Marcard scarcely ever transcended the position of his precurser, and in many of his anti-Jewish charges he simply paraphrases Rühs's onslaught. Still, the three decades that lie between the two men brought about obvious changes in conditions, which called for unprecedented responses on the part of the later author.

The rise of the liberal movement in the 1830s changed the intellectual atmosphere toward the Jewish problem. Not unconnected with this trend, changes occurred in the constitutional position of Jews, especially in south German states: Württemberg, Baden, and elsewhere. A whole group of Jewish intellectuals, baptized and unbaptized, writers, artists, and thinkers, entered the arena of public life, and their actions were placed to the account of Judaism even if they were baptized. Judaism itself seemed to be mutating—an ever-growing number of Jews neglected substantial parts of religious observances, and whole communities, led by their rabbis, altered the form of the religious worship.[6] How the participation of Jews in German cultural life was evaluated, we have considered in Chapter 14. The internal changes in Jewry and Judaism received no positive response from these Christian ideologists. "As to the educated modern Judaism, it is an absurdity, a mere negation of the Jewish Law as well as a negation of Christianity; it is a shallow deism lacking all definiteness and any tenets although differing from the absolutely fixed and delimited Theism of the Old Testament." Where is the source of this modern Judaism? As there is no answer to this query, the conclusion is that "contemporary Judaism is not a positive religion . . . that would be able to lend its adherents peace and support of any kind."[7]

It was typical of the exponents of the concept of the Christian state that whatever position they allotted the Jew in their scheme of things, the Jew they wished to have dealings with was of the old type, the observant Orthodox Jew. True, Frantz declared that since the adoption of reform in the Jewish religion was a matter of conscience, the state had to refrain

197

from either promoting or hindering it. Still, speaking about the historical role Jews were destined to fulfill in the future—meaning the salvation of the world that would coincide with the ultimate conversion of the Jewish nation according to the Christian tradition—he clearly stated that this would depend upon the Jews holding firm to their creed and not attempting to remodel it into a mere humanism and then "to smuggle themselves into the state through disgraceful sophistries." Similarly, Wolfart protested the use of religious reforms by Jews as a means of making themselves politically acceptable.[8]

If, in the deliberations of these authors, the problem of Jewish religious reform cropped up only occasionally, it still plays a central role in Wolfgang Bernhard Fränkel's bemoaning of the dissolution of Jewish tradition—and the consequences to be drawn from it. Fränkel, a doctor by profession, was a baptized Jew who in an earlier book had told the story of his conversion, or rather presented an ideological justification for it.[9] The bits and pieces of personal experiences related by Fränkel do not add up to a psychologically convincing account of a genuine conversion. After the fact, Fränkel clearly adopted the stance of a convinced Christian—the condemnation of the Judaism he had abandoned served as a prop for his new attachment to Christianity.

Fränkel's rejection of Judaism is unqualified; he rejects the old as well as the new interpretation—Orthodox or otherwise. Still, the main thrust of his criticism is directed against the secularized reform version that had appeared on the scene in modern times. Reform Jews had factually renounced the authority of both the Old Testament and the Talmud. But they had failed to establish a religious authority of their own, and their vagaries were a telling testimony to a lost cause, "of the religious anarchy of Jewry the more intelligent and better educated part of which has renounced all religion in order to be civilly emancipated." In fact, what they think to be the vehicle of their acceptance is the most powerful obstacle of their emancipation. Fränkel quotes approvingly the dictum of an opponent of emancipation in one of the recent debates: "Judaism as it developed in the progress of time is not only a negation of our church, but an overt contradiction of it." As the state cannot exist without the support of the church, it would be impossible for it to embrace at the same time its very opposite and denial, namely, Judaism.[10]

The idea of a Christian state is usually associated with Friedrich Julius Stahl. Stahl (1802-1861) was also a Jewish convert, but one who succeeded not only in being adjusted to and absorbed by his Gentile environment but even in attaining an outstanding position in it. He played a conspicuous role in the intellectual and academic life of Germany, as professor of law in the University of Berlin and as an outstanding political philosopher. He became a member of the Prussian Upper House and the leading ideologue of the Prussian Conservative party.[11]

Brought up in an Orthodox Jewish home in Munich, Stahl converted at the age of seventeen, upon entering the university. Though initially he seems to have been prompted by the usual secular motives of cultural and social adaptation, in the course of time he not only became a confessing Protestant, but made Christianity the basis of his social and political philosophy. The implications of his teachings with regard to Jews and Judaism are evident in many of his writings and are spelled out in detail in his *Der christlichen Staat und sein Verhaltniss zum Deismus und Judenthum* ("The Christian State and its Relation to Deism and Judaism") of 1847.[12]

The writing of this book was occasioned by a debate on the legal status of the Jews in the United Landtag of that year. Owing to historical and political circumstances, the Jews of the various districts of Prussia were subject to differing and conflicting laws and regulations. The government wished to put an end to this anarchy through a united and unifying legislation. Since the problem was on the agenda of the Landtag, the liberal-minded members proposed to forgo the attempt to circumscribe the rights and obligations of Jews within the state and to declare instead that civil rights should be independent of religious affiliation. The very idea of the Christian state thus came under attack, and it was in the defense of this concept that Stahl wrote.[13]

The line of defense of the idea of the Christian state began with the contention that the moral authority of royal government, no less than the acceptance of the social order and the subordination to judicial process, derived its source from Christianity alone: "The state is the molding of the human condition according to moral ideas, and since Christianity is the Divine manifestation of the moral ideas of these conditions of life, it stands to reason that Christianity must determine the nature of the state."[14] It is unnecessary for us to follow Stahl's reasoning in substantiating his theory or his attempts at refuting the logical and factual objections to it. Our main interest is to see what were the inferences with regard to Jews and Judaism that flowed from his accepted premises.

If the state be a Christian totality, no people of another religion—Jews or Deists—should have a place in it. Yet in speaking of the state, Stahl, like his predecessors, did not have in mind the population comprising it. It was, rather, the fabric of government, its arms and agencies, to which he referred. These and not the population, the passive object of the state's operation, must be Christian. Therefore, Jews and Deists may not only be admitted but have the right to enjoy all the benefits accruing from their membership—except that they cannot take part in the administration and distribution of these benefits.[15]

Not that Jews as human beings were incapable of fulfilling these tasks. Stahl takes issue with the opponents of Jewish emancipation who rested their objections on the peculiarities of Jewish character or the corrupting influence of the Jewish religion. Jews have their characteristics, like other nationalities, and Jewish peculiarities may be especially conspicuous. The current view on this matter "puts the Jewish national predisposition [*Volksanlage*] too high from the intellectual aspect and too low from the moral aspect." Stahl obviously sees no point in discussing this issue, which turns on the assessment of observable data. Instead, he resorts to the evaluation of the Jewish character as it is predetermined in the traditional Christian conception of the Jewish role in human history: "It is the chosen people of God, its mission is religious, to preserve belief in the true God in the midst of the pagan world . . . to raise up from its midst the savior of mankind." The Jewish character is accordingly a purely religious one. Its only moral justification is its fitness to meticulously preserve its religion. It is the religious consciousness in which it finds a moral support. This special quality continues to determine Jewish behavior even after its mission in preparing the world for Christianity and procuring its founders is fulfilled: "Therefore there are to be found up to this hour among the authentic Jews a type of very worthy men . . . men of deep religiosity, of conscientiousness in the way they openly conduct their lives." Stahl heaps on this type an almost unlimited measure of praise, which then serves as a foil for the condemnation of the Jew who has lost his moorings in his ancient religion: "There is also to be found among them a type repulsive beyond all measure . . . who having lost his most peculiar moral impulse . . . lacks any stability . . . a model of arrogance they find their satisfaction in the dexterity of their mind alone." Here we have the stereotyped image of the demoralized Jew underpinned by the theological conception of the exclusively religious destiny of the Jew who, once he has become disloyal to that destiny, must necessarily lose all moral restraint.[16]

This verdict on the moral polarity of Jewish personalities—clearly a result of the theological commitment—is mitigated by observation that by now most Jews have extricated themselves from their original mentality through a far-reaching adaptation to the mores and morals of their environment: "Once seclusion ceased, small groups could not keep clear from the moral atmosphere that surrounded them . . . All that comprises the thinking of present Europe transmitted itself for better or worse to the educated Jew who lived in the Christian environment [*Gemeinschaft*]." In short, Jews could function wherever a high standard of morality was required, but this was not due to their religious or human resources, but to their successful assimilation to their Gentile surroundings.[17]

In the same ambivalent fashion, Stahl disposes of the other traditional objection against Jewish political equality, Jewish national separation. The Jewish community, in its pristine status and composition, was not only unable but unwilling to participate in the social or political life of other nations. But the barriers have long since been broken down. "The Jew of today is in general not hindered internally from participation in the communal [*staatlich*] existence of the German nations, neither because of his religion nor through his way of thinking." This capacity has been acquired at the price of the abandonment of the "genuine Judaism, which no longer exists in Germany." Heavy as the price may have been, it was paid, and participation in the state purchased.[18]

What, then, was the obstacle to the full participation of the Jews in the active maintenance of the state? It was the moral symbiosis between the state and Christianity. Were the state a secular institution, as revolutionary France was declared to be, Jews would have been unreservedly accepted. The Germans, who were spared the tribulation of a revolution, were still in possession of a state of a higher moral order, and it would have been an audacity to demand its renunciation for the sake of political equality.[19]

Stahl no doubt made a conscious effort to arrive at a fair judgment concerning the affairs of his brethren in the flesh. If this had only a limited success, it was because of his unreserved commitment to the Christian theological conception, implying as this did a derogatory evaluation of its rival religion, Judaism. Stahl succeeded somehow in exempting contemporary Jewry from the moral consequences of this evaluation, but he retained it in full for the Jewish religion itself. Asked why Protestants were permitted to share the conduct of the state with Catholics, but not with Jews, he answered that Protestants and Catholics were divided as to the correct interpretation of the same revelation. The Jews denied the truth of the Christian revelation; they were adherents of another, obsolete, inferior religion. As, according to Stahl, the moral justification of the state was derived from its affiliation with the Christian religion, the toleration of its rival could not but be a qualified one. The imperfect religion might be sustained by its followers within the state, but it had no claim to be supported by the state. The idea that the state could accept both Christianity and Judaism, as the religions of different parts of the population, each of them guaranteeing the public morals of its adherents, does occur to Stahl but is rejected out of hand. Catholicism and Protestantism can regard each other as mutually complementary, "but it would never occur to a confessing Christian that Judaism or Deism is a supplement to Christianity." It would therefore be absurd to suggest that, alongside the Christian theological faculties maintained by the state, similar institutions should be established for the sake of Judaism.[20]

The allotted role of Christianity in the spiritual husbandry of the state provided a justification for treating Jews as second-rate citizens. It is perhaps of greater significance that, owing to the same conception, Jewish religion as such was relegated to a permanent and absolute inferior position.

16|The Jewish Stereotype and Assimilation

IN THE ARGUMENTS OF the German conservatives, the negative image of the Jew was linked to the demand for a diminution of his rights. Nevertheless, as the history of anti-Semitism in France has shown, the Jewish stereotype and its attendant ideologies persisted and developed whether or not there was any hope of diminishing Jewish rights. The desire to see the Jews adapt to the norms of the dominant culture was sufficient reason to present the negative image of the Jew and suggest it be erased by means of assimilation. Unlike the political struggle over rights, the argument over assimilation did not concern a defined concrete objective, and, accordingly, clear-cut verbal polemics were not employed. Instead, the disturbing spectacle of Jewish characteristics was presented through historiography or belles-lettres: the works of Michelet and Renan, in France, are examples of the former and, in Germany, the novels of Gustav Freytag and Wilhelm Raabe, *Soll und Haben* and *Hungerpastor*.[1] In both novels, Freytag's published in the mid-1850s, and Raabe's in the mid-1860s, Jewish figures play a central role. They are intentionally contrasted with their Gentile counterparts, and the contrast is invariably, in the prevailing literary fashion, black-and-white.

The country where Gustav Freytag's novel takes place is not named, but is easily recognizable as Silesia and its capital, Breslau. The plot reflects the three conspicuous social circles of the country: the landed aristocracy, the patriarchal Gentile merchants, and the Jews. The last two might appear to fall into the same socioeconomic category, since both Christian tradesmen and Jews are engaged in business. However, Freytag represents them not only as two separate social groups but as two different worlds. The first token of the Jews' dissimilarity is their cultural strangeness, evident, first of all, in their use of the language. With one exception, the "good Jew" about whom we shall hear later, not one of this class ever speaks a correct German sentence, even when making a conscious effort to do so, as does Veitel Itzig, the central figure among the Jews. All the Jewish men and women reveal a coarseness in taste and uncouthness in manners; their occasional attempts to improve themselves only make them ridiculous because of the discrepancy between pretension and reality.[2]

This aesthetically repulsive facade has its equivalent in the Jews' moral behavior. The main social intention of Freytag's novel is to condemn the aristocracy's unwarranted claim to excellence, honor, and preference, because those privileges have not been paid for in the currency of thrift, genuine honesty, and prudence. In Freytag's story, all the social virtues are concentrated in the businessmen of the established middle class, which is destined to replace the landed aristocracy as the model for society at large. In this undeclared struggle for leadership between the two groups in the Gentile world, the Jews play a most unsavory role. Uninhibited by notions of honor or precepts of morality, they become instrumental in bringing about the aristocracy's economic downfall and ethical deterioration. If not of an outright criminal character, the business dealings of the Jews are imminently susceptible of becoming so. In comparison with the Gentile businessmen, whose behavior conforms to the highest moral standards, the Jews of *Soll und Haben* are a kind of underworld prepared to exploit any weakness in the moral or economic structure of Gentile society. The ascription of this quality to the Jews is demonstrated through their association with a real criminal—the only one among the Gentiles—a destitute advocate who finds refuge in a Jewish tavern and initiates Veitel Itzig into dubious underhand practices.[3]

Freytag refrains from theorizing on the vices and virtues of his characters or on the ultimate causes from which they developed. Why Jews are what they are is not stated, either by the author or by any of the characters in the story. Still, some basic notions about how the Jewish characteristics originated are conveyed to the reader by inference or implication. That the Jewish peculiarities and shortcomings are neither racially conditioned nor ineradicable is demonstrated by the appearance of the "good Jew," the son of a rich dealer, Ehrenthal, who is exclusively dedicated to making money, but facilitates his son Bernhard's desire to pursue scholarship. This pursuit, though unrewarding because of the exclusion of Jews from a university career, is most successful as far as the formation of character is concerned. Bernhard, though living in the house of his parents, has shed all the negative Jewish peculiarities, including the moral ones. He is therefore found worthy of the friendship of the central figure of the novel, Anton Wohlfahrt, the paragon of all possible virtue and prowess. It is the "good Jew" Bernhard who on his deathbed points out to his father the moral shortcomings of himself and his whole class: "Since you left the house of our grandfather as a poor Jewish boy . . . you have thought of nothing but making money. Nobody taught you anything else, your faith kept you away from intercourse with those who understood better what gives value to life." It is only through contact with Gentiles that a Jew can acquire an appreciation of any values beyond the coarsest material ones. Judaism alone is not capable of giving its adherents morality or culture. This is the devastating conclusion that is conveyed by the story of *Soll und Haben*, from which millions of Germans for generations derived their impression of Jewish life or were at least influenced in their prejudices. The lesson to be drawn from this state of affairs is, according to the liberal-minded Freytag, the encouragement of contact between Jews and Gentiles and the removal of barriers preventing it. Since this consequence is at best implied, but nowhere made explicit, it is most probable that Freytag's popular novel served to strengthen the prevailing stereotype of the greedy, uninhibited Jew rather than remolding and reforming it.[4]

Raabe's *Hungerpastor* is a much simpler uncomplicated story than *Soll und Haben*. Here, the confrontation is only between the two main characters, the Gentile hero and the Jewish villain. The two become friends in early childhood when the Christian boy volunteers to protect his Jewish neighbor from the animosity of his comrades. Later in life, when the true character of the Jew becomes apparent, they turn out to be incompatible, and it is evident to all but the hero that the Jewish boy had never been worthy of the favor bestowed upon him. For while the Christian youth, though of extremely poor background, aspires to the highest ethical standards and seeks satisfaction in spiritual values, his Jewish counterpart is an absolute egoist, who uses his remarkable intellectual gifts for unrestrained self-aggrandizement. In Moses Freudenstein, who converts to Catholicism and becomes Theophilus Stein, we have the literary representation of the Jewish intellectual as reflected in the mind of his detractors: rootless in any society, uncommitted to any ideal, who, led by his cool calculating intellect, becomes a moral danger to his environment.

Where these Jewish qualities stem from is not clarified by Raabe—he certainly does not attempt a racial explanation. But that these qualities are inherent in the Jewish intellectual is stated in so many words by Moses Freudenstein himself and is also demonstrated through his connection with his father, a homeless huckster who secretly amasses his fortune for the benefit of his son, who is the most talented pupil in his class of Gentile schoolmates. The father foresees his son's future career and looks upon his acceptance into Gentile society as a compensation for the frustration that has been his own portion in life. The son, on the other hand, carries over his father's simpleminded acquisitiveness to the vast opportunities open to him in the highest ranks of Christian society. There is an obvious continuity between the behavior of the despised Jewish huckster, the father, and his son, the sophisticated doctor of philosophy.[5]

The utilization of literature for the study of social history is warranted, according to a well-sustained theory, because social types represented by successful authors are themselves a product of epitomized observation, a kind of artistic ideal-type not unlike what the social historian attempts to derive in his own way. Thus, the aristocrats and businessmen described by Freytag are modeled on what he observed in the social circles known to him. They therefore retain their historical authenticity even in novelistic garb. The question is whether this holds true for the Jewish characters appearing in the stories of Freytag and Raabe. The question does not pertain only to the credibility of the moral behavior of the Jews. There is also the bloodless schematism of the Jewish figures, the dullness of their psychological make-up, and the lack of texture and substance in their social life. Raabe attributes behavior to his Jew that is in direct contradiction to prevailing Jewish custom. A dying Jew is not attended to by the local rabbi but by the members of the Holy Association (burial society), and no Jew, corrupt as he may be at heart, would return to his worldly affairs after the burial of his father without observing the seven days of mourning. Unacquainted with the realities of Jewish life, Raabe has, in his portrayal, ascribed to individuals the collective features contained in the Jewish stereotype. This is the very reverse of the process required in the composition of the ideal-type, whether by the perceptive novelist or by the trained social historian. Gustav Freytag may have had more opportunity of observing Jews, but when it came to presenting them in his art, he revealed not the slightest sign of empathy. The Jews of *Soll und Haben* contrast strongly with the two other groups with respect to their moral standard, and apart from their immorality, the Jews are unreal, hardly human at all, and in fact no more than a kind of individualization of the prevailing prejudices about Jews. This distorted image of the Jew by two popular novelists could only have strengthened the tendency not only to pass judgment on Jews but also to think of them through the medium of preconceived notions and ideology.

Freytag's other characters reflect the various aspects of the lifestyle of their class, while the Jews only exhibit the solitary trait that categorizes them, according to the stereotyped concept, as immoral and uncultured. The Jews of these famous novels were born out of prejudices, and they doubtless further reinforced these prejudices in the readers' minds, though this may not have been the authors' intention. We do know that Gustav Freytag was an active liberal who, when the anti-Semitic movement broke out, was among those who vociferously condemned it. His view was that anti-Semitism would be halted by the adaptation of Jews to the German norms of behavior and culture. It stands to reason that when he presented a Jew in a strong negative light in his novel, his intention was to encourage adaptation. Thus the Jewish stereotype was enrolled in the service of assimilation.[6]

We find at this stage a clear link between the denigration of the Jew and the goal of adaptation, in the person of Wilhelm Marr. Marr, destined to become one of the founders of the anti-Semitic movement, was born in Hamburg in 1818 and resided in Switzerland in 1841-1845, where he joined the radical Young Germany group. On his return to Hamburg he became politically active as a writer; during the 1848 revolution, he was a member of the Council of Revolution, where he represented the atheist, social-reformist, radical position. When the tide of revolution subsided in 1852, Marr went into exile in Central America, but from 1859 on he was again politically active in his native city. Incidentally, in his political work at this time Marr had contact with Jews, some of whom were in the same camp, that of the radicals, while others, like Gabriel Riesser, were his political opponents. Thus, he was well-versed in the question of Jewish emancipation, which occupied the mind of the public all those years, especially in Hamburg. Moreover, his first wife was the daughter of an apostate Hamburg Jew—as were his second and third, but not his fourth.[7]

Marr's view of the future of the Jews and Judaism was clearly derived from his radicalism. He wanted a complete separation of Church and state. The situation in Hamburg, where the Jewish community still had the status of a corporation with legal force granted by the state, was in his eyes an anomaly that had to be abolished. This view was shared by a large segment of the community itself, which, in 1862, presented a memorandum to the communal leadership advocating the dismantling of the corporation—against the wishes of the Orthodox members. It was then that Marr wrote his polemical book *Judenspiegel*, which was directed against the Orthodox Jews, but which was interlarded with other motives to the degree that it became a general attack on Jews and Judaism. Marr argued that even the liberals among the Jews—for example, his personal and political rival Gabriel Riesser—were still deeply involved in Judaism and were not working to liberate human society from the net of religious tradition, an argument similar to that Bruno Bauer employed in his radical phase. Marr's argument hinged on racial characteristics, which, whether inherent or acquired, were clearly revealed physically, an idea explicitly based on Nordmann's theory, which will be described later.[8]

Germany, 1830-1873

Marr also drew copiously on Voltaire's Deistic moral criticism of Scripture and applied it to the Jews of his own time. At this stage, Marr had already taken hold of the principle components of the anti-Semitic ideology he was to evolve in the late 1870s. All the same, in retrospect he called his *Judenspiegel* a philo-Semitic work. Nor was this entirely untrue. The conclusion is not that Jews are without hope of improvement; on the contrary, there is an urgent need for them to shake off the burden of their past, to rid themselves of their distinctive Jewish ways and assimilate into their social environment. Clearly, anti-Semitism is still being brought into the service of assimilation.[9]

In its time, Marr's *Judenspiegel* fell flat, and his rivals in Hamburg found it unnecessary to react to it.[10] The ideas which, in the course of time and in a different context, were to reveal their hidden power of incitement, were neutralized for the time being. The 1860s and early 1870s were years in which the position and achievement of the Jews were strengthened. This does not mean that the negative image of Jews had disappeared, for it made a swift and powerful recrudescence in less than one generation. Anti-Jewish attitudes had only dropped out of sight for a time.

Robert von Mohl, an outstanding political scientist, moderately liberal and critical of Jewish emancipation, summed up the situation in 1869. He did so not in a polemic pamphlet, but in a chapter of a volume dealing with constitutional law and politics.[11] The promoters of Jewish emancipation, heedless of the real nature of the problem, von Mohl argued, had turned the former pariahs into full-fledged citizens. They did so in obedience to the abstract principle of human equality, disregarding the exceptional constitution of the Jewish group. This exceptionality expressed itself in two peculiarities, the double nationality of the Jew and his adherence to certain occupations. Von Mohl conceded that Jews might well possess the nationality of their adopted country; they would feel like Germans, French, or Italians, but at the same time they retained their Jewish nationality, their attachment to it having a dominating influence upon them. As to Jewish occupations, Jews concentrated in professions connected with trade and finance, with some expansion into artistic and intellectual activities. At any rate, they would never disperse among the whole population, sharing with the majority the toil of more burdensome and less lucrative employment.

Von Mohl saw the evolving situation as the result of a theoretical misconception and political mistakes. The political scientists had thought that a middle way was possible: granting the Jews citizenship without sharing with them the higher positions in state and society, channeling them instead into the more humble and—from the standpoint of society at large—less precarious employments. But once implemented, the steps taken led irreversibly to the full emancipation of the Jews. "Rights of liberation once granted can only be withdrawn in the wake of a complete subversion of all things in existence and not through a simple revision of legislation."[12] Von Mohl therefore dismissed in advance any possible practical consequences of his diagnosis. It was only in the service of "self-examination" (*Selbsterkentniss*) that his analysis had been offered. The reservation against Jewish emancipation was retained, though no remedy to rectify it was suggested. We have good reason to assume that this ambivalent attitude was not an idiosyncrasy of von Mohl, but rather an articulate expression of the climate of opinion prevailing in society at large. It explains the calm that descended upon Jews at that time and the storm that was to burst upon them in the not-too-distant future.

17 | The Conservatives' Rearguard Action

THE YEARS 1850-1871 were the period of the final struggle of German Jewry for formal political emancipation. The spokesmen of the 1848 revolution, assembled in the all-German Parliament of Frankfurt, proclaimed the principle that citizenship should be independent of religious affiliation. This principle had been incorporated in the constitutions granted by the respective governments—notably that of Prussia—under the pressure of circumstances. In the other states, too, concessions had been made toward full equality for Jewish citizens.[1]

The revolution having failed to achieve its objectives, the promises implied in the decisions concerning the Jews had no chance of being fully realized. Some of the liberties already enjoyed during the revolution—by citizens in general and by Jews in particular—had been canceled again; others had never even been introduced. Still, the nature of these reactionary measures was more administrative than legislative. Once the reaction toward the revolution had run its course, with the emergence of the so-called New Era in 1858, the tide turned in favor of Jewish advancement. With the unification of the northern states in 1866 and the establishment of the Reich in 1871 under the leadership of Bismarck, a new type of constitution was introduced, which, though distinctly nonrevolutionary, did embrace the principle of equality before the law for all citizens, irrespective of their religious affiliation.

In this period between the 1848 revolution and the foundation of the Reich, the Jewish problem, though still in the process of seeking an ultimate solution, had lost much of its public attention. Measures taken by the respective governments, whether favorable or unfavorable to the Jews, not having been conceived of as decisive matters of principle, did not elicit much comment for or against. The final acts of emancipation, on the other hand, were by-products of the new constitutions—the outcomes of momentous events, the Prussian-Austrian War of 1866 and the Franco-German War of 1870—and came into being almost unobserved. While during the preceding period, the 1830s and 1840s, public debates and polemics on the Jewish question were the order of the day, during the 1850s and 1860s they were almost totally absent. The *Allgemeine Zeitung des Judenthums*, the representative organ of German Jewry, could state repeatedly and with satisfaction that the previous steady flow of anti-Jewish pamphlets had become by 1865 a mere trickle.[2]

Anti-Jewish propaganda with a definite political objective was only forthcoming from the extreme right, the Prussian conservatives. Their representatives in the Landtag introduced a bill in 1852 and later in 1856 to amend the constitution to delete the principle that civil rights were independent of one's religious affiliation. In the view of the conservatives, the relevant clause of the constitution impaired the Christian character of the state and ought therefore to be deleted. The official organ of the party, the *Neue Preussiche Zeitung*, popularly known as the *Kreuzzeitung*, edited by Herman Wagener, the sponsor of the amendment to the constitution in the Landtag in 1856, did all it could to disseminate the idea of the Christian state and the concomitant exclusion of Jews from active participation in its conduct and administration. Wagener also summed up his ideas in a book on Judaism and the state (*Das Judenthum und der Staat*), the avowed purpose of which was the defense of the amendment, which failed to pass in the Landtag owing, according to Wagener's own testimony, to the "extremely vivid commotion" among Prussian Jews, who elicited no less than 264 petitions on behalf of Jewish communities.[3]

Wagener and his supporters basically adhered to the tenets of Friedrich Julius Stahl, except that in the evaluation of Jewish life they took an extremely critical view of modern developments in general and Reform Judaism in particular. Wagener tells us that he wrote his book "in association with a friend, an expert." In view of the book's intimate acquaintance with the internal problem of Judaism, it is likely that the friend was a Jewish convert; Samuel Holdheim's guess was that it was Selig Paulus Cassel.[4]

Wagener and his baptized friend wanted Jews to be loyal to their inherited tradition, for theological as well as for political reasons. The Christian doctrine expected Jews to fulfill an eschatological role on the second coming of Jesus, when the recognition of the Christian truth would lead them to exchange the Old Testament for the New; thus, in the meantime the Old Testament was to be observed by the Jews. Politically, Wagener assumed that traditionally observant Jews would more easily acquiesce in the passive role in state and society that could be allotted to them according to the concept of the Christian state. The Reform Jews and assimilationists, on the other hand, were a most dangerous social element. Their intellectual exponents applied the philosophical reinterpretation of religion to Judaism as well. Revelation, according to this view, was identical with the personal unfolding of human consciousness, and this resulted in connecting Judaism with the "widespread aim of presenting anti-Christian teachings under the guise of a religion." Jewish Reform thinkers who undermined the foundations of their own religion were, at the same time, endangering the existence of Christianity.[5]

The main danger, however, was not in the realm of theory but of social reality. Most Jews who joined a Reform community were unconcerned about the theories of the intellectuals. The great upheaval was evident in their behavior: "Once the tenacious energy of their nature has been directed away from religion, the bulk of the nation is bent only on acquisition and pleasure." They were "the representation of that Jewish degeneration that does not believe in anything but ready money and security bonds, and does not care about anything but good business." It was because of their "spiritual flabbiness and concern for familial and business connections" that conversion did not occur more often among Jews who had lost any genuine attachment to their own religion. They would perhaps not have minded at all "if the whole of Jewry would be absorbed by intermarriage with Christians." With the introduction of civil marriage by the secularized state, as in France, this was not improbable. True, even assimilated Jews seemed to object to intermarriage, but it was difficult to attribute this to religious motivation. Rather, one had to suspect "that in spite of all the lip-service to humanity and citizenship, they still intend to maintain themselves as a separate clique in order to get to the top through banding firmly together. Despite their enlightenment and denial of their Law they remain the conquering Jew."[6]

This is no doubt the voice of an apostate Jew whose despair at the inability of Judaism to stand up to new historical circumstances was at least one of the factors in bringing about his "change of heart." The conservative Christian Wagener made good use of the resentments and reflections of the former Jew. They conformed admirably to his own apprehensions of secularized Judaism, culminating, as the last sentence quoted above indicates, in the specter of the Jewish aspiration to dominate the whole world.

Herman Wagener ceased to edit the *Kreuzzeitung* in 1854 and parted company with the official leadership of the party. Instead he steered an independent course even more radically conservative. Indicative of this is his association with Bruno Bauer, who at this juncture is found, surprisingly, in the conservative camp. Wagener, for his part, would associate with anyone whose ultimate goals coincided with his own, notwithstanding differences of an ideological nature. It is therefore quite credible that the anonymous *Die Juden und der deutsche Staat* (Berlin 1861), later to be acknowledged by Johannes Nordmann as his own work, was written in collaboration with Herman Wagener.[7]

Nordmann's pamphlet went into many printings, and traces of its influence will be found in subsequent anti-Jewish publications. Its avowed political objective was to prevent Jews from holding public office—an issue still unsettled in Prussia as well as in some other German states. In justifying this demand, the author made only a fleeting reference to the Christian character of the state. He did not seem to regard a close tie between religion and state as an asset: "From a higher point of view this may appear to be a deficiency." But at any rate it was not religion as such that counted—"the myths are of no consequence." It was Christian morality that lent state and society its character, and as Jews were incapable of rising to the standard of this morality, they found themselves excluded.[8]

To substantiate his point, Nordmann set out to draw a picture of Jewish moral inferiority. Unrestrained as he was by Christian dogmatics, he took his cue from the Jewish adherence to the Old Testament, thus virtually joining the anti-Jewish trend of Deistic provenance. Nordmann declared that the proper evaluation of Biblical characters and the analysis of the Biblical teachings were better guides to Jewish mentality than haphazard observation of contemporary Jewry. Accordingly, he repeated all the charges of Jewish immorality based upon the conduct of the patriarchs and the behavior of the ancient Israelites toward other nations. The persistence of Jewish qualities through the ages is taken for granted; it is ascribed to the continuous detachment of Jews from their environment: "Seclusion and inbreeding over many thousand years strengthened the thorough domination of the race type and made the way of thought a part of it. Jewish blood and Jewish sentiment became inseparable and we have to conceive of Judaism not only as religion and congregation [*Kirche*] but also as the expression of racial peculiarity." To complete the picture, Nordmann attempts to portray the physical peculiarities of the Jewish race. The assumption is that "Jews, in contradistinction to the Germanic tribes, possess the deficiencies of the Southern races without their merits." From this premise a most disadvantageous description of the Jewish type could be concocted; Jews are simply assigned all possible physical defects and their intellectual and moral corollaries.[9]

Nordmann appears to have been the first in Germany to make the notion of race a pivot around which anti-Jewish ideology might turn. Still, at this juncture, the notion lacked the embracing significance it was to assume in later decades. It did not as yet carry with it the connotation of biological consistency and determinism. Indeed Nordmann, in spite of the pivotal role of race in his exposition, kept the door open for the Jew to join Gentile society through acceptance of Christianity. Though not of much religious significance, the conversion of the Jew would be tantamount to the "explicit avowal of his breach with the morality of his race . . . he would at the same time be detached from his tribe and made more susceptible to culture." The liberation of the Jew from his racial deficiencies was a possibility even without baptism, and Nordmann held out a hope that in the remote future the whole of Jewry might be so liberated: "We know and appreciate some Jews in whom the racial peculiarities have been reduced to such an extent that they no longer impair the human values. We are therefore very much inclined to admit exceptions . . . As for the time to come, when in a remote future a finer morality will enter into the heart of the chosen people . . . and the moral elevation of centuries will prove that it has broken with the inheritance of millenia . . . then our later descendants will have no possible reason to make a distinction between Germans and Jews."[10]

In view of the convergence between the racial concept and traditional expectations, it is quite understandable why Nordmann's exposition appealed to conservatives of Wagener's breed. It is less obvious how Wagener could stomach the much more radical, if less explicit, theorizations of Bruno Bauer. Still, the close cooperation between the two men is an overt fact. Both Wagener and Bauer shifted from their former positions and joined in an endeavor to influence society, through dissemination of their critical, conservative ideas. Two different vehicles were established by Wagener for this purpose; the periodical *Die Berliner Revue* and the encyclopedia *Staats und Gesellschaftslexikon*. In the periodical Bauer commented on current affairs as they occurred, and in the encyclopedia he furnished his readers with information on historical and philosophical subjects. Here and there he revealed an absolutely negative attitude toward Jews and Judaism past and present.[11]

Bauer turned his back on his Young Hegelian past and transferred his anti-Jewish sentiments into the context of his new conservative Weltanschauung, where they became even sharper than before. For him, criticism and even outright detraction of things Jewish became a habit bordering on obsession. The psychological process that led to this fixation is not sufficiently clear, but the mechanism of its functioning is visible enough. Bauer takes pleasure in deriding Judaism, dubbing Jews base, barren, and obsolete; he fixes on them any negative characteristic possible in whatever context he happens to encounter it.

The Conservatives' Rearguard Action

In Wagener's encyclopedia, Bruno Bauer wrote all the articles pertaining to Jews and Judaism and thus found ample opportunity to pass judgment on them. No Jew passes the tests of probity or originality. Heine and Börne "reveal only that repulsive insolence which makes it possible to absorb only a superficial tinge of the German environment and even that they only thresh about and dilute." Moses Mendelssohn exemplifies the Jew whose only title to honor derives "from an intercourse with the most important man of society which he maintains until such a time that he thinks it fit for himself to step to the head." This is a good example of how negative judgment on an individual Jew is extended to the Jew as a type, or rather, how the preconceived characteristics of the type are attached to the individual. The articles devoted to individual Jews are not confined to characterizing their subjects; judgments on Jews and Judaism in general are included. Then, there are the lengthy articles on Jewish history in different periods, where Bauer could expand at will. His article on the last period, called "Das Judenthum in der Fremde" ("Judaism abroad"), he found worth publishing (1863) as a separate pamphlet.[12]

Bauer's conception of Jewish history, its division into periods and the spiritual evaluation of them, apparently follows the Christian theological tradition, and it is under the cover of the traditional concepts that he clandestinely introduces his own idiosyncrasies. The first sign of submission to the Christian tradition is Bauer's treatment of the Biblical period. He finds nothing to impugn in the actions of the Old Testament heroes. The atrocities of the conquest of Canaan in the Book of Joshua are found to be providential and morally unimpeachable. This represents, no doubt, a reversion by Bauer to his pristine youthful attitude, and a tacit repudiation of his radical period, during which, following in the footsteps of the Deists, he made biting attacks on Biblical Judaism. It is not easy to decide whether, as suggested by his last biographer, Bauer assumed this forbearing attitude only in view of the conservative element among whom he now found himself. This change certainly did not involve a shift in his general attitude toward Judaism.[13]

At any rate, Bauer carried over all the charges against Judaism from his radical to his conservative phase, adding a few new ones, such as the putative Jewish inclination to revolutionize the world. Jews had acclaimed all modern revolutions, be they in France, Poland, Hungary, or Italy, with rejoicing. This, in Bauer's interpretation, was only an expression of the resentment against the Christian world order that had been inherent in Judaism ever since it was displaced from its dominant position by Christianity: "The Jew, the eternal Jew, the purest and most unadulterated representative of antiquity, the bearer of rancor and anger over the history of two millennia that was made without him and against his will is therefore a friend of every revolution." Thus, the widespread bias against Jews because of their alleged preponderance in revolutionary movements was given a Christian historical-philosophical sanction. Presented in the opening paragraph of the pamphlet *Das Judenthum in der Fremde*, this theory could not fail to strike a sympathetic chord in the heart of the conservative reader. For other people, however, in the 1860s, a revolutionary attitude was counted as a virtue rather than a vice; Bauer himself certainly did not lack admiration for the combatants who tried to renew European society through redeeming revolutionary acts. To forestall the pride of some Jews at their contributions to revolution, Bauer, at the close of his treatise, goes out of his way to prove that the practical participation of Jews in the 1848 revolution in Vienna, Budapest, or Berlin was negligible. Bauer wished to have it both ways. The Jews were the culprits of the revolution insofar as it was considered as an illegitimate interference in the traditional order. At the same time, their claim to have shared in its preparation was rejected where it was conceived of as a redeeming act. Though it was not their work, "Jews greeted the convulsion of the Christian world-order as the labor pains of their messianic time and the unmistakable harbinger of their world domination."[14]

Jews were ascribed the same passive but expectant attitude toward the Enlightenment that had opened European society to them. They made no original contribution to its emergence—not even Spinoza's philosophy was acknowledged as such—but they seized upon it as the vehicle that would carry them to their expected dominance of the world.[15]

The Jewish dream of world domination had already occupied Bauer's mind when he was writing his *Judenfrage* in 1842. At that time the dream had been derided as a chimerical expectation projected by the Jews themselves into the distant messianic future. Two decades later, noting the progress the Jews had made, Bauer described the dream as an immediate ambition of the Jews and an acute danger to the Gentile world. This prognosis of the Judenherschaft, "Jewish domination," was based not only and not primarily on the increasing wealth of the Jews. It was, rather, the supplanting of the "Christian order" by "humanistic fantasies" that stamped "a Jewish character upon the present time." Bauer hastened to assure the reader that humanism was in fact a product of Christian spirituality, as evidenced by the intellectual struggle of poets and thinkers since the time of the Reformation. It had, however, been mistakenly presented as its very contradiction and thus delivered into the hands of Jews to exploit for their own egoistic purposes.[16]

Resorting to the traditional Christian vocabulary, Bauer succeeded in lending the Jewish-Gentile dichotomy a spiritual significance. But far from being consistent in this, he drifted easily into a concept with a clearly non-theological basis. Alongside the Jewish-Christian confrontation, there appears in the course of his deliberations the Jewish-German tension, and in discussing the special nature of the body and soul of the Jews, the terms "blood" and "race" are repeatedly applied. These had not yet become the central concepts of an elaborate theory, but their use is indicative of the tendency to comprehend Jewish physiognomy and mentality as phenomena independent of the Jewish connection with Christianity. By the same token, the projection of contemporary Jewish peculiarities into the past became a logically cogent consequence: "The Jewish tribe did possess a different kind of blood from the Christian people of Europe. It had a different body and constitution; other inclinations and longings. Moreover, not unconnected with the different physical body was that alienation to which it was doomed not just since the destruction of Jerusalem but from the very beginning of its existence."[17]

In deriding the Jews as a race, Bauer was undoubtedly influenced by Nordmann's book. Since both worked under the influence of Wagener, each must have known what the other had written. Moreover, traces of Nordmann's influence on Bauer may be discerned in the details of his thought, despite the fact that in style and breadth of knowledge Bauer immeasurably surpassed his mentor. Essentially, Bauer held the view that the Jew combined in himself the defects of various races, and he came to dub the Jew a "white Negro." The assumption of the Jew's racial inferiority now served as a support for the negative cultural and moral evaluation of him. The penetration of this inferior minority into the ranks of European peoples, generally, and the Germans in particular, formed the central theme of his book, and, as he himself stated, robbed him of his equanimity.[18]

Bruno Bauer, like Richard Wagner before him, termed the cultural development of the recent decade "Judaization" (Verjüdelung). The main responsibility for this, however, did not rest with the Jews but with the Gentiles: "It cannot be said that the Jews obtruded themselves upon us when in the middle of the last century they appeared for the first time in society; rather it was us who called and introduced them and . . . made them presumptuous . . . We, we alone, and above all we Germans, are to be blamed that we have now to defend ourselves against the Jews."[19]

What practical form this defense should take, Bauer does not spell out. As in all his comments on public life, his criticism of the role of the Jews is marked by acute though arbitrary analysis, rather than the prescription of practical solutions. He explicitly defines his role in the preface of the pamphlet Das Judenthum in den Fremde as being to offer a cogent analysis of the situation, the lack of which until now had obviated the search for practical solutions. On the basis of the theory he presented, a solution could now be found—by others.[20]

In fact, instead of paving the way for a solution, Bauer's theory helped prevent one. In his radical period, though most critical of the petrified Jewish tradition, Bauer did not exclude the hope that Jews and Gentiles could be united in common humanity once both parties rid themselves of their respective religious fantasies. But when he came to recognize the positive role of Christianity in supporting the traditional order, this contingency was eliminated. Moreover, the racial interpretation of Jewish peculiarities disavowed the Christian expectation of the ultimate conversion of the Jews—the hoped-for result of Jewish emancipation in the imagination of many of its proponents. In contrast to them, Bauer never revealed any desire to see Jews converted to Christianity; he regarded them as an absolutely unassimilable social element, and he faced the logical consequences of his conviction.

In the closing paragraph of his pamphlet, Bauer comes as close as possible to an overt confession of his failure to offer a practical solution to the Jewish problem. Regarding the political status of the Jews, he perfunctorily endorses the official program of the Prussian conservatives. This boiled down to the request that the prevailing practice of excluding Jews from public office be formalized by legislation. Characteristically, Bauer did not base his endorsement on the concept of the Christian state as the conservatives had. Instead, he declared it a distortion of the German honor "to let the offices of dignity and conscience degenerate into a business" by delivering them into the hands of the Jews.[21]

But, whatever the justification, the restraint on the political advancement of the Jews was no answer to the problem posed by Bauer's radical criticism. Faced with a glaring discrepancy in his thought, between outright condemnation of Jewish existence and relative toleration of it, Bauer in the end declares Jews to be a kind of necessary evil, owing to their "profane and businesslike worldly sense [*Weltsinn*]," without which society could not well function: "The Lord of this world needs the Jews in order to accomplish his finite and profane objectives and his need is so strong that by now he does partly recruit his army from the ranks of Christians as well; were it not for the Jews we all would be constrained to take their place." This last sentence of Bauer's long treatise is clearly an anticlimax. It is an indication of the comparative harmlessness of a radical ideology when social reality fails to conform with it. Jewish advancement was so evident in the 1860s, owing to the political and social forces at work, that even an exponent of the radical ideology recoiled from drawing conclusions that were obviously at odds with social reality. Others could afford simply to ignore Bauer's ideology. It is a fact that while Bauer's *Judenfrage* in 1843, as we have seen, elicited a whole series of responses, his pamphlet of 1863 passed absolutely unnoticed. In historical retrospect, however, Bauer's radical thinking anticipates a trend that was destined to be sadly effective in a later time of changing circumstances.[22]

Wagener's conservative circle was not the only refuge for the anti-Jewish spirit in an age in which, on the general social scene, opposition to Judaism seemed to be progressively disappearing. Richard Wagner's "Judaism in Music" was repeatedly reissued—under the author's name—beginning in 1869. In 1871 Osman Bey's pamphlet *The Conquest of the World by the Jews* was published in Basel, first in French and immediately thereafter in German. At first, the pamphlet was ignored despite its clamorous title. It only became a widely disseminated instrument of propaganda with the rise of the anti-Semitic movement at the close of the 1870s. This is also what happened with the *Talmudjude* of August Rohling: when it first appeared in Münster in 1871 it attracted some attention, but it was only in the 1880s that it became the classic text of religiously oriented anti-Semitism, especially in Austria and Hungary.[23]

Rohling's assault on Judaism started in 1871 in his preface to a commentary on the Psalms, in which he collected several allusions from the Talmud that bore witness to a contempt for the Gentiles and demonstrated the manner in which Jews discriminated against them by virtue of Talmudic law. Some of these statements of this professor in the theological faculty of Münster Academy were quoted in the local paper, the *Westfälischer Merkur*. They aroused excitement in the Jewish community, and a controversy started between Rohling and Dr. Theodor Kroner, principal of the Jewish Teachers Seminary at Münster; they exchanged words first in the daily paper and afterward in separate pamphlets. Even before the outbreak of the anti-Semitic movement, Rohling's *Talmudjude* ran through several revisions and editions, ultimately becoming one of the most scathing anti-Jewish publications. As its author himself admitted, the book followed in the footsteps of Eisenmenger and other authors. However, this does not mean that Rohling was not himself able to read the Talmudic sources, as was charged against him in a subsequent disputation in Vienna. In his debate with Dr. Kroner, the latter did not always have the better of it. We have here a phenomenon similar to that of Eisenmenger: a Christian scholar—although certainly not of the stature of Eisenmenger—read the Hebrew texts correctly, but nevertheless blundered very seriously in the conclusions he derived from them.[24]

Rohling was an orthodox Catholic. His opposition to Talmudic Judaism was theological. According to his faith, Jews must adhere to the Mosaic Law as written or accept the teachings of Jesus, which were the legitimate continuation of the first revelation. Jews who adhered to the Talmud had sundered themselves from the Old Testament without attaining the level of the New Testament. The law by which they abided was a human invention, and it was not adapted to guide them to religious truth or moral action. On the contrary, the Talmudic tradition, since it was nothing but a collection of human opinions, was a supple instrument for justifying every superstitious idea, corruption, and iniquity. Rohling's declared objective was to persuade the Jews of their error and move them to abandon their religion and embrace Christianity. He sought to attain his objective by gathering extracts from the sources of the Jewish religion and, if not actually forging them, at any rate misrepresenting them and distorting the meaning they held for those who adhered to them. The naive reader of the pamphlet would see it as a poisonous attack on the Jewish religion and its adherents. Nevertheless, in its time, the influence of the pamphlet was limited. It only gained the attention of the Catholic press; and the *Allgemeine Zeitung des Judenthum*, the principal voice of the Jews, dismissed it as a local Münster phenomenon. Opposition to Judaism was not absent, but at this stage it did seem to have been swept into a corner.[25]

Part V: Austria-Hungary, 1780-1880

18|The Austrian Prelude

AUSTRIA WAS the first country in Europe to recognize, through Joseph II's Edict of Tolerance in 1782, the right of Jews to become naturalized subjects. However, the edict was far from granting the Jews more than a carefully circumscribed living space and choice of occupation, with a concomitant obligation to send their children to modern schools and to adapt culturally in other ways. Then, while in other European countries—France, Holland, Prussia, and the other German states—Jews made incisive advances toward full legal integration, Austrian Jewry remained for decades in the legal position in which the edict of 1782 had placed it. Only the revolution of 1848-1849 compelled the imperial government to budge from its extreme conservative position on the Jewish question as well as other overdue social and political issues. The constitution extracted by the revolutionaries granted equal rights to all citizens independent of their religious affiliation—a concession from which the government was quick to retreat once the revolution had been suppressed. Still, some of the most vexatious measures—the restrictions on the number of families to be established in Bohemia and Moravia, the strict control on the Jewish population of the capital and the prohibition against establishing a Jewish community there—were not reintroduced. In the following decades, until the granting of full emancipation in 1867 in the wake of the Austrian defeat by Prussia, were transitional; legal restrictions were loosened while formal emancipation was still withheld.[1]

The Jewish situation during the period of transition from 1782 to 1867 is characterized by the deep discrepancy between the factual conditions and their formal acknowledgment by the authorities. This was an attitude not untypical of the Austrian government and its agencies in general. In spite of the far-reaching legal restrictions, Jews had, even before the revolution of 1848, entered into positions barred to them according to the letter of the law. Vienna, theoretically closed to Jews except for those specially privileged, harbored thousands, to whose presence the authorities willingly closed their eyes. The upsurge in commerce and industry, to which Jews made a conspicuous contribution, rendered the presence of Jews in the capital an unavoidable necessity. The authorities were reluctant to change the laws, preferring circumvention.[2] Still, the discrepancy between factual conditions and their disregard by the law was too glaring to last. No wonder that the call for full emancipation voiced by Jews and their supporters, especially in the aftermath of the 1848 revolution, gained in weight and importance, ultimately achieving its final goal.

At the same time, there was no lack of opposition to Jewish advancement. Arising initially in response to Joseph II's Edict of Tolerance, it followed the progress of Jewish emancipation step by step. Ingrained anti-Jewish prejudices could not be expected to suddenly disappear in a country deeply immersed in Christian tradition. Yet, true to the climate of opinion prevailing in Joseph's era, the opponents often based their arguments on rationalistic grounds. Quoting Voltaire, a pamphleteer of Prague in 1782 declared that "a nation that got as far as being hated by all nations must necessarily have brought upon itself that hatred by its own fault." The author contended, as did another writer in Vienna a year earlier, that Jews would have to change their professions and moral habits before their acceptance into state and society could be seriously considered.[3]

Jews indeed changed, but not in the direction their critics had expected. Jews expanded their economic activity, the process of slow but steady industrialization and modernization having offered unheard-of opportunities in traditionally Jewish occupations: banking, trade, and capitalistic investment. Having gained access to modern educational facilities, Jews began to take an active part in the intellectual life of the great cities. They became conspicuous in the professions—especially law and medicine—as well as in the creation and promotion of the public press. Their initial advances in all these fields were made in the decades during which Jews were still laboring under legal and political disabilities. They may well have regarded their successes as a prelude to complete acceptance by society and full legal and political emancipation.[4] Their opponents, however, drew different conclusions from these preliminary experiments in cooperation with Jews under comparatively equal conditions. They viewed them as ominous indications of possible future developments.

The Austrian Prelude

Writing "On the Sources of Present Medical Discontent" in 1842 in the *Medizinische Jahrbücher des kais. königlichen österreichischen Staates*, Anton E. von Rosas found the disproportionate increase in Jewish doctors the main reason for the general deterioration of the profession. "Discounting the extremely few honorable exceptions," the Jewish doctors were said to be "inclined to charlatanism." Having been addicted for two thousand years to the spirit of mercantilism and having accepted material gain as the guideline for action, how could a Jew indeed rise to the ethical standard of "self-abnegation," indispensable for the medical profession. Conclusion: "The Israelite as he is may and should become peasant, artisan, artist, indeed anything in the world rather than doctor, jurist, or theologian for Christians." A preconceived notion of Jewish mentality served here as an ideological weapon in defense of the exclusive right of Christians to certain professions then endangered by Jewish competition.[5]

Even where the fact of Jewish achievement was conceded, its evaluation turned on the image of the Jews and the conception of their position in Gentile society. Since these were unfavorable, the very fact of Jewish success could easily be converted into an argument against legal emancipation, which would have been conducive to further Jewish advancement. To combat the request of Bohemian Jewry for the abolishment of a special Jewish tax imposed by the Empress Maria Theresa, a contributor to the *Revue österreichischer Zustände* (1842) actually adduced the immense success of Jews in "trade and business" (*Handel und Wandel*) to counter the Jewish demand. Jews were better off than any other part of the population. Jews were proud of their achievement and boasted of having brought the country's industry to a flourishing stage. This being true, it should not be put to their credit. For the real work in the factories was being done by Christians, while Jews only condescended to do the managing and supervision. Between the Jewish industrialist and his laborers, there was "no bond . . . of love or thanks but only that of self-interest. Whatever the relations might be, they both remained alien to each other, alien in faith, alien in love." Whatever advantage a Jew would derive from his work in the country and by whatever means, it would always remain in the nature of usurpation: "The benefits of a commonwealth should be allotted only to its inhabitants and not to the aliens, who may only claim protection but no rights."[6]

When accused by a critic of religious intolerance, the author of the article revealed himself as Count Ferdinand Schirnding, well known for his *Österreich im Jahre 1840*, a survey of the political, social, and cultural conditions of the Austrian empire where he had first presented his views on the Jewish question. Three years later, he found another opportunity

225

to return to the subject—the three versions representing a rejection of the Jewish claim to citizenship and equality in an ascending curve of animosi-ty.[7] A destitute aristocrat, Schirnding counted as a liberal, and his anti-Jewish arguments, too, are strongly reminiscent of those of his German counterparts of similar provenance (see Chapter 12).[8] Schirnding's main objection against Jews and his reason for opposing emancipation was Jewish economic, social, cultural, and religious exclusiveness. The phrase "state within the state" is a recurring formula in the count's writings and is repeatedly explained and expounded in all its aspects. In brief, once again it was the perception of Jews as a foreign social entity that was at the root of their opponents' unwillingness to accept them as equals. Once they were conceived of as strangers, no economic or other achievement was to their credit: rather, they counted against them as trespasses on the sphere of life of the autochthonous population.[9]

The liberal feature of this otherwise radical rejection of Jews and Judaism consisted of a theoretical acceptance of Jews on condition of the dissolution of the Jewish social entity. The instrument of dissolution was occupational dispersion and intermarriage. Wealth and education raised the status of the Jew but failed to make him eligible for posts and positions that were the domain of full citizens. "If the Jewish people wishes to be otherwise emancipated, then it must first amalgamate with the blood of Christianity." It must also give up its addiction to trade, finance, and the scholarly and artistic professions. "As long as it does not engage in agriculture and handicraft and as long as it separates itself in the close bond of internal marriage and the unification of blood, so long is the emancipa-tion of Judaism unthinkable."[10]

In proposing intermarriage between Jews and Christians, Schirnding knowingly put himself into conflict with Catholic orthodoxy. This lends some credibility to his repeated assurance that it was not the religious divi-sion between Jews and their neighbors that made him adopt the stand he did. On the intellectual level, liberals like him, following the trend initiated by Joseph II, transcended the position of the Catholic Church. Still, traces of the Christian teachings persisted, as was evident in Schirnding's attitude toward Jews and Judaism on the practical level. Although he did not, in fact, demand that Jews convert, he nevertheless could not see any way that they could persist in their Judaism, even in its Reform version. Jewish emancipation was conditional upon "acclimatization to Christianity." There could be only one explanation of this demand: Schirnding and others like him saw in the spreading culture a secular or semisecular transmutation of Christianity. Into this he sought to envisage the Jews, in theory at least, being swallowed up and disappearing.[11]

A more radical effort to eliminate Catholic influence from public life emerged in Austria only in the course of the 1848 revolution, to be answered immediately by an even more emphatic assertion of Catholic exclusivity. The laicization of the state being a declared aim of the revolution, Jewish emancipation seemed to be a necessary by-product of the upheaval. Still, it became an issue passionately discussed in leaflets and newspapers, which, with the abolition of censorship, flooded the capital. Many of the initiators of and contributors to the newly established press organs were Jews. Similarly, among the active participants in the revolution, the number of Jews exceeded by far their percentage of the population. Barely tolerated in the preceding years, Jewish intellectuals thought to mold Austrian society into a shape that would allow them unlimited freedom of activity.[12]

However, the heightened involvement of Jews in events of public interest elicited a negative reaction. The conspicuous part played by Jews in revolutionary activities had been used by the opponents of the revolution to discredit it. Jews were denounced as having instigated all the unrest in the hope of achieving what had been justly denied them as long as law and order reigned supreme.[13] Some argued for absolute negation of Jewish rights; Quirin Endlich who charged in a vitriolic pamphlet that instead of contributing to the welfare of the state, Jews exploited it for their own benefit. The repetition of such arguments became a habit, especially in periodicals and newspapers with a pronounced conservative and Catholic stance: for instance, the *Wiener Kirchenzeitung*, launched during the revolution by Sebastian Brunner, which continued to be published during the following decades of relative peacefulness and prosperity for Austrian Jewry. An ordained priest and preacher in the church of Vienna University, Brunner became the leading figure of militant neo-Catholicism in Austria. Resorting to modern terminology in the defense of Catholic doctrine and praxis, he came near to the type of the French publicist, common in France since the Restoration period. Like them, he tried to retain or recapture the former position of the Church in state and society, combating in the process of this struggle all manifestations of modernity. Naturally, Jewish emancipation and social advancement came in for censure.[14]

Condemnation, anti-Jewish remarks, and even outright defamation were scattered throughout the many literary works of Brunner. The *Wiener Kirchenzeitung* followed the political and social events in Austria as well as abroad and commented on them in the spirit of its editor. Jews and Judaism continued to serve as an ever-intriguing subject. The readers of the periodical were taught to regard Jews as the capital foe of the Catholic Church and the promoters of all that was evil and destructive in modern society.

Behind this anti-Jewish propaganda lurks, of course, the theological conception of the Jewish position in the world in Christian times. Occasionally this conception comes to the fore, as, for instance, in Brunner's introduction to the German translation of Louis Rupert's *L'Église et la synagogue*, prepared and published by him in 1864. Confessing full agreement with the views of the French theologian—who went so far as accepting the charge of Jewish ritual murder—Brunner epitomized his own evaluation of Jewish-Christian relations. Rupert's arguments were recommended as an answer to the Jewish-liberal accusation that the Church engendered the spirit of intolerance. The truth, according to Rupert and Brunner, was that the Church had always simply defended itself against the Jews' perennial claim to superiority, the latest manifestation of which was the seizure of both "the mastery of money and journalism in many states in Eastern and Central Europe." Jews were being assisted in their campaign by "enemies of Christian truth" among people "born in the womb of Christianity." It was the Jews, or rather Judaism as a spiritual entity, that always inspired "animosity and intolerance." "These are rooted in the spirit of the ancient synagogue, they are the natural product of the dark spirit that prevails in the Talmud . . . The synagogue takes upon itself the responsibility *for the way of action of its adepts.* For it is itself that instills into the Jew the inimical spirit against Christians as well as other nations."[15]

This is a concise formulation of the traditional appraisal of Talmudic Judaism, differing from that of Eisenmenger only in its more sophisticated wording. It justifies the fate the Jews have suffered at the hands of Christians. At the same time, it dismisses the modern attempts of Jews and Gentiles to change the Jewish position, through emancipation and social integration. The only way left for Jews to extricate themselves from their predicament is to accept Christianity. The closing sentence of Brunner's preface to Rupert's treatise is an appeal to the intelligent Jew to draw the right conclusion from the lesson contained in the book's argument, that is, to convert.[16]

In 1866, the editorship of the *Kirchenzeitung* passed into the hands of Albert Wiesinger, and the organ steered an even more radical course of anti-Jewish propaganda, at least as far as style and phraseology were concerned. Wiesinger was a popular writer, catering to the taste of a lower class of Catholic believers. In 1870 he gathered around him a group of like-minded authors for the publication of a series of pamphlets, the avowed purpose of which was the strengthening of the Catholic faith and the loyalty of the unsophisticated masses. The means by which this objective was to be achieved was the debunking and condemnation of what passed in state and society for liberal, modern, or progressive. Jews and Judaism were repeatedly discussed in these brochures, some of which were dedicated entirely to some aspect of the Jewish problem. The tone of reference was always critical or even inimical. The contents were the time-honored charges of the Christian tradition or their modern variation. The title of Wiesinger's own pamphlet, *Poor Christians and Starvelings, Jewish Capitalists and Spendthrifts*, characterizes the prevailing slant of these publications. In the headlines of another pamphlet the term *Judenpresse* ("Jewish press") appears.[17]

This propaganda seized upon the increased activity of Jews in advancing the economy beyond its traditional scope and their creation of vehicles for the expression of secular sentiments. These two processes were a source of bitterness to church-loyal conservatives and were even more strongly condemned because of the involvement of Jews in both of them. This anti-Jewish propaganda had no equal in other European lands in the liberal era, either for quantity or virulence. Despite all this, in its time it did not secure much attention. In 1860 Ignatz Kuranda, the editor of the *Ost Deutsche Post* and a noted public personality (later head of the Vienna Jewish community) attacked Sebastian Brunner sharply in his paper. When sued for this, he proved that Brunner had drawn from sources like Eisenmenger in order to calumniate the Jewish citizens. Kuranda was acquitted.[18]

In general, not much weight was attached to propaganda emanating from clerical sources. A leading article in the Jewish newspaper *Neuzeit* in 1872 ridiculed Wiesinger's *Kirchenzeitung*, saying it was read by Jews only for entertainment. It is doubtful whether this surmise was correct, but it does indicate the measure of Jewish self-confidence at that time. Since that propaganda was tied up with the Church, it was looked upon as a backward cultural phenomenon that was bound to disappear in the course of time.[19]

19|The Hungarian Prelude

IN THE LAST DECADES of the eighteenth century, Hungarian Jewry consisted of less than a hundred thousand souls, most of them scattered in villages and hamlets where they had been permitted to reside by the nobility or the magnates, the feudal lords of these estates. Only a small portion of these Jews were descendants of the medieval inhabitants of Hungary. Most of them had immigrated more recently from Bohemia and Moravia, the patrimonial dominion of the emperor in the West, or from neighboring Galicia in the North. Except for those who received special royal permits, Jews were absolutely excluded from most of the cities that were incorporated on the basis of royal charters. Only in towns under the direct jurisdiction of the landed aristocracy, such as Bratislava, which was owned by the Palfys, or Eisenstadt and the neighboring "seven communities" under the auspices of the Esterhazys, could larger Jewish communities develop.[1]

The formative stage of Hungarian Jewry was the period from the Edict of Tolerance by Joseph II until the formal emancipation in 1867. This period is characterized by a rapid growth in the Jewish population through natural increase and continuous immigration, and a corresponding expansion of the area in which Jews were permitted to live. These developments were a direct result, or rather an integral part, of the ongoing reform of the constitution, as well as economic, social, and cultural life, in Hungary.[2]

Although the reforms of Joseph II served to modernize Hungary, the process took a different course than that anticipated by its initiators. Instead of strengthening the ties that bound Hungary to the imperial center in

The Hungarian Prelude

Vienna, the reforms of Hungarian life and institutions tended to weaken or sever those ties. Rising nationalism added additional impetus to the modernization process, fostering and sanctioning the dissolution of traditional institutional structures and time-honored patterns of social and cultural life. It was in the name of the national renaissance that the introduction of new modes of economic behavior, social encounter, and political alignment were demanded. The removal of the physical and legal restrictions on Jews, and the admittance of their capital, their experience, and ingenuity to whatever purpose they might usefully be applied, were among the postulates of liberal national reformers.[3]

Some decisive changes in the Jewish situation were in fact achieved before the reform movement came to its culmination—and its temporary reversal—in the revolution of 1848. The most important change was the decision of the Hungarian Diet of 1838-1840 to grant Jews almost total residential mobility, opening the way for settlement in all towns except the few that were engaged in mining of metal. This decision paved the way for the establishment of most of the urban Jewish communities of Hungary, which drew into their orbit Jews from nearby villages, as well as the continuous stream of immigrants from the west and north.[4]

These newly established communities, along with the old ones, soon became scenes of strife and conflict between those who wanted to adapt to the new conditions and those who adhered to the inherited tradition. The proponents of adaptation identified themselves with the aspirations of the Hungarian patriots and became the standard-bearers of both the Hungarian national renaissance and Jewish assimilation. On the other hand, the traditionalists, though not unmindful of the tremendous improvement in the Jewish situation, resisted any change in what they regarded as essential to Jewish communal and private life.[5]

Though not unparalleled by what transpired in France and Germany some decades earlier, the dissension in the Hungarian Jewish communities was particularly grave. Warned by what had occurred in the west, the traditionalists, led by the strong personality of the Rabbi of Bratislava, Moses Sofer, who was himself of German origin, attempted to forestall the sweeping erosion of Jewish tradition. They developed an ideological position and erected institutional barriers behind which they could entrench themselves. These neotraditionalists were assisted by the majority of Hungarian Jewry in the northern districts, who were mostly of Galician origin and Hassidic persuasion and were deeply enmeshed in Jewish popular culture.[6]

The presence of the traditional Jews within Hungarian Jewry has to be taken into account in order to understand the nature of the debate on the possible integration of Jews into the Hungarian nation, which was taking place during the period of reform. The cultural gulf that separated the traditional Jew from society at large appeared insurmountable, and the negative image of the Jew tended to be reinforced rather than diminished through actual contact. The Jew appeared to be ethnically foreign, morally suspect, culturally unassimilable. Surveying the causes of the destitution of the Hungarian peasants in the eighteenth century, Lajos Kossuth, who was to be the leader of the 1848 revolution, found the ubiquity of the Jewish tavernkeeper, who allegedly seduced the peasants to drunkenness and thriftlessness, one of the main factors.[7] Although Kossuth claimed to base his observations on firsthand experience, there is no doubt that inherited prejudice also contributed to this generalization. Indeed, in passing judgment on Jewish behavior, Kossuth did not limit himself to the Jews he may have encountered in the northern counties, the scene of his early life. He spoke about the Jewish people in all places and ages, pitying them because of their homelessness and sufferings, and condemning them at the same time for their nasty traits, which they had developed as if to take revenge on their persecutors for their terrible sufferings: "This group of people which . . . has been preserved through the centuries without having merged with the nations among which it lived, like the fungus that absorbs the nourishing moisture of the vegetation. It has not even given a thought to nationalism."[8] As the last words indicate, Kossuth thought the Jews were totally remote from any sense of common national identity with the people among whom they lived. Accordingly, he discounted them as a possible constituent of the Hungarian nation, which was to be recreated by the national renaissance. As we shall see later, he reversed his position on this matter in later years, but similar attitudes were held by other prominent Hungarian nationalists, notably Count István Széchenyi, who was both the associate and the opponent of Kossuth.

Count Széchenyi initiated most of the ideas of reform that were destined to transform Hungarian society from a collection of rigidly structured estates into a community that, at least on principle, would allow for individual mobility, foster social contact between the members of different classes, and welcome innovative ideas in economic, scientific, and intellectual life. Born in Vienna in 1791 into the family of one of the great magnates of the realm, István absorbed most of the seminal ideas of his age through reading, and, more importantly, through personal contacts during his travels in the more advanced countries of Europe. Still, what was needed was the creative imagination of a genius to apply these ideas to the peculiar conditions of Hungarian society. What lent focus to Széchenyi's ideas was his faith in the national renaissance of Hungary, which he sustained in the face of the dismal and disheartening reality. This modernized aristocrat combined romantic nationalism with liberalism and the commitment to a humanistic Catholic Christianity. With this intellectual baggage, Széchenyi's attitude toward Jews and Judaism is not too difficult to explain.[9]

Through his European connections, Széchenyi had also come into contact with some of the Jewish parvenus, who, at that time, had already reached the fringes of upper-echelon Gentile society without necessarily having succeeded in dissipating anti-Jewish prejudices. At the Rothschilds in Paris in 1825 he met Alexander von Humboldt and disliked him, not least because the famous scholar and traveler "seemed to be an admirer and obedient servant of the Jew with whom he dined."[10] And this is not the only instance in which the designation "Jew" was used for personalities who found their way into his diary. In this he unmistakably revealed his approval of a formula by which the Gentile partner, by denying the Jew his individuality, continued to demonstrate his social distance from him. This practice was on the wane at this time, and Széchenyi would have avoided it publicly. Despite his personal view, he considered it useful to include educated Jews in the circle of the social elite from which the impetus for social reform would emerge. To facilitate the creation of such circles, the young count founded the National Casino in Budapest, which he expected would be emulated in the principal towns of the country, and he wanted to admit Jews to the casino but was unsuccessful because of the opposition of other members.[11]

Such social leniency was obviously intended for only a select few Jews, and it was a far cry from admitting Jews into the body of the Hungarian nation. The human substance for this body was to derive, first and foremost, from Hungarian stock. Still, Széchenyi's concept of nationality was not tied to the notion of race. The main factor in the renaissance of the nation was the revival of the neglected national language. Hungarian nationalism tended to be identified by Széchenyi and his contemporaries with a commitment to the Hungarian tongue. As a language can be adopted, they could not easily exclude the descendants of other ethnic groups from joining the nation. Indeed, it was through the process of linguistic assimilation—which the most radical Magyars argued should be forcibly imposed—that the Hungarian patriots expected to solve the problem of the other nationalities—the Slovaks, the Rumanians, the Germans, and others—whose presence among the Hungarians seemed to endanger national unity. Széchenyi, although opposed to forced assimilation, would not have rejected voluntary Magyarization of the other nationalities—with the exception of the Jews.[12]

Széchenyi aired his views on the Jewish question twice, once in 1839 in a gathering of the parliamentary representatives of the county of Pest in advance of the session of the Parliament of that year; the second in 1844, when the issue of Jewish emancipation was on the agenda of the Parliament. The full text of his second deliberation has been preserved, but of the first we possess only a summary of a police report.[13] Still, the two speeches complement each other and are revealing enough to convey Széchenyi's viewpoint and his ideological motivations.

Széchenyi conceded that Jews had made an effort to learn the Hungarian language, but he dismissed it as mere affectation or a studied device for the sake of the coveted emancipation. He did not accept it as the expression of the Jewish desire to become a part of the Hungarian nation. Jews were, in his estimate, too deeply imbued by the German spirit, the main obstacle to the Hungarian national renaissance. They could not be assimilated into the Hungarian nation, which was, owing to its Asian origin, of a unique oriental character.[14]

No doubt Széchenyi, perhaps unwittingly, conceived of a gulf separating Jews and Hungarians and tried to account for it in rational terms. This conception comes to the fore even more clearly in his observations on the subject at the Diet of 1844. Responding to the arguments of the supporters of Jewish emancipation, he rejected their humanitarian appeal on the grounds that obligation to one's own race must take priority. The granting of full civil rights to the Jews, at least at that juncture, would have endangered the Hungarian regeneration. In this respect, Hungary was unable to follow the example of France and England, who did emancipate their Jewish communities. The percentage of Jews in those countries, however, was negligible, while in Hungary the number of Jews was too great to be absorbed without damage to the Hungarian national character. It was in that connection that Széchenyi used the much-quoted simile of the bottle of ink that would leave no traces if poured into the ocean, but if added to a bowl of soup would render it unpalatable. This sounds like a purely quantitative argument, but a qualitative differentiation appears as well. There are significant differences of character and disposition between Jews and Hungarians. Jews possess "more intelligence and more industriousness" than Hungarians. These Jewish traits might well contribute to the material welfare of the nation, but the price for such contribution would be the loss of purity of Hungarian national characteristics, whatever those characteristics might be. For the distant future, Széchenyi was prepared to contemplate a state within which all human beings, including the Jews, would enjoy equal rights. For the time being, however, the weakness of the Hungarian nation, which had just begun to cultivate its values, necessitated its protecting itself against excessive external influences.[15]

There are ambiguities and signs of waverings in Széchenyi's attitudes toward the Jews. Although opposed to emancipation, he seems to be free of the anti-Jewish perceptions that would place him among the precursors of anti-Semitism. The qualities of character, intelligence, and diligence, which he marshals to argue against the acceptance of Jews, are positive rather than negative, and the exclusion of Jews from citizenship is to be temporary or, at least, not necessarily permanent. Indeed, Széchenyi would have disavowed any conscious, defamatory accusations against Jews. Still, there is good reason to believe that his reservations against including the Jews in the Hungarian nation had deeper roots than were revealed in his overt polemics. It is important that he contemplated the ultimate inclusion of the Jews in the state rather than the nation. This commonwealth of the future would serve as a political framework which, consonant with current liberal political philosophy, would be neutral toward religious and ethnic differences. The question raised during the debate on emancipation at that time, however, was whether Jews could join the Hungarian nation and not simply the Hungarian state. Széchenyi did not address himself directly to this question, but his answer to it—in the negative—can be inferred from his premises.

As mentioned above, Széchenyi considered Christianity—that is, Christianity in general, not its confessional variations, Catholic or Protestant—to be one of the elements that constituted the Hungarian nationality. Although he reduced Christianity to its common denominator, he was far from giving it a mere Deistic or humanistic reinterpretation. An ardent Catholic, it was concession enough for him to grant other Christian denominations an equal share in the national spirit. Non-Christians, Jews, or the adherents of other religions could well be included within the framework of the state, a formal organization that would cater to the welfare and the security of its members. But to join the nation, one had to be equipped not only with such visible tokens of the national culture as command of the Hungarian language, but also with more spiritual qualities derived from Christianity.[16]

Széchenyi's appeal for steady but cautious reform stirred favorable reactions at first, but ultimately was overtaken by events. These came in response to the dynamics of radicalism under the leadership of Széchenyi's rival Kossuth, which led to the 1848-1849 revolution in which Kossuth became both hero and victim. This shift is also reflected in Kossuth's changing attitude toward the Jewish question. Although prejudiced against Jews, probably no less than Széchenyi was, Kossuth, once he had settled on the idea of an immediate, radical transformation of society, included the Jews in his scheme as well. He therefore recommended unqualified emancipation, but made it dependent on the Jews divesting themselves of all peculiarities, religious or otherwise, that separated them from the bulk of the Hungarian people. More a Deist than a Christian,

Kossuth conceived of a comprehensive nationalism that would be capable of overcoming all residual religious or ethnic differences. Since Judaism, with its particularistic prescriptions, was an obvious impediment to national amalgamation, it was to be reformed to become compatible with the Hungarian nation. The dietary laws, the observance of festivals on different days, as well as the prohibition of marriage with non-Jews would have to be abandoned. Convinced of the overriding value of national unification, Kossuth felt that both Jews and Gentiles would see the logical as well as historical cogency of his proposition.[17]

Kossuth repeatedly expressed this conviction and was ready to act upon it while he was wielding political power during the revolution. Despite this, the revolutionary government deferred the decision on the Jewish question until the last moment, in the summer of 1849, when it became obvious that it would be defeated by the Austrians and the Russians; this failure was due to the unmistakable reluctance of non-Jews to accept Jews on equal terms. In the first months of the revolution, anti-Jewish riots broke out in Bratislava and other cities. In Budapest, Christian citizens refused to serve in the national guard alongside Jewish volunteers, despite the active participation of Jewish youth in the revolution. Cautioned by these and similar events, Kossuth's government, while still theoretically in favor of Jewish equality, postponed the declaration of it. The promulgation of the law at the hour of defeat was a demonstration of the government's belief in it. What is important to note is that the law granted Jews legal equality and obliged them at the same time to reform their religion. The government's declaration enjoined the Jewish community to convene a rabbinical assembly to lay down the principles of a reformed Judaism. Other governments in granting emancipation had entertained the expectation of a concomitant reform of Judaism, and Napoleon had even threatened revocation in order to force the rabbis to act. But the direct link between emancipation and reform is unique to the Hungarian revolution and clearly reflects Kossuth's radical and ultimately self-defeating views.[18]

The revolutionary legislation failed not only to bring about emancipation, but also to influence religious reform. The chief ideological promoter of Jewish emancipation, Count Joseph Eötvös—who recommended it as early as 1840—was destined, as the minister of cultural affairs in the Hungarian government after the compromise with Austria in 1867, to implement emancipation. Eötvös no doubt also considered that a far-reaching accommodation of the Jewish religion was necessary for complete integration. However, Eötvös' liberalism was of a different kind than Kossuth's. He combined it with a moderate, almost contemplative, temper—as befitted the intellectual of aesthetic leaning that he was—and he would have recoiled from imposing his will on a religious minority in exchange for political or social rights.[19] An assembly, the so-called Jewish Congress, was convened under his auspices, but its assignment was not to carry out a determined governmental policy but to erect an organizational framework for Hungarian Jewry. A majority in the congress favored reform, or at least some cultural accommodation to the new circumstances. However, a substantial and intransigent minority was unwilling to acquiesce in any cultural accommodation such as modern schooling, preaching in any language but Yiddish, or changes of real religious significance. The clash resulted in the secession of the Orthodox minority from the congress and the establishment of different organizations for each group, endorsed, though reluctantly, by the government. Thus, the religious and cultural polarization of Hungarian Jewry received a kind of official acknowledgment that helped widen the gap. While a substantial number of Hungarian Jews were quick to accommodate themselves religiously and culturally, the Orthodox entrenched themselves behind an institutional structure that retained the basic features of the traditional ghetto community. If Hungarian public opinion did not encourage this trend, it at least condoned it. The liberals, losing their original impetus, were ready to compromise, and much of the traditional society, based on the privileges of the ruling class and the supremacy of the church, persisted despite a general liberalization. Within this structure Jewish Orthodoxy could persist undisturbed. The demand for cultural and ethnic integration, which the initiators of emancipation had set as the price for equality, was tacitly or even explicitly relinquished.[20]

One has to keep the persistence of Jewish Orthodoxy in mind in order to understand the anti-Semitic reaction that first appeared in Hungary as early as 1875, less than a decade after formal legal emancipation. On the eighth of April of that year, Győző Istoczy, a member of the ruling liberal party, raised three questions in parliament. First, did the government intend to enact the often promised legislation that would prevent immigration of foreign Jews, who were inundating the country? Second, would the government condone or hinder a movement of nonviolent self-defense against this "aggressive caste [the Jews]"? Third, was the government intent on continuing the course, followed since the enacting of emancipation, of neutrality and indifference toward the Jewish problem, a policy that had turned out to be unjustifiable?[21]

To appreciate the first of the three questions, one has to bear in mind that, just like other countries willing to grant emancipation, Hungary was willing to do so exclusively to Jews who were already legal residents, thus precluding immigration from other states where Jews still suffered civil disabilities of various kinds. In Hungary this exclusivity was particularly

237

crucial because of the steady flow of immigrants that comprised a large part of Hungarian Jewry. At the same time, a legislative solution was even more difficult, since the immigrants were not technically foreigners, but came from Bohemia, Moravia, and Galicia, which were lands of the Austrian empire, to which Hungary also belonged. Thus, although anti-immigration legislation had been contemplated by the government when emancipation was granted, the idea had subsequently been abandoned. Istoczy, in raising the matter anew, knew that no practical result would be achieved. His questioning was only designed to air his views on the Jewish question, a subject on which he felt at odds with the majority of his party as well as with current public opinion.[22]

The main thrust of Istoczy's reasoning was a redefinition of Judaism, officially accepted as a religious confession. He saw it as "a closed social caste bound together as a tightly sealed entity by unity of blood, a tradition accepted from ancient times, the sharing of interests and religion." Judaism might pretend to be a religion only, and by accepting this defini- tion state and society granted it the protection due to all religious confes- sions in modern society. Religion, however, was only one element in Judaism, which had always preserved itself as a separate social unit. Istoczy was reluctant to call the Jews a nation, since they lacked the basic attribute of nationhood, a common language; yet he portrayed the Jews as pursuers of the perennial Jewish goal: the domination of the world, partial- ly realized already through Jewish preponderance in economics and in the press, the molder of public opinion in modern society.[23]

Istoczy ridiculed the naiveté of people who believed in the absorption of the Jewish community through assimilation and intermarriage. True, there were Jews who divested themselves of those traditional features of Jewish life that had inhibited their movement outside the Jewish social or- bit. Such Jews were willing to involve themselves in non-Jewish society even to the extent of intermarriage. But, in penetrating non-Jewish society they did not cease to be Jews; on the contrary, they exploited their newly won position to further the interests of their caste. Istoczy saw the division between the Orthodox defenders of rigidly preserved traditional life and the innovating group of the neologists as a mere fiction, a strategy employed to achieve a common goal. Here Istoczy was clearly resorting to a conspiracy theory of history such as we have encountered in the exposi- tions of des Mousseaux, by whom he may have been directly influenced. According to this theory, the Orthodox were allotted the task of preserving the core of the original Jewish social unit, which would serve as a refuge for those who wished to return to the fold from their adventurous mission in the strange world of the Gentiles. The neologists, on the other hand, were the emissaries sent out to facilitate Jewish world dominion through penetration of the innermost recesses of the world to be conquered.[24]

The Hungarian Prelude

The idea of Jewish world dominion is paramount in Istoczy's mind. He may have derived it, of course, from any of the German or French anti-Jewish writers he had read. In referring to the activities of the Alliance Israelite Universelle as an example of the practical realization of Jewish dominance, he betrays at least one of his literary sources, des Mousseaux, who pointed to the Alliance as the instrument of Jewish world domination. Yet, although influenced by German and French sources, Istoczy applied his theory to the special conditions of his own country. France and Germany, although less imperiled by Jewish domination than Hungary, had witnessed "the noise of more than one cry of alarm" and no doubt would, in the future, take practical measures of self-defense. For Hungary, however, such measures were overdue.[25]

In spite of this sense of urgency, Istoczy failed at the time to develop an anti-Jewish program. He rejected the idea of revoking the emancipation, because given the prevailing doctrine of political equality, it was unfeasible. Moreover, it would be ineffective in view of Jewish advances even prior to their emancipation. The state could not possibly curb Jewish activities as it did those of the socialists, a group far less dangerous than the Jews in Istoczy's view. The major action, however, ought to be taken not by the state but by society, which should organize itself in self-defense against the collective encroachments of the Jews on the rights and domain of the people. He only asked the state to condone organizations whose activities would be directed not against a religious community, but against a competing unit, a caste.[26]

Ideologically, there is nothing new in Istoczy's reasoning. He reiterates complaints about Jewish advances in France and Germany. The writings of anti-Jewish authors—Paulus, Bauer, and Wagner—are clearly reflected in his arguments. Like his predecessors, he saw the Jews as a distinct social group, foreign and unassimilable, which pursued its egoistic objectives regardless of the havoc and damage that resulted. His vocabulary also included the biological notion of the parasite, "which, incapable of existing for itself, continues to feed on vegetation until such a time as it completely destroys it." Basically, however, Istoczy's characterization of the Jew was derived from a wide variety of sources, including Christian traditions that had endowed the Jews with almost diabolical powers and propensities.[27]

What lent Istoczy's deliberations their special significance was his position and the arena in which he announced his ideas. His ideological forebears were more or less marginal intellectuals, whose writings could not possibly reach more than a certain section of the population. Istoczy, on the other hand, as a member of the ruling party of his country, addressed the whole Hungarian nation from the most advantageous position possible in terms of publicity. At that time, he was alone, if not in his conviction, at least in his determination to voice it. Prime Minister Béla Wenck-

239

heim, whose duty it was to respond, could designate Istoczy's three questions as ill-timed and inopportune, dismissing them as contrary to the principles on which the newly founded constitution rested: the independence of a citizen's rights from his religious affiliation, including Judaism. It was here that Istoczy wished to differ, and he did so fully aware of his isolated position. Why he adhered to this position so persistently is not entirely clear, but he had had some unpleasant experiences with Jewish litigants in his home county, in western Hungary. There he was a member of the lower gentry, which was losing ground because of the economic development that Jewish capital and capitalists were helping to promote. This may have led him to see history as a perennial conflict between Jews and Gentiles. Be that as it may, Istoczy was convinced that he had found the clue to the proper understanding of the contemporary situation. He used every opportunity to repeat his arguments, adapting and embellishing as context and circumstances required.[28]

A welcome occasion for one of his major speeches in Parliament arose during the 1878 Congress of Berlin, in which all the major European powers discussed the eastern question. At that time, Istoczy proposed that if one of the participants in the congress suggested establishing a Jewish state as a part of the settlement of the question of the Balkans and the Near East, the Hungarian government should resolve to support it. Istoczy claimed that the idea of using the present political situation to regather Jews in their ancient homeland was not his own. He attributed it to an English writer in the monthly *Nineteenth Century*. As the idea had been circulating at that time in certain quarters, it may have reached his ears through other channels as well. But, whatever its origin, in Hungary in 1878 the idea of a Jewish state seemed unimaginable. Thus, it was also far-fetched to ask Parliament to pass a resolution on the purely hypothetical assumption that the establishment of a Jewish state would be on the agenda of the congress. No wonder that Istoczy's listeners were more amused than impressed by his proposal and thus induced Istoczy to withdraw it, arguing that his main purpose had been simply to raise the Jewish question in general.[29]

That this intention was indeed the case is patently obvious upon closer examination of the contents of Istoczy's speech. True, the speaker spelled out the details of a political procedure for the foundation of a Jewish commonwealth, pointing at the same time to the psychological and material capability of the Jewish people for such a task. Reading some of these passages, one is strongly reminded of Theodor Herzl's proposals, as well as of some emphatic arguments of Zionist thinkers in favor of Jewish nationalism. Istoczy, however, mustered these details only to show that Jews possessed an alternative to change their destiny, but would not do so; he

240

insisted that although Jews had an opportunity and possessed the necessary financial means to establish their own state, they deemed "it more advantageous to pursue the Jewish will to dominate the European nations."[30]

The idea of Jewish world domination, in Europe and Hungary particularly, occupied Istoczy's mind almost to the point of obsession. To give it a semblance of rationality and substance, he cited statistical and other factual data. At the same time, he warned the Jews not to delude themselves as to the resistance they would encounter in attempting to achieve their objective. He referred to the examples of bygone centuries when similar circumstances led up to "the mass extermination of the Jews." Though unlikely to occur as long as the Jewish domination continued, it could well take place in case of "a great political upheaval or a social convulsion that would engulf the society of several states." No moral considerations would impede such a solution; in Istoczy's view it would be nothing but the exercise of the nations' right to defend themselves.[31]

These are shocking assertions, especially in historical retrospect, since we cannot fail to view them as foreshadowing the mentality that made Nazi atrocities possible. Istoczy shocked his contemporaries as well. While his lengthy deliberation on a Jewish state elicited only amusement from his listeners, and the minister whose duty it was to respond could dismiss it as a mere literary exercise, Istoczy's references to the medieval method of solving the Jewish problem took many people aback. The speaker of the house felt duty-bound to warn the orator that if he had indeed uttered the words the speaker believed he had, he must be called to order. To condone the use of force against Jews, even hypothetically, ran counter to good taste and was considered unparliamentary.[32]

Although Istoczy later came to play an important part in the anti-Semitic movement, both in Hungary and on the international scene, his utterances of 1875-1878 are still only precursors of the movement. First of all, even he regarded his ideas as purely theoretical; he was far from contemplating any action, organizational or otherwise. Although he may have struck a sympathetic chord in many Gentiles by expressing his resentment against a too rapid advancement of the emancipated Jew, such resentment did not necessarily lead to an anticipation of the catastrophic consequences envisioned by Istoczy. At any rate, no one felt impelled to act. Although Istoczy himself was convinced that the time for active anti-Jewish measures would arrive, it is doubtful that he thought it was imminent. It must have come to him as a surprise when less than half a decade after his first speech in the Hungarian parliament, the German anti-Semitic movement initiated by Adolf Stöcker more than fulfilled his prediction. Spurred by the German example, the Hungarian movement under Istoczy's leadership was organized, and when, in 1882, the first international meeting of anti-Semites took place in Dresden, Istoczy was destined to play a central role in the formulation of its program and its propaganda. Anti-Semitic ideas had entered the phase of active realization.[33]

Part VI: The Movement

20|The Incubation

THE YEAR 1879 is a turning point in modern Jewish history: it marks the beginning of modern anti-Semitism. The tangible signs of the phenomenon were the appearance of the court preacher Adolf Stöcker in Berlin as an anti-Jewish agitator and the publication, in the prestigious *Preussische Jahrbücher*, of a strongly biased analysis of the Jewish problem by the prominent historian and liberal politician Heinrich von Treitschke. These events, following one upon the other, in September and November, startled the public and stirred up widespread anti-Jewish activity.[1]

Contemporaries referred to the consequences of these events as the emergence of a "movement." The political and social activity headed by Adolf Stöcker in the ensuing years was called the "Berlin Movement"; and the word *movement* was applied to the enterprises of the anti-Jewish groups in general. Historians, however, studying the phenomena in retrospect, have eschewed the term. They have described, analyzed, and discussed these events under two other aspects: as ideologies (Weltanschaungen or philosophies) or as the programs of political parties. Thus, we possess studies of the rise and fall of the anti-Semitic parties, as well as inquiries into the nature, intellectual components, and historical origins of the anti-Semitic arguments. The term *movement*, the original designation of the phenomenon, is employed, if at all, only casually. It has never been made the main objective in an investigation of modern anti-Semitism.[2]

Of course, in comparison to an ideology or the program of a political

245

party, a movement is an uncertain and evasive concept.[3] A social movement presupposes the diffusion of ideas about the desirability of social change. On the basis of these ideas, political parties may be founded whose declared purpose is to introduce the desired changes. The number of people in sympathy with the ideas for change and prepared to assist in their realization is always greater than the number who join the political parties established for this purpose. As we shall see later, once the anti-Semitic ideology had been absorbed, it found many ways of social realization in addition to the channels of political endeavor. A social movement is characterized by the diffuseness of its boundaries, the range of commitment of its adherents, and the variety of means it employs to realize its goals.

Genetically, a movement appears on the scene as an eruption occasioned by some unforeseen but significant event. Such eruption is, however, preceded by a period of incubation, in the course of which the ideas destined to serve as the intellectual proppings of the movement are being developed by its prospective supporters. The movement proper involves a drive toward change in some aspect of society, which, during the period of incubation, has become the object of criticism. This criticism may be expressed by individual spokesmen or it may be evident in the general climate of opinion. The leading maxims that later govern the social action of the movement are in the air during the period of incubation. Any event interrupting the wonted course of life in society, or simply the appearance of a leader ready to capitalize on a situation, may serve as the stimulus that brings about a movement.

The anti-Semitic movement set as its goal the elimination of Jewish emancipation, or at least the neutralization of its social effects. Whether the law that granted Jews citizenship and equality of rights could or should be revoked was contested among anti-Semites; yet all agreed that the role Jews were permitted to play in the economic, political, and cultural life of German society went beyond tolerable limits. Hence the conclusion that emancipation, as implemented by the state and exploited by the Jews for their own benefit, was in need of some correction.

As described previously, broad segments of German society had objected to emancipation before it became a fact. Whole series of arguments had been marshaled in support of their objection. Those who deplored the emancipation or its consequences could simply refer to these arguments, pointing at the same time to the facts that allegedly substantiated them. The theories of post-emancipatory anti-Semitism are a direct continuation of these early versions. Between the two periods, that is, between the great debates on the Jewish question in the first decades of the nineteenth century and the outbreak of anti-Semitism in the late 1870s—there was an interval of almost two generations. During this time, in the wake of the unification of the German Reich, Jewish emancipation had been quietly introduced and accepted. Reservations or resentment were voiced mainly by ultraconservatives. Anti-Jewish sentiments seemed to be on the wane. To combat emancipation in the later period required the reawakening of anti-Jewish bias and the refreshing of anti-Jewish theories adapted to the new situation. This process took place during the years 1873-1879, the incubation period of political and social anti-Semitism.

The year 1873 is marked in European, and especially German, history as the date of the great bankruptcy, the failure of many financial enterprises established in the preceding years of unprecedented economic boom. This financial debacle ushered in the great depression of the Bismarck years, which lasted with some fluctuations until 1896. As the anti-Semitic movement emerged and flourished during this time, a causal connection between the two phenomena has been generally taken for granted, though the nature of the possible connection has remained unclarified. It was easy to blame the Jews for the widely ramified economic disaster, either because of their conspicuous participation in the phony economic boom preceding the catastrophe or because of the obvious link between Jewish interests and the political and economic liberalism of the system in which the debacle happened. The frustration engendered at that time by the economic recession could be said to have created a frame of mind for the acceptance of any theory that would account for peoples' suffering by fixing the guilt on some visible object. In this situation, the traditionally suspect Jewish minority almost automatically assumed the accustomed role of the scapegoat.[4]

In the years preceding the emergence of anti-Semitism proper, German Jewry seemed to have left behind the struggle for political and civil status. Not only had formal emancipation been granted, but Jews were allowed to play an important part in the shaping of the political destiny of the country. Bismarck was ruling with the help of the National-Liberal Party, two leading figures of which, Ludwig Bamberger and Eduard Lasker, were unconverted Jews. Although conscious of their Jewishness, these politicians, along with a multitude of other less prominent Jews, felt no inhibitions about sharing the responsibility for the affairs of state and society with other Germans. Thus it was Eduard Lasker who, in January and February of 1873, attacked the doubtful practices current among the promoters of economic enterprises, especially in connection with railway construction. Railway construction was still in private hands, but could be carried out only with the permission of the state authorities. The necessary capital was provided either by the great firms and banks or by joint-stock companies created ad hoc for the purpose. The last method was followed by Bethel Henry Strousberg, a Jew from Eastern Prussia who converted to Christianity and who in the sixties and early seventies enjoyed a meteoric economic and social career. Amassing an immense fortune through daring enterprises, Strousberg succeeded in entering the highest social circles of the Prussian aristocracy and even became an elected conservative member of the Reichstag. In his business practices, Strousberg claimed to have maintained the accepted standards of probity. He executed his projects under the supervision of the authorities and won the support of important and, as Lasker himself attested, impeccable personages. Yet at the time of Lasker's attack in the Prussian Parliament, Strousberg's reputation had already been damaged. He had undertaken the building of railways in Rumania, where he met with great difficulties, endangered the investments of his associates, and impaired the good name of German enterprise. As a failing upstart, he became an easy target for Lasker's weighty but nonspecific charges. In fact, the invective against Strousberg in Lasker's speeches served as the background to the indictment of another group of people, outstanding among them the privy councilor Herman Wagener. Under cover of their own high position, these people applied, in legally dubious fashion, the "Strousberg system" to their own benefit. Though unimpeached, Wagener had to resign his post, and the whole group of conspicuously conservative affiliation who were involved in the scandal stood exposed to public contempt. Lasker, on the other hand, was hailed as the undaunted defender of public morality.[5]

On the surface, the whole affair of the Lasker disclosure had no bearing on the Jewish question. The fact that the hero of the affair, as well as one of the villains, was Jewish—although the villain was baptized—could well have demonstrated the irrelevance of religious affiliation or ethnic origin as far as probity or moral standards were concerned. However, German society was far from adopting a detached attitude toward public figures and judging them purely on the basis of individual conduct and achievement. The Jewish origin of both Strousberg and Lasker was hardly overlooked. Congratulating Lasker on his performance in the sad affair, Adolf Stahr, a noted philologist who was the husband of the then-famous author Fanny Lewald, a baptized Jew, expressed his deep satisfaction that it was a Jew who passed judgment on the foul financial practices, the main beneficiaries of which are "the Pereires and Mires, the Strousbergs and consorts."[6]

In allowing the moral feat of one Jew to compensate for the faults of many others, Stahr did in fact predicate their collective moral responsibility. It was the continuous perception of the Jews as a collective social entity that was at the bottom of the defamation that set in, when, in the wake of the great debacle, the participants in the drama came under public

The Incubation

scrutiny.[6] The initiator of this scrutiny was the journalist Otto Glagau, with a series of articles starting in December 1874 in the widely read weekly *Gartenlaube*. The title of the articles, "Der Börsen- und Gründungsschwindel in Berlin" ("The Swindle of the Bourse and Promotion in Berlin"), does not reveal any special focus on the Jewish participation in the scandal. The main purpose of the articles was to expose the guilt of those who, as Glagau understood it, were responsible for the ruin of simple folk, seducing them to invest their savings in doubtful and even fraudulent enterprises. Glagau assumed a purely moral stance. Economists who tried to explain what happened in terms of their discipline, talking about the recurring waves of economic crises and the like, were spurned by him as collaborators of the promoters in covering up their guilt. Similarly, when it was pointed out to him that at the time of the great boom all parts and sections of the population counting on easy gain were seized by what an economist called the "fever of speculation," he emphatically denied the accountability of the victims of the debacle. All the fault lay with those who were engaged in promoting the business in the banks, the bourse, and the press. Limited as this outlook was, it could not fail to appeal to those who found themselves exonerated, the whole blame being put on others.[7]

Those blamed were originally not characterized as Jews in particular, and certainly not exclusively. In the first installments of the *Gartenlaube* series, the names of Jewish and non-Jewish promoters appear in seemingly innocent equilibrium. When accused of identifying promoters as Jews, Glagau could rightly point to "a series of Christian names" that appeared in every article alongside those of Jews. But nevertheless, he gave the impression of identifying Jews in particular as promoters, because, while Christian names usually appeared without any qualification, Jews were presented as such, either explicitly or through some humorous but pejorative epithet. Glagau may have originally intended this more as stylistic spice than as anti-Jewish propaganda. It was, of course, intriguing to learn that Bethel Henry Strousberg was originally called Bartel Heinrich Strausberg and was from the "chosen people." The editor of *Gartenlaube*, proud of the organ's reputation for decency, omitted some of the more obnoxious expressions. Still, enough remained, so that the promoters of Jewish origin were identified not simply as participants in the dubious economic enterprises, but also as Jews.[8]

Moreover, Glagau refers occasionally not only to the deeds of individual Jews, but to those of Jews in general. In a chapter entitled "Berlin becomes a metropolis," four promoters are introduced. For the three with good non-Jewish names—Hermann Gelber, Heinrich Qistrop, I. A. W. Carsten—no mention is made of their social background. The fourth promoter, Paul Munk, however, is singled out for special consideration. "Herr Paul Munk, as many of his coreligionists who made their fortunes [*Glückmachen*] here, stemmed from the district of Posen. Since 1866 almost the half of the Grand Duchy of Posen has emigrated to Berlin. The number of Jews here grew from 20,000 to almost 50,000. The Children of Israel multiply themselves in Berlin as rapidly as they once did in Egypt. They are almost all well-to-do and wealthy people; real poor Jews are not to be found there. The climate of Berlin . . . agrees with the descendants of Abraham exceedingly well, and if one should wish to palliate their grief of eighteen hundred years and lead them back today into the land that flows with milk and honey, they would say: 'Thank you, thank you very much!' "[9]

Such observations on Jews in general, added to the identification of individual promoters as Jews, created the impression that all Jews were to be blamed for the depression, if only by association. It was not simply the sensitivity to criticism that made Jewish readers of the *Gartenlaube* protest against the tone and content of Glagau's articles. Glagau's answer to these protests reveals the mechanics of anti-Jewish prejudice. Did he not also mention the names of Gentiles, even of aristocrats? "But it is not my fault that among the promoters and stockjobbers—as I shall indeed establish it with numbers—90 percent are certainly Jews and 10 percent at most are Christians." Here is another misleading identification, namely, between stockbrokers and promoters. The high percentage of Jews among those active at the stock exchange is taken as an indication that the same proportion holds among swindling promoters. That this was Glagau's reasoning becomes clear from the alleged proofs he offers for his contention. For though the problem at issue was that of the promoters, the facts adduced pertain to the stockbrokers: "Not only in Berlin, Vienna, Frankfurt am Main, not only in Germany and Austria-Hungary are nine-tenths of the stockbrokers Jews or baptized Jews. Jews dominate the stock exchanges of London and Paris. Here also business stands still 'on the Jewish High-Holidays'." With regard to the stock exchange, the proofs of Jewish influence were readily available. The evidence for a preponderance of Jews among the fraudulent promoters, Glagau, somewhat hesitantly, it is true, promised to adduce on another occasion. Meanwhile a striking slogan was born: "Ninety percent of the jobbers and promoters are Jews."[10]

The slogan had immediate reverberations. It was taken up by newspapers and periodicals, most importantly by the Catholic *Germania*, which launched a series of anti-Jewish articles, fed at least in part by the Glagau "revelations." The Catholics had their own special reasons to jump on the anti-Jewish bandwagon. They were engaged in the Kulturkampf against Bismarck, and the Jews who belonged to the liberal camp were among the supporters of the chancellor's anti-Catholic front.

Glagau cited those publications that echoed his own work as confirmation of its truth, even before he found the highly doubtful statistics he used to substantiate it. The promise was given in the introduction to a book containing the *Gartenlaube* articles, published in 1876. A sequel followed a year later, expanding the story of the doubtful enterprises of the boom years and their subsequent failure throughout Germany.[11]

Helmut von Gerlach, who later turned his back on anti-Semitism, likened Glagau's method in writing and reasoning to that of Eduard Drumont, the master of anti-Semitic agitation in France a decade later. Like Drumont, Glagau presented his material in a personalized fashion. The actors in his stories are always identified by name and locality, thus gaining credibility whether or not they actually existed. The coloring is always black and white, the victims of the machinations of the promoters are always innocent, the latter always guilty of conscious fraud. It is the moralistic tone of the condemnation, rather than the substantiation of facts, that is used to convince the reader of the truth of the charges. The argument that 90 percent of the promoters were Jews is contradicted even by the material selected for the direct purpose of proving it. It is the Jews' culpability, rather than their number, that is emphasized to make them appear the prime movers of the swindle. Initially, the Jews were not credited with such a prominent role.[12]

It was not the Jews' real or imagined share in bringing about the economic debacle that provoked Glagau's enmity. It was the conspicuous part they played in economic activity—banking, finance, the stock market—and their rapid rise to economic, social, and political prominence. This is evident in his introduction to the book publication of his articles, in which he recounts their genesis and history. In the book, the derogatory epithets and expressions suppressed by the journal editors are reinstated, and some unflattering observations on Jews added. The new closing chapter contains a humorous description of a visit to the Berlin stock exchange, in which the whole institution is made to appear an almost exclusively Jewish club, where only the service personnel are conspicuously non-Jewish. The ominous slogan of the "ninety percent" is presented here in a visualizable form.[13]

In his introduction and notes, Glagau undertakes to answer the objections raised to his observations about Jews, and in doing so, he only becomes more emphatic, until he has transcended the issue of Jewish participation in the recent economic debacle and has entered into a wholesale condemnation of the Jewish presence in German society. "No longer should we tolerate Jews pushing themselves everywhere to the foreground, to the head, seizing everywhere the leadership, the command. They push us Christians continuously aside, they press us to the wall, they take away the air we breathe. In fact, they exercise domination over us, they possess a dangerous supremacy and they exert an extremely unwholesome influence . . . The whole history of the world knows no other example of a homeless, definitively physically, and psychically degenerate people, simply through fraud and cunning, through usury and jobbing [*Schacher*] ruling over the orbit of the world."[14]

Here we have in a nutshell all the anti-Semitic phobias, apprehensions, and accusations that were to be expanded to dominate the anti-Semitic movement. It erupted in the course of a controversy initially not even directed against Jews as such. We may believe what Glagau asserted in the closing paragraph of his introduction, that in publishing his articles, he had a larger subject in mind than that of Jewish jobbery: he wished to expose "the corruption in a society that is permeated by unclean elements from top to bottom." During the publication of the articles it became clear that his attacks on Jews gained much more public attention than the general social critique. This was revealed both by the emotional Jewish reaction and by the adoption of the accusations in other periodicals, not to mention the approbation the author received privately. Thus his attention was turned toward anti-Jewish criticism, and in reissuing his articles, as well as in subsequent writings, he became an outstanding anti-Jewish propagandist.[15]

At this stage the anti-Jewish agitation was still outside the domain of party politics. Glagau conceded that Lasker had performed a service in revealing the foul practices of the promoters, but criticized him for having restricted his attacks to "Gründer" ("promoters") of the Conservative party. Still there is no indication that he wished to discredit by this criticism Lasker's party in favor of the Conservatives. Such a political maneuver was, however, initiated by the Conservatives themselves. In June-July 1875, five articles appeared in the *Kreuzzeitung*, the organ of the Conservative party, entitled "The Bleichröder-Delbrück-Camphausen Era and the New German Economic Policy." These articles amounted to an all-out attack on the economic policy of liberalism that was being carried out in Prussia by the two ministers named in the title of the article. Bleichröder, the third person mentioned, was head of the most important bank in Berlin and Bismarck's financial adviser in public as well as private matters.[16]

The Conservative opposition to the economic practices of the Liberal era was of course not new. Representing the aristocratic landowners, the Conservatives pleaded for a protectionist system contrary to the policy of free trade and unfettered individual enterprise that had been in vogue

The Incubation

since the political alliance of Bismarck with the National Liberals in the mid-sixties. Now, in view of the economic crisis descending upon the country in the wake of the great bankruptcy, a reversal of the Liberal trend seemed likely. The general disillusion would lead to the total discreditation of the Liberal Party, which was the obvious aim of the "Era-articles," as they became known. What is of interest for us is the method through which the authors thought they might best achieve this aim, namely, to pillory it as a Jewish invention. The tendency is enunciated with the utmost clarity in the opening paragraph of the first article, where the respective responsibility of the three men, Bleichröder, Delbrück, and Camphausen, for the prevailing economic policy is discussed. The two ministers, mistaken about the merit of the system, might have been proud to take responsibility, but in reality it rested with the only economic expert of the trio, Bleichröder, who suceeded in keeping himself in the background. However, versed as he was in the problems at issue by profession and tradition, he was in fact the mastermind behind the whole system: "Herr G. von Bleichröder, we should like to add in parentheses, is of the Mosaic faith and a dominating banker—the congruence, Jewish and banker, is almost automatic. After all, in Prussia in 1861, out of 642 bankers, only 92 were Christians, the other 550 were Jews." That Bleichröder was able to keep out of the limelight in an age of publicity was due to another aspect of Jewish domination, their control of the press: "Its most prominent organs are in the main in the hands of his coreligionists or in those of people more or less directly or indirectly dependent upon them." While other Jews used to be accused of seeking publicity through the press, Bleichröder is charged with the very contrary. What the author of these articles is driving at is to show that the conduct of the state in general is in Jewish hands, that German politics are in fact *Judenpolitik*. To substantiate this charge the author points to the crucial role that Jews like Eduard Lasker, Ludwig Bamberger, and H. B. Oppenheimer were permitted to play in the legislative bodies, the Prussian Landtag and the Reichstag. With finance, press, and legislation in Jewish hands, it was no wonder that the Reich was conducted "almost exclusively in favor of our co-citizens of the Mosaic faith and Jewish nationality." Unaware of the real state of affairs, the German public had up to then tolerated the prevailing regime. Once enlightened about its true nature, it would sweep it out of existence.[17]

The "Era-articles" appeared anonymously, but their author is known to have been Franz Fürchtegott Perrot, a consistent and outspoken critic of Bismarck's economic policy. Still, the articles were not one man's work. We know from the testimony of Perrot's brother that the publication of the series was discussed in advance with leading figures of the Conservative party. Then, in the ensuing polemics with critics of the five articles, the editor of the *Kreuzzeitung* joined in the fray and became even more outspoken. To discredit the system it was even insinuated that improper benefits had accrued to the Reichskanzler from his connection with Bleichröder. This may have been the reason why these articles aroused such immense public interest. Their significance in the history of anti-Semitism is, however, the presumption of their promoters that the harping on anti-Jewish sentiment would be an appropriate means of achieving their political purpose. The circle around the *Kreuzzeitung* let it be known that it had not given up its reservations about full emancipation. Jewish citizenship entailed the Jews' claim to hospitality and protection by the state, but not the right to positions of authority; this misconception about emancipation led to the anomaly of Jewish dominance. Knowing that misuse, once begun, is difficult to eradicate, they did not hope to eliminate emancipation at one stroke. "Still we want to keep such elimination always in view and prepare the way for it, and ultimately complete it . . . by gradual legislative repeal."[18]

This reservation against the full emancipation of Jews derives its ideological background from the concept of the Christian-German state, to which the representatives of the *Kreuzzeitung* circle openly confessed. The secular basis of the state, formally accepted at the founding of the Reich, had not dispelled the contradictory notions current in Conservative circles. The disapproval of the current political, social, and possibly even economic life was here an integral part of an inherited Weltanschauung. What was new in the events of the mid-1870s was that this disapproval was openly voiced in political polemics, and it was absorbed and adopted by people remote from Conservative circles and even opposed to them; Franz Perrot, C. Wilmanns, and Rudolf Meyer are examples.

As mentioned above, Perrot was an independent critic of the prevailing economic system and did not connect his antiliberal attitudes with anti-Jewish motives. He attacked financial operations based on the inflated evaluation of shares, as practiced by the promoters before the great collapse took place. In a book written in the first months of 1873, he concentrated on railway building, quoting Eduard Lasker's speech on the subject at length and favorably. Perrot argued that a state should not permit an undertaking of public interest to become the domain of private enterprise. Railway building had become a monopoly of the capitalists and a golden opportunity for adventurous promoters. Perrot spoke about the preponderance of the "International Bankocracy," condemning its practices and function, but ignoring the social or religious affiliation of those who kept it moving. Thus the Jewish question was kept out of the discussion. But later, in the "Era-articles," as we have seen, Perrot blamed the economic debacle on the Jews. By 1879 he had joined in the anti-Jewish agitation, publishing a pamphlet on Jews in the life of the German state and society. In the same year he launched a strong protest against the founding of the German Reichsbank, the result of Ludwig Bamberger's initiative. The protest, however, was not restricted to social or economic reservations; the Reichsbank was denounced as a deliberate invention to promote Jewish domination of Germany. Declaring himself to be free from Jew-hatred, Perrot explained that one "cannot be blind to the dangers connected with the fact that a people of an alien stock, alien nationality, alien religion, and alien tongue, though in the minority of one to eighty or a hundred of the population, nonetheless now seizes all the capital in Germany, dominates the public press and opinion, guides the Parliament and administration everywhere, and pushes its way into the top positions where for the time being they employ converted Jews in leading posts."[19] We shall later return to the perception of Jewish reality reflected in Perrot's statement. But first we have to adduce some other examples of social criticism focused on Jews.

C. Wilmanns and Rudolf Meyer were among the most severe critics of the prevailing economic policy and its political backing. Wilmanns' analysis of the situation reveals a penetrating insight into the interplay between economic and legislative factors, the protection of particularistic interests through parliamentary representation, and the social consequences thereof. He clearly conceived that a legal system granting unlimited freedom to investors of capital would lead to a radical reshaping of society. Those in possession of capital and ingenious enough to exploit it would ascend to the top. The historically established classes of artisans, peasants, and landowners would crumble away, and the newly arisen laborers, the proletarians, would be exposed to exploitation. His conclusion was that a new party of social reform had to be established, the goal of which would be the channeling of economic forces toward the development of a balanced and healthy society.[20]

Wilmanns' premises, as well as his conclusions, could have been presented and defended without so much as mentioning the Jews. Indeed, in the first part of the book, his diagnosis of society's ailment seems to be complete without referring to the Jewish factor. Capital runs its devastating course because of forces inherent in its nature. In an earlier pamphlet, of 1872, Wilmanns had already pointed to "the craft and cunning of the promoters and their agents" endangering the savings of the small capitalists, but there was no indication that the jobbers and their victims might be of different religious affiliations.[21] By 1876, however, the identification of Jews with bankers, promoters, jobbers, and the like had become almost a commonplace, and in the second part of his book Wilmanns too succumbed to the temptation. Wilmanns quoted Glagau's formula, that Jews made up 90 percent of the unscrupulous promoters, and complemented it with an assortment of hypotheses about the source of the Jewish propensity to fulfill the alleged Jewish function. Jews were ethically indifferent to, or even antagonistic toward others. To prove this allegation Wilmanns cited extensively Rohling's *Talmudjude*, and thus the traditional Christian concept of Jewish immorality was introduced into the new anti-Jewish campaign. No Jew, be he an adherent of religious reform or even a convert to Christianity, could possibly erase the Talmudic influence on his character. In the course of centuries this had assumed the nature of a racial characteristic: "their essence stands in glaring contrast to that of the Germanic and in general to that of the Occidental people." Incapable of amalgamation with other nations, Jews caused decomposition of the society within whose confines they happened to move—an assertion for which a misinterpreted but much quoted phrase of Theodor Mommsen is at hand. Describing the decline of the Roman Empire, Mommsen referred to the Jews as one of the "ferments of decomposition" of Roman society, a characterization later taken to be a racial trait. The more Jews are estranged from others, the more they maintain solidarity and cooperation among themselves on the local, as well as the international, level. They are the nucleus as well as the driving force of the "golden international," the existence and functioning of which Wilmanns set out to describe and condemn.[22]

The ascription of such an active role to one group in the capitalist system is hardly consistent with Wilmanns's insight into the historical forces at work in bringing about contemporary capitalism. Indeed, in the context of the book, his observations on Jews appear artificially grafted upon the corpus of his sociohistorical analysis. Nonetheless, this feature must have contributed to the book's success; it went through six editions within a few months of its publication. Its title, *The Golden International*, became an anti-Jewish slogan in the ensuing years of agitation.

Rudolf Meyer concluded his book *Political Promoters and the Corruption in Germany* (1877) with: "As long as Count Bismarck remains the sole mighty idol, so long will the German nation be sacrificed to the Reich and the Reich to the Chancellor—and the Chancellor belongs to the Jews and the speculators. Hence there is only one inevitable route for our politics: *Elimination of the present system and its carrier*" (italics in the original). As in the "Era-articles" of Perrot, anti-Jewish sentiments are here employed as a means of combating the system and its mighty prop and representative. In this book, Meyer fails to spell out his alternative to the prevailing system. But from his other publications we know that he pleaded for a strong control of the country's economy in order to protect the laborers. To demonstrate the necessity of control, he depicted the economy of the country as being in a state of chaos and public morality on the decline. The role of the Jews in handling the system and benefiting from it is repeatedly stressed by Meyer, but they are not seen as its initiators or its main beneficiaries. Nor do they serve as the main target of the attack. As far as its manifest objective was concerned, Meyer's campaign could have been conducted without connecting it to the Jewish question. But bringing in the Jews, the campaign gained an additional dimension, making it, as in the case of Wilmanns's book, more pungent and effective.[23]

Ludwig Bamberger in retrospect named the mid-1870s as the date when the anti-Jewish trend began making itself felt even in his own National Liberal party. Obviously, the literary expression of anti-Jewish sentiments created, or rather reflected, a social reality. How rapidly and deeply this new trend operated can be gauged from what we know about the shift of sentiments within the Masonic lodges. The fight for the admission of Jews to Freemasonry had gone on since the beginning of the century, parallel to the struggle for political emancipation. In the decades of ascending liberalism, there had been a steady progress in favor of unrestricted admission. More and more Masons had voted for opening their lodges to Jewish members. From the year 1875, however, the tide had been reversed. Not only had the balloting in favor of Jews shown a decrease, but outright anti-Jewish propaganda with strong racial overtones made its appearance in Masonic publications.[24]

The change cannot be attributed simply to the whims of some literary figures. The repercussions of the economic crisis, making people susceptible to suspicion, envy, and the seeking of scapegoats, do not explain why the Jews were singled out. It is true that the Jews were to be found at the centers of commerce, in trade, banking, and at the stock exchange, all of which served as the background for the dubious activities of the promoters who had brought about the crisis. Nevertheless, as we have seen, it did not immediately occur to the public or to those writers who subsequently became anti-Semitic propagandists to blame the Jews for the debacle. It was two or three years before accusations were made against them. Once the attention was focused on the Jews, it was not limited to the blame that might have been due them as promoters. The very presence of the Jews in German society became a target for attack.

The root cause of this outbreak of anti-Semitism is illustrated by Theodor Mommsen's reply to Heinrich von Treitschke, who in 1879 joined in the growing defamation of the Jews, making anti-Semitism respectable in the best academic circles. Mommsen, a staunch and outspoken Liberal, conceded that the Jewish community was far too peculiar, ethnically and culturally, to be easily integrated into the newly united German nation. The proper attitude to be taken by the rest of society was to ignore their oddness, hoping for a gradual adaptation and amalgamation. And this was exactly what the German public did, until the anti-Jewish propagandists intervened.[25]

In evaluating Mommsen's observation, a distinction must be made between the facts and the conclusions drawn from them. Mommsen was correct that, even after they had been subjected to cultural adaptation, the Jews were distinguishable as a separate social group. Mommsen also rightly stated that while liberalism was dominant, most of the German public had turned its attention away from the signs of internal unity among the Jews. This did not mean that they were satisfied with, or reconciled to, the existence of a separate Jewish community, but were quietly hopeful that it might dwindle away. The other conclusion of Mommsen, that this expectation would have been realized had not the anti-Semites intervened, was obviously hypothetical and, as experience proved, utopian. After all, the cultural adaptation of the Jewish community never, at any place, led directly to the total absorption of that community into the larger society. At any rate, what actually happened was that a deliberate indifference to the Jewish community consciously changed into an emphatic awareness of its existence, its status, and its unique character. Thereafter, all the images associated with the Jew before emancipation were revived, giving impetus to the new anti-Semitism.

This turnabout from indifference to a critical and hostile awareness of Jews came about in the context of an economic crisis and a political change from a liberal to a conservative regime. But context does not mean "cause." The economic crisis and the rejection of liberalism afforded an occasion for the expression of hostility toward the Jews, but did not create it. The decisive factor in the anti-Semitic eruption was the failure to fulfill the condition upon which the eradication of Gentile suspicions of Jews had been predicated, namely, the disappearance of the tightly knit Jewish community. Far from disappearing, this community only assumed a new metamorphosis, not all aspects of which were regarded favorably by the Gentiles. Though Jews were now active inside German society, in economic life, culture, and politics, they nevertheless remained conspicuous as a group. Their pursuits, never centrally planned or directed, were determined by historical and sociological factors. They filled economic positions consonant with their previous occupational experience. Culturally, they found their niche in callings open to all, such as journalism. They joined political parties whose aims coincided with their own interests. And despite their integration, they stood out as a closely knit group. I summarized the situation previously in *Out of the Ghetto*, in which I analyzed the process of emancipation and assimilation.

The Incubation

A look at Jews and the activities of Jews in the decades of the growing emancipation—between 1848 and 1880—shows that the picture is not a process of assimilation pure and simple. Assimilation, it is true, makes progress insofar as some Jews are coming into more intimate contact with non-Jews and all Jews more and more adopt the cultural patterns of their surroundings. But at the same time, Jews also create the instruments that continue to hold them together and help them maintain a separate social identity. The conception of Jews as a congregation existing merely by virtue of a common confession of faith functioned only on the theoretical level. In reality they retained the characteristics of a subgroup in society, recognizable by its ethnic origin, its economic concentration, its comparative social isolation, and by its nonconformist minority religion. The social countenance of this group differs greatly of course from the face the Jewish community presented a hundred years previously when Jews were a tolerated group, ecologically concentrated, economically strictly limited, and socially and culturally thoroughly isolated. At that time, the group was tightly organized and disciplined while religion served as a mighty force for unification. Now, in the second half of the nineteenth century, Jews were divided among themselves in point of religion—the common denominator may almost be said to have been the rejection of Christianity. Cultural isolation was almost completely gone, and the economic one-sidedness at least ameliorated. What remained unimpaired was Jewish inbreeding, the maintaining of exclusively Jewish family ties. This, and the residues of that religious nonconformity, comparative economic concentration, and social isolation, and some cultural peculiarity still gave the Jewish group a special physiognomy. If the group was different from what it had been a century before, it certainly had not assumed the characteristics expected by those who propounded the idea of fusion with Christian society.[26]

Thus, instead of completely disappearing as expected, the Jewish community merely underwent a transformation. And the old stereotypes were now revived. The wait-and-see attitude of the Gentile population, which involved the concealment and suppression of anti-Jewish sentiment, turned into overt resentment. This was the point at which anti-Semitism boiled over.

21|The Crystallization

IN FEBRUARY 1879, Wilhelm Marr's pamphlet *The Victory of Judaism over Germanism* appeared. By the fall of that year the pamphlet had gone into its twelfth edition, becoming the first anti-Semitic best-seller. Marr's thesis is clearly expressed in the title; Jewish dominance in Germany was not a danger to be feared for the future, it was already a fact. Jews had realized their perennial aim; they had conquered Germany, and they had done so through the fault of the Germans themselves. "You have elected the foreign rulers into your parliaments, you are making them legislators and judges, you are making them dictators of the financial system, you have surrendered the press to them . . . what do you really want? The Jewish people is flourishing [*wuchert*] with its talent and you are beaten. This is entirely in order and you have deserved it a thousand times."[1]

The sharp tone of the pamphlet, its intriguing title, and the apostrophizing of the German reader may have been instrumental in attracting attention to it. As far as the content was concerned, the pamphlet added nothing to the ideology or the argumentation of anti-Jewish writings of recent years. The significance was not in what it said but in what it left out. Marr extracted the anti-Jewish argument from its controversial political involvement. He did so in full consciousness, confessing that he had written his book in order "to take the Jewish question out of the fog of abstractions, and the quarrel of the parties."[2] Marr was convinced that the anti-Jewish argument—which he was soon to call anti-Semitic—was persuasive enough to unite its adherents without being tied to other controversial political and social issues. Marr's pamphlet was the first, since the reemergence of the Jewish question in the 1870s, to clearly announce its anti-Jewish tendency in its title. Anti-Semitism was now sailing under its own steam.

True, Marr pretended to doubt whether the fight against Jews was worthwhile, declaring their victory to be final and irreversible. This, however, was pure tactics. In fact he sensed, correctly as it turned out, that the social atmosphere was sufficiently saturated with anti-Jewishness to make an attack on Jews a promising political enterprise. In his pamphlet he urged the establishment of a periodical to propagate anti-Jewish ideology, and supported financially by conservative backers, he started his *Deutsche Wache* in October of 1879.[3] In its pages he announced the founding of an association called the Antijüdischer Verein. The term *jüdisch* was very soon replaced by *semitisch*, the word *Semite* for *Jew* having been in vogue for some time. The association then appeared under the name Antisemitenliga. Thus the fateful word anti-Semite was started on its way, not without its creator having an inkling, at least, of its destructive potential.[4]

That Marr intended to rally all the discontents of society around opposition to the alleged Jewish dominance is explicit in the statutes of his Antisemitenliga. The first paragraph states the association's goal: "To bring all non-Jewish Germans of all confessions, all parties, all positions in life to one common and close union, that will strive towards one goal . . . to save our German fatherland from complete Judaization."[5] What characterized this new phase of the anti-Jewish agitation was that it ascribed all evil in society to Jewish influence and promised to make the consequences disappear through the removal of their cause. It was not surprising that the formula, impressive by its very simplicity, should have been widely adopted. Alexander Friedrich Pinkert of Breslau circulated as early as April 1879 an appeal for the founding of a new party to be called the Deutsche Reform-Partei. The name is reminiscent of the party suggested by Wilmanns in his *Goldene Internationale*, to which Pinkert refers, and yet the stimulus that spurred him to action came from Marr's pamphlet and the new party was based on Marr's ideas. What Wilmanns had in mind was a comprehensive social reform, but Pinkert's attention was focused exclusively on the Jews. Indeed, the only practical step he envisaged was the creation "of a center for all the anti-Jewish exertions," whence a full-scale program would automatically emanate.[6]

Otto Glagau, too, was not blind to the complexity of the social problems indicated by the widely spread corruption he set out to expose. It was only gradually that the Jewish issue became the exclusive object of his preoccupation, as if from there the solution of all the problems could be derived. By 1879 he found a concise formula for his conception: "The social problem is simply the Jewish question."[7] The "social problem," that is, the unrest among labor evident in the growing strength of the Social-Democratic party, loomed large at this juncture in German public opinion. Glagau silenced it simply by subordinating it to the Jewish problem. Solve the Jewish question, and all other social problems would take care of themselves.

The capacity of the Jewish question to divert attention from broader problems of society was most eloquently documented in the well-known career of the court-preacher Adolf Stöcker and in the history of his party, the Christlichsoziale Arbeiterpartei.[8] A great orator, an ambitious personality endowed with a strong sense of social mission, Stöcker took the highly unconventional step, for a man of his position, of forming a political party. Through the combination of "Christian" and "social" he hoped to wean the working class from the socialists, who had made inroads on the rank and file of the proletariat in the capital. At first he had limited success. The working class, estranged from church and state, remained suspicious of the man who stood in the shadow of both. For the middle class, on the other hand, the party's program contained nothing intriguing or attractive. The Jewish question was not included in it, and Stöcker even avoided referring to it in his speeches; it can well be believed that he ultimately did so only at the request of some of his followers.[9] By the fall of 1879, the agitation of Marr and his colleagues had made the Jewish issue difficult to elude. Once having resorted to it, Stöcker turned out to be as critical of the Jews' reality as any anti-Jewish propagandist. He presented his views, it is true, in a more dignified, but at the same time most effective, fashion. His first speech took place on September 19, 1879 and was entitled, "What We Demand from Modern Jewry." The speech, whose ideological assumptions we shall analyze later, was a reflection on the demeanor of emancipated Jewry. According to the speaker, Jews misunderstood the act of emancipation, taking it as a license to behave as the equals or even the superiors of Germans. They ought to have recognized their position as that of tolerated strangers and conducted themselves accordingly.[10]

Judging by the enthusiasm with which it was received, Stöcker's discourse must have struck a sympathetic chord in the hearts of his listeners. Responding to the unexpected echo of his own words, Stöcker changed the course of his political effort. His party, instead of catering to the needs of the working class, became a rallying point for dissatisfied middle-class people, who believed they had found a panacea for all their afflictions—anti-Semitism. Stöcker himself became the central figure of what soon became known as the Berlin Movement.

The movement emanated from Berlin, but it embraced the whole of Germany and spread, as we shall see, beyond its borders. That it was a sociopolitical movement, in the strict sociological sense, is evident from contemporary descriptions of it, whether sympathetic to it or not. As early as November 1879 it was characterized by Heinrich von Treitschke as a "leidenschaftliche Bewegung gegen das Judentum," that is, a passionate agitation or movement—the word *Bewegung* may mean both—against Jewry. He pointed to three or four aspects of the phenomenon. First was the unwillingness of the electors to return Jewish representatives to parliaments—demonstrated by the recent elections to the Prussian Diet, where, among others, even Eduard Lasker lost his seat in Frankfurt and Breslau. Second, the creation of anti-Semitic associations—here was one of the first instances of the spontaneous use of the word *anti-Semite*. Third, the Jewish question was being discussed in agitated meetings. Finally, a flood of anti-Jewish pamphlets had inundated the market.[11] Treitschke's article itself revealed some aversion against the cruder forms of anti-Jewish activity, but he confessed himself to be in accord with its basic impulses and motivation. The article became a factor in strengthening the movement; published in the prestigious *Preussische Jahrbücher* by the much-adored liberal historian, politician, and publicist, it made anti-Semitism respectable in academic and intellectual circles.[12]

That academic youth joined the movement saddened those who saw anti-Semitism as an aberration of the German spirit, especially when they remembered the role played by German students during the revolutions of 1830 and 1848 that had ushered in the era of liberalism.[13] The same fact, however, confirmed the anti-Semites in their conviction that they represented the legitimate contemporary expression of the German spirit and carried with them the message of the future.

Two years after the emergence of the movement, Otto Glagau took stock of its progress, concluding with a kind of moral evaluation. He conceded that the basic motivation of most of the anti-Semites was the fear of Jewish competition or even actual suffering from the Jew-made economic system. "Yet to these materialistic motives there are added ideal, moral, and religious ones, too," to wit, the fear of Jewish intrusion into German society, undermining the autochtonic German culture and civilization. Youth especially was, according to Glagau, prompted by "pure noble enthusiasm" to join the anti-Semites.[14] In historical and sociological perspective, it is doubtful whether such a differentiation between materialistically and idealistically motivated anti-Semitism is in order. Students, too, had reasons to fear the competition of their Jewish colleagues, the flocking of Jewish students to secondary schools and universities, in excess of proportion in the population, being one of the recurring anti-Jewish complaints. On the other hand, though there was obviously some association between social affiliation and anti-Semitism, and the movement was characteristically middle-class, especially in its initial stages, this does not mean that cognizance of personal or class interest determined affiliation to the movement. Different members of a group reacted differently. We know, for instance, that a substantial minority of students in Göttingen protested the attachment of their association to the movement, but were outvoted by the majority; and this may have been the case elsewhere.[15] Whatever the hidden factors behind such decisions, the conscious motivation for joining the movement was the feeling that the Jews represented a danger to the material and spiritual welfare of German society. The anti-Semites saw themselves, paradoxical as it may sound, as a defensive movement. A considerable segment of German society acted as if a foreign invasion of the country were imminent. And this was no mere metaphor: the image of the Jew as the member of a strange and foreign nation dominated the mind of the anti-Semites.

Certain characteristics of the Jewish community—family exclusivity, professional concentration, emphatic mutual solidarity—no doubt enhanced the image of it as a separate and peculiar social entity. The anti-Semitic perception, however, endowed this entity with dimensions, qualities, and intentions that could be frightening in the extreme. This overblown vision of the Jewish community was, of course, the result of the historical burden that clung to it. For the anti-Semites, Jews were not simply an emancipated minority who, by entering civil society, became an energetic rival and competition for the majority. The Jews were the descendants of the New Testament Pharisees, sons and daughters of ghetto dwellers, the pariahs of European society, whose name conjured up a whole complex of negative connotations. This negative image of the Jew inherent in Christian tradition, deeply ingrained in the consciousness of European nations, had been knowingly subdued or discarded during the Liberal era. Once the political and intellectual climate had changed, the old image of the Jew in the Christian tradition, in a version adapted to the new situation, easily reasserted itself.

The traditional anti-Jewish attitude of Christianity, in its authentic theological version, was clearly the background of Adolf Stöcker's anti-Semitism. Though Stöcker devoted the greater part of his first anti-Jewish orations to the secularized modern Jew and Reform Judaism, the passion of his aversion is best demonstrated in what he has to say about Orthodox Judaism. This is "in its most internal core an atrophied form of religion, a lower grade of revelation, an outlived spirit, still to be revered but anulled by Christ and for the present no longer truth." Here was the unadulterated, unmitigated teaching of the Church about the superseding of Judaism by Christianity.[16]

As an orthodox Protestant, Stöcker took this thesis for an incontestable truth, and it was from it that his wrath against modern Judaism was derived. The spokesmen of the latter dared to claim a leading role in the shaping of the modern world, harping on the idea of a religious mission inherent in Jewish tradition. This claim was often combined with criticism of Christianity, which was said to be unfit for a similar historical assignment, because of its otherworldliness or some other feature. No greater offense was imaginable in the eyes of someone who believed in the divine rejection of Judaism, even in its original Biblical variation. The Jews' claim was an arrogant intrusion in the sphere of spirituality, and it was from this that their social arrogance derived. Moved by their alleged religious superiority, they felt entitled to occupy more and more prominent social positions at the cost of the Christian population. In the Christian theologian's view, their political and social success was a spiritual usurpation of almost blasphemous implications. It is no wonder that Stöcker wished the situation to be corrected; by what means and measures we shall see later.[17]

At the other end of the ideological spectrum was the theory of Eugen Dühring. A noted economist and philosopher, as well as a secularist and radical critic of Christianity, Dühring revealed his anti-Jewish attitude as early as 1875 in a short paragraph in one of his philosophical treatises. He expanded it in 1880, when the Jewish question became a public issue, into a vitriolic and acerbic frontal attack on Jews and Judaism. The pamphlet *The Jewish Question as a Question of Race, Morals, and Culture with a World Historical Answer* pretended to handle the problem while avoiding the Jewish-Christian confrontation altogether. In Dühring's view, Jews were a unique human species with marked physical and moral characteristics. All of these were negative, and they were evident in their record ever since the Jews had appeared on the scene of human history. Far from being original in this, Dühring took up the argument of Voltaire and his followers, especially Renan. Following in their footsteps, he derived the Jewish characteristics from the Bible as well as Jewish history up to recent times. Dühring disassociated himself from other anti-Semitic writers, who thought to find the source of Jewish immorality in the teachings of the Talmud. The Jewish Bible, held in awe by Christians, was testimony enough to the inferiority of the Jewish race in every possible respect. Dühring, a remarkable scholar, who even in his anti-Semitic pamphlet revealed a great measure of analytical acumen, believed in all seriousness that he was capable of recognizing in his contemporaries the recurring pattern of Jewish qualities depicted in the Bible. The truth is that, along with a high degree of intelligence, Dühring had the obvious features of a morbid mental constitution, accentuated probably by his complete blindness at the age of thirty. His irascible nature was undoubtedly a factor

265

in his quarrels and polemics with colleagues and opponents of his economic theories, among them Karl Marx and Friedrich Engels. At any rate, the supposed Jewish inferiority discovered in everyone known to be of Jewish descent, be it Ricardo, Spinoza, Heine, Börne, Stahl, Marx, or Lassalle, not to mention an unnamed multitude of contemporary politicians and journalists, points to an idée fixe. Hardly could it be accepted as the result of acute observation. That these claims derived from Dühring's obsessions is clearly demonstrated through his blunder in ascribing Jewish parentage to Gotthold Ephraim Lessing on account of the typically Jewish features supposedly revealed in Lessing's writings and conduct.[18]

If this were madness, it still had method. By predicating an unchanged and unchangeable inferiority in Jews, Dühring lent the recurring antagonism toward Jews—ancient, Christian, or modern—an air of universality. The recent anti-Semitism then appeared only as a new phase in the continuous self-defense of all Gentiles against the perennial Jewish danger. The Jewish-Christian conflict was thus divested of any special significance. It appeared to be one case among many.

On closer examination, however, it can be seen that Dühring the secularist was well able to employ the special Christian sensibility in order to heighten the effect of his anti-Jewish arguments. His theory had clearly absorbed elements of the Christian resentment against Jews and Judaism. Jesus was a victim of the "scribes' corruption in Jerusalem," the responsibility for which contemporary Jewish scribes would have liked to transfer to the Romans. Adding insult to injury, these modern Jewish scholars claimed superiority for the collected wisdom of the Talmud over the teachings of Jesus. Jewish writers were engaged in habitually mocking Christianity, showing disrespect in face of "the highest martyrdom of humanity." Dühring did not recoil from a philosophical tour de force in combining his own rejection of Christianity with a denigration of the Jews for their refusal to follow Christ. Other people did not need the self-crucifixion of nature recommended by Christianity: "The eternal Jew burdened with the curse of nature" missed the opportunity for self-purification through Christ.[19]

The link between modern anti-Semitism and its Christian antecedents is more complicated in Dühring's case than Stöcker's, but is still conspicuous. Dühring's type of anti-Semitism has been called "anti-Christian anti-Semitism."[20] Insofar as this suggests that those who opposed anti-Semitism also opposed Christianity, this appellation is correct, but not if it is taken to mean that this anti-Semitism derived from opposition to Christianity—in the same way as Christian anti-Semitism was bound up with adherence to Christianity—or that the opposition to Christianity and Judaism had a common root and equal weight. It is true that Dühring's criticism of religion fell on Judaism and Christianity alike, but the opposition to Judaism was conjoined with additional motivations. Judaism was found to be defective on two counts: It was proscribed among other religions and also bore the hereditary burden attached to it by virtue of its clash with its rival, Christianity. In the crystallization of the anti-Semitic movement, the criticism of religion played no decisive role. The anti-Jewish motivations alone did the trick. That is why men like Stöcker and Dühring, irreconcilably at odds in terms of Christianity, could regard themselves—and they did, as we shall see later—as belonging to the same movement, namely that of anti-Semitism. Others, even less consistent in their thinking, easily combined bits and pieces of ideological elements from whatever provenance as long as they seemed to support their anti-Jewish ideas.

All the anti-Semites were unanimous as to the alleged moral inferiority of Jews, but differed as to its cause. Stöcker, although aware of the traditional Christian evaluation of the Talmud as the source of Jewish exclusiveness and immorality, was judicious enough to concede that such an influence had to be discounted for the majority of modern Jewry, even if they did not repudiate Talmudic Judaism altogether. He explained the moral recklessness of the modern Jew, which he took as a hard fact, to be a result of his religious indolence and abandonment of all tradition, even that of Judaism.[21] Other anti-Semites, however, were not prevented by such obvious changes in the mental constitution of modern Jewry from quoting Talmudic passages as the source of the alleged Jewish moral insensibility. The reference to the Talmudic sources, usually based on Rohling's *Talmudjude*, became a steady feature of anti-Semitic propaganda. Rohling's book was cited by Perrot in the epilogue to his "Era-articles," by Constantin Frantz in his *Nationalliberalismus und Judenschaft*, and by Pinkert in his *Judenfrage*, to mention only a few of the most influential anti-Jewish writings of the period. Duhring, on the other hand, held, as we have seen, the Old Testament's teaching responsible for Jewish immorality and regarded the "recent citation of Talmudic instances" to be superfluous. In spite of these differences, the three schools of thought—the theological, the Christian ideological, and the secular—confessed to having a common goal, fighting Jewish immorality, the prevalence of which was taken for granted.[22]

As far as the creation of a movement was concerned, the appeal of Marr to overcome the differences of background and commitment can be said to have met with a remarkable measure of success. Christians and Atheists, Catholics and Protestants, Conservatives and Liberals, or former Liberals, joined the anti-Semitic cause.[23] Their conception of the Jews as the common enemy united them. In the initial phase of the movement, such sense of common sentiment would do. In the course of time, however, the movement tended to create its own organs to realize its objectives; at this point the unity of anti-Semites floundered. They were hopelessly divided on the definition of their aims as well as on the means to be applied for their realization.

Once again, we may resort to a comparison between two extreme tendencies, the one represented by Treitschke and Stöcker and the other by Dühring. Whether Treitschke should be called an anti-Semite is a matter of semantics. Highly critical of the results of emancipation, he still declared its revocation to be unthinkable. On the other hand, Treitschke's perception of Jewish reality is as negative as that of any other anti-Semite, and he lays the responsibility for all the Jewish shortcomings, with the Jews alone, who should and could do better if they only wanted. Stöcker concurred with the diagnosis, as well as with the suggested therapy, but would not have relied upon Jewish self-improvement. Initially he was reluctant to recommend the revocation of the law of emancipation, but demanded its amendment in some particulars: the number of Jewish judges should be limited and schools should be made altogether free of Jewish teachers. A year after Stöcker's first speech, the so-called anti-Semites' petition was submitted to Chancellor Bismarck. In addition to Stöcker's demands, it asked for the prohibition of Jewish immigration to Germany, the introduction of a special census for Jews living there, and the exclusion of Jews from positions of governmental authority. After some hesitation, Stöcker joined his signature to that of the 265,000 other people who endorsed it.[24]

As far reaching as the suggested measures were, they seemed moderate in comparison to what Dühring had in mind. When he first dealt with the Jewish problem in 1875, he offered no advice on how to solve it. Given the social system, Jewish emancipation and even dominance appeared an unalterable fact, while in the society of the future, which Dühring anticipated to be socialist, though not Marxist, the whole problem would lose much of its acuteness. But when, at the turn of the decade, the revocation of Jewish emancipation became the battle cry of the anti-Semites, Dühring adopted the slogan and became one of its most radical exponents. Far from awaiting the elimination of the problem through a general reform of society, he contended that nothing short of special anti-Jewish legislation would rectify it. The details of the suggested legislation amounted to the restriction of Jewish activity to the fringes of German society. Other civilized nations would follow the German example, but even this was only an intermediate measure. Basically Dühring denied the right of Jewish existence at all, be it among other nations or in a special

Jewish state in Palestine or elsewhere. Though not made explicit, the wish to eliminate the hateful race—in defense of humanity to be sure—was unmistakably conveyed in the closing paragraph of Dühring's pamphlet of 1880.[25]

A latent division between Stöcker and Dühring, later to become an open conflict between the two, appeared in their attitudes toward baptized Jews. Though spiced by rudiments of Christian theology, Dühring's basic conception was rationalistic. This is clearly evident in the pivotal position the notion of race was permitted to occupy in his system. By granting the notion of race a central role, the immutable character of Jewish mentality is implicitly predicated. The act of baptism could, accordingly, make no difference whatsoever. Dühring was not the only one who took this stand. It was inherent in the very term "anti-Semitism." Its creator, Wilhelm Marr, an atheist like Dühring, made no bones about the consequences, that is, the exclusion of religious affiliation from the definition of the Jew. Even men like Glagau, Perrot, Wilmanns and Rudolph Meyer, though not anti-Christian, made no distinction between baptized and unbaptized Jews. Glagau had no hesitation in placing converted Jews like Strousberg with the other Jewish jobbers, stating that "from the baptized minister to the last Polish schnorrer they constitute a united chain"—and the others expressed themselves in similar terms.[26]

The mundane motivation of many a convert being common knowledge, the point of classing them with their former coreligionists could easily be understood. Yet such classification implied an overt criticism of the Church, which admitted such quasi-converts to the Christian community. Publicists like Glagau and politicians like Wilmanns (a member of the Reichstag) could afford to cast a critical eye on the ecclesiastical praxis. Not so an officer of the church like Stöcker, the court preacher. According to the official doctrine of the Church, a man baptized, for whatever reason, was a Christian. If a bad reason, he had to be chastised for his misdeeds as a Christian, but under no circumstances could he be thrown back to the community of unbaptized Jews. Thus, when the chips were down and the anti-Semites had to decide whether baptized Jews were to be included among the targets of their anti-Jewish campaign, the conflict between Stöcker and the racially minded anti-Semites was inevitable.[27]

The anti-Semitic idea, absorbed by people of different social background, social philosophy, and religious conviction, turned out to be strong enough to rally all of them to a common sentiment, but not to direct them to common action, not even so far as the Jewish question was concerned. The promoters of anti-Semitism deluded themselves that they had found not only the solution of the Jewish question but the key to all the intriguing problems of German society. Anti-Semitism, in their conception, ought to have assisted in overcoming all social divisions and cementing an overall national unity.

Paradoxically, it was the great success of anti-Semitism in penetrating various layers and circles of society that exposed the falsity of this conception. Anti-Semitism served as a uniting bond in such associations as the Antisemitenliga, which embraced people of similar background and convictions. Yet each group of anti-Semites brought to the idea of anti-Semitism their own social outlooks, economic interests, and religious doctrines. These differences came to the fore whenever cooperation between such groups was attempted; and the unification of all parties on the basis of anti-Semitism was frustrated. The opponents' charge that, by projecting Jews as the universal cause of social adversity, anti-Semitism was distorting social reality, can be said to have been vindicated by events.[28]

If anti-Semitism turned out to be ineffective as a medium of unification, it proved to be a most successful principle for social segregation. The expansion of the anti-Semitic movement expressed itself when associations, parties, and fraternities whose manifest social objectives were of an absolutely neutral nature added more or less explicit clauses to their constitutions excluding Jews from membership.

The most publicized exclusion of this kind, at the start of the movement, was that of the students' unions, the Burschenschaften. Participation in the life of patriotic fraternities was a part of the education of every German student. During the liberal era, Jewish students too could avail themselves of this opportunity. Now, as student bodies succumbed to anti-Semitic agitation, and anti-Semitism became a regular feature in the unions' activities, Jewish students found themselves, overnight and in many cases in the crudest fashion, expelled from their former associations. The Jewish reaction to these events was the founding of special Jewish student organizations, thus demonstrating the separateness of Jews and Gentiles, even within the same institution.[29]

What occurred in the students' unions was paralleled by what transpired in the Masonic lodges. A change in the climate of Masonic opinion took place, as we have seen, as early as the mid-1870s. The shift grew into a reversal of the open-door policy, especially in the Prussian lodges. In the confessedly Christian branch of Freemasonry, the attempt to alleviate the religious requirement and admit Jews, formerly the declared objective at least of a minority of the members, was now abandoned. Where Jews had previously been admitted either as members or as visitors, Jewish candidates were now repeatedly rejected, demonstrating the real attitude of the Christian majority, and the Jewish members drew their conclusions and dropped out of the lodges. Such former Jewish

The Crystallization

Masons in Berlin were then instrumental in establishing the fraternity of B'nai B'rith, affiliated with the main branch of this organization in the United States. The rapid expansion of these exclusive Jewish lodges—with three years of its foundation in 1882, B'nai B'rith could boast of twenty-three chapters all over Germany—amply demonstrated the new trend of social isolation of German Jewry.[30]

The segregatory tendency also made itself felt in the domain of political parties and associations, though in a less formalized way. Of course, Jews could never be expected to disperse themselves evenly between all the political parties. The well-meant advice of Eduard von Hartmann, given after the eruption of political anti-Semitism, that in their own interest Jews should spread out across the whole political spectrum, revealed a great measure of naivete in the face of social reality. Even at the time of liberalism, the Jews' choices were limited, both by the exclusiveness of the right wing and by their own inclination toward the middle and the left. The Prussian Conservative party could be joined by baptized Jews; Julius Stahl ascended there to eminence and leadership—but it must have been extremely difficult for an unbaptized Jew to find his place there. But beside such obvious facts, von Hartmann's advice ignored the natural tendency of every social group to support the party whose program is in line with its own economic and political interest. Due to their professional orientation as well as their social positions, Jews were predestined to side with certain political parties to the exclusion of others. Their affiliation with the National Liberals, and not only through the leading role of men like Ludwig Bamberger and Eduard Lasker, was notorious. But the range of choice was, theoretically at least, a much broader one, and with the exception of the confessedly Christian parties, limited numbers of Jews were indeed to be found in the other camps as well. With the emergence of the anti-Semitic trend, Jewish political mobility was most severely restricted. Even the National Liberals were now reluctant to appoint Jewish candidates, since Jewishness counted as a liability in a contest with a non-Jewish opponent. Jews now leaned politically toward the left, the party of the radical Freisinnige and even the socialists. The spontaneous concentration of Jews in leftist politics gave rise to an imposed seclusion from the main scene of activity, thus completing the Jewish social segregation.[31]

From the mid-1870s, anti-Semitic propaganda served as a weapon, as we have seen, for Conservatives and Catholics to use in combating the Liberals. When, ultimately, the former succeeded in ousting the latter and replacing them as the parliamentary confederates of Bismarck, the impression could easily have arisen that the Chancellor benefited from the new trend and indeed condoned it. The personal attitude of Bismarck and other high officials to anti-Semitism was no doubt ambivalent. No condem-

271

nation of the movement ever emerged from these high quarters. The petition of the anti-Semites, practically an appeal for curtailment of Jewish equality, was rejected by the government on formal grounds, by reference to the constitution that guaranteed civil rights irrespective of religious confession. No word of disapproval of the intended defamation was uttered.[32]

Whether a more energetic repudiation on the part of the authorities would have stemmed the tide is a moot question. It is, however, not because of its silence that the government shares the responsibility for what happened. What should have been their direct concern was the implementation of the law, granting Jews equal rights with other citizens. But, in the domain of public administration, including appointments in the universities and promotions in the army, the law remained a dead letter, notably so in Prussia. This set the tone for the country as a whole. Even baptized Jews had difficulty in being accepted or promoted in the army and the public administration. This was the case even in the heyday of liberalism. At that time, it was explicable as the residue of former obstacles, which would be removed with the progressive democratization of state and society. Whether such a development was in the cards at all remains a matter of speculation. Once the anti-Semitic movement engulfed society, such liberalizing tendencies, if ever they really existed, were reversed. Instead of directing public opinion in favor of Jewish equality, the authorities sought justification for their own discrimination in the unwillingness of the public to permit Jews to occupy positions of teaching or administrative authority. The exclusion of the Jews from such positions, perhaps even more than their social and political segregation, demonstrated their exceptional and precarious situation, recalling once again the notion of the pariah.[33]

22 | The Hungarian Variation

THE OUTBREAK OF the anti-Semitic movement in Germany was by no means a local affair. It aroused international attention, its ups and downs being reported in the whole European and even American press. The tone of most of these reactions, especially in the West, conveyed a sense of surprise, that such things could still happen toward the end of the nineteenth century.[1] Yet those who were attuned to the music that reached them from Berlin had a sympathetic response. For Gyözö Istoczy, in Hungary, the report from Germany contained a most welcome message; it reassured him that what he had preached for half a decade—mostly to deaf ears—was not a product of his idiosyncratic animosity toward Hungarian Jews. Well-known representatives of the great nation of *Dichter und Denker*—poets and thinkers, court-preacher Stöcker, the noted historian Treitschke, and the militant philosopher Dühring—said substantially the same. It must have been most gratifying for Istoczy to find his own speech on the possible repatriation of Jews to Palestine quoted by the leading figure among the radical anti-Semites, Wilhelm Marr. He entered into correspondence with Marr, expressing the hope that the success of the anti-Jewish campaign in Germany would sustain his own efforts in his homeland.[2]

Confirmed in his conviction, Istoczy not only returned to his subject in his speeches in Parliament, but resorted to other means of propagating his ideas. In October 1880 he launched an anti-Semitic periodical and published the constitution of a "Central Association of Non-Jewish Hungarians." Istoczy's monthly, called *Twelve Circulars*, continued for the

273

next four years, providing reports on anti-Semitic activities in Hungary and abroad, as well as printing anti-Semitic articles and essays of indiscriminate provenance and merit. The statutes of the association were adapted from the constitution of Wilhelm Marr's Antisemitenliga with some important qualifications. People who wished to work secretly for the elimination of Jewish influence could join the association without their membership being publicized. Even more surprising, there was a provision for baptized Jews to be accepted, though only as undisclosed members. Both these provisions are indicative of the complex situation in Hungary, which precluded the division between Jews and their opponents along clear-cut social or other criteria.[3]

To what extent these efforts of Istoczy met with immediate success is not clear. Initially, at least, the constitution of his association served as a blueprint for the future rather than a reflection of concrete reality. Yet the mere proposal of an anti-Semitic association aroused sufficient attention to cause a member of Parliament to ask the government whether it was in accordance with the law of the country, and whether a permit for the association had been applied for and granted. Compared with the derisory reception accorded Istoczy's earlier attempts to make himself heard, the tone of the inquiry as well as the answer of Premier Tisza—though clearly not in favor of Istoczy's intentions as far as the government was concerned—did reveal a thorough shift in the situation. Istoczy's proposals were now seen as a possible danger to the peace of the country, not as the fantasies of a lunatic. Istoczy's periodical, too, though the extent of its distribution is unknown, at least persisted. This was in contrast to an earlier attempt, a year before the outbreak of the German movement, which Istoczy himself informs us was stillborn. Istoczy's most tangible success, however, was that he began to draw into his orbit other members of Parliament; by 1882 the anti-Semitic group numbered five members.[4]

That anti-Semitic agitation affected public life was clearly demonstrated in the student riots at the university in Budapest in the first month of 1881. Jewish students were attacked, the manifest reason being the Christian students' annoyance at the disproportionately high percentage of Jews in the school—36 percent of the medical students and 26 percent of the law students. Istoczy became the mentor as well as the living symbol for the anti-Semitic students. A petition, signed by some four hundred of them, was handed to him as the man best able to represent the students' complaints before the government and Parliament. All this conformed to the German pattern of the movement—with one important qualification. The Hungarian government took a firm stand against the noisiest manifestation of the movement. An assembly of the students, planned in the wake of the university riots, was prevented by the police on the direct order of Premier Tisza—a measure that elicited Istoczy's protest in the course of a parliamentary interpellation.[5]

Some people began to sense danger and tried to locate the cause of the rising anti-Semitism. A liberal member of Parliament ventured the opinion that the failure of the government to legalize civil marriage—because of the resistance of the Church and conservative elements in Hungarian society—had prevented the full integration of Hungarian Jews through intermarriage. Even some members of the government seem to have shared this view, for some weeks later a bill enabling civil marriage, restricted to cases where religious marriage was out of order, was submitted to Parliament. Yet even if such a law could have been enacted—in fact it was removed from the agenda—it would certainly not have accelerated assimilation sufficiently to eliminate the anti-Semitic attacks.[6]

Jewish assimilation had been progressing in Hungary. Instances of intermarriage[7] occurred, and these required that the Jewish partner convert. Still, the number of converts, through intermarriage and otherwise, though extensive in certain circles, remained marginal as far as the community as a whole was concerned. It left Hungarian Jewry at large a distinct minority, partly acculturated and partly even culturally aloof, but in all respects highly visible, especially because of its concentration in certain sectors of the economy and the professions. This conspicuousness exposed it to critical comment and observation.[8] Under the impact of the German example, these comments turned into overt anti-Semitism. In 1882 the movement received a mighty impetus from two sources, one from Russia, the other deriving from a local event, the blood-libel agitation of Tiszaeszlár.

In the spring of 1881, the first major Russian pogroms occurred in the wake of the assassination of Alexander II. If what has been suggested by some historians is true, that the anti-Jewish propaganda preceding the violence in Russia was also fed, if not initiated, by the reports from Germany, then the central significance of German anti-Semitism—not of course as an exclusive cause, but certainly as an igniting spark—would appear even more embracing. At any rate, the pogroms in Russia had a tangible influence on Hungary, already affected by the direct contact with Germany. Substantial numbers of Russian Jewish refugees—precursors of the great wave of emigration to the West that started as the aftermath of the pogroms—reached Hungary during the years 1881-1882. Hungarian public opinion had long been sensitive to the problem of immigration for a slow but steady influx of East-European Jews had arrived before and after emancipation. The improved political and economic situation of Hungarian Jewry presented an attraction to their less fortunate brethren of

Russia and Galicia. The wave of 1881-1882 was especially notable, if not because of its scope, then because of its origin: the notorious Russian atrocities. The Hungarian reaction was ambivalent. Liberal elements may have shared the indignation of the West about the inhumanity involved, but others were more apprehensive about the possibility that the Russian persecution of Jews stimulate an unwelcome immigration to Hungary. Indeed a number of counties of northeastern Hungary, through which the immigration proceeded, submitted a petition to Parliament asking for legislative protection against it.[9] The anti-Jewish sentiments aired in the course of the public debate on this issue became exacerbated when linked up with the agitation of the Tiszaeszlár blood-libel.

The small Jewish community of Tiszaeszlár, a town on the upper part of the river Tisza, consisted of Jews of the popular Hassidic type, who, even if accommodated to the Hungarian environment, were still regarded as of Galician provenance. It happened that a Gentile girl of fifteen disappeared on the Sabbath preceding Passover. The girl's mother, having no clue to the riddle of her daughter's disappearance, lent an ear to the ever-growing rumors that the Jews might have killed her for her blood, to be used on the approaching Jewish festival. The belief in the blood-libel as a recurring Jewish ritual was widespread in the Hungarian countryside. Many instances were cited in connection with the Tiszaeszlár case, both by defenders of the Jews—to show how past accusations had turned out to be unfounded—and their accusers—to substantiate the blood-libel's credibility by its persistence.[10]

The Tiszaeszlár case, like most others, would probably have petered out, even if the truth about the supposed victim had not eventually been discovered. In this instance, however, the allegation of the Jewish crime passed from the local to the national scene. The Catholic priest of Tiszaeszlár reported it to the press and appealed to Istoczy and his colleague, Géza von Onody, to help prevent the obstruction of justice by Jews, in whose culpability he firmly believed. The anti-Semitic propagandists, as well as news-mongering journalists, seized upon the sensation, lending it national prominence through interpellation in Parliament and extensive press reports. The local authorities turned into zealous persecutors of the Jewish defendants, so that even when the corpse of the lost girl was found in the water of the river Tisza, its identification was frustrated by psychological and juridical distortions.

The trial, which ended in the acquittal of the Jewish defendants, lasted well over a year. It aroused international interest and nationwide agitation, which did not subside with the judges' verdict. Convinced of Jewish culpability in advance, the Jew-haters, instead of being placated by the result of the process, were rather more excited by it. Attacks on Jews and

276

breaches of the public peace had already occurred during the early stages of the affair. The most severe among them was that at Bratislava in September 1882. The unrest assumed dangerous dimensions during the months following the acquittal. Bratislava was once again the main scene of the disturbances, which also engulfed the capital and many other cities and villages in different parts of Hungary. Jewish public opinion ascribed the unrest to the deliberate agitation of the propagandists. Indeed, there was no lack of that, but the disturbances were at the same time an expression of anti-Jewish prejudice and of resentment against the Jewish advances of recent times. It was thanks to the strong arm of the government, which was quick to take action when necessary, that the pogrom-like attacks of the mob were curbed and kept within limits.[11]

For anti-Semites like Istoczy, the events of 1880-1883 were highly gratifying. They seemed to confirm his conviction of the seriousness, and even centrality, of the Jewish question. The anti-Jewish agitation to which he amply contributed through his speeches and writings was taken by Istoczy as a sign that the time was ripe for political action to realize his more far-reaching objectives. His stand on the Jewish problem hardened. If in 1880 he still contemplated having baptized Jews join the movement, in the ensuing years his outlook became outspokenly racial. At the same time he made use of the traditional Christian arguments. He quoted Rohling in support of the blood-libel accusation and published articles about the immorality of the Jews, relying once again on the by then widely known *Talmudjude*.[12] Rohling himself, since 1876 professor of Hebrew antiquities at Charles University in Prague, played a part in the Hungarian affairs. The professor volunteered to testify before the court in session on the Tiszaeszlar case that Jews, according to their traditional sources, do indeed require Christian blood for their Passover ritual.[13] It is no wonder, given such views, that anti-Semitism became more and more extreme, on both the social and the political level.

As mentioned above, five other members of Parliament sided with Istoczy on the anti-Semitic issue. Istoczy continued to be a member of the Liberals, the party of the government. The other five belonged to the radical opposition, the Party of Independence—radical in this case because of its uncompromising stand on the question of Hungarian autonomy within the Austro-Hungarian Empire. That anti-Semitism could still be integrated with conflicting political trends and affiliations is an indication that it had not yet been raised to the rank of an embracing intellectual and political principle. Parties, too, could continue tolerating nonconformist views on a subject conceived of as a side issue. The anti-Jewish agitation, however, turned out to be a snowballing process. The anti-Semitic counties asked first for protection against Jewish immigration, but then a petition was submitted to Parliament demanding the repeal of the law of emancipation, a demand that the anti-Semitic members of Parliament adopted as their own. On this issue there was no possible compromise. The Liberals as well as the Party of Independence were committed to the principle of equality before the law, regardless of religious affiliation. Istoczy had left the Liberal party as early as 1882, the other anti-Semites joined him a year later to establish their own party.[14]

The subsequent history of the anti-Semitic party, the details of which it is unnecessary to tell here, demonstrates, as does the history of the anti-Semitic parties in Germany, that anti-Semitism was not effective in rallying people who differed on other social or political issues. The election of 1884 took place in the aftermath of the Tiszaeszlár affair and brought the membership of the Anti-Semitic party to its highest peak, 17 representatives out of 257. They were committed to the anti-Semitic plank, on which they had been elected, but once the relation to Austria—the shibboleth of Hungarian politics—became an issue, the unity of the anti-Semites crumbled. Convinced supporter of the Ausgleich—the basic political principle of the governing Liberals, to which he had belonged—Istoczy was unable to cooperate with those anti-Semites who held a contradictory view. He and two other members of the anti-Semitic party seceded. Atomized, the anti-Semitic parliamentary force lost whatever effectiveness it ever possessed.[15]

The historical significance of the wave of anti-Semitism that engulfed Hungarian society in the 1880s was that it halted the process of integration that had followed emancipation. Outwardly, the country quieted down toward the end of the decade, and the ruling Liberal party passed legislation designed to consolidate the Jewish position. In 1895 civil marriage was introduced and Judaism was given the status of a recognized religion, putting it on a par with the Christian churches. However, in both houses of Parliament, especially the upper chamber, these laws passed in the face of angry opposition from representatives of the Catholic Church and conservative Catholic circles. These now organized a new party, the People's party, which stood for the preservation of the Christian character of society and the state. These aims were emphatically anti-Semitic, and the party actively pursued the elimination of Jews from certain economic and other positions. Consumer organizations and financial institutions founded by the People's party were not only competing with Jewish concerns but promoting a new spirit of hostility to Jews and Judaism. The conservatives also strongly criticized the participation of Jews in Hungarian cultural life. In places where they exercised power, as, for example, in institutions of higher learning, they inhibited Jews from attaining positions consonant with their abilities and achievements. The failure of anti-Semitism to attain

278

its political goals did not bring about its demise. The residue of the anti-Semitic movement continued to show its strength as a divisive and subversive factor in Hungarian life, no less than it had in Germany where it had originated.[16]

Anti-Semitism, in showing its mettle on the Hungarian scene, seemed to disprove its opponents' contention that it was an exclusively German phenomenon. German as well as Hungarian anti-Semites, though spurred by local conditions, presented their ideas as relating to the life of all European Christian countries. Portraying Jews as a danger to all civilized nations, they offered anti-Semitism as the remedy to a universal social disease. To demonstrate the universal character of this movement, the idea of an international anti-Semitic congress emerged. Who was the first to suggest it is unknown, but when it was convened in September 1882 in Dresden the three Hungarian representatives, all of them members of the Hungarian Parliament, played an important role in the proceedings. Ivan von Simonyi served as one of the chairmen of the congress. He delivered a speech on "Anti-Semitism and the Laws of Human Society," and Istoczy composed a "Manifesto to the Governments and Nations of Christian States Endangered by Judaism." It wished to alert the non-Jewish world to be on its guard against the common enemy, the Jew.[17]

The congress of Dresden brought together some of the leading figures of the anti-Semitic movement: Stöcker, Ernst Henrici, and Pinkert-Waldegg from Germany; Karl von Zerboni (of whom we shall hear in the next chapter) from Austria; and Simonyi and Istoczy from Hungary. According to the congress report, some Russian representatives were also present; these, however, remained anonymous.[18] Though united in their animosity against Jews and Judaism, the representatives operated under different political conditions and could not hope to concur in a common practical program. Besides, the German representatives, Stöcker on the one side and Henrici on the other, were deeply divided among themselves as to the ideological foundations as well as the practical consequences of their anti-Semitism. Istoczy in his memorandum made an effort to reconcile the two differing trends. He presented the European nations' opposition to Judaism in religious as well as racial terms: "More and more does Judaism undermine the Christian religion that turned into a specific race-religion of the European-Aryan nations."[19] The draft of the manifesto was submitted to the representatives of the different schools of thought and its final version was no doubt the result of compromise.[20] The conclusions from the congress were necessarily of a limited nature. They consisted of an appeal to those who were aware of the "Jewish danger" to organize themselves into voluntary associations with the declared aim of setting a limit to Jewish dominance. These associations were expected to join the newly established Alliance Antijuive Universelle. The name of this organization was deliberately chosen as the counterpart to the Alliance Israelite Universelle, decried as the instrument of Jewish world domination. The myth of the Jewish world conspiracy was evidently among the leading ideas at the conference.[21]

The organizers' efforts to overcome the differences between conflicting ideologies had limited success, and very soon came under severe attack from one Dr. J. Amman in Berlin, a follower of Eugen Dühring. The fact of Istoczy's memorandum having been addressed to the Christian nation meant, in Amman's view, a regression to obsolete concepts, ignoring the more modern secular foundation of anti-Semitism evolved by Eugen Duhring.[22] The clash between the two opposing trends governed the discussion during the second international congress that took place a year later, in April 1883, in Chemnitz.[23] More international than the first, owing to the presence of some representatives from Rumania, Serbia, and France (the Austrians were absent), its transactions were even more Germany-centered. Though destined to take more concrete steps toward realization of its aims, the conference spent time patching up the ideological differences. Though upholding the principle that the commitment to anti-Semitism ought to unite Gentiles of all persuasions and nations, Otto Glagau, who presided over the assembly, conceded that it had seldom been followed in practice. The weakness of anti-Semitism as a principle of organizational unification had been demonstrated also on the international scene. What practical advice the participants could take with them boiled down to the recommendation of Liebermann von Sonnenberg that each of them should work for the social isolation and economic boycott of Jews in his own country. They should refrain from reading the Jewish press and refuse to join any association that would accept Jews as members.[24] It was in this way, and mainly on the local level, that anti-Semitism became an effective social factor at this time.

23│The Austrian Extension

IN SPITE OF AUSTRIA'S geographical and cultural proximity to Germany and similar economic unrest, the anti-Semitic movement was somewhat late getting started there. The great crash of 1873 began in Vienna. The devastating repercussions, especially for the small investors, were as severe there as in Germany; nor was the Jewish involvement in the artificial boom any less conspicuous. When the reckoning began and people were looking for scapegoats, Jews were mentioned. However, they were not made the villain of the piece as they had been in Germany. To be sure, there was obvious resentment and quite vociferous criticism of the spectacular advancement of Jews in business and the professions. This is well illustrated by Theodor Billroth's protest against Jewish preponderance in medicine. In 1876 Billroth, who was in charge of medical studies in Vienna, disqualified Jews for the profession on account of the alleged bad traits inherent in most of them. Though the professor wished his criticism to be distinguished from "popular [*beliebt*] modern *Judenschimpfen* ["grumbling about Jews"], there are obvious similarities. The professor's protest, as well as the favorable response to it by the Gentile student body, must be seen as a part of the widespread annoyance at the remarkable progress made by the Jews. Characteristically, Billroth's criticism had been rejected by virtually all the organs of liberal public opinion. These were published for the most part by Jews, a reflection of the identity of interests between the prevailing political and social order on the one hand and Austrian Jewish society on the other.[1]

A significant difference between the Jewish situation in Austria and

281

Germany derived from the different social makeup of the liberals, or at least their political leadership. Liberalism in Germany was in the main a product of the rising middle class, toward which Jews were oriented. Individual Jews such as Ludwig Bamberger and Eduard Lasker could and did rise to leading ranks in the Liberal party. Austrian liberalism, on the other hand, was rooted in the aristocracy, both high and low, a heritage of the time of Joseph II. These aristocrats willingly participated in the benefits of the economic and social modernization that had been prompted by Jewish capital and inventiveness, while retaining the political leadership within their own circles. In a letter to his son in 1872, Ignaz Plener, referring to an observation his son had made a year before that "Jews do not yet push themselves to politics," stated that things had changed in the wake of the recent elections. By then there were some Jews in the House of Representatives and two baptized ones in the government.[2] If Jews were mainly active in finance and the professions, members of the aristocracy too lent their names to those economic and financial enterprises, which, starting with the crash of 1873, had got into trouble. The close association with the aristocracy may have saved the Jews from being misrepresented. At any rate, in the first years of the economic crisis, open attacks on Jews still remained the preserve of the militant clerical cliques of the Sebastian Brunner school.[3]

For the time being, more serious Catholic thinkers, notably Karl von Vogelsang, held back from the anti-Jewish campaign. Asked in 1876 whether it would not be desirable for the weekly *Vaterland*, edited by him, to emulate its Berlin counterpart, the Catholic *Germania*, in "exposing the devastation wrought by Jews in politics and social and economic life" in Austria, he declined. What in fact came under severe attack at this juncture was liberalism as a system and a trend. It was attacked not only by the slowly emerging socialist movement, but also by Catholic thinkers who had become aware of the deep social problems created by the rule of free enterprise and capitalistic investment. Karl Vogelsang was the spiritual leader of this group, which expressed its ideas in the political journal *Vaterland* and, in greater depth, in the monthly *Österreichische Monatsschrift für Gesellschaftswissenschaft*, dedicated to economic and social problems. In the latter, in 1879, Anton Tschörner, a noted economist, published a comprehensive survey of working conditions and wages in various industries. He found that, unprotected by any law, especially in the newly created branches of industry, workers were being exploited by the capitalists. Tschörner charged that the beneficiaries of the system were oblivious of the hardship and suffering caused by their undertakings, unless made aware of them by the militant socialists. Written at the time when anti-Jewish propaganda in Germany—based on the alleged

Jewish culpability for all the evils of economic liberalism—reached its peak, Tschörner's indictment did not as much as mention Jews. Based on a realistic survey, Tschörner's findings applied equally to the branches of economy with a strong Jewish involvement—for example, the textile industry—and those,· especially heavy industry, where Jews were not involved at all.[4]

Though the social system as such was the direct target of criticism in Vogelsang's circles, this does not mean that Jews were held to be innocent in bringing it about. In 1875, explaining his refusal to join the Berlin *Germania* in its anti-Jewish campaign, Vogelsang said the situation in Austria was beyond being repaired simply by attacking or even eliminating the Jews. Liberalism as such was "imbued through and through by the Jewish spirit" and only by repudiating liberal institutions and innovations could society be liberated from its evil. The Jewish problem would then take care of itself.

The ideological moorings of this attitude have to be seen in Vogelsang's faith in an original social teaching of the Church which, refurbished and adapted to modern conditions, would remedy all the social harms and iniquities. Reminiscent of the doctrines of the French Catholic thinkers of the Restoration period, this thesis indicates the attempts of Catholicism to regain lost ground by relying on intellectually respectable reasoning. Vogelsang used it to establish the affinity of Judaism to liberalism and the repugnance of Christianity to it. Christianity is said to represent "the idea of mutuality and righteousness," while Judaism is the carrier of "the inferior spirit of individualism," a product of the divinely imposed exile of two thousand years. When liberalism was replaced with a "genuine Christian society," Judaism would fade out automatically. Since he trusted in a radical rectification of the situation, it was unnecessary for Vogelsang to engage in an anti-Jewish campaign along the lines of his Berlin counterparts. Still, negating a place for Jews in the society of the future meant the condemnation of Jewish existence in the present. The dissemination of such ideas could only create an atmosphere where active combating of Jews became the order of the day, and in which, ultimately, Vogelsang and his followers joined.[5]

The first attempts to draw practical consequences from anti-Jewish sentiment seem to have been made in the student unions or fraternities. During the era of liberalism, Jewish students saw the fraternities as an opportunity for social integration. Constituting a substantial part of the student body in the universities—21 percent in Vienna in 1870—Jews played an important part in the fraternities. On the occasion of the Billroth affair in 1876, the Leseverein Deutscher Studenten wished to send a supporting address to the much-criticized professor. It could only do so in the face of strong opposition from its Jewish members. The integration was obviously not complete, though officially at least the fraternities remained open to Jews. The first exclusion of Jews may have occurred as early as 1878, but most of the unions started discussing the subject only in 1880. In 1883, the anti-Jewish members of the fraternity Teutonia prevailed, and by the end of the decade all the unions became *judenrein*.[6]

The slowness of this development in the Austrian student body is in stark contrast to what happened in the German Burschenschaften, where the exclusion of Jews was carried out in all the universities in a matter of months. For Austria, however, this gradualness is typical; anti-Semitism penetrated slowly but thoroughly into the organizational fabric of Austrian society, accompanied only occasionally by a kind of spontaneous agitation according to the German pattern. This halting reaction to the stimulation coming from Germany is the more astounding as Austria, and especially Vienna, did not lack its own leaven for anti-Jewish fermentation.[7] The increase of the Jewish community from 6,200 in 1860 (2.2 percent of the population) to 72,600 in 1880 (10 percent)—compared to an increase from 3.5 percent to 4.8 percent in Berlin in the same period—was no doubt a strong irritation for people unsympathetic to Jews. In addition, the clerically inspired anti-Jewish indoctrination had continued in Austria unabatedly. If, nonetheless, anti-Semitism was slow to develop into a manifest political trend, the reason has to be sought in the peculiar sociopolitical conditions of the country.[8]

From the beginning of the liberal era in the late 1850s, Germany was characterized by sociopolitical mobility. Political trends were expressed in the creation of associations and parties. Thus, anti-Semitism could be harnessed—as indeed had been done in an exemplary fashion by Stöcker—to the service of political objectives, and it played at least an accessory role in ousting the former liberal regime. In Austria, the political regime rested on a most restrictive electoral system, which allowed only some 3 percent of the population, the aristocracy and the upper bourgeoisie, to have a say in the choice of government through sending representatives to the Reichsrat. The upper class was so dominant that it could rule without concern for the complaints of the lower classes or for criticism levied by their intellectual—Catholic or socialist—advocates. In fact, the change in the government and the subsequent shift in the electoral system was not a result of internal social pressure. The liberal Constitutional party was ousted in August 1879 in the wake of a disagreement with the Emperor Franz Joseph on a foreign policy issue: the occupation of Bosnia. The new head of the government, Count Taaffe, having no anti-liberal commitments, it was not at all clear what course he would steer in internal affairs. At any rate, the artisans and laborers who had been shunned by the liberals thought the time was ripe to encourage intervention in their favor. In October-November 1880, the first meeting of artisans, assembled by the watchmaker Buschenhager, took place in Vienna. It demanded the protection of the trained craftsmen against competition from Jewish hawkers. Out of these meetings there emerged a year later the founding of an Association for the Protection of the Artisan. In 1882 this association had become the Österreichischer Reformverein.

Reformverein was the term applied by the German anti-Semites to their association; and it was with the conscious adoption of their program and methods that the term was transplanted to the Viennese political scene. The leadership now went out of the hands of the simple artisans and was taken over by politicians like Robert Pattai, a lawyer, and Karl von Zerboni, the editor of the weekly *Österreichischer Volksfreund*, a periodical that propagated the association's aims in an effort to gain political power through the mobilization of popular support. This effort became a promising enterprise due to an unprecedented step taken by Minister-President Taaffe. Needing political support, Taaffe compromised with the Polish and Czech landed nobility who, up to then, had been largely excluded from the franchise. Under the new electoral system introduced in 1882, any man who paid a minimum of five guilden in direct taxation received the right to vote. Thus large numbers of people, previously neutralized politically, gained access to the forum of public affairs.[9]

Most of the new politicians who entered the scene now made ample use of the anti-Semitic sentiments that saturated Vienna. The Reformverein engaged in active agitation. In its slogan it demanded the expulsion of Jews from their political, economic, and social positions. This was to be done by refusing to vote for them, to buy from them, and to have any contact with them. The ideology sustaining this agitation consisted of bits and pieces of the current anti-Jewish arguments, strongly colored by the traditional Christian conception of Jews and Judaism. In a gathering of some five hundred participants in April 1882, a speaker named Franz Holubek declared that "The Jews have not shown themselves worthy of emancipation . . . The Jew is no longer a co-citizen. He made himself our master, our oppressor . . . Do you know what gives these people the right to put their foot on our neck? The Talmud, in which you Christians are called dogs, donkeys, and pigs." This invective provoked an uproar in the audience, causing the police to dissolve the meeting. Holubek was indicted for interreligious incitement but in the ensuing trial, defended by Pattai, he was found innocent. The line of defense was that the alleged invective conformed to scholarly established truth as stated in the learned treatise *The Talmudjude*, by August Rohling, professor of Hebrew literature at Charles University in Prague.[10]

285

Rohling's *Talmudjude* did not differ essentially from the many pamphlets and articles that had been issued earlier by Sebastian Brunner and Albert Wiesinger without eliciting much public attention. The court's verdict in the Holubek case, however, seemed to have corroborated the accusations against the Talmud, and the concomitant defamation of the Jewish community. Thus Adolf Jellinek and Moritz Gudemann, both scholars of rank and officiating rabbis of the Viennese community, protested the implied insinuation, while their less well known colleague Samuel Bloch, the rabbi of Florisdorf, a suburb of Vienna, decided to use the opportunity to discredit the pretended scholarly authority of Rohling. He therefore charged Rohling with having falsified the Talmudic sources, using in fact Eisenmenger's quotations, and with being unable even to read the original Aramaic text. A much publicized controversy between the professor and the rabbi arose and very soon transcended the Holubek affair. For meanwhile, the news of the Tiszaeszlár trial, in which Rohling had also been involved, began to occupy public attention. The Prague professor had volunteered to testify under oath, before the court in Hungary, that Jewish religious sources indeed contained the prescription for the ritual murder of Christians. Rabbi Bloch then accused Rohling of having proposed perjury, thus compelling the professor to sue him for libel.[11]

The affair concluded with the moral defeat of Rohling. Knowing he was unable to prove his point, he withdrew his suit, but not until 1885. Even then, those with anti-Jewish bias were not convinced of Rohling's failings, and meanwhile his *Talmudjude* and his other publications had gained unprecedented publicity. Indeed, such crude anti-Semitism reached its peak in Austria in those years. The government's attempts to contain it were of no avail, even though, among other actions, they forbade the circulation of Istoczy's anti-Semitic manifesto, which had been issued after the Dresden assembly. They also seem to have prevented Austrian representatives from attending the Chemnitz assembly.[12] Such administrative measures, however, could not stop the public agitation to which broad segments of the population seem to have responded. How deeply the situation had been affected can be gauged from Ernst Plener's observation about the dilemma in which the leadership of the Liberal party found itself. Having enjoyed the support of the Jews, especially the intelligentsia and those in ethnically mixed districts such as in Moravia, the party was expected to take a stand on behalf of the Jews in their hour of trial. To have done so, however, would have cost the party's candidates the votes of the petit bourgeoisie, who were still loyal to its program.[13]

The number of Liberal party members who abandoned their former commitment must have been legion. Some of these became instrumental in creating the opposing parties and adopting, in the course of time, an anti-Semitic stand.[14] The outstanding example is Georg Ritter von Schönerer, the founder of the German National party. Schönerer took as his political objective the ultimate affiliation of the German-speaking parts of Austria to the Reich. This long-range political goal implied some immediate consequences. It required the supremacy of the Germanic peoples over the other nationalities—the Hungarian, the Czechs, and the Poles within the Austrian Empire—and the loosening of the existing ties between them. Closer cooperation with the German Reich was presented as ideological as well as practical necessity. Though Schönerer pleaded for the protection of landed property and productive labor against "the Semitic domination of money," a proper anti-Semitic program had not yet crystallized. There were Jews who subscribed to the nationalist as well as the social aspects of this ideology and participated in establishing Schönerer's party. The final formulation of its political credentials, the Linz Program of 1882, was as much the work of the Jewish historian and publicist Heinrich Friedjung as it was Schönerer's.[15]

Still, the strong emphasis on nationalism modeled on the German pattern no doubt created an affinity for anti-Semitism. Anti-Semitism being in the ascendancy in public life, it was also good policy for any party to adopt it. Thus, in 1885 Schönerer added a paragraph to the party's program stating that its realization presupposed "the elimination of the Jewish influence in all areas of public life." As a former Liberal, however, Schönerer retained his strong anticlerical convictions. This prevented him from basing his anti-Semitism on the confessional presumptions represented by Karl von Vogelsang. Though not shunning the use of popular invectives against Talmudic Judaism, the main target of his attacks was the Jewish race, explicitly denying the possibility of Jewish assimilation through baptism.[16]

Adopting race and blood as the central terms of his propaganda, Schönerer consciously joined the radical anti-Semites of the Reich—Marr, Dühring, and others. Though German in origin, this radical movement did not lack representatives in Austria, especially in academic circles. In his *Babylonierthum, Judenthum und Christenthum* (1882), Adolf Wahrmund, lecturer at Vienna University and the Oriental Academy, while giving lip service to a spiritual orientation, avoided racial terminology. Factually, however, he invested Jews with ineradicable demonic qualities: "frantic haughtiness, intellectual imbecility, and inhuman harshness of heart." Thus there could be no possibility of change through baptism.[17]

It was mainly among the nationally minded students that Schönerer recruited the adherents of his consistently racist anti-Semitism. On the broader public scene, however, the religiously colored anti-Semitism inspired by Karl von Vogelsang prevailed. More an ideologist than an organizer, he nonetheless became actively involved in the founding of the Christian Socialist Organization in 1887. True to Vogelsang's conception, the organization sought to achieve the necessary social reforms on a positive Christian basis, which gave it necessarily an anti-Jewish slant. As mentioned previously, Vogelsang initially wished to combat the Jewish influence only by re-establishing the Christian base of Gentile society. Once he was engaged in practical politics, however, such distinctions lost their validity. The organization's spokesmen had no hesitation in resorting to all the anti-Semitic slogans in vogue since the outbreak of the anti-Semitic movement. Whether because of this agitation or the credibility of the organization's social program, it made rapid progress. The meetings drew exceptional numbers of people, and local chapters were established in several districts within and outside the capital. Because of its practical effectiveness, the organization was joined by one of the most popular political figures in Vienna, Karl Lueger, who made it a willing instrument of his political career.[18]

Lueger, like Schönerer, had belonged to the radical wing of the liberal camp. The members of this group sustained the principles of liberalism but were critical of the way they had been implemented by the ruling party in the national government as well as in the Viennese municipality. Lueger and his colleague, Ignatz Mandl, a Jewish lawyer, both members of the municipality, fought corruption and ineptitude as well as the moral insensitivity of the establishment to the suffering of the lower classes. Lueger's social attitude, having much in common with that of the Christian Socialists, must have made him feel some affinity toward them, while on the Jewish issue he seemed to have no firm convictions. The Christian Socialists for their part wished to see this popular figure, who also excelled as a speaker, in their ranks. At first Lueger, whether because of the anti-Jewish aspect of the organization or for other reasons, showed some reserve. But when, in 1887, he finally accepted an invitation to appear on the agenda of a public meeting of the organization, he outdid, in his anti-Jewish harangue, the speaker before him, who happened to be a well-known anti-Semite from Hungary. Lueger was now rapidly absorbed by the Christian Socialist camp. He became acquainted with Vogelsang, accepted his spiritual leadership, and acted as a loyal practicing Catholic. In return, he was granted uncontested leadership among the Christian Socialists and assumed a central role in the public life of the country and especially of the capital.[19]

Toward the end of the 1880s the monotony of the political scene was broken. By comparison with the ten previous years, the picture became spectacularly variegated. Though out of power, the Liberals retained important positions in the administration and in the economy as well as controlling public opinion through the press (*Neue Freie Presse*). This Liberal bulwark was attacked on the right by the Catholics, who were themselves divided between the clericals of the school of Sebastian Brunner, the Conservatives of mostly aristocratic background, and the Christian Socialists. On the left were the Radicals and the Social Democrats, the latter having established their party in 1889. Still active were the first promoters of anti-Semitism, the artisans and the adherents of the Reformverein. Distinct from all these, because of its German orientation, was Schönerer's German National party. The representatives of the Czechs and Poles in the Reichsrat added their own variations.

It was against this checkered background that the political struggle of the ensuing years was fought. One final outcome was that Lueger realized his ambition to become the lord mayor of Vienna. The Christian Socialist party, headed by Lueger, cut into the membership of its rivals the Radicals, the members of the Reformverein, and the German Nationalists. The only match for Lueger among the leaders of these parties was Schönerer, but his appeal to the national sentiments, though attractive to some, was repulsive to others, as it seemed to run contrary to Austrian loyalties. In addition, Schönerer antagonized people through his intransigency and committed tactical and other mistakes. Lueger, on the other hand, was a master of what today would be called public relations, skillfully attracting people from many quarters. Still, no party could have hoped to absorb all the others, and the ultimate success of Lueger rested on his limitation of his political objectives. Instead of striving for the unification of all the anti-Liberal forces, he was content with marshaling them for common political action on an ad hoc basis. He created a loose coalition between the many factions, under the name of United Christians. Though stressing the positive Christian aspect, the name became synonymous with anti-Semite. It was with protests against Jewish dominance of Viennese public life that Lueger compelled Emperor Franz Joseph, after repeated refusals, to confirm him in 1897 as the elected mayor of the capital.[20]

When one compares the political impact of anti-Semitism in Austria and in Germany, striking dissimilarities emerge. The deeper reason for these must be sought in the different stages of political development in the two countries engulfed by the movement. Anti-Semitism hit Germany shortly after it had achieved its unification in the Reich, which was accomplished, as pointed out by Helmuth Plessner, without its having evolved a compelling concept of commonwealth. The basis of unification was a purely national one. Jews, having retained some tokens of their own nationality, could not easily be counted as part of the unified nation. When anti-Semitism made people aware of this state of affairs, the social and political consequences, in the form of exclusion of Jews, followed immediately and thoroughly. German anti-Semitism reached its ideological as well as social peak at one stroke. Its temporary retreats and abatements were in the nature of compromises and the result of weariness. No concept that might have replaced the nationalist principle, and so might have secured the inclusion of Jews in the community, ever appeared on the scene.[21]

Jewish emancipation in Austria took place at a time when good citizenship was still expressed through loyalty to the idea of the Austrian empire, embodied and symbolized by the House of Hapsburg. In becoming citizens, Jews were expected to adapt themselves to modern conditions along the lines indicated when their integration had been proposed at the time of Joseph II. Integration did not mean, as it did in Germany and Hungary, assimilation into one of the nationalities of the empire. If assimilation took place—in most cases it was, rather, the adoption of the cultural pattern of the ruling German section of the population—it was spontaneous. A total merging with the autochthonous population was neither an explicit nor a tacit condition of emancipation. Thus, when the reaction to emancipation emerged, in the shape of the anti-Semitic movement, the resentment was directed against the economic and professional advancement attained by Jews, which, in their opponents' eyes, came at the cost of and detriment to others. This resentment was not accompanied, as it was in Germany, by a genuine or pretended disappointment over the insufficiency of Jewish assimilation. The Austrian resentment lacked a central principle that would have suddenly turned the scale against the Jews, such as the depiction of them as strangers.

To be ethnically or even culturally different was no reason to be excluded from any right in a country where loyalty still went to the ruling house and the idea of the historically established empire. True, this political principle was already being undermined by an emerging nationalism, and it is no coincidence that the most radical version of Austrian anti-Semitism evolved in the German nationalist movement of Schönerer. Once German nationalism was accepted as a substitute for the idea of the imperial constitution, the exclusion of Jews, according to the German pattern, followed suit. Others, who still kept to the old principle, justified their anti-Semitism by reference to the traditional distinction between Jews and Christians. This, however, did not mean a return to the pre-emancipatory conception of the role of religion in public life. Functionally, the significance of the term Christian was modified by its combination with *Socialist*. Christianity, it was assumed, was capable of helping to solve the social problems that were at least partly attributable to the preponderance of Jewish capital, spirit, and enterprise. This slanting of the meaning of *Christian* made the name palatable for people who would have recoiled from joining an organization with a purely religious objective. Hence, the Christian Socialist platform had an exceptionally broad appeal, promising as it did the answer to both the social and the Jewish problem.

The anti-Semitic movement arose when resentment of Jewish advancement turned into a sociopolitical impulse that found expression in the principles of nationalism and Christian Socialism. In Germany, the movement perfectly conformed to this pattern from its very beginning, while in Austria the preconditions for both principles emerged only slowly. That is why the anti-Semitic impulse, though it erupted in wild agitation in the early 1880s, did not have immediate social consequences. Jews were not excluded overnight from student fraternities or political associations, and the two central leaders of the movement, Schönerer and Lueger, parted company with their Jewish comrades Friedjung and Mandel only in 1887 and 1889, respectively. The emotional revulsion of anti-Semites against Jews, and their irrational resistance to Jewish integration, were the same in all countries, but the ideological justification and practical consequences drawn from it varied according to the intellectual climate and the political circumstances.[22]

24|French Anti-Semitism

THE FRENCH DAILY *Le Figaro* concluded its report on the first international congress of anti-Semites in Dresden with the following observation: "An anti-Semitic movement the like of which is presenting itself in some points of the world, would in France fall under public ridicule. In any case, if it would try to present itself, the government would not fold its arms nor would the courts remain inactive." Seen from the vantage point of enlightened public opinion, this seemed to be a well-founded assessment of the situation. The French press reported assiduously about the anti-Jewish commotion of recent years in Germany, the Tiszaeszlár affair in Hungary, and the pogroms in Russia, and most people were scandalized by what they saw as the outrageous behavior of culturally backward countries.[1]

Alongside such outright rejections of anti-Semitism, there appeared a tendency to emulate anti-Semitic propaganda and organization. During the Dresden conference, only journalists from France had been present, but the meeting in Chemnitz had been attended by some unnamed French representatives.[2] Two anti-Semitic weeklies were launched as early as 1881-1882. These ceased publication after a month or so, but the third, *L'Antisémitique*, started in June 1883, maintained itself for over a year. The weekly's publisher, A. Vrecourt, and his clique tried at the same time to establish an international anti-Semitic league and convene an anti-Semitic conference. Unwilling to cooperate with their German counterparts, they sought and received the consent of the Hungarian anti-Semite Istoczy and his colleagues. Yet all these plans came to naught. Transferred in January 1884 from the provincial town Montdidier to Paris, *L'Antisémitique* could not achieve permanence.[3]

The failure of *L'Antisémitique* was in glaring contrast to the immense success of Eduard Drumont's *La France juive* after the lapse of less than two years.[4] The discrepancy is, however, easily explained, in view of the different attitudes the two publications assumed with regard to the Christian tradition. *L'Antisémitique* used all the popular invectives against Jews, especially their alleged devastating role in the economic life of the country, but it underpinned its arguments by a Voltairian kind of anti-Semitism. It ascribed their noxiousness to qualities already evident in the laws and personalities of the Old Testament. Protests poured in from otherwise sympathetic readers. These were ready to accept the anti-Jewish accusations, but not at the price of the disparagement of what the Christian tradition also held in awe. By resorting to this profane version of anti-Semitism, Vrecourt antagonized those sections of the French public who were best predisposed to accept his arguments—the clergy and clerical Catholics.[5] The same may be said about Auguste Chirac, who in his *Les Rois de la République* took up the theme of Alphonse de Toussenel but linked it with rationalistic theories about the secular origin of all religions.[6]

The dogmatic Catholics always retained their reservations toward Jews and Judaism. The reaction in these circles to the emerging anti-Semitism abroad was at best only ambivalent. In reporting about the blood-libel of Tiszaeszlár the Catholic press wavered between reporting the facts, regretting only the vehement popular excesses, and outright confirmation of the defendants' guilt. Remembering what members of the Catholic right like Rupert and des Mousseaux had to say about the alleged truth of the blood-libel in general, this should not come as a great surprise. One paper at least, the legitimist *L'Union* welcomed the convening of the Dresden conference, expressing the hope that it would lead to an expansion of the anti-Semitic movement.[7]

Signs of the Catholic view of the Jews as an alien, malignant group were evident in the history of the bank L'Union Générale. Founded in 1878 by Eugene Bontou, a well-known public figure of strong Catholic principles, the bank recommended itself to its prospective clients not simply in businesslike terms, but also as a Catholic institution. Its purpose was to secure for confessing Catholics the financial power they sadly lacked hitherto, concentrated as it had been in the hands of "Protestants and Jews." Intrigued by this appeal, many Catholics, from bishops and the clergy down to simple folk, entrusted their fortunes and savings to the bank. When it went bankrupt in 1882, the theory that Jewish machination had caused the disaster found easy credence among the losers. Though there was no evidence of their involvement, the name of Rothschild loomed large in the rumors and overt accusations. The repercussions of the L'Union Générale affair prepared the ground for a growing receptivity to anti-Jewish propaganda, in certain circles at least.[8] Still, it took the propagandistic ingenuity of Eduard Drumont to realize the potential.

Drumont was a little-known journalist of petit bourgeois background when, in 1886, he published his two-volume *La France juive: Essai d'histoire contemporaine*. The book sold poorly for the first two months and the publisher was about to withdraw it when a review appeared in *Le Figaro*, characterizing the book as a Catholic counterattack on the republic's growing laicization. The book and the subject matter became the talk of Paris, indeed of the whole of France. The publicity was intensified following Drumont's duel with a Jewish journalist, Arthur Meyer, who, offended by some passages in *La France juive*, challenged its author. At any rate the book went through some hundred printings within one year, turning Drumont into one of the best known public figures in France.[9]

What earned this lengthy dissertation, consisting of haphazard quotations, gossipy stories, and spurious arguments, such immense public attention? Badly arranged as the material was, the book posited a central thesis that the Jews, the members of an inferior race, the adherents of a primitive and despised religion, had made themselves the masters of modern France. This sounds like an echo of Wilhelm Marr's slogan of the Jewish conquest of Germany. Yet, though Drumont spoke about "conquest juive" in the opening sentences of his book, he adopted the expression from the historian Hippolyte Taine. Taine had described the Jacobinic conquest; Drumont wrote, "I wish to describe the Jewish conquest." The impulse for launching the anti-Jewish attack no doubt derived from what had been going on in Germany and Austria-Hungary. Drumont referred in his introduction to Istoczy and Stöcker as "truly great men" who were unknown in France only because the press was in Jewish hands. He was also full of praise for the activities of the Alliance Antijuive Universelle, which in the long run would more than neutralize its Jewish counterpart, the Alliance Israélite Universelle. Though receiving some inspiration from foreign sources, in the main Drumont relied upon the French anti-Jewish tradition. Applying it with skill and embellishing it with his own imagination, he found it an adequate foundation upon which to build one of the most extensive and most vitriolic anti-Semitic treatises.[10]

La France juive contains quotations of and references to all the variants of French anti-Semitism—the popular Catholic, the socialist, and the liberal. The thesis of the economic dominance of Jews in modern France is supported by citations from the writings of the socialists Proudhon, Leroux, and especially Toussenel. The latter's *Les Juifs les rois de l'époque* is one of Drumont's star witnesses against Jews in general and the relentlessly pursued Rothschilds in particular. From Catholic sources Drumont borrowed the ancient indictment of the Jews for their deicide, their hatred of Christianity, and their moral insensibility, attributing to them every kind of crime against non-Jews, including the use of Gentile blood for ritual purposes. The identification of Jews and Freemasons was very popular by the mid-1880s. *L'Antisémitique* returned to it in almost every one of its issues. Drumont dedicated a full chapter of his book to this theme, quoting Chabouty as his source of information.

Unconcerned about intrinsic inconsistencies, Drumont blended the traditional Christian anti-Semitism with racial discrimination against Jews and Judaism. The principle exponent of this in France was Ernest Renan. Although Drumont despised him because of his slippery character and his friendly relations with Jewish notables, he nonetheless, or rather just because of that, cited him as an objective expert. Indeed, the opening paragraphs of *La France juive* introducing Jews as a branch of the culturally inferior and morally incorrigible Semitic race is based almost entirely on Renan's writings.[11]

The consistent definition of the Jews as a race would have precluded their possible conversion to Christianity. Drumont avoided the issue of conversion, but he was adamant in considering converts still Jews. Des Mousseaux, as we shall remember, divided the Jews between the orthodox and the nonobservant, but they remained one in their common endeavor to rule over the Gentiles. Drumont added a third category, the converted "who, Christians in appearance, are united with the preceding through the closest ties, delivering to their comrades the secrets which would serve them." To meet any possible objection by the Church to such an attitude toward converts, Drumont referred to the Jesuits' rule that barred membership to Jews and Saracens down to the fifth generation.[12] This was one of the many instances in which Drumont went out of his way to make his views and opinions palatable to confessing Catholics. Drumont's own attitude toward Christianity was not entirely clear. He was brought up in a rather laicized atmosphere and it was only later that he turned to religion. Still, his intercession for Catholicism was more in the nature of protecting a cultural heritage than defending a religious truth. No doubt, his complaints about the growing estrangement of people from the Christian tradition was genuine. So was his indignation over the contempt shown to the Church by the laicists, which he pointedly attributed to Jewish influence. At any rate, his harping on Christian sentiments unconnected with the demands of dogmatics drew into the orbit of anti-Semitism people outside of clerical circles. In avoiding any statement that could antagonize the Catholic of orthodox convictions, he gained the sympathy of believers inclined in advance to dislike Jews and Judaism. In presenting

295

anti-Semitism as a defensive action against foreign invaders about to undermine the strength, the culture, and the moral fiber of French society, he made an appeal that had an emphatically patriotic ring impressive to large sections of the population.[13]

The propagandistic effect of the happy combination of disparate ideological elements was complemented by a clever style. Expressing his theories and theses in pugnacious and pointed sentences, he spiced them well with stories and anecdotes to exemplify and substantiate their validity. Convinced of the merit of his cause, Drumont was absolutely unconcerned about the truth of his allegations. Whatever was out of harmony with what he deemed to be the original French culture and tradition he simply attributed to Jewish influence, and people who accepted such elements he declared to be Jewish. Proven to be wrong in one case, he was not deferred from using the same methods in the next one. He continued to throw out his challenges and accusations with his wonted audacity impressing no doubt the uninformed and uncritical public.[14]

Anti-Semitic propaganda was everywhere linked up with social criticism. The anti-Semites pointed to the shortcomings evident in society and ascribed them to Jewish influence. Drumont is outstanding in this respect; in painting French society as absolutely corrupt in politics, administration, police, and judiciary—all of this due to the Jewish poison—he outdid his contemporary anti-Semites of other countries. His vehement rhetoric is reminiscent of the Nazi propaganda in the Weimar Republic—and this similarity would yield the key to the understanding of Drumont's radicalism.[15]

In Germany, as well as in Austria and Hungary, the anti-Semitic objectives were to be realized within the prevailing system. The anti-Semites of these countries were always careful to emphasize their loyalty to their rulers—at the Chemnitz conference the proceedings began with an acclamation in honor of the German, Austrian, and Russian emperors.[16] An exception to this rule was perhaps Ritter von Schönerer of Austria, who wished to see a Germanized Austria in which Jews would be excluded from public life. Yet not even Schönerer openly denied the legitimacy of the prevailing political system or the authority of the established government.[17] This was, however, exactly what Drumont did in France. Drumont belonged to the right-wing politicians and publicists who, whether royalists or Bonapartists, regarded the Third Republic as an usurpatory political fabric void of legitimate or intrinsic authority. Drumont openly declared himself to be waiting for "the officer brave and strongly impressed by the humiliation into which our country has fallen, who would risk his life to raise it." Such a man and five hundred men from the suburbs, one regiment encircling the Jews' banks, would suffice to realize the most fruitful revolution of modern times.[18]

The very identification of the regime with the Jews served as an effective weapon against both of them. The term *Republic juive*, an anticipation of the *Judenrepublic* of the Nazis, was a Drumontian invention.[19] Not that the Nazis needed the French precedent in evolving their own propaganda, but the situation being the same—the denial of the right of the regime to govern, combined with the proscription of the Jewish minority loyal to it—led to the employment of similar weapons.

Its extremism in thought and expression brought *La France juive* immense public attention until the closing act of the Dreyfus affair in 1906. This is not surprising, for Drumont retained a central position in that agitation up to its very end. How far the interest in the book reflected a belief in its content is impossible to ascertain. Some of its readers recognized it as what it indeed was, the arbitrary interpretation of uncritically assembled facts in the service of a conspiratorial theory. Léonce Reynold, for instance, in his *La France n'est pas juive* (1886), demolished step by step the alleged factual statements as well as the logical conclusions built upon them. Reynaud was an experienced retired public servant committed to the ideals of civil equality in a secularized state and highly mobile society. Others, even if their predilections only partly conformed to those of Drumont, were less critical of his obvious exaggerations and extravagances.

Gabriel de Gonet, a socialist of Fourierist persuasion, though at variance with Drumont over the role of the Jew in modern society, welcomed *La France juive*. He saw in it a perhaps unintentional endorsement of Fourierism. To document the affinity between the two schools, de Gonet republished Toussenel's *Les Juifs les rois de l'époque*, which was an offshoot of Fourierism and was extensively quoted by Drumont. The greatest measure of sympathy towards *La France juive* was elicited in Catholic circles. The book was hailed by essentially the whole Catholic press, and Drumont boasted of the manifold expressions of support he received from the lower clergy and simple Catholic believers.[20]

Compared to the spectacular success of the book itself, the practical political results of its appeal were minimal and for Drumont highly disappointing. Believing in the overriding importance of his diagnosis, he was persuaded that those who consented to it would rally around him despite their attitudes toward other issues, political, social, or religious. This indeed happened in the case of Jacques de Biez, who, though a republican, offered Drumont, on the publication of *La France juive*, his services in the anti-Semitic cause. After three years they founded La Ligue Nationale Antisémitique de France. Eligibility for membership in the league was based on devotion to anti-Semitism, irrespective of political or religious considerations. The same principle was applied in the choice of those who served on the staff of *La Libre Parole*, the anti-Semitic daily with strong Catholic leanings launched by Drumont in 1892. Raphael Viau tells us that

The Movement

La France juive converted him to anti-Semitism, but otherwise though for years on the staff of *La Libre Parole* he remained what he was before, "ni religieux ni anticlerical, mais plutot *areligieux*" (italics in the original).[21]

Confessing Catholics, and especially the members and adherents of the religious orders, such as the Assumptionists, kept aloof. Their support for Drumont exhausted itself in encouragement of his fight against the supposed enemies of the Church. They were, however, reluctant to join hands with one who had evolved his own brand of Catholicism with regard to doctrine as well as practice and was prepared to cooperate with anyone on the basis of anti-Semitic commitment alone. Drumont's readiness to engage in dueling, which was strictly proscribed by the Church, made him ineligible to represent the Church in any way. This was demonstrated as clearly as possible when the members of the newly established anti-Semitic league headed by Drumont wished to be elected to the Paris Municipality Council in 1889. Lacking the support of the religious establishment, all of them, including Drumont, failed to be elected. Drumont, for his part—at least from then on—though upholding Catholicism on principle, was often critical of the religious establishment, reprimanding the higher clergy for compromising with the new aristocracy of money. Thus, the main source of possible political patronage for Drumont was neutralized.[22]

The sphere of influence that remained open to Drumont was literature and journalism. A whole series of books published after *La France juive* served to spread his ideas. Even more effective was *La Libre Parole*, whose role in creating the anti-Jewish atmosphere before and during the Dreyfus affair is difficult to overrate. Drumont's paper accused the Jewish officers of the army of disloyalty to their country and even of outright espionage two years before the arrest of Captain Dreyfus. When the arrest occurred, it was naturally hailed as a vindication of the anti-Semitic thesis. Uncommitted to the program of any of the political parties on the right—the royalists, the Bonapartists, and others—it supported all those who contested the legitimacy of the Republic and its secularist tendency.[23]

Drumont attained a political role of his own only once, and that only for a short period, when the Dreyfus affair and the concomitant anti-Jewish agitation reached its climax. In 1899 Drumont was elected to the Chamber of Deputies from Algeria, where anti-Semitism was even more virulent than in the mother country. Together with Drumont, a group of eighteen other members openly committed to an anti-Semitic program entered the Chamber. Drumont served as the center of the group, which, however, failed to constitute itself into a formally organized party. Even as a loose coalition it lasted only until the next election in 1902, when most of them, including Drumont himself, failed to be re-elected.[24]

In Germany, Hungary, and even in Austria, anti-Semites of differing

298

political convictions tried to organize parties. In France anti-Semitism became effective only as a complementary feature to other political movements. When anti-Semitism reached its zenith in 1897-1901, several anti-Semitic societies were established. Drumont's Anti-Semitic League, which had collapsed shortly after its foundation in 1890, was revived as the Grand Occident de France, a name that hinted at its opposition to the Freemasons, who operated under the direction of the Grand Orient. There were also Jeunesse Antisémitique and Patrie Française. Morès and Guérin, the leaders of the Grand Occident, hoped it would become the nucleus of a party that would embrace anti-Semites of all political leanings: "monarchists, republicans, Catholics and freethinkers." But each of the groups only attracted those of its own political persuasion. Apparently Drumont had already despaired of direct political activity; even when he was a member of the Chamber of Deputies he showed no initiative and functioned apathetically. The anti-Semitic groups had different leaders. Even *La Libre Parole* had a rival, *Antijuive*, edited by Jules Guérin, who was also the leading spirit in the Grand Occident. Drumont's talent lay in the art of criticism, slander, and provocation, but he lacked the capacity to execute political activity.[25]

The functioning of anti-Semitism varied according to the social and political conditions of each country, as well as the actual positions Jews occupied in it. French Jews, especially those against whom the anti-Semitic charges were directed, namely, the financiers and intellectuals, were thoroughly part and parcel of French society in the 1880s and 1890s, although their Jewish origin was clearly marked. This was paradoxically documented by the fact that the anti-Semites, especially Drumont and his coterie, when challenged by Jews, granted them satisfaction through dueling—a privilege open to the members of the elite in any society in which dueling is an accepted way of settling conflicts and differences. In Austria, the non-Jewish student organizations denied their Jewish colleagues the right to challenge non-Jewish students to duels, and in Germany, too, the exclusion of Jewish students from Burschenschaften meant an absolute social ostracism.[26]

With the annexation of Alsace by Germany after the 1870 war, the focal point of the Jewish community disappeared, as did the typical Jewish stereotype that had served as the prime target of anti-Jewish activity. Two-thirds of the 60,000 Jews left in France dwelt in Paris. The remaining 20,000 were dispersed in the east of the country and a few districts in the north and south. The map of the spread of anti-Semitism in the 1880s and 1890s by no means coincided with the places where Jews lived. It covered towns and areas where it is doubtful if the inhabitants had ever had direct contact with a Jew. This was an entirely different situation from that of

Germany and Austria-Hungary, where the proportion of Jews was much higher and their visibility in certain districts was very great. In France, too, gusts of enmity did find concrete objectives, and certain assaults almost assumed the dimensions of riots. Essentially, however, French anti-Semitism was directed against an abstract concept of Judaism, represented by the Jewish economic elite and intelligentsia. This type of anti-Semitism had the capacity of growing in doctrine and in extremity.[27]

French anti-Semitism, though more radical than its German counter-part as far as its ultimate goals were concerned, had fewer immediate social consequences.[28] The political goals of Drumontian propaganda, epitomized in the motto of *La Libre Parole*, "La France aux Français," is reminiscent, as mentioned above, of that of the Nazis. If the results were altogether different—and by the end of the Dreyfus affair in 1906, political anti-Semitism in France seemed to be absolutely discredited—this was the result of an altogether different political atmosphere. French anti-Semites identified Jews and Freemasons; this was a myth. The charges directed against Jews were linked to the general attack against the republic and especially against the laicization of France. In response to this, Jews found themselves allied with all those who found their ideals and interests to be compromised by the anti-Semitic movement. Thus, the Jews' cause found involuntary defenders. At any rate, as the republic and the laicizing trend prevailed—to the satisfaction of some of the more realistic Catholics as well—the attempt to proscribe the Jews came to naught.[29]

Still, the wave of anti-Semitism left its traces in France as it had in the other countries it had engulfed. If the noisy propaganda of *La Libre Parole* of Drumont had been silenced, the paper having changed hands as well as direction since 1910, it was replaced by the more sophisticated insinua-tions of *L'Action française* of Charles Maurras, Leon Daudet, and others. They were striving for the renaissance of France on the basis of a *na-tionalisme integral*, which embraced some elements of Catholic spirituality and therefore excluded Jews automatically. Through such ideas, hostility toward Jews was kept alive until the pre-Nazi and the Nazi period, when it once again assumed a political and later even physically destructive form.[30]

Part VII: Culmination

25 | Racism and the Nazi Climax

WITH THE FAILURE OF the anti-Semitic political parties in Hungary, France, and Germany—Austria was an exception, owing to Lueger's success in Vienna—the anti-Semitic movement seemed to lose its impetus. Indeed, several of the movement's initiators—Istoczy in Hungary, Marr in Germany, and most of Drumont's associates in France—withdrew in disappointment.[1] There was reason enough for their disappointment. Jewish citizenship, the major target of the anti-Semitic attack, remained intact. Far-reaching social exclusion of Jews, and a certain degree of economic pressure exerted on them, were the only effects of the anti-Semitic propaganda. Though these were in themselves welcome phenomena, a vicious circle resulted, abrogating the anti-Semitic objectives. Even more than before, Jews were now compelled to concentrate both socially and economically. Professions open to them, such as medicine and law, now attracted more Jews, not fewer. Moreover, the historical and sociological forces that were instrumental in securing the relative preponderance of Jews in various branches of the economy and public affairs continued to be active. Jews continued to play a conspicuous role in banking, at the stock exchange, and in management of the press. The great warehouses introduced in the last decades of the nineteenth century were a Jewish commercial innovation publicly demonstrating the Jew's role in the process of modernization. For those who regretted the passage of a more restful way of life, or felt economically and otherwise threatened by the new developments, this very process was a thorn in the flesh. Given the basic tenet of anti-Semitism, that Jews comprised an alien

303

and pernicious element in society, the concentration of vital public functions in Jewish hands must have been intolerable to them.[2]

The concept of pernicious Jewish alienism lay at the bottom of the anti-Semitic grumbling and propaganda, which continued despite the failure of the anti-Semitic parties to realize their objectives. One school of thought from its very inception pinned its hopes on the ultimate effect of propaganda. It maintained that its aims could be realized only after various circles in society had absorbed anti-Semitic ideas. Theodor Fritsch was the main proponent of this school. His role in undermining the position of Jews by distorting their religion, their character, and their mentality cannot be overrated.

Fritsch, an engineer by training and profession, joined the anti-Semitic movement in 1881 at the age of twenty-nine, when he wrote his first anti-Jewish pamphlet.[3] In contrast to other anti-Semitic leaders, such as Glagau, Stöcker, and Dühring, who grafted the anti-Semitic ideology onto their previous world view, Fritsch adopted it as his exclusive intellectual concern and single-minded endeavor. He persisted in his efforts right up until his death in 1933, a few months after Hitler's ascendance to power, thus serving as a living bridge between the inception of the movement and its disastrous culmination.

Fritsch possessed an outstanding talent for propaganda. He could be articulate on different intellectual levels, adapting his fluent and always striking style to his audience. More clear-sighted than his colleagues, he did not believe that an anti-Semitic party would amass sufficient political power to realize its objectives. He relied, rather, on the slow but methodical indoctrination of anti-Semitic ideas, which he believed could be absorbed by the adherents of any political party, social trend, or religious conviction. He advocated this view at the 1885 anti-Semitic congress, but was overruled by a majority vote for the establishment of the anti-Semitic German Reform party. Fritsch accepted the post of party manager, but used it mainly as a vehicle for propaganda, an activity that had preoccupied him before, and which continued to do so after he left the party in 1894.[4]

The basic aim of Fritsch's propaganda was to discredit the Jewish character and mentality. He strove to convince his contemporaries that Jews, a pernicious and destructive species, must be fought in self-defense, as sanctioned by all considerations of morality. His very first pamphlet, made up of rhymed verses coined for popular consumption, depicted the Jew as a deceitful, parasitic creature, an enemy of mankind, incapable of reforming himself, either by baptism or otherwise. By way of an apology for the gross language in the text, the author included in his preface various Talmudic quotations, taken probably from Rohling's *Talmudjude*, to demonstrate the manner in which the Jews' religious book referred to Gentiles. In later publications, aimed at a better-educated reading public, Fritsch underpinned his thesis with the theory of races, applying the by-then current differentiation between degenerate and subhuman Semites and physically and mentally perfect Aryans. In his *Anti-Semite Catechism*, later renamed the *Handbook of Anti-Semitism*, Fritsch brought together attestations, assertions, and alleged disclosures from all the available anti-Jewish literature, some of Christian, others of rationalistic provenance, but all ideologically rooted either in religion or in the theory of races. Published in 1896, the *Handbook* went through thirty-six editions before the First World War and no doubt reached millions of readers.[5]

Indiscriminate in his choice of material, Fritsch nonetheless conceded that the best hope for success was to disparage the Jewish mentality as it was reflected in the Talmudic tradition. Jews possessed all the capital and controlled the press, therefore it was futile for the time being to try and fight these forces directly. "Yet Judaism has an enormous weakness, the *Talmudic moral*. Rabbinism is the Achilles heel of the Jewish world dominion, and it is only here that the foe can be mortally wounded. Only here can he be seized, at his core and essence, at the roots of his demonic power."[6]

With respect to religion, Fritsch called himself *freireligioes*, an epithet designating those critical of the teachings and conduct of the Church, who were nevertheless willing to allow religion a limited place in their own life and in the life of the collective.[7] While one would have thought such a posture to be incompatible with intolerance, its most predominant proponent at the time was Paul de Lagarde (1827-1891), who in fact combined devastating criticism of traditional Christianity (both Protestantism and Catholicism) with deep-seated animosity not only toward Judaism as a religion, but also toward Jews as a group.[8] A Biblical scholar and Orientalist of rank, Lagarde appreciated the prophetic religion reflected in the Old Testament. But the study of the ancient sources was meant to stimulate only an immediate relation to God, a religious experience. The same was true even of the Gospels and of the figure of Jesus himself. No ethical teachings or forms of worship could be directly derived from them. These had to evolve out of the autochthonous national tradition and culture. The German "religion of the future" was to be created in the image of their own intrinsic nature, to the exclusion of all foreign elements introduced by Christianity, especially those stemming from its Jewish heritage.[9] Jews, being a foreign nation could naturally have no share in the German religious creation. Their very presence in German society was detrimental to its revitalization, a process of which Lagarde, at any rate, very nearly despaired. His religious and social criticism was negativistic. He

305

castigated society in the harshest terms, but proposed no tangible solutions. Nor did he have any positive conception as to what was to be done about the Jews, and his assertions about them were restricted to violent invective.[10]

Fritsch made ample use of Lagarde's anti-Semitic assertions, which, extracted from their context, sounded even more vehement than in their original setting.[11] On an altogether different plane, Fritsch can be said to have pursued a religious line not unlike that of the great scholar. In this connection, he freely attacked not only the Talmud, but also the Old Testament, and evoked misgivings among the more conservative elements of the anti-Semitic camp. Disrespect toward any part of the Bible would discredit the anti-Semitic propaganda in the eyes of unsophisticated believers, and especially the rural clergy.[12] This may indeed have been the case, but only in those circles where Christian orthodoxy remained intact. For those whose commitment to Christianity was no more than an attachment to the central symbols of the faith could identify with Fritsch's anti-Semitic tenets. He certainly retained a respectful and even worshipful stance toward what he maintained to be the original core of Christianity. This he declared to be of non-Semitic, indeed of Aryan, character, possibly even of Aryan origin. "Surely Christian teaching arose as a protest of the Aryan spirit against the inhumane Jew-spirit."[13] Unconcerned with historical evidence, Fritsch was one of the first anti-Semites to ascribe to Jesus an Aryan descent. Even with regard to the Old Testament, he sought a way not to offend the sensibilities of the faithful: only the morally objectionable parts, said to be of Jewish creation, were to be rejected. Portions containing lofty teachings or reflecting genuine religious sentiments were claimed to be of Aryan origin and only adopted by Jews.[14]

Crude as such methods may have been, they served the purpose of reconciling Christian predilections with a racially oriented anti-Semitism. Traditionally minded Christians may have been scandalized by such a high-handed approach to their faith, and even Jews felt entitled to denounce it as un-Christian in spirit;[15] the fact remains, however, that exactly this type of reinterpretation of Christianity was becoming popular and preparing the ground for a racial outlook on human history in general, and on the Jewish question in particular.

On quite a different level, but with the same anti-Jewishness, a racial interpretation of Christianity was the central theme of the most renowned anti-Semitic treatise of the age: *Foundations of the Nineteenth Century*, by Houston Stewart Chamberlain. English by birth, German by choice, Wagner's son-in-law by his second marriage, Chamberlain was an adept of the Wagnerian cult. He became the prophet of German national ascendancy. This ascendancy was to be achieved through the correct comprehension of the forces at work in the shaping of human history. The thousand-page *Foundations* claimed to be a historical and philosophical guide to just such comprehension, a diagnosis of the state of affairs reached by human history at the close of the nineteenth century.[16]

The chief intellectual device employed by Chamberlain, as by Fritsch, was the notion of race, but with a difference. While Fritsch and other anti-Semites before him relied on the dichotomy between the lowly and despicable Semites and the gifted and highly estimable Aryans, Chamberlain developed a more sophisticated approach. According to Chamberlain, positive or negative qualities were not the innate endowments of any race. They were rather, the result of a propitious or unpropitious blending of races with different virtues. A felicitous apportionment of the races would lead to the highest standards of human qualities and achievements, as was the case with the Germanic peoples. The reverse was true of the Jews, who suffered from racial bastardization and all its consequences.[17]

It took the audacity of an ideologue convinced of the validity of his insight to put forth such a theory as the basis for his view of the world. Many contemporary thinkers regarded intuition as a higher source of knowledge, and Chamberlain was especially inclined to accept it as such. Self-educated but well-read in science, the history of religion, philosophy, and other areas, he professed his immediate synoptic understanding to be superior to the findings of specialized experts. "Not as a scholar have I approached these subjects, but as a child of the present time who wishes to understand his living presence."[18]

Though ultimately relying on what he conceived to be his intuitive insight, Chamberlain nevertheless amassed an enormous amount of anthropological and historical data to support his theory. The material dealing with Jews took up a substantial part of the book and fell into two categories. One explained the physical constitution of Jewish stock, culminating in what was said to be the bastardization of the race. The other category was descriptive and showed the mentality of the Jews, their cultural barrenness, moral inferiority, and utter lack of religious sensibility. Unlike popular-minded anti-Semites such as Fritsch, Chamberlain emphasized the religious point, denying that Jews ever possessed even the rudiments of what could truly be called religion. "No people in the world are so utterly devoid of genuine religion as the Semites, and particularly their half-brothers, the Jews."[19] In denying Jews what had been considered their special claim to creativity, Chamberlain exposed their absolute mental poverty, confirming the assumption of their racial degeneration.

In treating the physical and mental data of Jewish life, Chamberlain moved freely between one set of facts and another, drawing conclusions of one type of inferiority from another, and vice versa. The first link in the chain of reasoning was undoubtedly Jewish mental inferiority, as reflected in the religious impotence of Jews. On this point the author could rely on a well-established tradition. The *Foundations* are indeed full of quotations and references to deprecatory characterizations of the Jewish religion. Such characterization was the fruit of the perennial Judeo-Christian conflict, and modern Biblical scholarship only added to this heritage. Though undogmatic, Biblical scholars such as Renan, Wellhausen, and others retained Christianity's self-evaluation as the consummation of Judaism, which it had left behind at an inferior stage of development. These scholars were Chamberlain's chief witnesses, and they testified to Judaism's depravity.[20] At the same time, Chamberlain did not deny having found positive elements in the Jewish tradition. But true to his methodology of subjective discrimination, he attributed these to foreign sources, or rather foreign blood—the Ten Commandments to Egyptian origin; the undeniable charm, boldness, and visionary enthusiasm of King David to the heritage of a hypothetical Amorite mother, and so on, and so on.[21]

The disparagement of Judaism went hand in hand with the glorification of Christianity. Though Chamberlain had reservations about the doctrines and dogma of the church, even rejecting them at times, he insisted on his right to be considered a follower of Christ, not because he had accepted any part of the teachings of Christ but rather because of his approach to the personality of Christ, which he saw as a source of spiritual, possibly even mystical, inspiration. After quoting passages from the Sermon on the Mount, Chamberlain exclaimed: "No one before had ever spoken thus, nor has anyone since done so." He then went on to explain that the passages had no doctrinal content. What the sermon conveyed to those who had heard it, and what it continued to convey to all those impressed by it still, was the inspirational quality of the speaker's unique personality: "We do not know exactly what he said, but his unmistakable, unforgettable tone beats at our ears and forces its way into our hearts."[22]

The figure of Christ was thus turned into a stimulus to the highest order of religious experience. Jews, incapable of such exaltation, could have no share in such an experience. Their rejection of Jesus was therefore no accident. It resulted from the unbridgeable chasm between their racially conditioned mentality and the experience transmuted through the personality of Jesus. True to the concept of racial and mental parallelism, Chamberlain could not possibly credit Jews with having produced Jesus, even if only biologically. He was declared to have been, probably, of Aryan origin. To make this historically plausible was of course not beyond the powers of Chamberlain's pre-eminent intuition.[23]

Racism and the Nazi Climax

While working at a high level of historical generalization, Chamberlain at times touched on social reality. Any reader, if inclined to anti-Semitism, could easily derive from the book's principles justification for the prevalent discrimination against the Jews. The author more than hinted at the destructive influence Jews would have on Aryan culture. The idea of law and justice as embodied in the jurisdiction of the Aryan nations was beyond Jewish comprehension. The anti-Semitic objection to having Jews appointed as judges was therefore not at all unfounded, Chamberlain assured the reader in one of his asides.[24]

The *Foundations* had a broad impact and lasting effect. It attracted immediate attention, and by the end of the First World War it had sold more than one hundred thousand copies. Though many of its critics pointed out its intrinsic weakness—the attachment of subjective judgments to quasi-scientific data—only a very few dismissed it as ideological bunk. One of these, a Jew it is true, explained the book's warm reception, despite its obvious defects, by quoting Goethe: "Any assertion which gratifies self-conceit and expedience is enough to ensure a wide following among the ordinary multitude."[25]

Chamberlain's exposition indeed gratified German national sensibility. Germans were said to be the embodiment of the best Aryan racial qualities, destined to redeem human culture from its present state of destitution. Chamberlain's chapter on "The Entry of the Jews into the History of the West" alone assured him a grateful welcome. By weaving Jewish inferiority into a system that seemingly embraced all of human history, he endowed the widely held anti-Jewish prejudices with scientific foundation and philosophical dignity. At the same time he did not sever the anti-Jewish bias from its historical roots, the Judeo-Christian conflict, from which it derived its emotional appeal and passion. Chamberlain, though no Christian in any strict sense of the word, not only retained Christianity's central symbol, Christ himself, but placed him on the highest pedestal in his own system. This paved the way for practicing Christians to embrace Chamberlain's theory, as did the Emperor William II, who hailed the *Foundations* as a revelation to understanding of the present world. More dogmatically oriented believers would, of course, be repelled by many of Chamberlain's unorthodox assertions. Ordinary Christians, unconcerned with ecclesiastical niceties, were, like the emperor, satisfied with Chamberlain's minimal Christian identification and went along with his welcome exposition.[26]

The circulation of the *Foundations* and the concomitant dissemination of the racial doctrine took place between 1900 and 1914, when political anti-Semitism in Germany was at its lowest ebb. Nevertheless the doctrine served a social function. It secured and warranted the containment of the

Culmination

Jewish minority within circumscribed social and economic boundaries. In the future, with the ascendance of the Nazis, it was destined to fulfill a political function of unprecedented intensity and consequence.

The racial theory as an intellectual tool for interpreting historical phenomena is connected with the name of Gobineau and his *Essai sur l'inégalité des races humaines* (1853-1855). Gobineau's theory was not prejudicial to Jews. On the contrary, he depicted the Semites as one of the gifted and culturally productive variations of humanity. Gobineau's essay, though predicating innate differences between groups of different racial descent, had no concrete and contentious social objectives. Ideologically, it aimed only at accounting for the putative decline of human society through the loss of racial purity on the part of the Aryans, the master race and fountainhead of superior culture. Race became an intellectual tool of discrimination only when Aryans were depicted in opposition to Semites, the latter including the Jewish minority, practically their only tangible representative on the European scene. This confrontation between Aryans and Semites as the two extremes on the scale of racial evaluation had begun with Renan, prior to the publication of Gobineau's essay. Once published, however, Gobineau's captivating literary work gave a tremendous boost to the credibility of the notion of race as an explanatory factor in past and present human society. Those concerned with the role of Jews in human history felt themselves on sure ground when using it, even though they gave it a slant unanticipated by the author of the essay.[27]

Additional confirmation of the legitimacy of the race concept came from an entirely different source, as a side effect of Charles Darwin's *On the Origin of Species* (1859). Stimulated by the idea of natural selection, scholars tried to trace the physical and cultural criteria for different types of man—in short, the development of the races.[28] Anti-Semitic ideologues did not wait for results of scientific research. Taking the notion of race as their starting point, each developed a theory of his own, often in direct contradiction to the theories of others. Most theoreticians regarded each race as static in its physical and mental characteristics, though they differed as to what these characteristics were and where they stemmed from. Chamberlain, however, declared the notion of an originally fixed racial character to be a figment of the imagination. He took his cue from Darwin's concept of natural selection and, as we have seen, maintained that it was the peculiar combination of racial elements that produced the respective constitutions of Aryan, Semite, and Jew.[29]

Practically the only point on which all anti-Semitic theoreticians agreed was that Jewish racial qualities were of a patently negative nature. Since such characterization was part and parcel of the anti-Jewish tradition prior to the emergence of the theory of races, it is this tradition, and not the

310

notion of race per se, which must be regarded as the determining factor in racial discrimination against the Jews. In modern usage, the term *race* and its derivative, *racism*, ordinarily connote discrimination. Originally, however, *race* was a neutral term, and even when it was applied to the classification of primitive non-European tribes it lacked overt disparaging connotations. It acquired such nuances only after it was used in the sociopolitical campaign against a minority, the Jews, and then the term became associated with the notion of inferiority and wretchedness. Far from having fathered anti-Semitism, the concept of race indeed received its own negative connotation from being linked with it.

Chamberlain's and Fritsch's racial visions were not easily translatable into a concrete plan of action. Proceeding on an abstract plane, Chamberlain could remain vague as to how his religious-racial renaissance was to be achieved. Even Fritsch, that clever propagandist, could not see beyond the dissemination of his ideas. At times he hinted that unless state authorities would curb Jewish influence, "the lower strata of the population would attempt to solve the problem in their own fashion."[30] What he had in mind was the eruption of uncontrolled violence against Jews rather than the change of a system that granted Jews the legal protection due citizens of the state. But both Chamberlain and Fritsch lived to see the German Reich open up unthought-of possibilities and gave their ideas a chance of being realized.

Both the First World War and its aftermath, the 1918 revolution, had an ambivalent impact upon the social and political position of Jews in Germany. The initial enthusiasm at the outbreak of the war gave rise to a sense of national unity that seemed to embrace Jews as well, though Theodor Fritsch, no doubt voicing the sentiments of the hard-core anti-Semites, could not keep from showing his dissent even at this hour. As the struggle unexpectedly dragged on for years, more and more questions were raised about the real share contributed by Jews to the national effort. Jews were accused of shirking their duty, sitting back behind the front lines, and profiteering in the black market. In response to these charges, the minister of war in the Prussian Parliament, in November 1916, demanded a so-called Jew-count—counting the number of Jewish soldiers serving on the front and the Jews who did not contribute to the war effort.[31] The results, even if uncontested, could not, of course, settle the issue either way. The significance of the Jew-count lay in the fact that it showed the Jews were far from being accepted into the German nation, whether because they were socially anomalous or because the derogatory image of the Jew persisted, or both. It was this fact that continued to govern events, even though circumstances changed fundamentally when, in the wake of the revolution, imperial rule was replaced by the Weimar Republic.

Culmination

The German revolution of 1918, resulting as it did in the wake of physical and mental exhaustion both at the front and at home, left the new rulers facing enormous difficulties. They had to meet the political conditions imposed by the victorious allies on the vanquished nation. The vast sum of reparations to be paid prevented economic recovery, and led to the runaway inflation of 1923, which ended in the absolute devaluation of German currency. Any chance, however, of ameliorating the situation was prejudiced in the first instance by the fact that the new form of government enjoyed only limited public support. The Social Democrats and the Democrats had to contend with both leftist and rightist opposition to the principle of majority rule. The radical socialists envisaged dictatorial rule patterned on the Russian system, and belittled the achievements of the revolution. The rightists, consisting of many subgroups, represented two main political streams. The more conservative clung to the vestiges of former empire and held the republic and all it represented in unmistakable contempt. The second stream, made up of newly emerging veterans' groups and other socially unaligned elements, adhered to radically nationalistic, and at times also socialistic, ideals, and they too aspired to wrest the government from the hands of the despised republicans. There was no lack of attempts to achieve this by force. In the first years of the republic, political assassinations were the order of the day, and several attempts were made at a coup d'état, the most famous being Adolf Hitler's abortive putsch in Munich, in November 1923.[32]

From the Jewish viewpoint, the establishment of the republic was undoubtedly a decisive improvement—at least it looked to be for the foreseeable future. For the first time since Bismarck had cooperated with the Liberals, Jews could play more than a marginal role in politics. Jews held leading positions in both the defeated radical socialist groups and in the parties initially entrusted with the running of the new state. Hugo Preuss, an expert on constitutional law who under the Kaiser had no proper academic appointment, could now become secretary of state of internal affairs and be responsible for the drafting of the republic's constitution.[33]

The active participation of Jews in the affairs of the Weimar Republic was formally due to no more than a disregard of birth and religion, as prescribed in the constitution. Nevertheless, this participation was seen by the republic's rightist opponents as evidence of the un-Germanic nature of the republic. Anti-Jewish and anti-republican bias coalesced, and the two continued to sustain one another. All the right-wing political parties, whether monarchic, reactionary, or revolutionary, added some anti-Jewish planks to their platforms and programs. The military defeat, and the nationalistic reaction to it, engendered an atmosphere ripe for a scapegoat. It was in the aftermath of the war that the slogan "Jews and Freemasons," originally French, found fertile ground in Germany. The theory of a Jewish-Masonic conspiracy for world dominion, intimated in the slogan, found further support in the *Protocols of the Elders of Zion*. Concocted in Czarist Russia, the *Protocols* were transplanted to the West at this juncture. It spread and was believed despite the fact that its fictitious nature had been repeatedly exposed. The *Protocols*, however, was only one of numerous anti-Semitic pamphlets, fly-sheets, and articles that flooded the country following the war and the revolution. Their ready and popular reception only testifies to the negative spiritual climate engendered by the shattering historical events. It was also the result of studied machinations of the propagandists, who exploited the credulity of the masses in order to harness them to their political objectives. Outstanding among these, in energy, inventiveness, and lack of moral restraint, was Adolf Hitler.[34]

Austrian by birth, Hitler served in the German army during the war. For over a year after the revolution he was retained in Munich as an educational officer. His superiors, though in the service of the republic, actively supported the right-wing organizations, and it was because of this that Hitler, having exhibited extreme nationalistic tendencies, was employed. After leaving the army, he joined one such organization, the German Labor Party, soon to become one of its directors and then its exclusive leader. The organization modified its name by adopting the National Socialist epithet, and the party's program promised to attend to both the national and social problems of Germany. Paragraph 4 of the program stated: "Only members of the nation [*Volksgenosse*] can be citizens of the state. Only those of German blood, regardless of denomination, can be members of the nation. Jews can therefore not be members of the nation." Paragraph 5 added that noncitizens would be tolerated in Germany only as guests and be subject to special legislation.[35]

Through hard work, cunning, and a peculiar magnetism that charmed most people who came into contact with him, Hitler succeeded in increasing his party following. By the end of 1923 he felt sufficiently strong to make his first bid for power by forcefully seizing the government in Munich. The putsch was thwarted, a number of his followers were killed, and he himself was apprehended. His career seemed to be at an end. However, he continued to enjoy popular sympathy. The Bavarian authorities even allowed him to use his trial to disseminate his ideas and, moreover, attack the very foundations of the prevailing system. In prison he was permitted to dictate *Mein Kampf*, a large biographical volume outlining his plans for the future.[36]

Hitler's account of his youth has been found to be totally deceptive

313

and unreliable. Still, careful study reveals the make-up of his strange personality and its underlying motives. He had an enormous capacity for internalizing ideas, perceptions, and factual knowledge by reducing them to their simplest formulas. At the same time, his will power was such that he could convince himself of his ability to realize the goals born of these beliefs. During his Vienna years, he was determined to create some grandiose work as an artist and architect. During this period he involved himself in political and social problems, in the course of which some of his basic convictions took shape, radical anti-Semitism among them. With no prospects of showing his mettle, and little opportunity for an ordinary career, he must have been in his own eyes—as he certainly was in the view of others—an utter failure. The unforeseen circumstances of the revolutionary situation finally gave him, possibly to his own surprise, the chance to show what he was capable of doing.[37]

Hitler may be accurate in his account of how the encounter with Jewish life in Vienna, and with the reactions to it of leaders like Lueger and Schönerer, determined his attitude. Whether he consulted literary sources on the Jewish question, whether he studied the anti-Semitic classics of Chamberlain or others, remains unclear.[38] What he himself had to say about Jews and Judaism was a checkered collection of inconsistent anti-Semitic contentions. The alleged Jewish unbelief in the hereafter, the Jews' clash with Jesus and their killing of him, was as readily repeated as the Jewish lust after Christian women, the destructive influence of the Jewish press, the Jewish drive for world dominion with the assistance of the Freemasons, and so on. There was, however, one underlying conception that lent all these charges a unifying plausibility. This was the assumption that there was a peculiar, demonic racial quality at work in every Jew, in all aspects of Jewish life and in all phases of Jewish history. Hitler absorbed the racial ideology and gave it a simplified and crude formulation. While Chamberlain attributed the different qualities of different races to their more or less propitious blend, thus leaving room for shades, transitory stages, and the like, Hitler posited an absolute cleavage between Aryans and Semites. Ayrans were said to have all the virtues and be the source of all creativity; Jews were the embodiment of evil and destructiveness.[39] The Austrian anti-Semitic scholar Adolf Wahrmund, speculating on the origin of the Jewish mentality, attributed it to their emigration from country to country. He called Jews the eternal nomads. Referring to this theory, Hitler declared that "parasite" was the only description that fit Jews, since it indicated their incapacity to survive except at the expense of others.[40]

Cautioned by the failure of his putsch, Hitler abandoned the idea of seizing the government by force. Instead, he decided to use all the means of propaganda to enlarge his following so that it would comprise a majority of the population and vote him into power. To achieve this he needed suitable catchwords to appeal to the great masses. The simplified version of the racial theory aptly suited his purpose. The Christian elements that filtered through to the racial theory, the very name of Jesus at the masthead of the Aryan protest against Jews, were all part of a studied effort to play on the Christian sentiments of his audience.[41] Though highly indelicate in his selection of elements from the anti-Semitic tradition, he consistently avoided that school which combined anti-Semitism with criticism of Christianity because of its indebtedness to Judaism. Nor did he disparage the Old Testament in order to discredit Jews. Still he tolerated, though barely, the use by his associates of measures that antagonized serious Christians. From a religious point of view, the Nazi movement was far from monolithic. Theodor Fritsch joined it and continued to agitate in his *freireligioes* direction. Alfred Rosenberg, one of the first members of the Nazi movement, took an even more radical stand. In his *Myth of the Twentieth Century* (1930), he tried to imitate Chamberlain and drape his racial world-view in quasi-Christian garb but, where Chamberlain succeeded, he failed.[42] The book, to Hitler's displeasure, evoked the protest of devout Christians, both Catholics and Protestants.[43] Judging by its considerable circulation—it ultimately sold some half a million copies—the book's main theses must have been in line with the prevailing trend. It prognosticated a racial renaissance for Aryans after they had purged themselves of the Semitic element and its pernicious influence. To this, Hitler certainly subscribed. It stands to reason that his reservations about Rosenberg's treatise were of a strategic nature. At any rate, their differences centered on their approach to Christianity. With regard to Jews, they spoke the same language. Rosenberg too applied the parasitic epithet to Jews, but unlike his mentor Chamberlain, he regarded the Jewish race and its deleterious traits to be intrinsically determined from the beginning.[44]

Ideologically, Nazi anti-Semitism added nothing new to the prewar variety. Its extremism lay in the fact that it was geared toward a well-defined and, at the same time, a revolutionary political objective: the overthrow of the republic. Released from prison in December 1924, Hitler began reorganizing his party. For the following eight years, until his appointment as chancellor of the Reich, the party's fortunes fluctuated. At times, it looked as though the Nazis would dwindle and disappear, leaving the field clear to the moderate incumbents. Later, when the German masses turned more radical as a result of the 1929 economic crises, it looked as though the Nazis would be crushed by the Communists, their contenders for state control. In the struggle to gain the support of the masses, anti-Semitism was one of the major weapons employed by Hitler and his party henchmen. Whatever their opponents stood for—democracy, the parliamentarianism of the moderates and the socialism of the radicals, the basic institutions of the republic—was labeled a Jewish invention and as such pernicious by its very nature.[45] Jews were repeatedly condemned for whatever could be characterized as Jewish, and their condemnation was unceasingly reiterated, both verbally and in writings, but especially at Hitler's emotionally charged mass meetings, until their blameworthiness became commonplace.

There appeared to be no recourse against such a studied campaign of anti-Jewish defamation. The tactics available—to appeal to the courts or to disseminate enlightening information on Jews and Judaism, as Jewish defense organizations had done since prewar days—were now totally inadequate to the task at hand.[46] German Jewry, troubled by events but not unduly alarmed, placed their hopes on the expectation that the republic would survive. It seemed incredible that the destiny of a great nation should be delivered into the hands of a man of Hitler's stature. When the incredible became imminent, Jews could still hope that once in power and involved with the affairs of state, Hitler and his party would abandon, or at least moderate, their anti-Jewish platform, which had served the purposes of propaganda. This anticipation, though widely shared by most contemporary observers, among them people who in one way or another had helped Hitler come to power, misjudged the nature of the Nazi movement and, even more, the mentality of its leader.[47]

In retrospect—but only in retrospect—it is not difficult to see that Hitler, in many respects a man of exceptional ability, was possessed by a Jew-hating mania which was a basic element in his psychological make-up. Nor was the anti-Semitic ideology an incidental feature of his world view, but a central motive in his thinking and imagination. It was a conviction he shared with other founders of the movement, who had been nurtured by the same intellectual sources in their formative years.[48] The contention that Jews were absolutely depraved had so often been reiterated by theologians, cranks, philosophers, and demagogues, that it had finally become internalized by revolutionaries determined to act upon it. They were not troubled by doubts about the validity of the contention or the wisdom of its consequences. Linked to the racial theory, which was for them a comprehensive Weltanschauung, the anti-Jewish doctrine was an incontestable truth. Thus the paragraph in the Nazi party program that denied Jews the right of German citizenship was immediately put into operation. But this was no more than the openly declared consequence of the racial theory. Not yet mentioned, but already contemplated, in Hitler's mind at least, was the physical annihilation of the Jews. The basic principle of radical anti-Semitism, the denial to Jews of the right to exist, came here to a wholly unexpected, but not inconsistent, fruition as the policy of a government.

26 | Anti-Semitism Through the Ages

HAVING FOLLOWED THE evolution of anti-Jewish attitudes in modern times, we must ask whether this inquiry has yielded an answer to the question that launched it. That question may be restated as follows. The Jewish emancipation granted in the European countries, beginning at the end of the eighteenth century, presupposed the disruption of the ideological web that supported the prevailing anti-Jewish attitude. That web seemed to be intimately interwoven with the traditional Christian outlook, which contained a negative image of Jews and Judaism, in particular of their religious beliefs and morality. The acceptance of Jews as members of the modern state and society seemed, on the other hand, to indicate that the whole complex of Christian reservations against Jews had been abandoned. How, then, could anti-Jewish agitation re-emerge in the last decades of the nineteenth century, sustaining itself on images and prejudices apparently obsolete for a century and more?

The answer arrived at in the course of our inquiry can now be summarily stated. First, it is true that Christianity had lost its former hold on people's minds and its determining influence on state and society. The state and its agencies ceased to be institutionally linked to the Church, and the dynamics of society were no longer governed or controlled by Christian convictions. The leading elites operating in both these frameworks now were under the influence of more secular forces. Still, the recession of Christian influence was not tantamount to its eclipse. Even in its dogmatic version, Christianity was not entirely defunct. It still provided the universal discourse and spiritual atmosphere for some in society, for whom the traditional conception of the role of the Jew in history remained valid. The negative image attached to the word *Jew* thus retained its ideological moorings. It could at least live on latently and if occasion arose be pointedly actualized. This indeed happened with the emergence of the anti-Semitic movement in the nineteenth century. As documented in the course of our inquiry, there was a whole series of strictly orthodox Christians between the leaders and precursors of the anti-Semitic movement: Stöcker, Rohling, Vogelsang, and others, not to mention the intermediaries like de Bonald and des Mousseaux in France, Julius Stahl and Herman Wagener in Prussia, and Sebastian Brunner in Austria, who, before the outbreak of the anti-Semitic movement, served as a kind of bridge between the traditional hatred of the Jew and its modern metamorphosis.

The second variety of Christian backing for modern anti-Semitism is found among those who were unconcerned about the dogmatic truth of Christianity. They nevertheless sustained religion as a component of nationalism, presenting Christianity as the only possible guarantee for personal or public morality, or they adhered to it for other not strictly religious reasons. Christianity of this kind, even if thoroughly diluted, was found to retain the doctrine of Christian superiority over Judaism, and this was easily transformed into overt anti-Semitism. Such more or less transparent connections between anti-Semitic arguments and their Christian background are found abundantly in the works of men like Glagau, Istoczy, Drumont, and others. Not Christians in the strict denominational or dogmatic sense, these men were sufficiently immersed in Christian tradition to draw upon it in substantiating their theories and strengthening their convictions. The thesis of the moral insensibility of Jews, their putative drive for world domination and the like, even if fostered by contemporary stimuli—the social distance between Jews and Christians and the actual economic success and political advancement of Jews—was clearly derived from traditional Christian concepts of Jewish mentality and Jewish messianic aspirations.

In a broader sense, modern anti-Semitism turned out to be a continuation of the premodern rejection of Judaism by Christianity, even when it renounced any claim to be legitimized by it or even professed to be antagonistic to Christianity. The wish to base anti-Semitism on grounds beyond the Jewish-Christian division remained in fact a mere declaration of intent. No anti-Semite, even if he himself was anti-Christian, ever forwent the use of those anti-Jewish arguments rooted in the denigration of Jews and Judaism in earlier Christian times. In historical perspective at least, Christianity always appeared as the higher religion—an evaluation apparent even in the thinking of thoroughly secularized anti-Semites like Voltaire, Bruno Bauer, and Eugen Dühring.

Culmination

Such paradoxical combinations should not be too much of a surprise; they are in the nature of rationalistic secularization. Rationalism was capable of demolishing the intellectual structure of the traditional world-view while maintaining the underlying emotional layers and even the basic conceptual configurations, and modern anti-Semitism can be seen as a case of secularization on a grand scale. For it was the image of the Jew that was inherited from Christianity that determined the secular perception of the Jew. The difference was that on the cognitive level this perception had to be supported by reasoning derived from the newly evolved systems of thought. It was this composite character of modern anti-Semitism—an absolute archaic image covered by a layer of justifications—that made it an irrational phenomenon inaccessible to overt, logically oriented argumentation.[1]

The evidence that the anti-Jewish notions of the pre-emancipatory Christian era were carried over into post-emancipatory anti-Semitism is not found only in the domain of ideological justification. The social situation of the recently emancipated and grudgingly accepted minority provoked the animosity of the majority because of the pariah status the Jewish community had had before emancipation, when it had lived at the margin of Christian society. The term "pariah," suggested by Max Weber for a description of the Jewish status in medieval society, though it does not exactly accord with its original Indian connotation, well characterizes the situation of the Jews. It hints at ritualistically secured socioeconomic separation, combined with social degradation. The pariah status implies, or at least explains, the Jew's image in Gentile eyes, which assumed in the course of time an increasingly sinister and even diabolical character. The socially degraded Jew, close physically but remote culturally, was held capable of perpetrating any deed and committing any crime. At times, in Gentile eyes, the Jews ceased to be human at all.[2]

During the period under consideration here—that is, from the emergence of the idea of Jewish emancipation in the last decades of the eighteenth century to its full implementation in the Western countries a hundred years later—the Jew was conceived of as a former pariah who had moved from the margin of society to its very center, where he occupied, or at least competed for, positions formerly the property of others. This perception, though often exaggerated and distorted, was no mere product of the imagination. Emancipation, whether formally completed at one stroke as in France or acquired only gradually and amid more or less prolonged wrangling, as in Germany, Austria, and Hungary, meant the expansion of the living space of the Jews, physically, economically, socially, and intellectually. From the beginning of the emancipation, Jews settled in streets, towns, and districts where they had been previously excluded. They gained access to occupations and sources of livelihood out-side those allotted to them in former generations. They now aspired to be admitted to social circles, to join clubs, lodges, and societies, or simply to frequent cafes, restaurants, theaters, and the like that had hitherto been both inaccessible and of no interest to them. At the same time, having ac-quired the language of the larger society and adopted the basic elements of its culture, they began to take part in its intellectual and artistic life. A great many Jews became patrons of culture, at times constituting an important part of the theater audiences and the readership of books and periodicals. The gifted among them became themselves active in intellectual and ar-tistic creativity.

Anti-Semites wished to perpetuate the inferior position of Jews or even reinstitute some features of their pre-emancipatory situation. Thus, even if they negated the Christian motives responsible for the creation of the situation, anti-Semites still took it as the basis of their operation. There is a patent historical continuity between the two phases of the Jewish predicament.

The word "responsible," used in the previous paragraph, has a moralistic ring: applied deliberately, it transfers the subject of anti-Semitism from the domain of history to ethical accountability. It implies that Chris-tianity is accountable for all the enormities of modern anti-Semitism, including its culmination in the Holocaust. There are historians and theologians who have accepted this verdict and drawn conclusions from it. They are best represented by the French historian Jules Isaac, who in the title of his book *The Teaching of Contempt* epitomized its central thesis: the dissemination of the Church's doctrine of the contemptible character of Jews and the Jewish mentality prepared the ground for the defamation and ultimate proscription of Jews in modern times. Isaac was a secular Jew who was stirred to investigate the Jewish question only because of the Nazi persecution to which his own family fell victim. Isaac's indictment of Chris-tianity is strongly colored by his emotions and philosophical convictions. Astonishingly enough, he succeeded in attracting into his orbit theologians and believing Christians.[3]

The historian who seeks to assess the question of responsibility cannot content himself with a recital of the facts while withholding moral judg-ment. Once he becomes involved in the question of responsibility, he is no longer dealing with the facts alone. He is, rather, concerned with deter-mining the causal connection between events. He must pay attention to what might seem to contradict his judgment. The most powerful argument that has been adduced, by Christian apologists as well as by anti-Semitic ideologues, to acquit Christianity of the charge of having fostered anti-Semitism is the fact that anti-Jewish sentiments and even atrocities existed in Hellenistic Alexandria, as well as in the Roman world long before Christianity. The application of the term *anti-Semitism* to these ancient phenomena gave additional weight to this reasoning. If animosity against Jews in antiquity was basically the same as in Christian and modern times, then anti-Semitism could not be attributed to a factor that emerged only later. The only permanent feature that was present in all the three phases, the pre-Christian, the Christian, and the modern, was the Jews themselves. Thus, it was easy for the anti-Semitic pundits to conclude that because of their hateful character and behavior the Jews were the cause of their own misfortune throughout their extended history.[4]

Irrespective of the issue of responsibility, I regard the very presence of the unique Jewish community among the other nations as the stimulus to the animosity directed at them. The responses to this stimulus, however, have varied from time to time and from place to place, and insofar as these variations relate to each other chronologically, one can speak of a history of anti-Semitism. It is by comparing the modes and expressions of anti-Jewishness of different ages and by tracing the impact of former modes and expressions on their later mutations that the measure of historical responsibility can be assessed. The history and characteristics of ancient anti-Semitism in this sense becomes relevant for the appraisal of its Christian and modern variants. Elements of the ancient anti-Jewish tradition we have up to now encountered only as they have been transmitted through the channel of its Christian sequel. If the ancient phase of anti-Semitism is to be compared with the later phases, it will have to be viewed in its own historical context.[5]

In the ancient world also, Gentiles expressed animosity toward the Jews living among them; it went beyond the wonted tension between ethnic groups competing for the means of livelihood, political influence, and the like. Jews were singled out by Hellenists and Romans for acrimony and contempt, because of their strange rituals, circumcision, Sabbath observance, and dietary laws. The adherence to these religious prescriptions strengthened the social isolation of the Jewish community, of which one of the main elements was the absolute prohibition on intermarriage with members of other groups. The fact is, of course, that Jews entered the world of Gentiles first through contact with their neighbors and conquerors in their own land and then as Diaspora minorities committed to a religiously sanctioned exclusiveness unparalleled in the ancient world. Unlike other nationalities, Jews refrained from taking part in the religious exercises of their neighbors, condemning and ridiculing them as the outrageously sensual rites of the spiritually blind. This exclusiveness heightened their own social cohesion and was probably instrumental in securing them a better chance for group survival in an alien and hostile environment. At the same time, this very guarantee of their survival elicited or intensified a peculiar brand of social animosity which, because of some similarity to its modern counterpart, has been accorded the name *anti-Semitism*. The first stimulus to the animosity in both cases has been the social cohesion and compactness of the Jews. As a reaction to it, the complex of imaginary notions about the Jewish mentality and other characteristics arose. Some aspects of ancient and modern anti-Semitism are similar, but a close examination reveals differences, most of which can be attributed to the Christian anti-Semitism that operated during the extended period separating modern anti-Semitism from its ancient counterpart.

That Christian anti-Semitism—that is, the stigmatization of Jews on the basis of Christian doctrines and world views—is no simple continuation of its ancient precursor is patently clear. To the previous charges, Christian animosity added indictments that arose out of the religious conflict between Judaism and Christianity, which was focused on the rejection of the Christian Messiah by the Jews; this carried with it the charge of deicide. All the other charges against Jews, including those current already in the ancient world, such as their hatred of the Gentiles and their moral insensibility toward strangers, now appeared combined with their religious guilt and their putative abandonment by God. The condemnation of Jews thus gained a quasi-metaphysical dignity unprecedented in the ancient world. This religious sanctioning of anti-Semitism then had its social consequences. Linked as it was to the central tenets of Christianity, with its all-pervasive influence, the hatred of Jews spread throughout society. Ancient anti-Semitism may have had a religious tinge produced by the Jewish contempt of the pagan gods. Still, it could not equal its Christian counterpart in emotional intensity, in the depth and breadth of its social expansion.

On the other hand, Christian anti-Semitism, transcending its pagan antecedent quantitatively and qualitatively, had redeeming features. Its condemnation was not unqualified; it kept open an escape hatch for Jews who would accept Christianity. The very toleration of Jews by the Church, otherwise fanatically exclusive toward heretics and the adherents of other religions, was warranted by the belief in the ultimate conversion of the Jews at the end of days. Pagan anti-Semitism lacked any such qualification of its condemnation of Judaism. The consistent adherence to the definition of the Jews as the enemy of mankind left no room for tolerating them. At times, this led to theoretical recommendations for the total destruction of the Jewish people; practically, it resulted in their being persecuted when their religious nonconformity became especially provoking. If such hostile reactions remained an exception, and Jews as a rule were left unmolested, even welcomed and at times privileged, it was because of the marginal nature of anti-Semitic theory in the world view of antiquity. The Jews'

323

nonconformity and exclusiveness may have been an irritant, but the objection to Jewish existence did not assume the character of a principle. The latent animosity needed some special occasion to become socially or politically activated.[6]

Modern anti-Semitism combined the worst features of both its ancient and Christian antecedents. Emerging in the wake of Christian anti-Semitism, it inherited its mental and social pervasiveness. A measure of reserve toward Jews, oscillating between a sense of uneasiness and outright animosity, remained even where the intellectual texture of the Christian world view had worn thin. Yet Christianity's weakening hold implied also the dissolution of the Christian conception of the Jew's role in the history of mankind, from which the vindication of their presence in the midst of Gentile society as well as the anticipation of their future conversion to Christianity derived. The vision of the ultimate Jewish conversion was replaced by the expectation of the Jews' acculturation and assimilation in the not too remote future. The Christian belief in the spiritual efficacy of conversion—the cleansing of the converted Jew of all his supposed vices and shortcomings—as well as the acceptance, as an article of faith, of the certainty of the universal conversion of Jews in the future was sustained in face of a contradictory reality. Its rationalistic substitute, however, the expectation of Jewish assimilation, was open to empirical verification. The scrutiny of Jewish behavior in the decades following the emancipation, to see whether Jews were undergoing their expected metamorphosis, was the overt aspect of this verification.[7] It was, at the same time, a manifestation of latent anti-Semitism. For if Jewish integration had to be vindicated by observable facts, the conclusion could only be that Jews, as individuals and certainly as a collective, continued to retain some of their characteristic features. As the fundamental badness of the Jewish personality had been taken for granted, it followed that the continued existence of the Jews in the Gentile world was indefensible.

This conclusion had its theoretical basis in the racial theory, which, from the 1860s, assumed a quasi-scientific garb. The premises were that races were distinctively different, that their differences vitally influenced human history, and that there was a necessary confrontation between the Semitic and Aryan races. Originally, these hypotheses were only employed intellectually, for historical and linguistic research. But unfortunately the confrontation between the Semite and the Aryan coincided with the traditional distinction between the Jew and the Christian; everything that had been said about the Jew was now applied to the Semite, and the contrary was always said about the Aryan. Thus the condemnation of Jews and Judaism was transferred from its original religious-historical framework into a supposedly scientific context. Thence it was transferred again to the public arena. In the nineteenth century, there were no political-social applications of the racial theory except to the Jews; even in regard to the Jews, the theory was not of prime importance. It did not create the contrast between the Jews and the rest of society, nor the criticism of Judaism by its detractors. This criticism, with its numerous arguments and justifications, amounted to the metamorphosis of the anti-Jewish tradition, which the racist theory now endowed with an explanation derived from ideas of the nature of peoples and the historical laws that govern them. Thus, the theory was not the cause of the situation but only its ideational accompaniment. Thoughts of eliminating the Jews arose among unrestrained anti-Semites long before the racial theory emerged. The theory simply helped these thoughts to crystallize into a clear idea—this idea was realized with the extermination of Jews by the Nazis.

Of course, it took the mentality of the Nazis, combined with the special historical circumstances under which they operated—both unpredictable in advance—to act upon the principles inherent in the situation.[8] The principles themselves, in more or less pungent terms, have been made explicit by the ideologues of the anti-Semitic movement in the late nineteenth century and by some of their earlier precursors. Still, it is only through the prism of hindsight that the anti-Semitism of the nineteenth century appears as a harbinger of the Hitlerite catastrophe. The anti-Semites of that time, especially the more radical among them, were demagogues who eschewed responsibility for the implementation of their ideas as well as for whatever impact they might have on other peoples' thoughts and actions. Hitler was taken by most of his contemporaries for such a demagogue. Who could surmise that he possessed the diabolic determination he did, and, a considerable further step, that he would also acquire the necessary power to carry out his will?

The anti-Semitic movement of the nineteenth century, which culminated in the Nazi period, stands revealed as the product of a peculiar constellation of historical circumstances. It consisted of the overt reaction to Jewish emancipation in countries where the millennial Christian resentment against Jews and Judaism remained a latent but mighty force. This constellation was a unique one—as every constellation depending on many factors always is—having no chance to recur in the same way a second time. Indeed, even if all the factors that constituted the constellation were to reappear, the situation would be different, for it would include the inevitable reaction to the consequences of the first constellation. The attempt to foresee the future on the basis of its analogies with the past is a futile undertaking.

What the historian can do, beyond the critically controlled reconstruction of the past, is to assess the extent to which the elements involved in a past constellation of events are still operative in the present and how the reactions to its consequences seem to shape up—without pretending to know what new combination may emerge out of these and other unapprehended elements.

The reactions to the culmination of anti-Semitism in the Holocaust are evident both in the Gentile and the Jewish world. As to the first, one conspicuous reaction was the heart-searching of theologians and intellectuals, spurred by Jules Isaac, who have tried, with modest success it is true, to influence the Vatican to delete some of the most offensive anti-Jewish passages of the Catholic ritual. The criticism of these Christian thinkers concerning the anti-Jewish attitude of the Church is more far-reaching than their criticism of ritual. It touches on the whole Christian tradition, demanding a radical revision of the Gospels' portrayal of Christianity emerging against the background of a deteriorated and God-forsaken Judaism. Although supported by the results of modern historical research, which might justify a change on the basis of historical facts, it is doubtful whether such a revision is at all possible theologically. It has been cogently argued by critics of the trend to eradicate anti-Semite inferences that such a revision would subvert the whole doctrinal edifice of Christianity. It has also been pointed out that the presentation of Christian doctrine even by the most sophisticated modern theologians retains the idea of Christian superiority, implying a concomitant negative evaluation of Jews and Judaism. It is more probable, therefore, that the revisionary trend, seeking a rehabilitation of Judaism within the framework of Christianity, will remain an esoteric exercise restricted in its impact to an intellectual elite.[9]

Shifts in the relations between religious groups like Christians and Jews are not the result of actions planned by intellectuals. As modern society has undergone considerable secularization since the anti-Semitic movement of the nineteenth century, the anti-Jewish predilections of Christianity may have died down in spite of the continuous doctrinal negation of Judaism. Whether this can be taken as a sign of the impending demise of anti-Semitism is, however, highly doubtful, even if the continuing decline of Christianity could be taken for granted; for anti-Semitism has simultaneously been weaning itself from its Christian roots. It has certainly survived the paralyzation of Christianity as an organized religion in Soviet Russia and in the other Communist countries of Eastern Europe.

In his day, Schopenhauer had theorized that, because of the peculiar cohesion of its adherents, Judaism would endure even if its rival, Christianity, should completely disappear.[10] The validity of this theory is still untested. For, even where Christianity has declined, the residue of its anti-Jewish aspects has persisted, and thus Jewish cohesion and the inimical reaction to it have continued to feed off each other. This is certainly true for those countries where anti-Semitism has become virulent, reaching the dimensions of a movement and allowing the millennial Christian resentment to metamorphose into its modern form. It is less true of those countries to which Jews immigrated only in the age of secularization, and where they could become citizens with equal rights and unlimited opportunities for advancement.[11] Still, even in these countries, they remained a nonconforming minority of exceptional cohesion. Nor is there any guarantee that the memory of their pariah existence before emancipation will not affect their status in the future.

Zionism has aimed at a radical change, prompted by the conception of anti-Semitism as inherent in the Jews' status as a minority. But, though successful in establishing a Jewish state, Zionism has not achieved its ultimate goal, the elimination of the Diaspora. Instead of relieving Jews of their minority status, the state of Israel has added to their exceptionality— Jews who have not emigrated there are identified not only with their own country, but with Israel. Israel itself, as a newcomer on the international scene, owing its existence to most peculiar historical circumstances, is a target of constant attack. In the ideological expression of these attacks, anti-Semitic motives are routinely intermingled. These attacks inevitably affect the situation of Diaspora Jewry, which for better or worse is associated with the state. Thus, even where in their relations with Gentile society Jews are free of any discrimination, they may still feel themselves under attack and suspicion because of their connection with the state of Israel. Where, on the other hand, anti-Semitism, nourished by local stimuli, has survived, its expressions are colored by reactions to the Jewish state. Since anti-Jewish animosity has always trailed the path of Jewish history, and the last phase of it is characterized by the creation of the Jewish state, the new metamorphosis is hardly surprising. Whether this recent variant of anti-Semitism is the aftereffect of bygone revulsions or the portent of new ones is a question that imposes itself on our mind.

Notes

Abbreviations

AZJ   *Allgemeine Zeitung des Judenthums*
BLBI *Bulletin des Leo Baeck Instituts*
HUCA *Hebrew Union College Annual*
JSS   *Jewish Social Studies*
LBIYB *Leo Baeck Institute Year Book*
MGWJ *Monatsschrift für die Geschichte und Wissenschaft des Judenthums*
REJ   *Revue des études juives*

Introduction

1. For a comprehensive discussion of the origin of the term, see Chapter 21.

2. The basic facts of the process of emancipation can be found in any book on modern Jewish history. For a more detailed account, see Simon Dubnov, *History of the Jews,* trans. Moshe Spiegel (South Brunswick: Joseloff, 1967-1973), vols. 4 and 5.

3. Jacob Katz, "The Term 'Jewish Emancipation': Its Origin and Historical Impact," in *Studies in Nineteenth-Century Jewish Intellectual History,* ed. Alexander Altmann (Cambridge, Mass.: Harvard University Press, 1964), pp. 1-25, reprinted in Jacob Katz, *Emancipation and Assimilation: Studies in Modern Jewish History* (Farnborough: Greggs, 1972), pp. 21-45. See also Reinhard Rürup, *Emanzipation und Anitsemitismus* (Göttingen: Vandenhöck and Ruprecht, 1975), pp. 126-132.

4. For details, see Chapters 20-24.

5. Jacob Toury, *Die politischen Orientierungen der Juden in Deutschland*

(Tübingen: Mohr, 1966), pp. 170-245; Michael Marrus, *The Politics of Assimilation: A Study of the French Jewish Community at the Time of the Dreyfus Affair* (Oxford: Oxford University Press, 1971), pp. 122-140.

6. Ismar Schorsch, *Jewish Reactions to German Anti-Semitism 1870-1914* (New York: Columbia University Press, 1972), pp. 17, 39-42.

7. See the preface in Theodor Herzl, *The Jewish State* (New York: Herzl Press, 1970), and Leo Pinsker, *Autoemancipation! Mahnruf an seine Stammesgenossen von einem russischen Juden* (Berlin, 1882). An English translation of Pinsker by D. S. Blondheim appears in *Road to Freedom*, ed. Ben-Zion Netanyahu (New York: Scopus, 1944).

8. The first version was proposed by Bernard Lazare, *L'Antisemitisme, son histoire et ses causes* (Paris, 1894). See also Andrew G. Whiteside, *The Socialism of Fools: Georg Ritter von Schönerer and Austrian Pan-Germanism* (Berkeley: University of California Press, 1975), pp. 89-90.

9. The scholarly literature on the subject is extensive. For an analysis and summary of the research, see Ismar Schorsch, "German Anti-Semitism in the Light of Post-War Historiography," *LBIYB* 19 (1974): 257-271.

10. A summary and bibliography may be found in Salo Wittmayer Baron, *A Social and Religious History of the Jews* (New York: Columbia University Press, 1952), I, 188-195. In Chapter 26, I will discuss the part played by ancient anti-Semitism in later developments.

11. Christian anti-Semitism is an integral part of medieval Jewish history; nevertheless, even specific works on the relations between the two groups, as well as the hostile and Satanic image of the Jew, are quite numerous. The latest attempt of this type is Leon Poliakov, *The History of Anti-Semitism*, 3 vols. (London: Routledge and Kegan Paul, 1974-1975).

12. I have described the process of *embourgeoisement* and its social impact in *Out of the Ghetto: The Social Background of Jewish Emancipation, 1770-1870* (Cambridge, Mass.: Harvard University Press, 1973).

1. The Christian Tradition: Eisenmenger

1. Such was the method, for example, of Leon Poliakov in his *The History of Anti-Semitism*, 3 vols. (London: Routledge and Kegan Paul, 1974-1975), as well as of many others who have presented the history of anti-Semitism in the form of a summary, such as Bernard Lazare, *L'Antisemitisme, son histoire et ses causes* (Paris, 1894); James Parkes, *Antisemitism* (London: Valentine Mitchell, 1963); Friedrich Heer, *God's First Love: Christians and Jews over Two Thousand Years* (London: Weidenfeld & Nicolson, 1970); Salo W. Baron, "Changing Patterns of Anti-Semitism," *JSS* 38 (1976): 5-38.

2. Johann Andreas Eisenmenger, *Entdecktes Judenthum*, 2 vols. (Königsberg [Berlin], 1710).

3. Jacob Katz, "The Sources of Modern Anti-Semitism: Eisenmenger's Method of Presenting Evidence from Talmudic Sources," in *Proceedings of the Fifth World Congress of Jewish Studies* (Jerusalem, 1972), II, 210-211.

4. Heinrich Graetz, *Geschichte der Juden von den ältesten Zeiten bis auf die Gegenwart* (Leipzig, 1878-97), X, 282-286; Gerson Wolf, "Der Prozess

Eisenmenger," *MGWJ* 18 (1869): 378-384, 425-432, 465-473; Leopold Loewenstein, "Der Prozess Eisenmenger," *Magazin für die Wissenschaft des Judenthums* 18 (1891): 209-210.

5. Graetz, *Geschichte der Juden,* X, 276.

6. Meyer Kayserling, "Les hébraisants chrétiens du XVIIe siècle," *REJ* 20 (1890): 261-268; Shmuel Ettinger, "The Beginning of the Change in the Attitude of European Society towards the Jews," *Scripta Hierosolymitana* 7 (1961): 193-219; Hans Joachim Schoeps, *Philosemitismus im Barock* (Tübingen: Mohr, 1952), pp. 134-162.

7. This section is based on my book *Exclusiveness and Tolerance: Studies in Jewish-Gentile Relations in Medieval and Modern Times* (Oxford: Oxford University Press, 1961), especially part I, pp. 3-63.

8. Eisenmenger, II, 397-400.

9. Ibid.

10. Ibid., II, chapters 13-14.

11. Ibid., I, chapters 2-4, 7.

12. Ibid., I, chapter 12; II, chapters 3, 11.

13. Katz, *Exclusiveness and Tolerance,* pp. 59-63.

14. See the article "Zchirat Maaseh Amalek" ("Remembrance of the Deed of Amalek") in *Encyclopaedia Talmudica,* XII, 217-223.

15. Eisenmenger, II, 189-193, 200-218. Also cf. I, 654-659, 691-693, 748-754.

16. Katz, "Eisenmenger's Method," n. 22; Eisenmenger, II, 206-210.

17. Eisenmenger, II, 220-225, 227-234, 469-472, 501-515, 574-613.

18. Ibid., chapter 18, especially pp. 1017-1025; also pp. 647-668, 1208.

19. The words were first used by Johann David Michaelis (1717-1791), the Orientalist from Göttingen, in his criticism of Dohm's book (see Chapter 4) and appeared in *Orientalische und exegetische Bibliothek* 19 (1782): 9.

20. Selma Stern, *Der preussische Staat und die Juden* (Tübingen; Mohr, 1963), I/1, 75-88.

21. Robert Anchel, "La Tolerance au moyen-age," in his *Les Juifs de France* (Paris: T.B. Janin, 1946), pp. 93-124.

2. The Rationalist Reorientation

1. Paul Hazard, *The European Mind, 1680-1715* (London: Hollis and Carter, 1953); Basil Willey, *The Seventeenth Century Background* (London: Chatto and Windus, 1962).

2. Jacob Katz, *Out of the Ghetto: The Social Background of Jewish Emancipation, 1770-1870* (Cambridge, Mass.: Harvard University Press, 1973), pp. 38-39.

3. In this I am anticipating the conclusions of Chapter 3 on Voltaire and Chapter 13 on the German radicals.

4. Leo Strauss, *Die Religionskritik Spinozas als Grundlage seiner Bibelwissenschaft: Untersuchungen zu Spinozas theologisch-politischem Traktat* (Berlin: Akademie Verlag, 1930), pp. 90-91.

5. Ibid., pp. 126-128, 255-260.

6. On the history of biblical criticism, see Hans-Joachim Kraus, *Geschichte der*

historisch-kritischen Erforschung des Alten Testaments von der Reformation bis zur Gegenwart (Neukirchen: Buchhandlung des Eriziehungswesens, 1956), pp. 36-37, 52-55.

7. Jacob Guttmann, "Jean Bodin in seinen Beziehungen zum Judentum," *MGWJ* 49 (1905): 315-348, 459-489; Georg Röllenbeeck, *Offenbarung, Natur und jüdische Überlieferung bei Jean Bodin* (Gütersloh: G. Mohr, 1964); Roger Chauviré, *Jean Bodin, auteur de la "République"* (Geneva: Slotkin, 1969), pp. 141-170; Henri Baudrillart, *Bodin et son temps: Tableau des theories politiques et des idées économiques au XVIème siècle* (Aalen: Scientia Verlag, 1964), pp. 190-221.

8. Benedict Spinoza, *A Theologico-Political Treatise,* chapters 5 and 18. An entire literature has been written on Spinoza and his attitude toward the Bible; see, for example, Manuel Joel, *Spinozas theologisch-politischer Traktat* (Breslau, 1870); Sylvain Zac, *Spinoza et l'interpretation de l'écriture* (Paris: Presses universitaires de France, 1965).

9. John Toland, *Nazarenus, or Jewish, Gentile and Mahometan Christianity,* 12th rev. ed. (London, 1718); Leslie Stephen, *History of English Thought in the Eighteenth Century* (London, 1902), I, 103-104; Gotthard Victor Lechler, *Geschichte des englischen Deismus* (Stuttgart and Tübingen, 1841), pp. 468-471; Max Wiener, "John Toland and Judaism," *HUCA* 16 (1941): 215-242. Cf. Shmuel Ettinger, "Jews and Judaism as Seen by the English Deists of the Eighteenth Century," *Zion* 29 (1964): 188-190.

10. On the history of the Deists, see John Orr, *English Deism: Its Roots and its Fruits* (Grand Rapids, Mich.: Erdmans, 1934); Norman L. Torrey, *Voltaire and the English Deists* (New Haven, Conn.: Yale University Press, 1930); Roland Stromberg, *Religious Liberalism in Eighteenth-Century England* (London: Oxford University Press, 1954), pp. 52-87; and Lechler, *Geschichte des englischen Deismus.*

11. The later studies have increasingly come to question viewing the Deist trend as monolithic. See A. R. Winnet, "Were the Deists 'Deists'?" *Church Quarterly Review* 161 (1960): 70-77. Profound analyses of the various Deist writers are found in Günther Gawlick's introductions to editions of their works being published by Friedrich Frommann, Stuttgart-Bad Cannstatt.

12. Details and bibliographies on these writers may be found in the literature cited above, n. 10.

13. A kind of division of labor exists among the various authors: Toland concentrates on historical problems posed by tradition, Woolston attacks tradition because of its miracle tales, while Tindal and Morgan criticize it on moral grounds. See the chapters devoted to each of them in Torrey, *Voltaire and the English Deists.*

14. Thomas Woolston, *A Fourth Discourse on the Miracles of Our Saviour in View of the Present Controversy between Infidels and Apostates* (London, 1728), pp. 28-43; idem, *A Fifth Discourse on the Miracles of Our Saviour in View of the Present Controversy between Infidels and Apostates* (London, 1728), pp. 42-56. The following year saw the matter continued in yet a sixth discourse. Contemporaries, of course, saw through the ruse of the fictitious rabbi, and it will suffice here to cite two sources: William Gardiner, *A Short Answer to a Long Rabbinical Letter, Supposed to be Wrote to Mr. Woolston* (London, 1729), views the rabbi as

an obviously imaginary character, as does Woolston's biographer H. Chr. Lemker, *Historische Nachricht von Thomas Woolstons Schicksal, Schriften und Streitigkeiten* (Leipzig, 1740), pp. 113-114, 304-310.

15. Peter Annet, "Supernaturals Examined," in *A Collection of the Tracts of a Certain Free Enquirer* (London, 1734), pp. 109-119. A rabbi also appears in Morgan's book (see n. 18), but as though the author had forgotten about him completely, he does not partake in the conversation of the adversaries.

16. See B. Smalley, *The Study of the Bible in the Middle Ages* (Oxford: Oxford University Press, 1964), pp. 1-13.

17. Ettinger, "Jews and Judaism," pp. 184-188.

18. Thomas Morgan, *The Moral Philosopher* (London, 1737), I, 247-248.

19. See the summary by Günther Gawlick in the facsimile edition of *The Moral Philosopher* (Stuttgart-Bad Cannstatt: Friedrich Frommann, 1969), pp. 17*-20*.

20. On Shaftesbury's place among the Deists, see A. O. Alridge, "Shaftesbury and the Deist Manifesto," *Transactions of the American Philosophical Society*, n.s., 41, pt. 2 (1951).

21. Anthony of Shaftesbury, *Characteristicks of Men, Manners, Opinions, Times* (London, 1732), I, 357.

22. Ibid., p. 358.

23. Ibid.

24. Walter Rex, *Essays on Pierre Bayle and Religious Controversy* (The Hague: Nighoff, 1965), pp. 197-255.

25. *The Life of David, the History of the Man after God's Own Heart* (London, 1761). The book appeared anonymously and several writers were credited with its authorship, but research has concluded that it was written by Annet. See Torrey, *Voltaire and the English Deists*, pp. 187-195. Later, the subject remained of interest to the rationalists as well; see Hermann Samuel Reimarus, *Übrige noch ungedruckte Worte des Wolfenbüttlischen Fragmentisten, ein Nachlass von Gotthold Ephraim Lessing* (n.p., 1787), who devotes a lengthy sketch to David, subjecting him to deadly moral criticism. Annet's influence is clearly discernible in the method of the tale's presentation.

26. Matthew Tindal, *Christianity as Old as Creation* (London, 1730), pp. 92-96; Annet, *The Free Enquirer* (London, 1826), pp. 28-30. The material has been gathered and the motif analyzed for all the Deists in Günther Gawlick, "Abraham's Sacrifice of Isaac Viewed by the English Deists," *Studies on Voltaire and the Eighteenth Century* 57 (1967): 577-600.

27. Whether his declaration of earnestness should indeed be taken at face value remains questionable. See Stromberg, *Religious Liberalism*, p. 73.

28. For a summary of Tindal's work, see Torrey, *Voltaire and the English Deists*, pp. 104-129.

29. For an analysis of Morgan's teachings, see Gawlick's introduction (cited in n. 19). On his attitude to Biblical Judaism, see Ettinger, "Jews and Judaism," pp. 197-202.

30. See Lechler, *Geschichte des Deismus*, p. 387; see also Gawlick's comments, pp. 22*-23*.

31. The contrast is highlighted in the full title of the book: *The Moral Philos-*

opher: Dialogue between Philalethes, a Christian Deist and Theophanes, a Christian Jew. See Gawlick, p. 9*, n. 21, and Stromberg, *Religious Liberalism*, p.71, n. 1.

32. The entire matter is discussed in detail in Thomas Perry, *Public Opinion, Propaganda and Politics in Eighteenth Century England* (Cambridge, Mass.: Harvard University Press, 1962), especially pp. 72-122 and appendix B, pp. 194-199.

33. Ibid., pp. 11-12, 75-76, 87-88, 99, 178-180, 194-199.

34. As according to Ettinger, "Jews and Judaism," p. 206.

35. See Archaicus, *Admonitions from Scripture and History from Religious and Common Prudence, Relating to the Jews* (Oxford, 1753).

36. E. (J), *Some Considerations on the Naturalisation of the Jews* (London, 1753), discriminates between the Sephardic Jews and the Polish, who are considered worse than the Sephardic.

37. Bernard Glassman, *Anti-Semitic Stereotypes without Jews: Images of the Jews in England, 1290-1700* (Detroit: Wayne State University Press, 1975), traces the transmission of prejudice in England during the period when Jews were completely absent from the land.

38. Christian [pseud.], *Case of the Jews Considered with Regard to Trade, Commerce, Manufactures and Religion, etc.* (London, 1753), p. 12.

39. Opposed to these arguments is the author of *Unprejudiced Christian's Apology for the Jews* (London, 1753), p. 35.

40. Josiah Tucker, *Letter to a Friend Concerning Naturalisation, etc.* London, 1753), pp. 16-17.

41. Convincing proofs are presented by Edgar R. Samuel, "The Jews in English Foreign Trade: A Consideration of the 'Philo Patria' Pamphlets of 1753," in *Remember the Days: Essays on Anglo-Jewish History Presented to Cecil Roth*, ed. J. M. Shaftesley (London, 1966), and the literature cited there.

42. Philo Patria, *Further Consideration on the Act to Permit Persons Professing the Jewish Religion to be Naturalized by Parliament. In a Letter from a Merchant in Town to his Friend in the Country, etc.* (London, 1753), p. 100.

43. Ibid., p. 86.

44. George M. Trevelyan, *History of England* (London: Longmans, Green and Co., 1943), pp. 187-188.

45. Herbert Schöffler, *Abendland und Altes Testament: Untersuchung zur Kulturmorphologie Europas, insbesondere England* (Bochum: Pöppinghaus, 1937).

46. Various scholars have noted in passing the influence of the Deists on later thinking, but only Shmuel Ettinger, in his "Jews and Judaism," gathered together the anti-Jewish material from the Deist literature, drawing attention to the problem with appropriate emphasis.

3. Voltaire

1. The literature on Voltaire, both biographical and topical, is vast. Two of the most recent biographies are Theodore Besterman, *Voltaire* (London: Longmans, Green and Co., 1969), and Ira O. Wade, *The Intellectual Development of Voltaire* (Princeton: Princeton University Press, 1969).

2. On the turning point in Voltaire's life see Besterman, *Voltaire*, p. 360, and Wade, *Intellectual Development*, p. 253, but also cf. p. 559.

3. René Pomeau, *La Religion de Voltaire* (Diss., Paris, 1956), part I, pp. 74-115.

4. Norman L. Torrey, *Voltaire and the English Deists* (New Haven, Yale University Press, 1930), proves in detail Voltaire's dependence on English literature, but shows as well that he was careless in his citations and at times even took liberties with the English writers, using their names for his polemical needs. Voltaire's dependence on the English Deists in Jewish matters is the main thesis of Shmuel Ettinger, "Jews and Judaism as Seen by the English Deists of the Eighteenth Century," *Zion* 29 (1964): 182-207. Ettinger reached his conclusions independently of Torrey.

5. Peter Gay, *Voltaire's Politics: The Poet as a Realist* (Princeton: Princeton University Press, 1959), pp. 239-241, has remarked on the significance of the term.

6. On Voltaire as a historian, see Friedrich Meinecke, *Historism: The Rise of a New Historical Outlook* (London: Routledge and Kegan Paul, 1972), pp. 54-89; J. H. Brumfitt, *Voltaire Historian* (Oxford: Oxford University Press, 1958); and Wade, *Intellectual Development*, pp. 451-515.

7. Meinecke, *Historism*, pp. 62-71.

8. Voltaire, *Essai sur les moeurs et l'esprit des nations* (Paris: Garnier, 1963), I, 203, II, 806. Here he determines that man's spirit is influenced by climate, government, and religion.

9. Meinecke, *Historism*, pp. 77-81.

10. For example, "Nous ne toucherons le moins que nous pourrons à ce qui est divin dans l'histoire des Juifs; ou si nous sommes forcés d'en parler, ce n'est qu' autant que leurs miracles ont un rapport essentiel à la suite des évènements. Nous avons pour les prodiges continuels qui signalèrent tous les pas de cette nation le respect qu'on leur doit; nous les croyons avec la foi raisonable qu'exige l'Eglise substitueé à la Synagogue; nous ne les examinons pas; nous nous en tenons toujours à l'historique." *Essai*, I, 135-136.

11. See Walter Engemann, *Voltaire und China: Ein Beitrag zur Geschichte der Völkerkunde und zur Geschichte der Geschichtsschreibung sowie zu ihren gegenseitigen Beziehungen* (Diss., Leipzig, 1932), pp. 121-122, and *Essai*, I, 216-218.

12. Voltaire's opinion of Biblical personages is summarized nicely in Hanna Emmrich, *Das Judentum bei Voltaire* (Breslau: Pribatsch, 1930), especially pp. 128, 135, 142, and 178. A systematic study of Voltaire's method and achievements in Biblical research is produced by Bertram Eugene Schwarzbach, *Voltaire's Old Testament Criticism* (Geneva: Librairie Droz, 1971).

13. On the question of whether Moses ever lived, see Emmrich, *Das Judentum*, p. 25; on the historical truth of Phineas's deed and Korah's rebellion, see pp. 60-61.

14. Voltaire's moralistic approach has been stressed by many scholars: see Meinecke, *Historism*, pp. 71-74; Jerome Rosenthal, "Voltaire's Philosophy of History," *Journal of the History of Ideas* 16 (1955): 151-178; and Schwarzbach,

335

Criticism, pp. 232-254; *La Bible enfin expliquée par plusiers aumoniers* in *Oeuvres complètes de Voltaire* (Paris, 1824), XXXIII, 242.

15. See Voltaire, *Dictionnaire philosophique,* ed. R. Pomeau (Paris: Garnier, 1964), pp. 22-25, 294-298. On the human sacrifices, see *Essai,* I, 129-130, and Emmrich's *Das Judentum,* pp. 178-179; on superstitions, Emmrich, pp. 112-116. For the basis of Voltaire's claim in the matter of the human sacrifices, see Schwarzbach, *Criticism,* pp. 244-250.

16. See Emmrich, *Das Judentum,* pp. 10-21, 104-116; *Essai,* I, 98, 136, II, 797; and *Dictionnaire,* pp. 298-299.

17. Gay's book, *Voltaire's Politics,* corrects somewhat the notion that Voltaire was incapable of political judgment, but even Gay admits that it was not one of the outstanding features of his character.

18. See the summary by Emmrich, *Das Judentum,* pp. 99-103.

19. Gay, *Voltaire's Politics,* pp. 159-172.

20. See for example *Essai,* I, 140-141 and the summary by Emmrich in *Das Judentum,* pp. 161-166. Voltaire stresses the utility of belief in the immortality of the soul in *Essai,* I, 41 where he also declares that "the Pharisees did not come to believe in the immortality of the soul, in the dogmas of reward and punishment after death, only near the Hasmonean period." See also *Essai,* I, 60.

21. See the summary in Emmrich, *Das Judentum,* pp. 28-50. Voltaire refers to post-Biblical Jewish history in several places, for example *La Bible enfin expliquée* in *Oeuvres complètes,* XXXIII, 434-492; *Essai,* I, 148-152, 163-165, II, 61-64.

22. *Sermon du Rabbin Akib* in *Oeuvres complètes,* XXXI, 470-471.

23. Cited by Gay, *Voltaire's Politics,* pp. 351-352, from the article "Tolérance" in *Questions sur l'Encyclopédie.*

24. *Philosophie* in *Oeuvres complètes,* XXXI, 410.

25. Cited by Schwarzbach, *Criticism,* p. 109.

26. Evaluations of the Jews are found in Gay, *Voltaire's Politics,* p. 351. See Voltaire, *Dictionnaire,* pp. 136-138, and *Essai,* II, 61.

27. See the summary in Emmrich, *Das Judentum,* pp. 144-146. Schwarzbach, *Criticism,* p. 104, n. 42, suggests Voltaire's analysis of Jewish prayers in the Psalms in *Philosophie de l'histoire* as the source of his notion of domination in the Bible. Whoever reads the Psalms with an open mind, however, surely will not find future domination as their leitmotif; and even Voltaire placed greater emphasis on the will to revenge their enemies than on their hopes of mastering them. See the critical edition of the text in *Studies in Voltaire and the Eighteenth Century* 28 (1963): 227-229.

28. For particulars see the biography of Besterman, pp. 112, 311-312. On the Hirschel affair, see Wilhelm Mangold, *Voltaires Rechtsstreit mit dem Königlichen Schutzjuden Hirschel* (Berlin, 1905).

29. Cited by Arthur Hertzberg, *The French Enlightenment and the Jews* (New York: Columbia University Press, 1968), pp. 134-135, n. 174, from *Correspondence,* I, 146-147. Also cf. Besterman, *Voltaire,* p. 86.

30. See Gay's appendix to *Voltaire's Politics,* pp. 351-354, and his *The Party of Humanity: Essays in French Enlightenment* (New York, 1964), pp. 97-108, where the idea is more fully developed. Gay tries to resolve the paradox, but without success; see Hugh Trevor-Roper's review of Hertzberg's book in *The New York*

Review of Books, 22 August 1968, pp. 11-14, and Hertzberg's rejoinder, 24 October 1976, pp. 37-38.

31. Pomeau, *La Religion de Voltaire,* pp. 110-111, 358-359.

32. Gay wants to present a Voltaire actively involved in social affairs, but precisely this approach highlights that he is no revolutionary at all.

33. See Jacob Katz, "The Term 'Jewish Emancipation': Its Origins and Historical Impact," in *Nineteenth-Century Jewish Intellectual History,* ed. Alexander Altmann (Cambridge, Mass.: Harvard University Press, 1964), pp. 4-9. On Montesquieu, see Hertzberg, *French Enlightenment,* pp. 273-276, and Katz, *Out of the Ghetto: The Social Background of Jewish Emancipation, 1770-1870* (Cambridge, Mass.: Harvard University Press, 1973), pp. 28-41.

34. De Pinto's objections appeared first in Amsterdam in 1762 as *Apologie pour la nation juive, au reflexions critiques sur le premier chapitre du VIIe tome des oeuvres de M. de Voltaire au sujet des Juifs. Par l'auteur de "l'Essai sur le luxe"* and was reprinted with Voltaire's reply and the editor's notes by Antoine Guénée, *Lettres de quelques juifs portugais et allemands à M. de Voltaire* (Paris, 1769). See also Hertzberg's analysis, *French Enlightenment,* pp. 280-308.

35. *Essai,* II, 63.

36. Emmrich, *Das Judentum,* p. 201.

37. *Essai,* II, 66-67.

38. On Marx's view, see Chapter 13.

4. Ideological Counterattack

1. The reference to the two canons of Judaism, the Old Testament and the Talmud respectively, is a sure indication of later anti-Semitic religious attitudes.

2. Jacob Katz, *Out of the Ghetto: The Social Background of Jewish Emancipation, 1770-1870* (Cambridge, Mass.: Harvard University Press, 1973), pp. 161-175, and "The Term 'Jewish Emancipation': Its Origins and Historical Impact," in *Nineteenth-Century Jewish Intellectual History,* ed. Alexander Altmann (Cambridge, Mass.: Harvard University Press, 1964), pp. 21-45.

3. Ignatz Klingler, *Über die Ünnütz- und Schädlichkeit der Juden im Königreiche Böhmen und Mähren* (Prague, 1782).

4. Christian Wilhelm Dohm, *Über die bürgerliche Verbesserung der Juden* (Berlin, 1781); Volkmar Eichstädt, *Bibliographie zur Geschichte der Judenfrage* (Hamburg: Hanseatische Verlagsanstalt, 1938), pp. 8-15.

5. Friedrich Traugott Hartmann, *Untersuchungen ob die bürgerliche Freiheit der Juden zu gestatten sei* (Berlin, 1783); Johann Heinrich Schulz, *Philosophische Betrachtung über Theologie und Religion überhaupt und über die jüdische insonderheit* (Frankfurt and Leipzig, 1784).

6. On France, see chapter 8. On Holland, *Actenstücke zur Geschichte der Erhebung der Juden zu Bürgern in der Republik Batavien* (Neustrelitz, 1797); on Prussia, Ismar Freund, *Die Emanzipazion der Juden in Preussen,* 2 vols. (Berlin: H. Poppelauer, 1912).

7. This will be discussed in the next chapter.

8. Abraham Cahen, "L'Emancipation des Juifs devant la Societé Royale des Sciènces et Arts de Metz en 1787 et M. Roederer," *REJ* 1 (1880): 88-89.

9. On Friedländer and his suggestion, see Michael Meyer, *The Origins of the*

Modern Jew (Detroit: Wayne State University Press, 1967), pp. 57-78; Jean André de Luc, *Lettre aux auteurs Juifs d'un Memoire adresse à Mr. Teller* (Berlin, 1749), p. 6.

10. Christian Ludwig Paalzow, *Die Juden nebst einigen Bemerkungen über das Sendschreiben an Herrn Probst Teller zu Berlin* (Berlin, 1799), p. 51; idem, *Der Jude und der Christ—eine Unterhaltung auf dem Postwagen* (Berlin, 1803), p. 83; Schulz, *Philosophische Betrachtung*, p. 221; Friedrich Wilhelm Grattenauer, *Über die physische und moralische Verfassung der heutigen Juden* (Leipzig, 1791), pp. 6-7.

11. Christian Ludwig Paalzow, *Über das Bürgerrecht der Juden* (Berlin, 1803), pp. 98-102, 116; Grattenauer, *Über die physische und moralische Verfassung*, pp. 40-47; Paalzow, *Die Juden nebst einigen Bemerkungen*, pp. 14-21; Friedrich Buchholz, *Moses und Jesus* (Berlin, 1803), p. 145.

12. Grattenauer, *Über die physische und moralische Verfassung*, pp. 19-20, 24-25, 114-115.

13. Buchholz, *Moses und Jesus*, pp. 208-209.

14. Friedrich Traugott Hartmann, *Untersuchungen*, pp. 11-20, 40, 117-122.

15. Johann Gottlieb Fichte, *Beitrag zur Berichtigung der Urteile des Publikums über die französische Revolution* (Jena, 1793), p. 101.

16. Hartmann, *Untersuchungen*, p. 17-19.

17. Ernst Traugott von Kortum, *Über Judenthum und Juden hauptsächlich in Rücksicht ihres Einflusses auf bürgerlichen Wohlstand* (Nuremberg, 1795), pp. 50, 54-56.

18. The following is a summary of my essay, "A State within a State, the History of an anti-Semitic Slogan," *Israel Academy of Sciences and Humanities Proceedings* 4 (1971): 29-58, reprinted in J. Katz, *Emancipation and Assimilation: Studies in Modern Jewish History* (Farnborough: Gregg, 1972), pp. 47-76.

19. Schulz, *Philosophische Betrachtung*, p. 222.

20. Katz, "A State within a State," pp. 30-38.

21. Fichte, *Beitrag zur Berichtigung*, p. 188.

22. Herder's *Sämmtliche Werke*, ed. B. Suphan (Berlin, 1886), XXIV, 63; ibid. XIV, 67, 283-284. Contrary to the accepted view of Herder's attitude toward Jewish emancipation, it is clear from his comment of 1802 (XXIV, 63-64) that he was strongly against it. See F. M. Barnard, "Herder and Israel," *JSS* 28 (1966): 25-33.

23. Hartmann, *Untersuchungen*, pp. 155-186.

24. Kortum, *Über Judenthum und Juden*, pp. 63-85, 90, 93.

25. Ibid., p. 83.

5. Philosophy the Heir of Theology

1. On Tindal, see Chapter 2.

2. This thesis is nicely emphasized in Jacob Fleischman, *The Problem of Christianity in Jewish Thought from Mendelssohn to Rosenzweig* (Jerusalem: Magnes Press, 1964).

3. Mendelssohn's caution in his expressions on Christianity is apparent in his famous argument with Lavater. See Alexander Altmann, *Moses Mendelssohn: A Biographical Study* (University: University of Alabama Press, 1973), pp. 209-283.

See also Jacob Katz, *Die Entstehung der Judenassimilation in Deutschland und deren Ideologie* (Diss., Frankfurt, 1935), pp. 72-73, reprinted in Katz, *Emancipation and Assimilation: Studies in Modern Jewish History* (Farnborough: Greggs, 1972), pp. 260-267.

4. Johann Heinrich Schulz, *Philosophische Betrachtung* (Frankfurt, 1784), pp. 11-36, 42-52, 58, 71-75, 76-100.

.5 *Allgemeine Deutsche Biographie,* XXXII, 745-747; Altmann, *Mendelssohn,* pp. 634-640. Schulz approved granting citizenship to Jews only on the condition that they abandon their teachings and traditions; see *Philosophische Betrachtung,* especially pp. 218-223.

6. Friedrich Buchholz, *Moses und Jesus* (Berlin, 1803), pp. 11, 34, 58, 84-85.

7. The following is based on my article "Kant and Judaism, the Historical Context," *Tarbiz* 41 (1972): 219-237; see also Nathan Rotenstreich, "The Image of Judaism by Kant," *Tarbiz* 27 (1958): 288-305.

8. Immanuel Kant, *Die Religion innerhalb der Grenzen der blossen Vernunft,* cited hereafter according to the Karl Vorländer edition (Leipzig: Felix Meiner, 1922). Kant's conception of the essence of religion has often been discussed; see Emanuel Hirsch, *Geschichte der neuen Evangelischen Theologie* (Gütersloh: Bertelsmann, 1952), IV, 55ff.

9. Kant, *Religion,* p. 145, and see Rotenstreich, "The Image of Judaism," pp. 397-401.

10. Katz, "Kant and Judaism," p. 227.

11. Ibid., pp. 232-235; Ernst Traugott von Kortum, *Über Judenthum und Juden* (Nuremberg, 1795), pp. 30-34.

12. Saul Ascher, *Eisenmenger der Zweite: Nebst einem vorangesetzten Sendschreiben an den Herrn Professor Fichte in Jena* (Berlin, 1794), pp. 35, 77. See also Katz, "Kant and Judaism," pp. 236-237.

13. See Hermann Nohl, ed., *Hegels theologische Jugendschriften nach den Handschriften der Kgl. Bibliothek in Berlin* (Tübingen: Mohr, 1907), pp. 21-47. Most of the book has been translated into English as G. W. F. Hegel, *Early Theological Writings,* trans. T. M. Knox (Chicago: University of Chicago Press, 1948). On Hegel's attitude toward the Jews, see Nathan Rotenstreich, "Hegel's Image of Judaism," *JSS* 15 (1953): 33-52; Hans Liebeschütz, *Judentum im deutschen Geschichtsbild von Hegel bis Max Weber* (Tübingen: Mohr, 1967); and Yirmiahu Yovel, "Hegel's Concept of Religion and Judaism as the Religion of Sublimity," *Tarbiz* 45 (1976): 301-326.

14. *Jugendschriften,* pp. 32-33.

15. *Early Theological Writings,* p. 186.

16. Ibid., pp. 187-200, 205ff.

17. Ibid., pp. 199-200. The concrete significance of this sentence has, as far as I can see, escaped previous scholars.

18. See Shlomo Avineri, "The Hegelian Position on the Emancipation of the Jews," *Zion* 25 (1960): 134-136.

19. This has been clarified in a convincing presentation by Yovel in "Hegel's Concept."

20. Schopenhauer's hostility to Judaism is well-known and mentioned often,

but is rarely given attention in the scholarly literature. See Isak Unna, "Stellung Schopenhauers zum Judentum," in *Jüdische Studien: Josef Wohlgemuth zu seinem sechzigsten Geburtstag gewidmet* (Frankfurt: Kaufmann, 1928), pp. 103-119; the Nazi author J. Denner, "Schopenhauer und die Juden," *Archiv für Judenfrage 1* (1943): 39-62; and Henry Walter Brann, *Schopenhauer und das Judentum* (Bonn: Bourier Verlag, 1975), where the relevant material has been gathered, although the author takes an apologetic stance.

21. Arthur Schopenhauer, *Sämtliche Werke: Die Welt als Wille und Vorstellung* (Wiesbaden: Brockhaus, 1949-1966), I, 134-136, 275; II, 378-379, 412-414, 716-718; and Brann, *Schopenhauer*, pp. 23-26.

22. Brann, *Schopenhauer*, p. 4.

23. Ibid., pp. 76-110. Hegel was a guest of the banker Beer, the father of the composer Meyerbeer, while his brother was on intimate terms with him, as was the author Moritz Gottlieb Saphir even before his conversion. Günther Nicolin, *Hegel in Berichten seiner Zeitgenossen* (Hamburg: Franz Meiner, 1970), pp. 233-234, 296, 344, 451-453.

24. Schopenhauer, II, 279-81; Brann, *Schopenhauer*, pp. 58-61. The latter wishes to ascribe a sort of Zionist vision to Schopenhauer's definition of Jewry as a nation, which in its historical context is entirely anachronistic.

6. Nationalism and Romanticism

1. On France, see Chapter 8.

2. Salo Baron, *Die Judenfrage auf dem Wiener Kongress* (Vienna and Berlin: Löwit, 1920), pp. 6-7.

3. Ibid., pp. 7-23, 146-177.

4. Ibid., pp. 23-45.

5. Friedrich Rühs, *Über die Ansprüche der Juden an das deutsche Bürgerrecht* (Berlin, 1816), pp. 3-4.

6. Ibid., pp. iv-vi.

7. Benno Offenburg, *Das Erwachen des deutschen Nationalbewusstseins in der preussischen Judenheit von Mendelssohn bis zum Beginn der Reaktion* (Diss., Hamburg, 1933), pp. 56-64.

8. Rühs, *Ansprüche*, pp. 2, 4; Rühs answered his critics in *Die Rechte des Christenthums und des deutschen Volks, vertheidigt gegen die Ansprüche der Juden und ihrer Verfechter* (Berlin, 1816).

9. Rühs, *Ansprüche*, pp. 10-12, 23, 25, 31-32, 35, 38.

10. Ibid., pp. 3-5.

11. Ibid., pp. 4-5; *Salomon Maimon, Geschichte des eigenen Lebens* (Berlin: Schocken, 1935), p. 156. The book was first printed in 1792.

12. Rühs, *Ansprüche*, pp. 5-6.

13. Ibid., pp. 2, 33-35.

14. The Spinozistic origin of the idea has been pointed out already by Saul Ascher, *Die Germanomanie Skizze zu einem Zeitgemälde*, (Berlin, 1815), p. 59; see Julius Guttmann, "Mendelssohns Jerusalem und Spinozas Theologisch-politischer Traktat," in *Bericht der Hochschule für die Wissenschaft des Judentums* (Berlin, 1931), pp. 31-67.

15. Jakob Friedrich Fries, *Über die Gefährdung des Wohlstandes und Charakters der Deutschen durch die Juden* (Heidelberg, 1816).

16. Ruhs, *Anspruche*, p. 6; Fries, *Gefahrdung*, pp. 3, 8, 21, 23-24.

17. Fries, *Gefährdung*, p. 21.

18. Ibid., pp. 14-15, 22.

19. Jakob Friedrich Fries, *Von deutscher Philosophie, Art und Kunst, ein Votum für Friedrich Heinrich Jacobi gegen F. W. J. Schelling* (Heidelberg, 1812), pp. 38-39; Ernst Ludwig Theodor Henke, *Jakob Friedrich Fries, aus seinem handschriftlichen Nachlass zusammengestellt* (Leipzig, 1867), pp. 147-148; J. F. Fries, *Zwei politische Flugschriften, 1814 und 1817* (Münster, 1910).

20. Fries, *Gefährdung*, pp. 11, 23. The anti-Semitic views of Rühs and Fries have been often referred to as identical; see Selma Stern-Täubler, "Der literarische Kampf um die Emanzipation in den Jahren 1816-1820 und seine ideologischen und soziologischen Voraussetzungen," *HUCA* 23 (1950-1951): pp. 171-196. Rühs himself pointed to the differences between himself and Fries; Rühs, *Die Rechte*, p. 5.

21. J. Kracauer, *Geschichte der Juden in Frankfurt a.M. (1150-1824)* (Frankfurt: Kaufmann, 1927), II, 355-431, 432-521; S. Scheuermann, *Der Kampf der frankfurter Juden um ihre Gleichberechtigung (1815-1824)* (Kallmünz: Lassleben, 1933).

22. Georg Friedrich Karl Robert, *Kurze Erledigung des sogenannten Nachtrags zu der an die Hohe Teutsche Bundesversammlung gerichteten Beschwerdeschrift der Frankfurter Judenschaft, . . .* (Frankfurt, 1817), pp. 42, 44; Jucho and Johann Isaac von Gerning, *Ansichten und Bemerkungen über die bürgerlichen Rechtsverhältnisse der Juden in der freyen Stadt Frankfurt a.M.* (Teutschland, 1816), p. 11; Leonard von Dresch, *Betrachtungen über die Ansprüche der Juden auf das Bürgerrecht insbesondere in der freien Stadt Frankfurt a.m.* (Tübingen, 1816), pp. 4-10, 17, 37; for a similar dark prophecy, see Johann Friedrich Benzenberg, *Über Verfassung* (Dortmund, 1816), p. 505; *Erneuerter Abdruck eines Gutachten der Juristen-Facultät auf der grossherzoglich Hessischen Universität zu Giessen . . .* (n.p., 1817), p. 86; *Die Judenschaft von Frankfurt und ihre Rechte*, p. 4.

23. Robert, *Kurze Erledigung*, p. 31.

24. Schreiber, *Über die Ansprüche*, p. 3.

25. *An die Hohe Deutsche Bundesversammlung, Beurkundete Vertheidigung der Rechte der Bürgerschaft zu Frankfurt a.M.* (Frankfurt, 1817), appendix 20, pp. 39-40. Also quoted by Dresch, *Betrachtungen*, p. 8, and Rühs, *Die Rechte*, pp. 81-82; Schreiber, *Über die Ansprüche*, pp. 11-19, 32-33; *Was soll bei der neuen Verfassung aus den Juden werden?* (Frankfurt, 1815), pp. 17-18; *Die Judenschaft von Frankfurt und ihre Rechte* (n.p., 1817), pp. 6-7.

26. *Was soll aus den Juden werden*, p. 2; *Die Judenschaft von Frankfurt*, p. 7.

27. Robert, *Kurze Erledigung*, p. 32.

28. *Was soll aus den Juden werden*, pp. 18-19. See also Dresch, *Betrachtungen*, p. 18; Schreiber, *Über die Ansprüche*, p. 4; Johann Christian

Ehrmann, *Das Judenthum in der M-Y, eine Warnung an alle deutschen* . . . (n.p., 1816).

29. *Abdruck der Gegen-Erklärung des Senats der freien Stadt Frankfurt a.M. an die Hohe Deutsche Bundesversammlung* (Frankfurt, 1817), p. 38; *Erneuerter Abdruck*, p. 34, n. 32; Georg Aquilin Rapp, *Versuch einer rechtlichen Prüfung der sogenannten bürgerlichen Rechte . . . der Frankfurter Judengemeinde* (Frankfurt, 1817), pp. 4-5; Schreiber, *Über die Ansprüche*, p. 6; Johann Georg Rössing, *Historisch-juridische Entwicklung der unveränderten Unterthanspflicht der jüdischen Gemeinde zu Frankfurt a.M. und des Rechtsbestandes aller eigenthümlichen Juden-Gefälle dieser freien Stadt* (Frankfurt, 1817), p. 134.

30. Schreiber, *Über die Ansprüche*, pp. 22-26; *Die Judenschaft*, pp. 6-7, 52; Weissen-Becker, *Die Christen und die Juden oder Richterspruch der Vernunft über das Leben, Dichten und Trachten der Juden* (Frankfurt, 1819), p. 85; von Gerning, *Ansichten und Bemerkungen*, p. 15.

31. Karl Borromaeus Alexander Sessa, *Unser Verkehr, eine Posse in einem Akte* (Leipzig, 1815), pp. 15-16, 104.

32. Johannes Hahn, *Julius von Voss* (Berlin, 1910), pp. 40-53; Julius von Voss, *Neue Possen und Marionettenspiele* ("Das Judenkonzert in Krakau"; Berlin, 1826), pp. 237-294.

7. Incitement and Riot

1. *Nemesis: Zeitschrift für Politik und Geschichte* 8, pt. 1 (1816): 3.

2. Ludolf Holst, *Über das Verhältnis der Juden zu den Christen in dek deutschen Handelsstädten* (Leipzig, 1818), pp. 3, 35-49, 55-59, 68-69, 112-117. Holst's book had been used by Selma Stern-Täubler, "Der literarische Kampf um die Emanzipation in der Jahren 1816-1820 und seine ideologischenund soziologischen Voraussetzungen," *Huca* 23 (1950-1951): 171-196. On Holst see Hans Schröder, *Lexikon der hamburgischen Schriftsteller bis zur Gegenwart* (Hamburg, 1857), III, pp. 332-333.

3. Holst, *Über das Verhältnis*, pp. 32-39, 291.

4. Ibid., pp. 55, 287-290.

5. G. Merkel, *Über Deutschland wie ich es nach einer zehnjährigen Entfernung wiederfand* (Riga, 1818), p. 144.

6. Ibid., pp. 157-158.

7. Ibid.

8. G. Merkel, *Briefe über einige der merkwürdigsten Städte im nördlichen Deutschland* (Leipzig, 1801), I, pp. 282-291.

9. Merkel, *Über Deutschland*, pp. 152-153.

10. Ibid., pp. 161-162.

11. Ibid., pp. 162-163.

12. Alexander Lips, *Über die künftige Stellung der Juden in den deutschen Bundesstaaten* (Erlangen, 1819), p. 20; Salomon Jakob Cohn, *Historisch-kritische Darstellung des jüdischen Gottesdienstes und dessen Modifikationen von den ältesten Zeiten an bis auf unsere Tage* (Leipzig, 1819), pp. xx-xxi.

13. Karl August Varnhagen von Ense, *Denkwürdigkeiten des eigenen Lebens, die Karlsruher Jahre 1816-1819*, rev. ed. H. Häring, 1904 (Baden: Müller, 1924), pp. 370-371.

14. Wolfgang Menzel, *Denkwürdigkeiten* (Blelefeld and Leipzig, 1877), p. 96.

15. The following is based on my article "The Hep-Hep Riots in Germany in 1819: The Historical Background," *Zion* 38 (1973): 62-115.

16. Theodor A. Scheuring, *Das Staatsbürgerrecht der Juden* (Würzburg, 1819).

17. Katz, "The Hep-Hep Riots," pp. 65-70.

18. Ibid., pp. 74-99.

19. Ibid., pp. 74-80.

20. Ibid., pp. 80-90.

21. Ibid., pp. 91-98.

22. Leonore Sterling, "Anti-Jewish Riots in Germany in 1819: A Displacement of Social Protest," *Historia Judaica* 12 (1950): 105-142.

23. Katz, "The Hep-Hep Riots," pp. 100-104.

24. Georg Sartorius, *Über die Gefahren welche Deutschland bedrohen, und die Mittel ihnen mit Glück zu begenen* (Göttingen, 1820), especially p. 169.

8. The Revolutionary Promise and the Catholic Reaction

1. Reinhard Rürup, *Emanzipation und Antisemitismus* (Göttingen: Vandenhöck and Ruprecht, 1975), p. 30.

2. See Chapter 5.

3. See Introduction, n. 2.

4. Patrick Girard, *Les Juifs de France de 1789 à 1860* (Paris: Calmann-Lévy, 1976), pp. 70-86.

5. Bernhard Blumenkranz, ed., *Les Juifs et la revolution française, problèmes et aspirations* (Toulouse: Privat, 1976), pp. 12-18, 48.

6. François Hell, *Observation d'un Alsacien sur l'affairs présente des juifs d'Alsace* (Frankfurt, 1779).

7. Ibid., p. 100; see Jacob Katz, "A State Within a State, the History of an Anti-Semitic Slogan," *Proceedings of the Israel Academy of Sciences and Humanities* 4 (1971): 38.

8. *La Revolution française et l'emancipation des juifs* (Paris: EDHIS, 1968), VII.5, "Opinion de M. le Prince de Broglie sur l'admission des juifs à l'état civil," p. 4; ibid., VI.7, "Lettre au Comité de Constitution sur l'affaire des juifs par M. de Bourge, representante de la Commune de Paris," 19 May 1790, pp. 31-33.

9. Ibid., VII.3, "Opinion de le Comte Stanislas de Clermont-Tonnère, député de Paris," 23 December 1789, p. 13.

10. Ibid., VII.5, "Opinion de M. le Prince de Broglie, député de Colmar," pp. 6-8.

11. Ibid., VI.7, "Lettre au Comité de Constitution sur l'affaire des juifs par M. de Bourge," p. 43.

12. Blumenkranz, *Les Juifs et la revolution française*, pp. 105-119.

13. Ibid., pp. 14-18.

14. Poujol, *Quelques observations concernant les juifs* . . . (Paris, 1806).

15. Ibid., pp. 42-53, 56-70, 150-151.

16. Ibid., pp. 132-136, 153.

17. Ibid., pp. 124-132.

18. Ibid., p. 140.

19. Ibid., pp. 124-136, 153-155.

20. On de Bonald, see J. Hours, "Un précurseur oublié de l'antisemitisme français, le Vicomte de Bonald," *Cahiers sioniens* 4 (1950): 165-170.

21. De Bonald's article is included in his collected works, M. de Bonald, "Sur les juifs," *Oeuvres complètes* (Paris, 1859), III, 934-948.

22. De Bonald, *Oeuvres*, III, 936, 939-940, 942, 958.

23. Ibid., p. 947.

24. Ibid., pp. 943-944.

25. Frederick R. Artz, *France under the Bourbon Restoration, 1814-1830* (New York: Russel and Russel, 1967), pp. 104-112.

26. De Bonald, *Oeuvres*, I, 552.

27. On Lamennais' relations to Jews, see Arnold Ages, "Lamennais and the Jews," *Jewish Quarterly Review* 63 (1972): 158-170.

28. F. de La Mennais, *Essai sur l'indifférence en matière de religion*, 3 vols. (Paris, 1825).

29. Ibid., III, 56-57.

30. The idea is, of course, not peculiar to France, but the linguistic expression is more common in French than in other languages.

31. Ernest Sevrin, *Les Missions religieuses en France sous la Restoration (1815-1830)* (Paris: Vrin, 1948). The lasting effect of Catholic education has been shown by Paul Demann, *La Catechese chrétienne et le peuple de la Bible* (Paris: Cahiers sioniens, no. 6, 1952), pp. 1-220.

32. J. Katz, "Religion as a Uniting and Dividing Force in Modern Jewish History" in *The Role of Religion in Modern Jewish History* (Cambridge, Mass.: Association for Jewish Studies, 1975), pp. 4-8.

33. Paul Klein, "Mauvais juif, mauvais chrétien," *Revue de la pensée juive*, April 1951, pp. 57-102; Pierre Blanchard, *Le Venerable Libermann* (Paris: Desclée, De Brouwer, 1960); P. Theotime de Saint-Just, *Les Frères Lemann, juifs convertis* (Paris, 1937).

34. Theodore Ratisbonne, *Mes souvenirs* (Rome: Congregation de Notre-Dame de Sion, n.d.).

35. Louis Bautain, *Philosophie du christianisme, correspondance religieuse* (Paris, 1835), I xxxiii-lxii.

36. Ratisbonne, *Mes souvenirs*, pp. 69-75.

37. Bautain, *Philosophie du christianisme*, I, 69.

38. A. Cerfberr de Médelsheim, *Ce que sont les juifs de France* (Paris, 1844).

39. Ibid., p. 46.

40. His response is given on pp. 127-167, especially pp. 141-142.

9. The Socialist Indictment

1. On the demography of French Jewry, see Patrick Girard, *Les Juifs de France de 1789 à 1860* (Paris: Calmann-Lévy, 1976), pp. 105-114.

2. Ibid., pp. 121-132.

3. Nicholas von Riasanowsky, *The Teaching of Charles Fourier* (Berkeley: University of California Press, 1969); Edmund Silberner, *Sozialisten zur Judenfrage* (Berlin: Colloquium Verlag, 1962), pp. 16-27.

4. Riasanowsky, *The Teaching of Fourier*, pp. 1-31.

5. *Publication des manuscrits de Charles Fourier* (Paris, 1853-1856), III, 24; Silberner, *Sozialisten zur Judenfrage*, pp. 22-25.

6. Charles Fourier, *Le Nouveau monde industriel et societaire* in *Oeuvres complètes* (Paris, 1846-1848), VI, 421; idem, *Théorie des quatre mouvements* in *Oeuvres complètes*, VI, 61; ibid. vol. 1, p. 253.

7. *Théorie des quatre mouvements*, p. 61.

8. *Le Nouveau monde*, p. 421; *Publication des manuscrits*, II, 34-37.

9. *Publication des manuscrits*, II, 36.

10. Charles Fourier, *La Fausse industrie* (Paris, 1836), pp. 660, 783.

11. G. D. H. Cole, *A History of Socialist Thought* (London: Macmillan, 1955), I, 71-74; Silberner, *Sozialisten zur Judenfrage*, pp. 28-43; Alphonse Toussenel, *Les juifs rois de l'époque, histoire de la foedalité financière* (Paris, 1845), pp. 328-377.

12. Toussenel, *Les Juifs*, pp. 4, 173-180.

13. Ibid., p. vii; *Archives Israelites* (1845), pp. 752-754.

14. Toussenel, *Les Juifs*, preface to 2nd ed., pp. i-ii.

15. Ibid., pp. ii-iii.

16. 1st ed., pp. 73, 201-202.

17. Ibid., p. 74.

18. 2nd ed., pp. xii-xiii.

19. Ibid., pp. 122-132, especially pp. 123, 132.

20. Ibid., p. xvii. See also his references to Jews in *Travail et faineantise, programme démocratique* (Paris, 1849), pp. 12-17.

21. *Les Juifs*, p. 148.

22. Satan [Georges-Marie Mathieu-Dairnvaell], *Histoire édifiante et curieuse de Rothschild 1er roi des juifs* (Paris, 1840), and *Rothschild 1er, ses valets et son peuple* (Paris, 1846), p. 35.

23. Silberner, *Sozialisten zur Judenfrage*, pp. 44-55; Pierre Leroux, *Malthus et les économistes* (Boussac, 1849).

24. Leroux, *Malthus*, pp. 15-18.

25. Silberner, *Sozialisten zur Judenfrage*, pp. 56-64.

10. The Liberal Ambiguity

1. George Weill, *Histoire de l'idée laique en France au XIXe siècle* (Paris: F. Allan, 1929).

2. Mary Elisabeth Johnson, *Michelet et le christianisme* (Paris: Nizet, 1951), pp. 17-59, 63-145; Gabriel Monod, "Michelet et les Juifs," *REJ*, 53 (1907): i-xxv

3. Jules Michelet, *Bible de l'humanité* (Paris, 1890).

4. Ibid., pp. 375-376.

5. Ibid., p. 366.

6. Michelet, *Bible*, pp. 379, 381-382. On Voltaire's observations, see Hanna Emmrich, *Das Judentum bei Voltaire*, (Breslau: Pribatsch, 1930), pp. 46, 101; Monod, *Michelet et les Juifs*, p. xvii.

7. Adolph Franck, *La Kabbale où la philosophie religieuse des Hébreux* (Paris, 1843); Michelet, *Bible*, pp. 383-385.

8. Michelet, *Bible*, pp. 373-374, 376.

9. Max Weber, *Gesammelte Aufsätze zur Religions soziologie* (Tübingen: Mohr, 1947), III, 281, and *Grundriss der Sozialoekonomie, Wirtschaft und Gesellschaft* (Tübingen: Mohr, 1947), pp. 636-637. On the validity of the thesis see Chapter 26, n. 2.

10. Michelet, *Bible*, pp. 380, 382-383.

11. H. W. Wardman, *Ernest Renan: A Critical Biography* (London: Athlon Press, 1964). On Renan's attitude toward Jews and Judaism, see S. Almog, "The Racial Motif in Renan's Attitude toward Judaism and the Jews," *Zion*, 32 (1967): 175-200; Ernest Renan, *Histoire du peuple d'Israel*, 5 vols. (Paris, 1887); idem, *De la part des peuples sémitiques dans l'histoire de la civilisation* (Paris, 1862), p. 23.

12. Edmond Renard, *Renan, les étapes de sa pensée* (Paris: Bloud et Gay, 1929), pp. 64-71; Renan, *Peuples sémitiques*, p. 22.

13. Ernest Renan, *Vie de Jésus* (Paris, 1863), especially p. 64; Paulus Cassel, *Über Renans Leben Jesu* (Berlin, 1864), pp. 1-9; Rabbin Levy, *La Synagogue et M. Renan* (Luneville, 1863), pp. 9-11.

14. See Chapter 5.

15. Renan, *Vie de Jésus*, pp. 410, 412.

16. Jaques Barzun, *Race: A Study in Superstition* (New York: Harper and Row, 1965), pp. 17-33, 47-105; Janine Buenzod, *La Formation de la pensée de Gobineau et l'essai sur l'inegalité des races humaines* (Paris: Nizet, 1967), pp. 283-289; Leon Poliakov, *The Aryan Myth: A History of Racist and Nationalist Ideas in Europe* (New York: Basic Books, 1974), pp. 17-36, 188-214; Michael D. Biddiss, *Father of Racist Ideology: The Social and Political Thought of Count Gobineau* (London: Weidenfeld & Nicolson, 1970).

17. Renan, *De l'Origine du language* (Paris, 1848), pp. 28-36, 2nd ed. 1858, pp. 104-190; Renan, *Histoire général et système comparé des langues sémitiques*, 2nd ed. (Paris, 1858), p. 4; Christophe Lassen, *Indische Altertumskunde* (Bonn, 1847), pp. 414-417.

18. Renan, *Histoire général et système comparé*, pp. 5, 7.

19. Ibid., p. 7.

20. Ibid., pp. 9, 12.

21. Ibid., pp. 13, 15.

22. Ibid., p. 16.

23. Renan, *De l'Origine*, 2nd ed., pp. 199-209, and *Histoire des langues sémitiques*, pp. xv-xvi. Renan cooperated with Adolphe Neubauer in scholarly publications. His lecture, "Le Judaisme et le Christianisme," was delivered in 1883 before La Société des Études Juifs. See Almog, "The Racial Motif," p. 178.

11. Jews and Freemasons

1. Drach's basic polemical treatise is *L'Harmonie entre l'église et la synagogue* (Paris, 1849).

2. Luigi A. Chiarini, *Théorie du judaisme, appliquée à la réforme des Israelites de tous les pays de l'Europe, et servant en même temps d'ouvrage preparatoire à la version du Thalmud de Babylone*, 2 vols. (Paris, 1830). On the circumstances of

this publication, see S. M. Dubnow, *History of the Jews in Russia and Poland* (Philadelphia: Jewish Publication Society, 1918), pp. 100-115.

3. For the main facts of the Mortara case, see Ismar Elbogen, *A Century of Jewish Life* (Philadelphia: Jewish Publication Society, 1966), pp. 30-31.

4. Louis Veuillot, *Mélanges religieux, historiques, politiques et litteraires*, 2nd ser. (Paris, 1860), vol. 5.

5. Ibid., especially pp. 189-202; Veuillot (p. 191) lists a number of books from which one could learn about the Talmud. His quotations, however, come only from the two French sources. Veuillot's attacks elicited a series of Jewish responses, and not only in the press. Salomon Klein, the Rabbi of Colmar, answered them in his *Le Judaisme ou la vérité sur le Talmud* (Mulhouse, 1895).

6. L. Rupert, *L'Eglise et la synagogue* (Paris, 1859), especially p. 233; Sebastian Brunner, *Die Kirche und die Synagoge* (Schaffhausen, 1864).

7. Rupert, *L'Eglise*, pp. 256-257, 265-310.

8. Ibid., p. 240.

9. Patrick Girard, *Les Juifs de France de 1789 à 1860, de l'émancipation a l'égalité* (Paris: Calmann-Lévy, 1976), pp. 97-132.

10. Theodore Ratisbonne, *La Question juive* (Paris, 1868), pp. 8-9.

11. Ibid., pp. 27-31.

12. Gougenot des Mousseaux, *Le Juif, le judaisme et la judaisation des peuples chretiens* (Paris, 1869); R. Byrnes, *Antisemitism in Modern France* (New Brunswick, N.J.: Rutgers University Press, 1950), pp. 113-114.

13. Des Mousseaux, *Le Juif*, pp. ix, 36, 40, 47, 57, 230-231, 242-243.

14. Ibid., pp. 60, 85, 129, 181, 351-353.

15. I have described the process of coalescence of the two objects of propaganda in my book *Jews and Freemasons in Europe, 1723-1939* (Cambridge, Mass.: Harvard University Press, 1970).

16. Ibid., pp. 18-19, 153-159, 219-220.

17. Des Mousseaux, *Le Juif*, pp. 262-272, 504-509; Katz, *Jews and Freemasons*, pp. 153-157.

18. E. H. Chabouty [C. C. de Saint André], *Franc-Maçons et juifs, sixième age de l'église d'après l'Apocalypse* (Paris, 1880). On the author, see Byrnes, *Antisemitism*, pp. 70-71, 718-735.

19. Katz, *Jews and Freemasons*, pp. 157-159; des Mousseaux, *Le Juif*, pp. 494-499; Chabouty's book is dedicated to attempting to prove the approaching advent of the millennium and the fulfillment of all Christian aspirations.

12. The German Liberals: Image of the Jew

1. Isaak Marcus Jost, *Neuere Geschichte der Israeliten in der ersten Hälfte des 19. Jahrhunderts*, 3 vols. (Breslau, 1846-1848), is still very valuable for this period. Modern monographs include: Ismar Freund, *Die Emanzipation der Juden in Preussen* (Berlin: Poppelauer, 1912), I, 229-240, on Prussia; S. Schwarz, *Juden in Bayern im Wandel der Zeiten* (Munich and Vienna: G. Olzog, 1963), pp. 181-274, on Bavaria; Isidor Kracauer, *Geschichte der Juden in Frankfurt* (Frankfurt: Kaufmann, 1925-1927), II, 432-521, on Frankfurt; Helga Krohn, *Die*

Juden in Hamburg, 1800-1850, ihre soziale, kulturelle und politische Entwicklung während der Emanzipationszeit (Frankfurt: Europäische Verlagsanstalt, 1967), on Hamburg; and M. L. Bamberger, *Beiträge zur Geschichte der Juden in Würzburg-Heidingsfeld* (Würzburg, 1905), on Würzburg.

2. See J. H. Claphan, *Economic Development of France and Germany, 1815-1914* (Cambridge, Mass.: Harvard University Press, 1968), pp. 29-52, 82-103. On the role of the Jews, see Jacob Toury, "Der Eintritt der Juden ins deutsche Bürgertum," in *Das Judentum in der deutschen Umwelt 1800-1850*, ed. Hans Liebeschütz and Arnold Pauker (Tübingen: Mohr, 1977), pp. 139-242. On the part played by the Rothschilds in advancing the cause of the Jews in Frankfurt, see Kracauer, *Juden in Frankfurt*, II, 488, 503-505. An example of the interrelation of economic factors and the achievement of emancipation is offered by Reinhard Rürup, "Die Emanzipation der Juden in Baden," in his *Emanzipation und Antisemitismus* (Göttingen: Vandenhoeck und Ruprecht, 1975), pp. 37-73.

3. Friedrich Wilhelm Riemer, *Mitteilungen über Goethe aus mündlichen und schriftlichen gedruckten und ungedruckten Quellen* (Berlin, 1841), pp. 428-429.

4. On Pfaff see *Allgemeine deutsche Biographie*, XXV, 582-587.

5. Conrad Friedrich von Schmidt-Phiseldeck, *Über das Verhältnis der jüdischen Nation zu dem christlichen Bürgerverein und dessen künftige Umgestaltung. Zwey Abhandlungen* (Copenhagen, 1817), pp. 123-126.

6. Christoph Heinrich Pfaff, "Uber das Verhaltnis christlicher Regierungen und Staaten gegen die Juden in dem gegenwärtigen Zeitpuncte," *Kieler Blätter* 1 (1819): pp. 124, 141-142.

7. Ibid., p. 141; Schmidt-Phiseldeck, *Über das Verhältnis*, p. 62.

8. Pfaff, *Über das Verhältnis*, p. 142.

9. Ludolph Holst, *Judenthum in allen dessen Theilen aus einem staatswissenschaftlichen Standpuncte betrachtet* (Mainz, 1821).

10. Alexander Lips, *Über die künftige Stellung der Juden in den deutschen Bundesstaaten* (Erlangen, 1819).

11. Ibid., pp. 30, 33.

12. Johann Baptist Graser, *Das Judenthum und seine Reform als Vorbedingung der vollständigen Aufnahme der Nation in den Staatsverband* (Bayreuth, 1828). On Graser, see *Allgemeine Deutsche Biographie*, IX, 584-585. On 2 November 1819, in a letter to M. Ehrenberg, Zunz writes, "Die Juden für die Lips seine herrliche Schrift geschrieben . . ." See Nahum N. Glatzer, *Leopold Zunz, Jude-Deutscher-Europäer, ein jüdisches Gelehrtenschicksal des 19. Jahrhunderts in Briefen an Freunde* (Tübingen: Mohr, 1964), p. 102.

13. Schmidt-Phiseldeck, *Über das Verhältnis*, p. 66.

14. Pfaff, *Über das Verhältnis*, p. 123.

15. Lips, *Über die künftige Stellung*, p. 21.

16. Graser, *Das Judenthum*, pp. 27, 46.

17. Holst, *Judenthum*, pp. 20, 146-147, 423.

18. Schmidt-Phiseldeck, pp. 20, 26, 32-36; Lips, p. 14; Graser, pp. 36-38.

19. The Jewish *maskilim* were in agreement on this issue and strove to correct it. The book by the pedagogue and publicist, Anton Rée, *Die Sprachverhältnisse der heutigen Juden im Interesse der Gegenwart und mit bes. Rücksicht auf Volkser-*

ziehung besprochen (Hamburg, 1844), is dedicated to the problem of uprooting traces of the special Jewish language. The book was received enthusiastically in *AZJ* 9 (1845): 93-94, 106-108, 126-127, 141-142 and in *Israelit des neunzehnten Jahrhunderts* 7 (1845): 63-64, 121-124.

20. Schmidt-Phiseldeck, *Über das Verhältnis*, pp. 48-49, 112.

21. Pfaff, *Über das Verhältnis*, p. 124; Graser, *Das Judenthum*, pp. 31-32, 35.

22. Holst, *Judenthum*, pp. 115-116, 166, 225-226.

23. Ludwig Börne, "Der ewige Jude," in his *Gesammelte Schriften* (Leipzig, n.d.), II, 171.

24. Jacob Katz, "The Term 'Jewish Emancipation': Its Origins and Historical Impact," in *Nineteenth-Century Jewish Intellectual History*, ed. Alexander Altmann (Cambridge, Mass.: Harvard University Press, 1973), pp. 21-25.

25. On Paulus, see Emanuel Hirsch, *Geschichte der neueren evangelischen Theologie* (Gütersloh: C. Bertelsmann, 1954), V, 27-36.

26. Heinrich Eberhard Gottlob Paulus, *Die jüdische Nationalabsonderung nach Ursprung, Folgen und Besserungsmitteln* (Heidelberg, 1831), pp. 11, 13, 24, 28, 46, 50-54, 88.

27. Ibid., p. 20.

28. See Rürup, "Emanzipation," pp. 54-55, for reform in this direction in Baden.

29. Paulus, *Jüdische Nationalabsonderung*, pp. 40-42, 65.

30. Ibid., pp. 6-7, 47, 118.

31. Ibid., pp. 114-115, 147.

32. Ibid., pp. 15, 119, 122-123.

13. The Radicals: Feuerbach, Bauer, Marx

1. Strauss's opinions are unknown, but in any case he was quite popular among people like Abraham Geiger. See Max Wiener, *Jüdische Religion im Zeitalter der Emanzipation* (Berlin: Philo, 1933), p. 51. Feuerbach will be treated later in this chapter; on Carové, see Shlomo Avineri, "Hegel's Views on Jewish Emancipation," *JSS* 25 (1963): pp. 150-151. Karl Grün openly stated his position in his *Die Judenfrage* (Darmstadt, 1844) and "Meine Stellung zur Judenfrage," in *Neue Anekdota* (Darmstadt, 1845), pp. 283-297. On Ruge, see Edmund Silberner, *Sozialisten zur Judenfrage* (Berlin: Colloquium Verlag, 1962), pp. 116-117.

2. They will be discussed further on in this chapter; on Bauer, see also Chapter 17.

3. On the term, see Jacob Toury, " 'The Jewish Question': A Semantic Approach," *LBIYB* 11 (1966): pp. 85-106.

4. Hans Joachim Schöps, *Das andere Preussen, konservative Gestalten und Probleme im Zeitalter Friedrich Wilhelm IV* (Berlin: Hande und Spenerische Verlagsbucchandlung, 1974), pp. 176-218.

5. Heinrich Leo, *Vorlesungen über die Geschichte des jüdischen Staates* (Berlin, 1828), p. 8.

6. Ibid., pp. 8, 15.

7. Ibid., pp. 16, 54.

8. Ibid., p. 68.

9. Ludwig Feuerbach, *Das Wesen des Christenthums* (Leipzig, 1843). For an analysis of his thoughts in general and on his attitude toward Judaism, see Eugen Kamenka, *The Philosophy of Ludwig Feuerbach* (London: Routledge and Kegan Paul, 1970), pp. 15-32.

10. See Kamenka, *Feuerbach*, pp. 35-68.

11. *Das Wesen des Christenthums*, pp. 167-169.

12. Ibid., p. 168.

13. Wilhelm Bolin, *Ludwig Feuerbach, sein Wirken und seine Zeitgenossen* (Stuttgart, 1891), pp. 12, 312-313.

14. For a biography of Bauer, see Ernst Barnikol, *Bruno Bauer, Studien und Materialien: aus dem Nachlass ausgewählt und zusammengestellt von Peter Heimer und Hans Martin Sass* (Assen: Van Gorcum, 1972).

15. Bruno Bauer, "Die Prinzipien der mosaischen Rechts- und Religionsverfassung," *Zeitschrift für spekulative Theologie* 2 (1837): 292-305.

16. Bruno Bauer, *Die Religion des Alten Testaments in der geschichtlichen Entwicklung ihrer Prinzipien* (Berlin, 1838), I, 1-11, II, 7-9.

17. Ibid., II, 37.

18. Biographers of Bauer have often dealt with his spiritual turnabout. Recently Zvi Rosen, "The Anti-Jewish Opinions of Bruno Bauer (1838-1843), their Sources and Significance," *Zion* 23 (1968): 66-67, n. 51, has suggested that Bauer had been influenced by Johann Christian Edelmann's *Moses mit aufgedecktem Angesicht* (1742) which he had come across at this time. Edelmann had been one of the first rationalist critics of religion in Germany—in particular, of Christianity and Judaism—and served as a sort of sanctioning authority for Bauer during his critical period. Although such a critical approach to Scriptures was not unfamiliar to him—he had been acquainted with it, as we have seen, through the writings of the English Deists—nevertheless, during his orthodox phase, he had rejected it in an apologetic fashion.

19. Hermann König, *Die Rheinische Zeitung von 1842-43 in ihrer Einstellung zur Kulturpolitik des Preussischen Staates* (Münster: Coppenrath, 1927), p. 81.

20. This important letter is cited by G. A. van den Bergh van Eysinga, *Godsdienst-Wetenschappelijke Studien* (Haarlem, 1952), XII, 29-30. Victor Riquetti de Mirabeau, *Sur Moses Mendelssohn, sur la reforme politique des juifs et en particulier sur la revolution tentée en leur faveur en 1753 dans la grande Bretagne* (London [Strassburg], 1787).

21. Bruno Bauer, *Die Judenfrage* (Brunswick, 1843). See Nathan Rotenstreich, "For and Against Emancipation: The Bruno Bauer Controversy," *LBIYB* 4 (1959): pp. 3-36.

22. Bauer, *Judenfrage*, pp. 60-61.

23. "Die Fähigkeit der heutigen Juden und Christen frei zu werden." The article first appeared in the collection Georg Herwegh, *Einundzwanzig Bogen aus der Schweiz* (Zurich and Winterthur, 1843) and was reprinted in *Bruno Bauer, Feldzüge der reinen Kritik*, ed. Hans Martin Sass (Frankfurt: Suhrkamp, 1968). The latter edition will be cited hereafter; see pp. 193-194.

24. Karl Grün, *Die Judenfrage, gegen Bruno Bauer* (Darmstadt, 1844), pp. 13-15.

25. Bauer, *Judenfrage,* pp. 4-5, 9, 12-16, 55-59 and *Feldzüge,* pp. 178, 187.

26. *Judenfrage,* pp. 103-104, and *Feldzüge,* pp. 185-186.

27. *Judenfrage,* pp. 75, 78, and *Feldzüge,* pp. 181, 188.

28. *Judenfrage,* p. 43, and *Feldzüge,* p. 181. For an example on the attitude of Jewish rationalists, see Jost's letter in Nahum N. Glatzer, "On an Unpublished Letter of Isaak Marcus Jost," *LBIY,* 23 (1977), 132.

29. Bauer replied to his critics in the journal he edited, *Allgemeine Literatur-Zeitung,* December 1843, pp. 1-17. Cf. Rothenstreich, "For and Against Emancipation," pp. 11-18.

30. Karl Marx, *Zur Judenfrage,* will be cited according to Saul K. Padover, ed., *Karl Marx on Religion* (New York: McGraw-Hill, 1974), pp. 169-192.

31. Silberner, *Sozialisten zur Judenfrage,* pp. 108-109. Among the numerous biographies of Marx, see especially Werner Blumenberg, *Karl Marx in Selbstzeugnissen und Bilddokumenten* (Hamburg: Rowohlt, 1962).

32. Albert Massiczek, *Der menschliche Mensch, Karl Marx's jüdischer Humanismus* (Vienna: Europa-Verlag, 1968).

33. Silberner, *Sozialisten zur Judenfrage,* pp. 108-109.

34. The petition was published in Adolf Kober, "Karl Marx's Vater und das napoleonische Ausnahmegesetz gegen die Juden 1818," *Jahrbuch des Kölnischen Geschichtsvereins,* 14 (1932): pp. 111-125.

35. Lewis Feuer, "The Conversion of Karl Marx's Father," *Jewish Journal of Sociology,* 14 (1972): pp. 149-166; Heinz Monz, *Karl Marx und Trier, Verhältnisse-Beziehungen-Einflüsse* (Trier: Neu, 1964), pp. 180-181.

36. In a letter dated 3 February 1837, the father describes the son's living conditions, contrasting them with the hardships of his own youth which he had had to overcome. The nature of the hardships is not mentioned. On Marx's revealing confusion concerning his Jewishness, see Silberner, *Sozialisten zur Judenfrage,* pp. 112-115.

37. Monz, *Karl Marx,* pp. 181-183.

38. König, *Die Rheinische Zeitung,* pp. 74-84; Blumenberg, *Karl Marx,* pp. 58-59. Text of the letter is cited in Silberner, *Sozialisten zur Judenfrage,* pp. 116-117.

39. The difference between the approaches of Marx and Bauer is explained well by Lothar Koch, *Humanistischer Atheismus und gesellschaftliches Engagement: Bruno Bauer's "kritische" Kritik* (Stuttgart: Kohlhammer, 1971), pp. 72-81.

40. Such was the approach of Marx's classic biographer, Franz Mehring, *Marx, Geschichte seines Lebens* (Leipzig: Soziologische Verlagsanstalt, 1933), pp. 43-98.

41. See Chapter 9.

42. Padover, *Marx on Religion,* p. 187.

43. Silberner, *Sozialisten zur Judenfrage,* pp. 125-127, 140-142.

44. The various opinions about Marx and his Jewish origins are summed up by Monz, *Karl Marx,* pp. 184-186. See also Robert Misrahi, *Marx et la question juive* (Paris: Gallimard, 1972).

14. The Scandal of the Artist: Wagner

1. On Mendelssohn, see Alexander Altmann, *Moses Mendelssohn: A Biographical Study* (University: University of Alabama Press, 1973), pp. 698-712; on Ascher, see Ellen Littmann, "Saul Ascher, First Theorist of Progressive Judaism," *LBIYB* 5 (1960): 107-121. Ascher's *Germanomanie* was attacked by Friedrich Ruhs, *Über die Anspruche der Juden an das deutsche Burgerrecht* (Berlin, 1816), pp. 17-18.

2. Sigmund Kaznelson, *Juden im deutschen Kulturbereich* (Berlin: Jüdischer Verlag, 1959), pp. 23-24, 150, 217, 875.

3. On Young Germany, see Helmut Koopmann, *Das junge Deutschland, Analyse seines Selbstverständnisses* (Stuttgart: Metzger, 1970); on Börne and Heine's publicist activities, see Gerard Ras, *Börne und Heine als politische Schriftsteller* (Groningen and The Hague: Woltens' V.M., 1926).

4. Eduard Meyer, *Gegen L. Börne, den Wahrheit-, Recht- und Ehrvergessenem Schriftsteller aus Paris* (Altona, 1831).

5. Ludwig Börne's *Briefe aus Paris* were published during the period 1830-1833; Heine's *Reisebilder,* during 1826-1831. On Börne and Young Germany's attitude toward Goethe, see Koopmann, *Das junge Deutschland,* pp. 114-131; see the index there on Saphir, as well as n. 2 above; and Meyer, *Gegen Börne,* pp. 5, 12-13.

6. Meyer, *Gegen Börne,* pp. 13-14.

7. Ibid., p. 14.

8. On Menzel, see the index to Koopmann, *Das junge Deutschland.*

9. Erwin Schuppe, *Der Burschenschaftler Wolfgang Menzel* (Frankfurt: G. Schulte, 1952), pp. 108-109.

10. *Votum Über das "Junge Deutschland,"* pp. 27-31.

11. *Die jeune Allemagne in Deutschland* (Stuttgart, 1836), pp. 9, 14-15. The identity of the author was established by Volkmar Eichstädt, *Bibliographie zur Geschichte der Judenfrage* (Hamburg: Hanseatische Verlagsanstalt, 1938), p. 216.

12. *Jeune Allemagne,* pp. 11, 19-23.

13. Ibid., pp. 26-27.

14. Wolfgang Menzel, "Herr Börne und der deutsche Patriotismus," *Morgenblatt für gebildete Stände,* 30 (1836): Literaturblatt, pp. 145-148. See Koopmann, *Das junge Deutschland,* index, S.V. "Wienbarg."

15. Jacob Weil, *Das junge Deutschland und die Juden* (Frankfurt, 1836); Berthold Auerbach, *Das Judenthum und die neueste Literatur* (Stuttgart, 1836); Gabriel Riesser, *Börne und die Juden: Ein Wort der Erwiderung auf die Flugschrift des Herrn Dr. Eduard Meyer gegen Börne* (Altenburg, 1832).

16. Heinrich Laube, *Struensee* (Leipzig, 1847) cited after his *Cesammelte Werke* (Leipzig, 1909), XXIV, 123-145.

17. Ibid., pp. 130-131.

18. Ibid., pp. 131-132.

19. Ibid., p. 132.

20. Ibid., pp. 130-131.

21. The most comprehensive biography of Wagner is Ernest Newman, *The Life of Richard Wagner,* 4 vols. (New York: Knopf, 1933-1946).

22. Ibid., I, 384-387.

23. *Abend-Zeitung,* 2-4 August 1841. A photocopy of the article can be found in the Schocken Library, Jerusalem, in a collection of unpublished articles on Heine by Erich Löwenthal on occasion of the sixtieth anniversary of Salman Schocken, in 1937.

24. Richard Wagner, *Das Judenthum in der Musik* (Leipzig, 1869), p. 10.

25. Richard Wagner, *Mein Leben,* 2 vols. (Munich: List, 1963), I, 338.

26. The two articles are "Die Kunst und die Revolution" and "Das Kunstwerk der Zukunft," both included in Wagner's *Gesammelte Schriften und Dichtungen* (Leipzig, 1907), III.

27. *Judenthum in der Musik,* pp. 10, 13, 15, 22. "Wir hatten uns das unwillkürlich Abstossende, welches die Persönlichkeit und das Wesen der Juden für uns hat, zu erklären, um diese instinktmässige Abneigung zu rechtfertigen" (p. 10). A similarity to Bauer's ideas is discernible in other matters as well, as we shall see below. See *Judenthum in der Musik,* p. 13.

28. Bauer, *Judenfrage,* p. 114; Saul K. Padover, ed., *Karl Marx on Religion,* (New York: McGraw-Hill, 1974), p. 122. That the Jews no longer need emancipation had already been said by Paulus, *Jüdische Nationalabsonderung,* pp. 4-5, but he had not attributed their actual freedom to their economic power.

29. *Judenthum in der Musik,* p. 12; see Christoph Cobet, *Der Wortschatz des Antisemitismus in der Bismarckzeit* (Munich: Fink, 1973), p. 147. The author failed to note that the 1869 text has its origin in an 1850 publication.

30. *Judenthum in der Musik,* pp. 12-13. On Meyerbeer, see n. 22; Mendelssohn-Bartholdy's name appears on pp. 25, 30. In the body of the article, only the unacceptable artistic methods of Meyerbeer are discussed; in an appendix (pp. 41-43), however, an added accusation of social plotting to further Meyerbeer's success is hurled at the composer. An entire book has been written on the relationship of Heine and Meyerbeer: Heinz Becker, *Der Fall Heine-Meyerbeer* (Berlin: W. de Gruyter, 1958).

31. *Judenthum in der Musik,* p. 20-21.

32. Ibid., p. 18.

33. Ibid., pp. 14-15. Fichte developed this theory in his "Speeches to the German Nation" in 1809. H. C. Engelbrecht, *Johann Gottlieb Fichte: A Study of his Political Writings with Special Reference to his Nationalism* (New York: Columbia University Press, 1933), pp. 112-121.

34. *Judenthum in der Musik,* pp. 21-22. Bauer devotes an entire chapter to the "freezing of the Jewish popular consciousness," *Judenfrage,* pp. 32-35.

35. *Judenthum in der Musik,* p. 31. See above n. 26.

36. Ibid., p. 17. In this, too, Wagner follows Bauer. See *Judenfrage,* p. 38.

37. *Judenthum in der Musik,* p. 17.

38. Ibid., p. 31.

39. Ibid., pp. 31-32.

40. Ibid., p. 32.

41. Ibid. The use of the figure of Ahasuerus, the Eternal Jew, as the symbol of the end of Israel's wanderings, was widespread in this period and also served Berthold Auerbach in his historical novel *Spinoza*. See Schopenhauer as well: *Parerga und Paralipomena*, II, 278.

42. Newman, Richard Wagner, I, 275-277.

43. *Judenthum in der Musik*, p. 20.

44. L. Stein, *The Racial Thinking of Richard Wagner* (New York: Philosophical Library, 1950) and Otto Dov Kulka, "Richard Wagner und die Anfänge des modernen Antisemitismus," *BLBI* 4 (1961): 290-296.

45. *Judenthum in der Musik*, pp. 34-36, 57.

46. *AZJ* 4 (1840): 545; Gustav Pfizer, "Heines Schriften und Tendenz," in *Deutsche Viertel-Jahresschrift* (1838): 216.

47. Ibid., p. 217. See n. 39.

48. *Judenthum in der Musik*, p. 29.

49. The Bavarian economist, Ignatz von Rudhart, claimed that Jewish peddlers helped the farmer to exploit the by-products of his labors which otherwise would have gone to waste. See his *Über den Zustand des Königreichs Bayern nach amtlichen Quellen* (Stuttgart, 1825-1827), I, 67-89.

50. Meyer, *Gegen Börne*, p. 10; Pfizer, *Heines Schriften*, p. 216; and n. 45 above.

15. The Christian State

1. Wolfgang Bernhard Fränkel, *Die Unmöglichkeit der Emanzipation der Juden im christlichen Staate: Als Entgegnung historisch nachgewiesen* (Elberfeld, 1842); H. E. Marcard, *Über die Möglichkeit der Juden-Emanzipation im christlich-germanischen Staat* (Minden, 1843); Constantin Frantz, *Ahasverus oder die Judenfrage* (Berlin, 1844); and see the analysis in Johanna Philipson, "Constantin Frantz," *LBIYB*, 13 (1968): 102-119; Philipp Ludwig Wolfart, *Über die Emanzipation der Juden in Preussen* (Potsdam, 1844) and idem, *Art und Ziel der öffentlichen Stimme in der preussischen Judenfrage* (Potsdam, 1844).

2. See Chapter 12.

3. Karl Streckfuss, *Über das Verhältniss der Juden zu den christlichen Staaten* (Halle, 1833) and idem, *Über das Verhältniss der Juden zu den christlichen Staaten: 2. Schrift unter diesem Titel* (Berlin, 1843).

4. Wolfart, *Über die Emanzipation*, p. 7; Fränkel, *Die Unmöglichkeit der Emanzipation*, p. 110; Frantz, *Ahasverus*, p. 18; Marcard, *Über die Möglichkeit*, p. 37.

5. Marcard, *Über die Möglichkeit*, pp. 6, 22-23.

6. Ibid., p. 31.

7. Frantz, *Ahasverus*, pp. 33-35.

8. Wolfart, *Art und Ziel*, pp. 28-30.

9. Wolfgang Bernhard Fränkel, *Das Bekentniss des Proselyten: Das Unglück der Juden und ihre Emanzipation in Deutschland* (Elberfeld, 1841).

10. Fränkel, *Die Unmöglichkeit*, pp. 119-126.

11. Gerhard Masur, *Friedrich Julius Stahl: Geschichte seines Lebens: Aufstieg und Entfaltung 1802-1840* (Berlin: Mittler, 1930); Robert A. Kann, "Friedrich

Julius Stahl: A Re-examination of his Conservatism," *LBIYB*, 12 (1967): 55-74; and Hamburger, *Juden im öffentlichen Leben, Deutschlands* (Tübingen: Mohr, 1968), pp. 197-206.

12. Friedrich Julius Stahl, *Der christliche Staat und sein Verhältniss zu Deismus und Judenthum: Eine durch die Verhandlungen des Vereinigten Landtags hervorgerufene Abhandlung* (Berlin, 1847).

13. Martin Philippson, *Neueste Geschichte des jüdischen Volkes* (Leipzig, 1907), I, 272-275.

14. Stahl, *Der christlichen Staat*, pp. 8-15.

15. Ibid., pp. 31-56.

16. Ibid., pp. 40-41.

17. Ibid., p. 42.

18. Ibid., pp. 43-44.

19. Ibid., pp. 65-66.

20. Ibid., pp. 60-61, 68-69. Since 1837, the Jewish public had been demanding the establishment of a theological faculty or a seminary under government sponsorship. See J. M. Jost, *Neuere Geschichte der Israeliten* (Breslau, n.d.), III, 152-153.

16. The Jewish Stereotype and Assimilation

1. Freytag's book *Soll und Haben* appeared in 1855 and will be cited hereafter according to the Berlin, Schreiter edition; Wilhelm Raabe, *Der Hungerpastor*, 25th ed. (Berlin, 1906).

2. A socio-historical analysis of the novel may be found in Ernst Kohn-Bramstedt, *Aristocracy and the Middle-Classes in Germany, 1830-1900* (London: P. S. King, 1937), pp. 132-141. See also George L. Mosse, "The Image of the Jew in German Popular Literature: Felix Dahn and Gustav Freytag," in his *Germans and Jews* (New York: Howard Fertig, 1970), pp. 61-76 and Pierre Angel, *Le Personage juif dans le roman allemand (1855-1915). La Racine littéraire de l'antisémitisme Outre-Rhin* (Paris: Didier, 1973), pp. 11-34, 161-177.

3. Freytag, *Soll und Haben*, pp. 119-132.

4. Ibid., p. 432. For Jewish reactions to the appearance of Freytag's book, see *AZJ*, 19 (1855): 633-634. See n. 6 for Freytag's stance on anti-Semitism.

5. Raabe, *Der Hungerpastor*, pp. 107-108.

6. See Kohn-Bramstedt, *Aristocracy*, pp. 1-8; Gustav Freytag, *Über den Antisemitismus: Eine Pfingstbetrachtung* (Berlin, 1893), pp. 13-16. Angel, *Le Personage juif*, pp. 179-185, brings additional proof that the personal views of Freytag and Raabe did not correspond to the tendencies of their books.

7. Vague and baseless claims abound in the literature on Marr. They are finally corrected conclusively in the outstanding article by Mosche Zimmermann, "Gabriel Riesser und Wilhelm Marr im Meinungsstreit," *Zeitschrift des Vereins für Hamburgische Geschichte*, 61 (1975): 59-84. For Marr's biography, see pp. 63-64.

8. On the background of Wilhelm Marr, *Der Judenspiegel* (Hamburg, 1862), see Zimmermann, "Riesser und Marr," pp. 76-78. The similarity to Bruno Bauer's views may, of course, also be explained as an expression of a parallel intellectual situation; nevertheless, it seems that Marr was familiar with Bauer's book. On Nord-

mann, see the next chapter. Marr builds on his ideas and adds that the racial degeneration of the Jews was the product of racial mixture. See pp. 39-40.

9. Voltaire is quoted on p. 26; see also pp. 7-29. Zimmermann, "Riesser und Marr," p. 77, cites Marr's handwritten memoirs on his evaluation of the *Judenspiegel* as philo-Semitic. It is the willingness to integrate Jews via assimilation which bolsters this claim. See also *Judenspiegel,* pp. 45-52.

10. Zimmermann, "Riesser und Marr," p. 20.

11. Robert von Mohl, *Staatsrecht, Völkerrecht und Politik* (Tübingen, 1869), III, 673-679.

12. Ibid., p. 680.

17. The Conservatives' Rearguard Action

1. On this and the following section, see Simon Dubnow, *History of the Jews,* trans. Moshe Spiegel (South Brunswick: Joseloff, 1967-1973), V, 255-274.

2. *AZJ* 29 (1864): 566.

3. Herman Wagener, *Das Judenthum und der Staat, eine historisch-politische Skizze zur Orientierung über die Judenfrage* (Berlin, 1857), pp. 1-2. On Wagener, see Adalbert Hahn, *Die Berliner Revue, ein Beitrag zur Geschichte der konservativen Partei zwischen 1855-1875* (Berlin: Ebering, 1934).

4. Wagener, foreword to *Das Judenthum;* Immanuel Heinrich Ritter, *Beleuchtung der Wagener'schen Schrift: Das Judenthum und der Staat* (Berlin, 1857), p. 8. Paulus Cassel was a Jewish scholar who converted, it appears, out of conviction. He was involved in missionary activity, but at the outbreak of anti-Semitism, he came to the defense of the Jews, as we shall see below. On his life, see *Allgemeine Deutsche Biographie,* XLVII, 465-466.

5. Wagener, *Das Judenthum,* pp. 5, 36-39, 68.

6. Ibid., pp. 34-35, 60.

7. Johannes Nordmann, *Die Juden und der deutsche Staat,* 2nd ed. (Berlin [Posen], 1861). On Wagener's part, see the testimony of Theodor Fritsch in the introduction to the 13th ed. of Nordmann (Leipzig, 1920), p. 2.

8. Nordmann, *Die Juden,* pp. 5-6, 9.

9. Ibid., pp. 20-21, 28, 32.

10. Ibid., pp. 61-63, and the introduction to the 3rd ed., p. 7.

11. Hahn, *Berliner Revue,* pp. 88-91; Herman Wagener, *Staats- und Gesellschaftslexikon* (Berlin, 1859-1867).

12. Wagener, *Lexicon,* s.v. "Börne," p. 302; and s.v. "Mendelssohn," p. 217. Bruno Bauer, *Das Judenthum in der Fremde* (Berlin, 1863).

13. *Lexikon,* "Judenthum," p. 605; Barnikol, *Bruno Bauer,* p. 351.

14. Bauer, *Das Judenthum in der Fremde,* pp. 2, 71-76. See *Lexikon,* "Jacobi" and "Fischoff."

15. Bauer, *Das Judenthum in der Fremde,* p. 7. In his *Judenfrage,* p. 9, he refused to credit Spinoza's contribution to the Jews, since the philosopher was no longer Jewish by the time he created his system.

16. *Judenfrage,* p. 44; *Judenthum in der Fremde,* pp. 3-5, 12-13.

17. *Judenthum in der Fremde,* pp. 8-9.

18. Ibid., p. 10. On the change in Bauer's opinions, between his *Judenfrage*

and his *Judenthum in der Fremde,* in the direction of racism, see Rothenstreich, "For and Against Emancipation: The Bruno Bauer Controversy," *LBIYB,* 4 (1959): 35.

19. *Judenthum in der Fremde,* pp. 4-5.

20. Ibid., p. 111.

21. Ibid., p. 77.

22. Ibid. See also Rothenstreich, p. 36.

23. See chapter 14. Osman-Bey [pseud.], *La Conquête du monde par les Juifs* (Basel, 1871) and, in German, *Die Eroberung der Welt durch die Juden* (Basel, 1873).

24. August Rohling, *Die Psalmen übersetzt und erläutert* (Munster, 1871), pp. i-viii. On Rohling, see I. A. Hellwing, *Der konfessionelle Antisemitismus im 19. Jahrhundert in Österreich* (Vienna: Herder, 1972), pp. 71-76. The polemic in the newspaper is from 3-15 May 1871, and the pamphlets are: Kroner, *Entstelltes Unwahres und Erfundenes in dem "Talmudjuden" Prof. Dr. August Rohlings nachgewiesen von Rabbiner Dr. Kroner* (Munster, 1871); *Offener Brief an . . . August Rohling als Antwort auf sein Pamphlet "Der Talmudjude" von einem Münsterischen Juden im Namen Vieler* (Munster, 1871); and the various editions of the *Talmudjude.* See 3rd ed., pp. 8-9; Rohling's reply to Kroner in the appendix to the 2nd ed., pp. 63-83, was deleted in the following editions.

25. Such ideas are scattered throughout the book and summed up in particular in the introduction to the third edition. On p. 5 of this edition, Rohling lists the newspapers which "agreed" with his views. With the exception of the Berlin conservative newspaper, the *Kreuzzeitung,* they are all Catholic papers. *AZJ* 35 (22 August 1871): 674. Rohling's declared aims concerning conversion already appear in the introduction to the first edition, p. 4.

18. The Austrian Prelude

1. A concise survey of the relevant facts can be found in Hans Tietze, *Die Juden Wiens* (Leipzig: Tal, 1933), pp. 113-206.

2. A lively description of the situation can be found in Sigmund Mayer, *Ein judischer Kaufmann, 1831-1911* (Leipzig, 1911); idem, *Die Wiener Juden, Kommerz-Kultur-Politik, 1700-1900* (Vienna and Berlin, 1917).

3. Ignaz Klinger, *Über die Unnutz- und Schadlichkeit der Juden in Konigreich Bohmen und Mahren* (Prague, 1762), p. 69. *Die Juden, wie sie sind und wie sie seyn sollen,* 2nd ed. (Vienna, 1781).

4. Tietze, *Die Juden Wiens,* pp. 143-177.

5. Anton von Rosas, "Beobachtungen und Abhandlungen aus dem Gebiet der Natur- und Heilkunde" in *Medizinische Jahrbücher des kaiserlich königl. osterreichischen Staates* (Vienna, 1842), pp. 1-19.

6. "Soll die Judensteuer in Böhmen aufgehoben werden?" in *Revue österreichischer Zustände* 1 (1842): 7-42, especially 21-24.

7. Ferdinand Schirnding, *Österreich im Jahre 1840. Von einem österreichischen Staatsmanne,* 4 vols. (Leipzig, 1840-1844); idem, *Die Juden in Österreich, Preussen und Sachsen* (Leipzig, 1842); idem, *Das Judenthum in Österreich*

und die böhmischen Unruhen (Leipzig, 1845). In the introduction to the first book listed (pp. iii-iv), Schirnding accepts authorship of the article in the *Revue*.

8. On Schirnding, see Konstantin Wurzbach, *Biographisches Lexikon des Kaiserthums Österreich*, XXX, 36-38.

9. *Österreich im Jahre 1840*, pp. 42-43; *Revue*, pp. 29-30; *Die Juden in Österreich*, pp. 53-55, 73-74, 103-104; *Das Judenthum in Österreich*, pp. 11-12, 56, 82-85.

10. *Österreich im Jahre 1840*, pp. 42-43.

11. *Das Judenthum in Österreich*, pp. 131-132, 124-126; *Österreich im Jahre 1840*, p. 58.

12. Salo Wittmayer Baron, "Impact of the Revolution of 1848 on Jewish Emancipation," *ISS* 11 (1949): 195-248. Freiherr von Helfert, *Die Wiener Journalistik im Jahre 1848* (Vienna, 1877), pp. 145-147.

13. Jacob Toury, *Turmoil and Confusion in the Revolution of 1848* (Merhavyah: Moreshet, 1968), pp. 42-44, 138-143; Johann Quirin Endlich, *Der Einfluss der Juden auf unsere Civilisation mit besonderer Rücksicht auf Industrial-Anstalten in Österreich* (Vienna, 1848).

14. On Brunner, see Erika Weinzierl, "On the Pathogenesis of the Anti-Semitism of Sebastian Brunner (1814-1893)" in *Yad Vashem Studies on the European Jewish Catastrophe and Resistance*, L. Rothkirchen, ed. (Jerusalem: Yad Vashem, 1974), X, 217-239; Sebastian Brunner, *Die Kirche und die Synagoge. Aus dem Französischen des L. Rupert* (Schaffhausen, 1864).

15. Brunner, *Kirche und Synagoge*, pp. iii-iv, vii.

16. Ibid., p. viii.

17. Albert Wiesinger, "Arme Christen und Hungerleider, jüdische Kapitalisten und Geldvergeuder," in *Weckstimmen für das katholische Volk*, IV, (Vienna, 1870); Heinrich von Hurter, "Der moderne G'schaftelhuber im Gewande der Judenpresse," ibid., II.

18. *Presseprozess Sebastian Brunner contra Ignaz Kuranda* (Vienna, 1860).

19. *Die Neuzeit*, 18.10.1872, pp. 463-464.

19. The Hungarian Prelude

1. Nathaniel Katzburg, "History of the Jews of Hungary" in *Pinkas Hakehillot, Encyclopaedia of Jewish Communities: Hungary* (Jerusalem: Yad Vashem, 1976), pp. 7-12.

2. Ibid., pp. 19-24.

3. Bálint Hóman and Gyula Szekfü, *Magyar történet* [Hungarian History] (Budapest: Egyetemi Nyomda, 1935-1936), V, 257-302; C. A. Macartney, *Hungary: A Short History* (Edinburgh: University Press, 1962), pp. 122-154 and Katzburg, "Jews of Hungary," pp. 20-22.

4. Katzburg, "History," p. 22.

5. Ibid., pp. 24-28.

6. Joseph Ben-David, "Beginning of Modern Jewish Society in Hungary During the First Half of the Nineteenth Century," *Zion*, 17 (1952): 101-128 and Jacob Katz, "Contributions Towards a Biography of the Hatam Sofer" in *Studies in Kabbalah and the History of Religions Presented to Gerschom Scholem* (Jerusalem: Magnes Press, 1968), pp. 115-148.

7. István Barta, ed., *Kossuth Lajos ifjúkori iratok* [Louis Kossuth's Youthful Writings] (Budapest: Akadémiai Kiadó, 1966), pp. 179-180.

8. Ibid., p. 179.

9. On Széchenyi, see the introduction to his diary (see n. 10) by the editor, Gyula Viszota, which constitutes a complete biography in itself, and George Barany, *Stephen Széchenyi and the Awakening of Hungarian Nationalism, 1791-1841* (Princeton: Princeton University Press, 1968). On his attitude to Jews, see Nathaniel Katzburg, *Anti-Semitism in Hungary* (Tel-Aviv: Dvir, 1969), pp. 25-28.

10. Gyula Viszota, ed., *Grof Széchenyi István Naploi* [Diaries of Count Stephen Széchenyi] (Budapest: Magyar Történelmi Társulat 1926-1939), II, 545-546, IV, 431.

11. On the establishment of the casino, see Viszota's introduction, ibid., V, xxxviff; on the Jews, III, 318, n. 2 and Barany, *Stephen Széchenyi*, p. 171, n. 111.

12. Gyula Szekfü, *A mai Széchenyi* [Today's Széchenyi] (Budapest: Magyar Kulturális Egyesületek, 1935), pp. 293-295 and Barany, *Széchenyi*, pp. 222-223.

13. The first is summarized by Viszota in *Széchenyi Naploi*, V, 271-272, n. 3, while the second may be found in János Török, ed., *Széchenyi István politikai iskolája saját müveiböl összeállitva* [Stephen Széchenyi's Political School Drawn Upon his Own Work] (Pest, 1864), II, 387-392. The contents of the two speeches are analyzed by Barany, *Széchenyi*, pp. 357-359.

14. *Széchenyi Naploi*, II, 272 and *Politikai iskolája*, II, 388-389, 391.

15. His views on religion: *Naploi*, II, cv-cxii and Barany, *Széchenyi*, pp. 90-93.

16. Árpád Károlyi and Vilmos Tolnai, eds., *Gr. Széchenyi István döblingi irodalmi hagyatéka* [Count Stephen Széchenyi's Posthumous Papers of Döbling], (Budapest: Magyar Történelmi Társulat 1921-1925), I, 362. See also pp. 438, 442, and II, 275, 412-413, note.

17. István Barta, *A fiatal Kossuth* [Young Kossuth] (Budapest: Akadémiai Kiadó, 1966). Kossuth's views on the Jews are summarized by Katzburg, *Anti-Semitism in Hungary*, pp. 24, 30-32. These were accepted views in liberal circles; see for example Bárándy, *Über Ungarns Zustände* (Pressburg, 1847), pp. 32-37; Katzburg, "History of the Jews of Hungary," pp. 22-24; and Jacob Toury, *Turmoil and Confusion in the Revolution of 1848* (Merhavyah: Moreshet, 1968), pp. 42-55.

18. There is a certain parallel here to the ordinances of Saxe-Weimar in 1823. See J. M. Jost, *Neuere Geschichte der Israeliten* (Breslau, n.d.), I, 226-232.

19. Paul Bödy, *Joseph Eötvös and the Modernization of Hungary, 1840-1870* (Philadelphia: American Philosophical Society, 1972).

20. Nathaniel Katzburg, "The Jewish Congress in Hungary," *Hungarian-Jewish Studies* 2 (1969): 1-33.

21. Nathaniel Katzburg, *Anti-Semitism in Hungary*, pp. 53-55, 81-84. Istoczy's speeches have been collected in Gyözö Istoczy, *Országgyülési beszédei, inditványai és törvény javaslatai* [Parliamentary Speeches, Motions and Proposals] (Budapest: Buschmann, 1904). The text of the interpellation is on pp. 12-14.

22. *Istoczy*, p. 16.

23. Ibid., pp. 2, 5-6.

24. Ibid., pp. 6-8. See also Chapter 11 and further on in this chapter.
25. Ibid., p. 4, and Chapter 11.
26. Ibid., pp. 10-12.
27. Ibid., p. 9.
28. Katzburg, *Anti-Semitism in Hungary*, p. 53, n. 1; Istoczy, pp. 14-16.
29. The text of the speech is in *Istoczy*, pp. 42-63, especially pp. 42, 54, 63.
30. Ibid., p. 46.
31. Ibid., pp. 44-53, 58-59.
32. Ibid., p. 63.
33. Ibid., pp. 17, 63.

20. The Incubation

1. This will be detailed in Chapter 21.

2. For example, two titles by contemporary writers are Erich Lehnhardt, *Die antisemitische Bewegung in Deutschland, besonders in Berlin, nach Voraussetzungen, Wesen, Berechtigung und Folgen dargelegt. Ein Beitrag zur Lösung der Judenfrage* (Zurich, 1884); Max Liebermann von Sonnenberg, *Beiträge zur Geschichte der antisemitischen Bewegung vom Jahre 1880-1885* (Berlin, 1885). A historian of the first type is Kurt Warzinek, *Die Entstehung der deutschen Antisemitenparteien (1873-1890)* (Berlin: Ebering, 1927). The second type is exemplified by George L. Mosse, *The Crisis of German Ideology, Intellectual Origins of the Third Reich* (New York: Grosset and Dunlap, 1964). See also Uriel Tal, *Christians and Jews in Germany: Religion, Politics and Ideology in the Second Reich, 1870-1914* (Ithaca, N.Y.: Cornell University Press, 1974). On the state of research in general, see Ismar Schorsch, "German Antisemitism in the Light of Post-War Historiography", *LBIYB* 19 (1974): 257-271; Reinhard Rürup, *Emanzipation und Antisemitismus* (Göttingen: Vandenhoeck und Ruperecht, 1975), pp. 115-125.

3. See the article "Social Movements," *International Encyclopedia of Social Sciences*, XIV, 438-452, and the bibliography there. The fact that anti-Semitism is chiefly negatively directed does not, from a sociological standpoint, exclude it from the principal characteristics that apply to any other social movement.

4. A detailed account of the events can be found in the book by the contemporary economist, Max Wirth, *Geschichte der Handelskrisen* (Frankfurt, 1874), II, 538-655; Hans Rosenberg, *Grosse Depression und Bismarckzeit* (Frankfurt: Ulstein, 1976). The connection between the economic crisis and the rise of anti-Semitism is generally accepted by all researchers, and is especially emphasized by Paul W. Massing, *Rehearsal for Destruction, a Study of Political Antisemitism in Imperial Germany* (New York: Harper, 1949). See also Rürup, *Emanzipation*, pp. 87-90; Rosenberg, *Grosse Depression*, pp. 88-117; and Schorsch, "German Antisemitism," pp. 262-263. On Lasker, Bamberger, and Strousberg, see Ernest Hamburger, *Juden im öffentlichen Leben Deutschlands* (Tübingen: Mohr, 1968), pp. 260-261, 269-278, 284-296.

5. On the political activities of Jews during this period see Hamburger, *Juden*, and Jacob Toury, *Die politischen Orientierungen der Juden in Deutschland* (Tübingen: Mohr, 1966), pp. 110-169. Lasker's speeches have been published in the

booklet, *Laskers Rede gegen Wagener . . . gehalten im Abgeordneten-Hause am 7. Februar 1873 . . .* (Berlin, 1873). See Strousberg's memoirs in *Dr. Strousberg und sein Wirken. Von ihm selbst geschildert* (Berlin, 1876). Hamburger became caught up in the negative opinion on Strousberg following his losses and Lasker's accusations—but there is room for revising this judgment. See Karl Ottmann, "Bethel Henry Strousberg, Eisenbahnkönig der Privatbahnzeit," *Archiv für Eisenbahnwesen* 70.2 (1960): 167-195. New light has recently been shed on Strousberg: Fritz Stern, *Gold and Iron: Bismarck, Bleichröder and the Building of the German Empire* (New York: Knopf, 1977), pp. 358-369. Strousberg appears as a daring initiator rather than as a scoundrel. Wagener described the events from his viewpoint in Herman Wagener, *Erlebtes, meine Memoiren aus der Zeit von 1848-1866 und von 1873 bis jetzt* (Berlin, 1884), pp. 55-62.

6. Paul Wentzcke, *Deutscher Liberalismus im Zeitalter Bismarcks, eine politische Briefsammlung* (Bonn: K. Schröder, 1962), II, 15.

7. Otto Glagau, "Der Börsen- und Gründungsschwindel in Berlin," *Gartenlaube*, December 1874, pp. 788-790. The articles were collected in a book of the same title and published in Berlin in 1876. The same theme appears in all Glagau's works, in particular, *Des Reiches Noth und der neue Culturkampf* (Osnabrück, 1879), p. 15. The director of the Statistics Institute in Saxony suggested that an institution be founded to keep track of processes with a view to predicting crises. Glagau massed his scorn against the suggestion: "In Manchesterian economic eyes economic and commercial crises are on no account the fruit of deception and failing but are a natural phenomenon such as storms and thunder which must be anticipated and heralded."

8. Glagau, *Gründungsschwindel in Berlin*, p. xxiii. *Gartenlaube* (1874): 789. An account of Glagau's negotiations with his editor is given in the introduction to *Gründungsschwindel in Berlin*, p. xxxiii. Glagau also wrote a play which described the machinations at the bourse, *Akteen, Historisches Schauspiel* (Leipzig, 1877). The play was written immediately after the outbreak of the crisis and, according to the author, had he succeeded in having it staged, he would not have written the articles in *Gartenlaube*. The two protagonists, a Christian and a Jew, play equal parts in the deceptions, but the image of the Jew follows the stereotype.

9. *Gartenlaube* (1885): 525.

10. Details can be found in the introduction to *Gründungsschwindel in Berlin*, pp. xix-xxiii, xxv, and, on pp. xxiii-xiv, Glagau's response to the attack on himself in the *Schlesische Presse* newspaper. According to him, he had to force the newspaper to publish it. This response was immediately taken up and widely quoted by other newspapers.

11. Amine Haase, *Katholische Presse und die Judenfrage* (Munich: Verlag Dokumentation, 1975), p. 178. *Gründungsschwindel in Berlin*, pp. xxv-xxviii. Otto Glagau, *Börsen und Gründungsschwindel in Deutschland* (Leipzig, 1877).

12. Helmut von Gerlach, "Vom deutschen Antisemitismus," *Patria* (1904). Surprisingly enough Glagau's books are even quoted in the professional literature: A. Sartorius von Waltershausen, *Deutsche Wirtschaftsgeschichte* (Jena: Fischer, 1920), pp. 276-279. A brief glance at this work suffices to reveal the author's utter carelessness in quotation.

13. *Gründungsschwindel in Berlin*, pp. 294-322.

14. Ibid., p. xxx.

15. Ibid., p. xxxv. Detailed evidence of this is given on p. xix and in the ensuing description. Besides the four books mentioned in nn. 7 and 8, at least three more appeared between 1880 and 1883. Wawrzinek, *Die Entstehung der Antisemitenparteien*, pp. 92-93. From 1883 to 1887 Glagau edited the monthly *Kulturkämpfer* and was preoccupied with Jews and Judaism. Glagau's name is mentioned in anti-Semitic history books, but not enough attention was paid to his central function and sophisticated propaganda.

16. Constantin Frantz, *Der National-liberalismus und die Judenherrschaft* (Munich, 1874). He apparently conjoins opposition to Jews with opposition to the ruling party, but his writings here, as in his other publications during this period, lack an active political direction. His background in protest remained what it had been in the forties, an adherence to the idea of a Christian state. See Chapter 15, n.3. *Gartenlaube* (1875): 745-746. *Gründungsschwindel in Berlin*, p. x. Glagau's observation here took on an anti-Jewish tinge. The articles were collected and published in *Die Aera Bleichröder-Delbrück-Camphausen* (Berlin, 1876). See Stern, *Gold and Iron*. The attack on Bleichröder is discussed on pp. 187 and 502.

17. *Aera Bleichröder*, pp. 4-6.

18. Franz Perrot, *Bismarck und die Juden* (Berlin, 1931). For details see the introduction, pp. 11-56, and p. 270. *Aera Bleichröder*, pp. 7-8, 52-53.

19. Franz Perrot, *Der Eisenbahn-Actienschwindel, Resultate des Actiensystems im Eisenbahnwesen* (Rostock, 1873), pp. 104-120, 221-224. Franz Perrot, *Die sogenannte deutsche "Reichsbank," eine priviligierte Aktien-Gesellschaft von und für Juden* (Berlin, 1876), pp. 35-36.

20. C. Wilmanns, *Die "goldene" Internationale und die Nothwendigkeit einer sozialen Reformpartei*, 2nd ed. (Berlin, 1876), pp. 35-37, 105-107.

21. C. Wilmanns, *Zur Reform der deutschen Banken* (Berlin, 1872), p. 11.

22. Wilmanns, *Die Goldene Internationale*, pp. 58, 59-61, 61-62. On the use of Mommsen's sentence by anti-Semites, see Renate Schaefer, "Zur Geschichte des Wortes 'zerzetzen' ," *Zeitschrift für deutsche Wortforschung*, 18 (1962): 63-65.

23. Rudolph Meyer, *Politische Gründer und die Corruption in Deutschland* (Leipzig, 1877), p. 204. Rudolph Meyer, *Der Emancipationskampf des vierten Standes*, 2 vols. (Berlin, 1875). Meyer, *Politische Gründer*, pp. 4, 19, 57-61, and in other places throughout the book.

24. Ludwig Bamberger, *Erinnerungen* (Berlin, 1899), p. 258. Jacob Katz, *Jews and Freemasons in Europe, 1727-1939* (Cambridge, Mass.: Harvard University Press, 1970), pp. 128-159.

25. Theodor Mommsen, *Auch ein Wort über unser Judenthum* (Berlin, 1880), pp. 8-13. This was also the view of Ludwig Bamberger, who feared the far-reaching effects of Treitschke's intervention: "The process of social and spiritual blending could be stopped and destroyed by the spill of only a single gnawing drop," *Deutschthum und Judenthum* (Leipzig, 1880), p. 36. The two articles have recently been reprinted in Walter Böhlich, *Der Berliner Antisemitismusstreit* (Frankfurt: Insel, 1965), pp. 176-179, 215-220.

26. Jacob Katz, *Out of the Ghetto: The Social Background of Jewish Emancipation, 1770-1870* (Cambridge, Mass.: Harvard University Press, 1973), pp. 213-214. See also Jacob Toury, *Sociale und politische Geschichte der Juden in Deutschland* (Dusseldorf: Droste, 1977), pp. 69-161.

21. The Crystallization

1. Wilhelm Marr, *Der Sieg des Judenthums über das Germanenthum* (Bern, 1879), p. 46. A mistaken date of publication is sometimes assigned to this book. The exact timing is known from the reactions of the *AZJ* on 18 March 1879, close to the appearance of the book.

2. Ibid., p. 48.

3. On conservative support for Marr's initiative, see Werner Jochmann, "Struktur und Funktion des deutschen Antisemitismus," in Werner E. Mosse, ed., *Juden im Wilhelminischen Deutschland, 1890-1914* (Tübingen: Mohr, 1976), pp. 409, 476.

4. On the appearance of the word, see Christoph Cobet, *Der Wortschatz des Antisemitismus in der Bismarckzeit* (Munich: Fink, 1973), p. 221; Rürup, *Emanzipation und Antisemitismus*, pp. 95, 177. The replacement of the term *anti-jüdisch* by *Antisemit* makes the word's path of emergence strikingly clear.

5. *Statuten des Vereins, "Antisemiten-Liga"* (Berlin, 1879), p. 1.

6. Egon Waldegg [Alexander Pinkert], *Die Judenfrage gegenüber dem deutschen Handel und Gewerbe* (Dresden, 1880), 5th ed., pp. 40-42.

7. Otto Glagau, *Des Reiches-Noth und der neue Culturkampf* (Osnabrück, 1879), p. 282. This sentence, which Glagau printed in capital letters, later became a marketable slogan.

8. On Stöcker, see Walter Frank, *Hofprediger Stöcker und die christlichsoziale Bewegung*, 2nd ed. (Hamburg: Hanseatische Verlagsanstalt, 1935).

9. Jochmann, "Struktur und Funktion," pp. 412-413.

10. Adolf Stocker, *Das moderne Judenthum in Deutschland, besonders in Berlin, Zwei Reden in der christlich-sozialen Arbeiterpartei* (Berlin, 1880), pp. 17-19.

11. Heinrich von Treitschke, *Ein Wort über unser Judenthum* (Berlin, 1881). It was reprinted in Walter Böhlich, *Der Berliner Antisemitismusstreit* (Frankfurt: Insel, 1965); the term *Bewegung* is from that edition (pp. 6-7).

12. Ibid., pp. 237-263. Treitschke's real part in promoting the movement has been clarified by Andreas Dorpalen, *Heinrich von Treitschke* (New Haven: Yale University Press, 1957), pp. 240-247.

13. A student from Göttingen spoke out against the change of climate among the youth since the 1848 revolution. He was the anonymous author of the manuscript *Die Antisemiten-agitation und die deutsche Studentenschaft* (Göttingen, 1881), pp. 12-15. The protest declaration of November 1880 against the anti-Semitic propaganda, which was signed by seventy-five public figures, among them Treitschke's colleagues, cried out against the abandonment of "Lessing's heritage." In an emotional speech in honor of the Kaiser's birthday, Mommsen expressed his disappointment at the pattern of Germany's historical trend on 18 March 1880. See Böhlich, *Antisemitismusstreit*, pp. 203, 243-246.

14. *Der Kulturkampfer* (1881), p. 74.

15. A complaint against the increasing number of Jewish students may be found in Stöcker's second speech in *Das moderne Judenthum*, p. 39; C. Wilmanns, *Die "goldene" Internationale und die Nothwendigkeit einer sozialen Reformpartei*, 2nd ed. (Berlin, 1876), pp. 66-68; Franz Perrot [Hilarius Bankberger], *Die Juden im deutschen Staats- und Volksleben* (Frankfurt, 1879), pp. 30-35. Jochmann's "Struktur und Funktion" is, to a large extent, devoted to clarifying the social standing of the bearers of anti-Semitism. See *Die Antisemiten-agitation*.

16. Stöcker, *Das moderne Judenthum*, p. 6.

17. Ibid., pp. 7-9, 16-19.

18. Gerhard Albrecht, *Eugen Dühring, Ein Beitrag zur Geschichte der Sozialwissenschaften* (Jena: Fischer, 1927), pp. 5-10. Dühring, *Cursus der Philosophie als streng wissenschafliche Weltanschauung und Lebensgestaltung* (Leipzig, 1875), pp. 390-393. Dühring, *Die Judenfrage als Rassen- Sitten- und Culturfrage* (Karlsruhe and Leipzig, 1881), pp. 24-25, 46-72, 94-95. Dühring expanded the subject of Lessing in *Die Überschatzung Lessings und dessen Anwaltschaft für die Juden* (Karlsruhe, 1881).

19. *Judenfrage*, pp. 26, 113-114.

20. Uriel Tal, *Christians and Jews in Germany: Religion, Politics, and Ideology in the Second Reich, 1870-1914* (Ithaca, N.Y.: Cornell University Press, 1975), pp. 223-282.

21. Stöcker, *Das moderne Judenthum*, pp. 10-15.

22. Perrot, *Die Juden*, pp. 76-89; Wilmanns, *Die "goldene" Internationale*, pp. 59-61; Frantz, *Der Nationalliberalismus*, pp. 50-51.

23. Stöcker, *Das moderne Judenthum*, p. 4.

24. Stöcker, *Das moderne Judenthum*, pp. 19-20. Walter Böhlich, *Der Berliner Antisemitismusstreit* (Frankfurt: Jurel, 1965), pp. 8-12, 258-259; Schmeitzner's *Internationale Monatsschrift* (1883), II, 314-316; Frank, *Hofprediger Stöcker*, pp. 118-121.   x

25. Dühring, *Cursus der Philosophie*, pp. 390-393, and *Die Judenfrage*, pp. 94-117, 157-158. Dühring has long been regarded as the prototype of the Nazi anti-Semite, and this thesis, moreover, gained corroboration through his use of language. Ingeborg Seidel, "Eugen Dühring als Vorläufer der Nationalsozialisten," in *Im Dienste der Sprache, Festschrift für Victor Klemperer* (Halle: Niemeyer, 1958), pp. 383-396.

26. Dühring, *Die Judenfrage*, pp. 1-4. Marr, *Der Sieg des Judenthums*, p. 6. Glagau, *Gründungsschwindel in Berlin*, p. xxx.

27. Ernst Henrici, *Was ist der Kern der Judenfrage?* (Berlin, 1881), pp. 4-6. The conflict broke out as the second anti-Semitic congress proceeded. I will discuss this in Chapter 22.

28. Richard S. Levy, *The Downfall of the Anti-Semitic Political Parties in Imperial Germany* (New Haven: Yale University Press, 1975). In this connection see also the first party historian, Kurt Wawrzinek, *Die Entstehung der deutschen Antisemitenparteien (1873-1890)* (Berlin: Ebering, 1927), pp. 82-83. This was the socialist position, comprised of two distinct components: the criticism of anti-Semitism and the conclusions drawn from it to verify socialist theories. See Introduction.

29. Adolph Asch and Johanna Philippson, "Self-Defense in the Second Half of the 19th Century: The Emergence of the K. C.," *LBIYB* 3 (1958): 122-138.

30. Jacob Katz, *Jews and Freemasons in Europe, 1723-1939* (Cambridge, Mass.: Harvard University Press, 1970), pp. 164-169.

31. Eduard von Hartmann, *Das Judenthum in Gegenwart und Zukunft*, 2nd ed. (Leipzig, 1885). Jacob Toury, *Die politischen Orientierungen der Juden in Deutschland* (Tübingen: Mohr, 1966), pp. 110-123; Hamburger, *Juden im öffentlichen Leben*, pp. 251-256.

32. Hamburger, *Juden im öffentlichen Leben*, pp. 34-35. Bismarck especially was accused of maintaining silence in the face of anti-Semitic propaganda; see Hamburger, p. 561. On Bismarck's attitude toward Jews much has been written, but after Fritz Stern's monograph no doubt can remain as to his position. It condenses the typical Junker disdain for Jews and Bismarck's detachment from principles which is so characteristic of him in all things. Stern, *Gold and Iron*, especially pp. 501-507, 516-519.

33. Hamburger, *Juden im öffentlichen Leben*, pp. 32-68, 69-97.

22. The Hungarian Variation

1. On France, see Chapter 24, nn. 1 and 2. A good source for England is the *Jewish Chronicle*, which often prints news from the general press. On America, see M. Eisler, *Die Judenfrage in Deutschland* (New York, 1880). Eisler's reactions to events in Germany are based on the news in the American press.

2. Wilhelm Marr, *Vom jüdischen Kriegsschauplatz, eine Streitschrift* (Bern, 1879), pp. 42-44. On Istoczy's contact with Marr see Werner Jochmann, "Struktur und Funktion des deutschen Antisemitismus," in Werner E. Mosse, *Juden im Wilhelminischen Deutschland, 1890-1914* (Tübingen: Mohr, 1976), pp. 420-421. My description is based on Istoczy's letters to Marr. Professor Jochmann was kind enough to provide me with those which he mentioned in his article.

3. See the first periodical, *12 Röpirat, Havi folyoirat* [12 *Flysheets, Monthly*], 15 October 1880. *Statuten-Entwurf des Central-Vereins des Nichtjuden-Bundes von Ungarn*, pp. 4-5.

4. See Nathaniel Katzburg, *Antisemitism in Hungary, 1867-1914* (Tel Aviv: Dvir, 1969), pp. 86, 89-90. The following description is based on Katzburg's study and that of Judit Kubinszky, *Politikai Antiszemitizmus Magyarországon, 1875-1890* (Budapest: Kossuth Könyvkiado, 1976).

5. Katzburg, pp. 95-96; Kubinszky, pp. 131-162.

6. Katzburg, pp. 97-98.

7. On the process of assimilation in Hungary of minorities including Jews, see Peter Hanak, "Polgarosodas es asszimilacio Magyarországon a XIX században," *Történelmi Szemle* 17 (1974): 513-536.

8. Jacob Katz, "The Uniqueness of Hungarian Jewry," *Forum* (1977), 45-53.

9. Katzburg, *Antisemitism*, pp. 99-104. Kubinszky, *Politikai Antiszemitizmus*, pp. 68-104.

10. On the blood-libel of Tisza-Eszlar, see Paul Nathan, *Der Prozess von Tisza-Eszlár* (Berlin, 1892). Katzburg, *Antisemitism*, pp. 106-120. Kubinszky, pp. 88-104.

11. Katzburg, pp. 140-155. Kubinszky, pp. 105-130.

12. This development may be followed in the articles of the monthly *12 röpirat*, and in his parliamentary speeches which were compiled in Istoczy, *Országgyülési beszédei*. See Chapter 19, n. 21.

13. I. A. Hellwing, *Der konfessionelle Antisemitismus im 19 Jahrhundert in Österreich* (Vienna: Herder, 1972), pp. 105-109.

14. Katzburg, *Antisemitism*, pp. 159-162.

15. Ibid., pp. 173-177.

16. Nathaniel Katzburg, "The Struggle of Hungarian Jewry for Religious Equality in the 1890s," *Zion*, 22 (1957): 120-148. Katzburg, *Antisemitism*, pp. 182-190.

17. A list of the conveners is given in the report of the first Dresden congress at the end of the manifesto (see pp. 11-12). Ivan von Simonyi, *Der Antisemitismus und die Gesetze der menschlichen Gesellschaft, Antisemiten-Kongress zu Dresden* (Pressburg, 1884). *Manifest an die Regierungen und Völker der durch das Judenthum gefahrdeten christlichen Staaten* (Chemnitz, 1883).

18. Only the names of the conveners and the chairmen are listed at the bottom of the manifesto, but the press, such as *Le Figaro* (see below, Chapter 24, n. 1) and the *AZJ*, mentions additional names. *Manifest*, p. 12.

19. *Manifest*, p. 4.

20. Evidence of this may be found in the report of the second congress in Chemnitz (below, n. 23), p. 263. The theses of Stöcker (and of another member) are given at the end of the manifesto in order to bridge the opposing views.

21. *Manifest*, pp. 7-10.

22. J. Ammann, *Die Irrefuhrung des Antisemitismus* (Berlin, 1883). This pamphlet, which does not appear in most of the anti-Semitic bibliographies, contains one of the most extreme formulations of anti-Semitic ideology from the anti-religious camp.

23. A full report on the congress was printed in *Schmeitzner's Internationale Monatsschrift, Zeitschrift für die allgemeine Vereinigung zur Bekampfung des Judenthums* 11 (May 1883), pp. 255-321, (June) 323-326. *Der Kulturkampfer, Zeitschrift für öffentliche Angelgenheiten*, 7 (1883): 26-35.

24. *Schmeitzner's Monatsschrift*, pp. 255, 294, 310-311. *Der Kulturkampfer*, 27. On the absence of the Austrians, see Chapter 23.

23. The Austrian Extension

1. Th. Billroth, *Über das Lehren und Lernen von medizinischen Wissenschaften an den Universitäten der deutschen Nation* (Vienna, 1876), p. 152. *Prof. Dr. Billroth's Antwort auf die Adresse des Lesevereines der deutschen Studenten Wiens* (Vienna, 1876); Hans Tietze, *Die Juden Wiens* (Vienna: Tal, 1933), p. 227.

2. Paul Molisch, *Briefe zur deutschen Politik in Österreich von 1848 bis 1918* (Vienna and Leipzig: Wilhelm Braumüller, 1934), p. 80.

3. Menachem Z. Rosensaft, "Jews and Antisemites in Austria at the End of the Nineteenth Century," *LBIYB*, 21 (1976), p. 64.

4. Anton Tschörner, "Die materielle Lage des Arbeiterstandes in Österreich," *Österreichische Monatsschrift für Gesellschaftwissenschaft*, 1 (1879). The Jews played a relatively important role in the clothing industry, but their part in the pro-

duction of metals and construction was small. See Simon Kuznetz, "Economic Structure and Life of the Jews," in L. Finkelstein, ed., *The Jew* (New York: Harper and Row, 1966), pp. 1611-1614, 1628-1631; Karl von Vogelsang, *Gesammelte Aufsätze über sozialpolitische und verwandte Themata* (Augsburg, 1886), I, 113.

5. Vogelsang, *Gesammelte Aufsätze*, pp. 113-115; Wiard Klopp, *Leben und Wirken des Sozialpolitikers Karl Freiherr von Vogelsang* (Vienna: Typographische Anstalt, 1930), and *Die sozialen Lehren des Freiherrn Karl von Vogelsang* (St. Polten, 1899).

6. Paul Molisch, *Die deutschen Hochschulen in Österreich und die politisch-nationale Entwicklung nach dem Jahre 1848* (Munich: Drei Masken, 1922), pp. 117-123.

7. Arthur Ruppin, *Soziologie der Juden* (Berlin: Jüdischer Verlag, 1930), II, 115; Rosensaft, *Jews and Antisemites in Austria*, p. 59. Richard Charmatz, *Österreichs innere Geschichte von 1848-1907* (Leipzig: Teubner, 1918), I, 40-58.

8. The course of events pertaining to the Austrian anti-Semitic movement has been often described. See Rudolf Kuppe, *Karl Lüger und seine Zeit* (Vienna: Österreichische Volksschriften, 1933), pp. 92-94; Dirk van Arkel, *Antisemitismus in Austria* (Diss., Leiden, 1966); Peter G. J. Pulzer, *The Rise of Political Antisemitism in Germany and Austria* (London: John Willey, 1964), pp. 144-147.

9. Kuppe, *Karl Lüger*, pp. 93-98; Charmatz, *Österreichs innere Geschichte*, pp. 49-52. The connection between the change in the electoral system and anti-Semitism has been noted by D. van Arkel, *Antisemitism in Austria*, pp. 34-37.

10. Kuppe, *Karl Lüger*, pp. 95-97; *Acten und Gutachten in dem Prozesse Rohling contra Bloch* (Vienna, 1890), II, 1-4.

11. *Acten*, pp. 5-29ff.

12. *Schmeitzner's Internationale Monatsschrift* (1883), II, 264. In the report on the participants who failed to attend, the Austrians Schönerer and Pattai are mentioned, and their absence is attributed to the "österreichische Gesetzgebung," p. 162.

13. Ernst Plener, *Erinnerungen*, 2 vols. (Stuttgart: Deutsche Verlagsanstalt, 1911-1921); *Parlamentarische Taetigkeit 1873-1891*, p. 234.

14. Observations on the liberal background of the anti-Semitic leaders Schönerer and Lüger, and also socialists such as Victor Adler, were made by Adam Wandruszka, "Österreichs politische Struktur, die Entwicklung der Parteien und politischen Bewegungen," in Heinrich Benedikt, *Geschichte der Republik Österreich* (Munich: Verlag für Geschichte und Politik, 1954), pp. 291-297.

15. Andrew G. Whiteside, *The Socialism of Fools: Georg Ritter von Schönerer and Austrian Pan-Germanism* (Berkeley: University of California Press, 1975), pp. 91-93. For a biography of Schönerer and a collection of his views on Jewry and Judaism, see Eduard Pichl, *Georg Schönerer* (Oldenburg: Gerhard Stalling, 1938), III, 410-417; Klaus Berchtold, *Österreichische Parteiprogramme* (Munich: Oldenbourg, 1967), pp. 185-203.

16. Berchtold, *Parteiprogramme*, p. 203. See sources in n. 15.

17. Adolf Wahrmund, *Babylonierthum, Judenthum und Christenthum* (Leipzig, 1882), pp. viii, ix, 257-259.

18. Paul Molisch, *Geschichte der deutschnationalen Bewegung in Österreich*

von ihren Anfängen bis zum Zerfall der Monarchie (Jena: Gustav Fischer, 1926), pp. 143-144; D. van Arkel, *Antisemitism in Austria*, pp. 56-67. On Luger see Kuppe, *Karl Lüger.*

19. Kuppe, *Karl Lüger*, pp. 99-101. This has been described many times, e.g., van Arkel, *Antisemitism*, pp. 67-80, and Pulzer, *Rise of Political Antisemitism*, pp. 162-170.

20. Van Arkel, *Antisemitism*, pp. 81-107, 186-192; Pulzer, *Rise of Political Antisemitism*, pp. 171-188.

21. Helmuth Plessner, *Das Schicksal deutschen Geistes im Ausgang seiner bürgerlichen Epoche* (Zurich: Niehaus, 1935), pp. 35-48, 183-185.

22. Pulzer, *Rise of Political Antisemitism*, p. 174; Whiteside, *The Socialism of Fools*, p. 121.

24. French Anti-Semitism

1. Jeannine Verdes-Leroux, *Scandale financier et antisémitisme catholique* (Paris: Le Centurion, 1969), pp. 118-122.

2. See Chapter 22, nn. 23-24.

3. Verdes-Leroux, *Scandale financier*, p. 118. A copy of most of the publications of *L'Antisémitique* is available at the National and University Library in Jerusalem. The publication of 28 July 1883 includes an appeal to the public concerning the League, and the following issues repeat it. See the issues of October 6 and 27. An announcement on the anti-Semitic conference appears in the December 1 issue and is reprinted several times thereafter. According to Verdes-Leroux, p. 118, the weekly donned new clothing in the form of *Le Peril social*, but this publication also soon ceased to appear.

4. Edouard Drumont, *La France juive, essai d'histoire contemporaine*, 2 vols. (Paris, 1886).

5. Articles of this type appeared in almost every publication. A reader's letter of the same sort appears, for example, in the issue of 3 November 1883.

6. Auguste Chirac, *Les Rois de la république* (Paris, 1883). This book appeared in an enlarged version in 1890. The author continued to publish anti-Semitic books and articles, and Drumont was often wont to quote him in his later books. See Edouard Drumont, *La Fin d'un monde* (Paris, 1889), and *Le Testament d'un antisémite* (Paris, 1891). Verdes-Leroux, *Scandale financier*, pp. 120-121, 221-222. Pierre Sorlin, *"La Croix" et les juifs, 1880-1899* (Paris: Grasset, 1967), closely follows the Jewish issue in the publications of the Catholic press. On Tisza-Eszlar, see pp. 78, 135-136.

7. See Chapter 11; Verdes-Leroux, *Scandale financier*, p. 119.

8. Verdes-Leroux's excellent book is devoted to a description of the scandal surrounding the bankruptcy. The purpose of the bank is defined on p. 24. See also pp. 58-59, 115-117.

9. Much has been written about Drumont. He has been drawn in extremely contradictory terms. See Pierre Pierrard, *Juifs et catholiques français* (Paris: Fayard, 1970), pp. 31-79. His two former partners provide biographical data: Jules Guérin, *Les Trafiquants de l'antisémitisme: la Maison Drumont and Co.* (Paris, 1905); Jean Drault, pseud. [Alfred Gendrot], *Drumont, La France juive et*

la Libre parole (Paris: Société Française d'Editions Littéraires et Techniques, 1935). Both draw a character sketch of Drumont, the first with unrestrained hostility, the second with critical sympathy. The reviewer's text has been published in Drault, pp. 7-9. According to Pierrard, p. 31, it was Alfonse Daudet who intervened with the editor of *Le Figaro* to try to sell the book to the public. See also Robert F. Byrnes, *Antisemitism in Modern France* (New Brunswick, N.J.: Rutgers University Press, 1950), pp. 190-192. The incident of the duel is outlined in the memoirs of Arthur Meyer, *Ce que mes yeux ont vu* (Paris: Plon, 1911), pp. 251-254. Meyer later converted and was sympathetic to anti-Semitism (Meyer, pp. 108-134). *La France juive*, I, v. The third part of Hippolyte Taine's book, *Les Origines de la France contemporaine* (Paris, 1881), is "La conquête jacobine"; see pp. vi, xvi, 137. *L'Antisémitique* of 5 January 1884 carried an article called "La Conquête de la France et de l'Europe par les juifs." Drumont nowhere mentions *L'Antisémitique*, but it is difficult to believe that he did not know it.

10. Israel Schapira, *Der Antisemitismus in der französischen Literatur, Edouard Drumont und seine Quellen* (Berlin: Philo, 1927). Schapira here suggests Drumont's major sources. A discussion of the problem can be found in Norman J. Clary, *French Antisemitism during the Years of Drumont and the Dreyfus Affair, 1886-1906* (Diss., Ohio State University, 1970), pp. 75ff.

11. The extent to which these sources were used can be deduced from the index in *La France juive*. Proudhon is quoted seven times, Leroux once, and Toussenel nine times. See especially II, 382-426, 309-348, and I, 3-23, of which pp. 13-14 deal with Renan's attitude.

12. *La France juive*, I, 50-52. In his later books Drumont explicitly denied conversion to Jews, and this is one of the reasons the consistent Catholics took exception to him. Sorlin, *"La Croix" et les juifs*, pp. 49-56.

13. The question of Drumont's inner relations with Catholicism is extensively discussed in Pierrard, *Juifs et catholiques*, pp. 49-56. Pierrard's conclusion is close to my own. The attraction of Drumont's anti-Semitic propaganda for various circles had been nicely interpreted as early as 1892 by Gariel Terrail [Mermeix], *Les Antisemites en France* (Paris, 1892), pp. 7-19.

14. The most salient incident was his identification of Gambetta, whom he despised, as both a Jew and one responsible for the existence of the republic. See Pierrard, *Juifs et catholiques*, pp. 41-44. In the later editions of *La France juive* the author added revisions to the identification of several figures as Jews, but this experience did not teach him to tread more carefully later.

15. The closeness in style between the French anti-Semitic propaganda and that used by the Nazis has sometimes been noticed. Hannah Arendt, *The Origins of Totalitarianism* (Cleveland, World Publishing Company, 1958), pp. 93-94; Ernst Nolte, *Der Faschismus in seiner Epoche* (Munich, 1963), pp. 61-190.

16. *Schmeitzner's Monatsschrift* (1883), pp. 257, 260.

17. See Chapter 22.

18. *La France juive*, I, 526.

19. The term reappears in Drumont, for example, *La France juive*, I, 430, 432.

20. Léonce Reynaud, *La France n'est pas juive* (Paris, 1886). Reynaud published a second book in response to Drumont's second composition, *Les Juifs fran-*

çais devant l'opinion (Paris, 1887). Gabriel de Gonet reprinted Toussenel's book in 1888 with an introduction. A typical book is that of Arsène Guérin, À propos de la France juive (Paris, 1886). Despite several defects from a Catholic point of view, the author sees Drumont as an important defender of Catholicism. On the attitude of the Catholic press to the Jews of France, see Sorlin, "La Croix," pp. 202-207.

21. Jacques de Biez, La Question juive (Paris, 1886), pp. 1-3. The author defines himself as a republican even after Drumont's call and suggests joining forces. The announcement on the formation of the League was printed in the first issue of the monthly, L'Alliance anti-juive pour la defense sociale et religieuse (1891), pp. 10-13. Raphael Viau, Vingt ans d'antisémitisme, 1889-1909 (Paris: Fasquelle, 1910), p. 2. See Sorlin, "La Croix," pp. 202-207. Drumont compromised; he never challenged anyone to a duel, but he accepted if he was called out. Pierrard (Juifs et catholiques, p. 503) calls this "strange casuistry on the part of an opponent of the Talmud."

22. C. Pontigny, ed., L'alliance anti-juive pour la defense sociale et religieuse, November 1890-October 1891, pp. 9-13. The criticism of the higher clergy, especially the Pope, which Sorlin ("La Croix," p. 207) mentions cannot yet be found in La France juive. It is the result of disappointment with the support of formal church circles. The development of Drumont's thinking is traced in Drault, Drumont, pp. 76-82.

23. Besides the two books mentioned above in n. 6, there appeared, even before the founding of Libre parole, the book La France juive devant l'opinion (Paris, 1886). Ernest Crémieux-Foa, La Campagne antisémitique, les duels, les responsibilités (Paris, 1892), pp. 24-27. Following this attack on Jewish officers, they challenged several of the writers of Libre parole to duels. One of these, Armond Mayer, was killed by Morès, a nobleman and close acquaintance of Drumont, an event that caused a great stir in influential circles. Details in Cremieux-Foa, pp. 30-53. The role of Drumont's newspaper in the instigation against Dreyfus has been described in the literature on the trial. A very detailed account is given by Patrice Boussel, L'Affaire Dreyfus et la presse (Paris: Colin, 1960).

24. Clary, French Antisemitism, pp. 200-211, 236-250; Viau, Vingt ans, pp. 292-301.

25. Guérin, Les Trafiquants de l'antisémitisme, p. 138. See also the relevant parts dealing with the societies mentioned, according to the index. See also Viau, Vingt ans, pp. 190-199. In 1903, Drumont himself attempted to found the Fédération Nationale Antijuive (Viau, p. 321), but by then the movement was already in its decline. See the appraisal and evidence given by Drault, Drumont, pp. 232, 240, 278-279.

26. Viau's Vingt ans is replete with reports of the various duels. Drumont compelled his associates to participate in duels which were regarded as a means of doing battle. See the International Encyclopedia of the Social Sciences, VI, 508-509; Michael R. Marrus, The Politics of Assimilation: A Study of the French Community at the Time of the Dreyfus Affair (Oxford: Oxford University Press, 1971), pp. 153-154; Dirk van Arkel, Antisemitism in Austria (Diss., Leiden, 1966), pp. 157-177.

27. See Sorlin, "La Croix," p. 122, for a map of the distribution of the anti-

Semitic groups. On the disturbances in France, see Marrus, *Politics of Assimilation*, pp. 208-210.

28. This was the accepted view among Jews and among some of the anti-Semites themselves. On the Jews, see J. Levoillant, "La Génese de l'antisemitisme sous la Troisième Republique," *REJ* 54 (1907): lxxvi-c. This was the text of a lecture presented to the Société des Études Juifs, and it appears that the Society, like the author himself, viewed the phenomenon as a bad dream, by now ended. With regard to the anti-Semites, Viau's *Vingt ans* had been written in an atmosphere of parting from a period that was over.

29. Alexander Sedgwick, *The Ralliement in French Politics, 1890-1898* (Cambridge, Mass.: Harvard University Press, 1965).

30. Drault, *Drumont*, pp. 300-328; Eugen J. Weber, *Action française; Royalism and Reaction in Twentieth-Century France* (Stanford, Calif.: Stanford University Press, 1962); Ernst Nolte, *Der Faschismus in seiner Epoche, Die Action française, Der italienische Facschismus, Der Nationalsozialismus* (Munich: Piper, 1963), pp. 61-190.

25. Racism and Its Nazi Climax

1. On Istoczy, see Judit Kubinszky, *Politikai antiszemitismus Magyarországon 1875-1890* (Budapest: Kossuth Könyvkiado, 1976), p. 219. On the despair of Marr and his colleagues see Jochmann, "Struktur und Funktion des deutschen Antisemitismus," in Werner E. Mosse, *Juden im Wilhelminischen Deutschland, 1890-1914* (Tübingen: Mohr, 1976), pp. 417-418; Levy, *The Downfall of the Anti-Semitic Parties*, pp. 243-244.

2. On the economic situation of German Jewry: Werner E. Mosse, "Die Juden in Wirtschaft und Gesellschaft" in *Juden im Wilhelminischen Deutschland*, pp. 57-113. On the romantic longings, see Fritz Stern, *The Politics of Cultural Despair* (Berkeley: University of California Press, 1961).

3. For biographical details, see *Festschrift zum fünfundzwanzigsten Bestehen des Hammer* (Leipzig: Hammer, 1926). Thomas Frey [Theodor Fritsch], *Leuchtkugeln, Altdeutsch-antisemitische Kernsprüche* (Leipzig, 1882).

4. See his article from 1912, "Vom parteipolitischen Antisemitismus," in Paul Lehmann, *Neue Wege, aus Theodor Fritsch's Lebensarbeit* (Leipzig: Hammer, 1922), pp. 280-288.

5. Fritsch, *Leuchtkugeln*, pp. 7-9; The awareness of the racial issue is called by Fritsch "One of the most important achievements of the human perception"; Thomas Frey (Theodor Fritsch], *Zur Bekämpfung zweitausend jähriger Irrtürmer*, (Leipzig, 1886), p. 45.

6. Lehmann, *Neue Wege*, p. 285.

7. Fritsch used the term *freireligiös* to describe his own religious stand. He enlarged upon it in a 1909 article "Religion?" in Lehmann, *Neue Wege*, pp. 95-106.

8. On Lagarde, see Stern, *Politics of Cultural Despair*, pp. 3-36; Robert W. Lougee, *Paul de Lagarde 1827-1891* (Cambridge, Mass.: Harvard University Press, 1962); Uriel Tal, *Christians and Jews in Germany* (Ithaca, N.Y.: Cornell University Press, 1974), pp. 271-273.

9. "Die Religion der Zukunft" is the title of an article from 1878 included in Paul de Lagarde, *Deutsche Schriften* (Göttingen: Lüder Horstmann, 1904), pp. 217-247.

10. Details in Lougee, *Paul de Lagarde*, pp. 210-215.

11. See the index to Fritsch's *Handbuch der Judenfrage* in any of its more than forty editions.

12. Lehmann, *Neue Wege*, p. 283.

13. Thomas Frey [Theodor Fritsch], *Brennende Fragen* (Leipzig, 1885), no. 15, p. 7.

14. *Festschrift Hammer*, pp. 44; Fritsch, *Zur Bekämpfung zweitausendjähriger Irrtümer*, pp. 69-76; the relevant chapter is "Die Vorläufer der Bibel."

15. *Mitteilungen aus dem Verein zur Abwehr des Antisemitismus*. The Verein was founded in 1890 by non-Jewish opponents of anti-Semitism with the cooperation of Jews. The *Mitteilungen* repeatedly pointed to the "unchristian" character of anti-Semitism; see Tal, *Christians and Jews*, p. 227.

16. Houston Stewart Chamberlain, *Die Grundlagen des neunzehnten Jahrhunderts* (Munich: F. Bruckmann, 1900); Gerd-Klaus Kaltenbrunner, "Houston Stewart Chamberlain," *The Wiener Library Bulletin*, 29 (1967-1968): 6-12.

17. *Die Grundlagen*, pp. 343, 386, 345-421, 465-531.

18. Ibid., p. 17.

19. Compare also *Die Grundlagen*, pp. 18, 220.

20. On Renan see above, Chapter 10. On Wellhausen, see Tal, *Christians and Jews*, pp. 179-180, 31. Tal deals extensively with this in Chapter 4.

21. *Die Grundlagen*, pp. 223, 369.

22. Ibid., p. 201 and the whole chapter on Jesus' appearance, pp. 189-251.

23. Ibid., pp. 211-237.

24. Ibid., p. 171.

25. Houston Stewart Chamberlain, *Briefe 1882-1924 und Briefwechsel mit Kaiser Wilhelm II* (Munich: Bruckmann, 1928), I, 308. The reviews were collected by the publisher and repeatedly printed; Chamberlain, *Die Grundlagen des neunzehnten Jahrhunderts und Immanuel Kant, kritische Urteile* (Munich: F. Bruckmann, 1909); H. C. Heinrich M. Cohen, *Houston Stewart Chamberlain, die Grundlagen des neunzehnten Jahrhunderts* (Dresden and Leipzig: E. Pierson, 1901), p. 44.

26. *Die Grundlagen*, pp. 323-459, and *Briefe*, II, 131-275; Lamar Cecil, "Wilhelm II und die Juden" in Mosse, *Juden im Wilhelminischen Deutschland*, pp. 330-332.

27. See Chapter 10.

28. *International Encyclopedia of the Social Sciences*, XII, 86-87.

29. Chamberlain refers explicitly to Darwin; *Die Grundlagen*, pp. 264-266, 278-287.

30. Jochmann, "Strucktur und Funktion," p. 427. In 1904 Fritsch still maintained that the Jewish problem could only be solved by way of legislation. See Lehmann, *Neue Wege*, p. 289.

31. Werner Jochmann, "Die Ausbreitung des Antisemitismus," in *Deutsches Judentum in Krieg und Revolution, 1916-1923*, Werner Mosse, ed. (Tübingen: Mohr, 1971), pp. 409-410, 425-427. Lehmann, *Neue Wege*, pp. 301-303.

32. Georg Franz-Willing, *Ursprung der Hitlerbewegung 1919-1922* (Preussisch Ollendorf: K. W. Schütz, 1974).

33. Werner T. Angress, "Juden im politischen Leben der Revolutionszeit," in Mosse, *Deutsches Judentum in Krieg und Revolution*, pp. 137-149, 184-193.

34. Franz-Willing, *Ursprung der Hitlerbewegung*, pp. 66-83; Jochmann, "Die Ausbreitung des Antisemitismus," pp. 455-484; Jacob Katz, *Jews and Freemasons in Europe, 1723-1939* (Cambridge, Mass.: Harvard University Press, 1970), pp. 174-196.

35. Franz-Willing, *Ursprung der Hitlerbewegung*, pp. 90-136, especially p. 118.

36. Karl Dietrich Bracher, *Die deutsche Diktatur, Entstehung, Struktur, Folgen des Nationalsozialismus* (Cologne and Berlin: Kiepenheuer & Witsch, 1970), pp. 117-132.

37. Ibid., pp. 60-72; August Kubizek, *Young Hitler: The Story of Our Friendship* (London, Allan Wingate, 1954); Franz Jetzinger, *Hitler's Youth* (London: Hutchinson, 1958); Franz-Willing, *Ursprung der Hitlerbewegung*, pp. 97-109; Adolf Hitler *Mein Kampf*, (Munich: Zentralverlag der NSDAP, 1943), pp. 58-68, 105-116, 119-137.

38. The attempt by Wilfried Daim, *Der Mann, der Hitler die Ideen gab* (Munich: Isaar Verlag, 1958), to identify Hitler's sources is unconvincing. It lacks necessary knowledge of the history of anti-Semitism.

39. *Mein Kampf*, pp. 264-267, 311-362.

40. Adolf Wahrmund, *Das Gesetz des Nomadentums und die heutige Judenherrschaft* (Berlin, 1892).

41. *Mein Kampf*, pp. 336-338.

42. Alfred Rosenberg, *Der Mythus des 20. Jahrhunderts* (Munich: Hoheneichen-Verlag, 1934); on Rosenberg, Robert Cecil, *Myth of the Master Race: Alfred Rosenberg and the Nazi Ideology* (London: B. T. Batsford, 1972).

43. Raimund Baumgärtner, *Weltanschauungskampf im Dritten Reich* (Mainz: Grünewald Verlag, 1977), pp. 154-190, 206-230. On Hitler's attitude towards the *Mythus*, ibid., pp. 106-111. See also Cecil, *Myth of the Master Race*, pp. 100-104.

44. Rosenberg applies the term *Schmarotzer, Schmarotzertum* as synonymous to *Parasit*. For the history of this kind of expression, see Alex Bein, "Der jüdische Parasit, Bemerkungen zur Semantik der Judenfrage," in *Vierteljahreshefte für Zeitgeschichte* 2 (1965): 121-149.

45. Hitler used this stratagem throughout his book, and the same was done by other Nazi propagandists. See Jochmann, "Die Ausbreitung des Antisemitismus."

46. Ismar Schorsch, *Jewish Reactions to German Anti-Semitism, 1870-1914* (New York: Columbia University Press, 1972).

47. On the illusions of Conservative elements supporting Hitler, see Bracher, *Die deutsche Diktatur*, pp. 209-218.

48. Baumgärtner, *Weltanschauungskampf*, pp. 106-108.

26. Anti-Semitism Through the Ages

1. Secularization does not mean here simply the removal of some domain of life from the scope of religion, but rather the retaining of its emotional appeal even

in that domain's secular metamorphosis. See Hermann Lübbe, *Säkularisierung, Geschichte eines ideenpolitischen Begriffs* (Freiburg: Alber, 1965).

2. The use of the term *pariah* in the Jewish connection has been often taken exception to—for no good reason in my opinion, if one is careful not to equate it with its original meaning in the Indian context. See Salo W. Baron, *Social and Religious History of the Jews* (New York: Columbia University Press, 1952), I, 23-25, 297; Werner J. Cahnman, "Pariahs, Strangers and Court-Jews: A Conceptual Clarification," *Sociological Analysis*, 1974, pp. 154-166.

3. Jules Isaac, *L'Enseignement du mépris* (Paris: Fasquelle, 1962)—English version: *The Teaching of Contempt, Christian Roots of Anti-Semitism* (New York: Holt, Rinehart and Winston, 1964); Wolf Dieter Marsch and Karl Thieme, eds., *Christen und Juden, ihr Gegenüber vom Apostelkonzil bis heute* (Mainz: Matthias Grünewald, 1961). A summary of Isaac's activities is given in Claire Huchet Bishop's introduction to his English book, pp. 3-15.

4. This argument was formulated by Ignatz Klinger (see Chapter 18, n. 3) and has been reiterated by many: Friedrich Rühs, *Über die Ansprüche der Juden an das deutsche Bürgerrechte* (Berlin, 1816), pp. 6-12; Jakob Friedrich Fries, *Über die Gefahrdung des Wohlstandes und Charakters der Deutschen durch die Juden* (Heidelberg, 1816), pp. 3-4; Bauer, *Die Judenfrage*, pp. 4-5. The idea has been well summarized by Hans Paul Bahrdt as the anti-Semitic apology: "Soziologische Reflexionen über die gesellschaftlichen Voraussetzungen des Antisemitismus in Deutschland," in *Entscheidungsjahr 1932, zur Judenfrage in der Endphase der weimarer Republik,* ed. Werner E. Mosse (Tübingen: Mohr, 1966), p. 136.

5. There is abundant literature on anti-Semitism in ancient times. The definitive study remains that of Isaak Heinemann, "Antisemitismus," Supplement 5, "Pauly-Wissowa," in *Real-Encyclopaedie der klassischen Altertumswissenschaft* (Stuttgart, 1929), pp. 3-43. The relevant source material has recently been compiled and annotated in Menahem Stern, *Greek and Latin Authors on Jews and Judaism* (Jerusalem: Israel Academy of Science and Humanities, 1976), vol. 1. A summary and analysis can be found in Ralph Marcus, "Antisemitism in the Hellenistic-Roman World," in *Essays on Antisemitism*, ed. Koppel S. Pinson (New York: Jewish Social Studies, 1946), pp. 61-75. See also J. N. Sevenster, *The Roots of Anti-Semitism in the Ancient World* (Leiden: Brill, 1975).

6. Stern, *Greek and Latin Authors*, p. 183; Sevenster, *Roots of Anti-Semitism*, pp. 11-12; Salo Wittmayer Baron, *A Social and Religious History of the Jews* (New York: Columbia University Press, 1952), I, 230-33, II, 100-101. The difference between ancient anti-Semitism and its Christian version has been much discussed in the literature cited in n. 4. My own view is close to that of Edward H. Flannery, *The Anguish of the Jews* (New York: Macmillan, 1965), pp. 22-24.

7. The study of the extent of integration of the Jews is a recurring motif among most of the anti-Semitic authors whose writings I have examined for this work. Striking examples are Paulus, Treitschke in Germany, Drumont in France, and Istoczy in Hungary.

8. I dealt with the problem of predicting the Nazi coming in my article "Was the Holocaust Predictable?" *Commentary* 59 (1979). Dühring, in particular, has long been recognized as a harbinger of Hitler (see Chapter 21). But at the Chemnitz

Congress, Glagau referred to Dühring as a secluded scholar whose views on the Jewish question "deviated from what is practical or possible to implement." *Schmeitzner's Internationale Monatsschrift* (1883), II, 288.

9. Rosemary Rüther, *Faith and Fratricide: The Theological Roots of Antisemitism* (New York: Seabury Press, 1974); Charlotte Klein, *Theologie und Antijudaismus: Eine Studie zur deutschen theologischen Literatur der Gegenwart* (Munich: Kaiser, 1975).

10. Arthur Schopenhauer, *Sämtliche Werke, Parerga und Paralipomena* (Wiesbaden: Brockhaus, 1961), II, 280.

11. On the difference in status of American Jewry following the struggle for emancipation, see Benjamin Halpern, *The American Jew: A Zionist Analysis* (New York: Theodor Herzl Foundation, 1956).

Index

377

Index

the press and, 128, 273-274, 292-293, 298-300; international congresses, (1882) 242, 279, 286, 292, 293, (1883) 280, 286, 292, 296, (1885) 304; "incubation period" of, 245-259; Christian responsibility for, 320-321; in ancient world, 322-323. *See also entries for individual countries*

Archives Israélites (periodical), 124

Armed forces, Jews in, *see* Occupations, Jewish

Aryan race, 135, 136, 137, 279, 305-310, 314, 315, 324. *See also* Race and racism

Ascher, Saul, 68, 175

Ashkenazim: in France, 108, 171

Assembly of the Estates (Munich, 1819), 98

Assimilation, 6, 82, 126, 157, 171, 231, 258-259, 290, 324; occupational dispersion and, 47, 208, 226; intermarriage and, 56, 61, 73, 212, 226, 236, 238, 275, 322; Wagner's views on, 187-188, 191-192; Jewish stereotype and, 203-209; linguistic (in Hungary), 233, 234, 235; denial of, through baptism, 287. *See also* Baptism; Conversion of Jews; Cultural life, Jewish participation in; Social contacts

Association for the Protection of the Artisan, 285

Assumptionists (religious order), 298

Atheism, 24, 32, 207, 267, 269

Auerbach, Berthold, 176, 182-186

Austria: Prussian victory over (1866), 2, 211, 223; Jewish emancipation in, 3, 52, 98, 107, 223-229, 236, 290, 320; hostility against Freemasonry in, 143; anti-Semitism movement in, 219, 280, 281-291, 296, 298, 303, 314; -Hungary relation, 236, 279; -Germany affiliation sought, 287; nationalism in, 290-291

Austria-Hungary, 238, 277; Jewish emancipation in, 1, 2-3, 250; defense of Jewish community in, 4; anti-Semitism movement in, 294, 300. *See also* Hungary

Babylonia, Jews in, 16, 156, 162

Babylonierthum, Judenthum und Christenthum (Wahrmund), 287

Baden (German state), 52, 156, 197

Bamberger, Ludwig, 247, 253, 255, 257, 271, 282

Banking, *see* Capitalism

Baptism, 65, 66, 68, 158, 214, 304; anti-Semitist view of, 56-57, 269, 272, 274, 277; and Mortara case, 140, 141; as "obsolete ritual," 169, 170; of Marx family, 171; of Jewish intellectuals, 177, 178, 184, 187, 188, 193, 197, 198, 211, 248, 271; assimilation by, denied, 287. *See also* Conversion of Jews

Barruel, August, 143

Bauer, Bruno, 159, 160, 164, 169-170, 172, 174, 188, 195, 207, 213, 319; writings of, 165-168, 170, 214-218, 239; influence of, on Wagner, 186, 188, 214, 217

Bautain, Louis, 117, 118

Bavaria, 313; Jewish emancipation in, 2, 52, 147,150-151; "Hep Hep" riots in, 97-103, 147, 150, 154

Bayle, Pierre, 23, 29

Beer, Michael, 182

Behr, Joseph, 98, 99

Berlin: Jewish status in, 54, 55, 94-95, 148, 183, 252, 271; Jewish population in, 250, 284; anti-Semitism movement in, 250, 251, 273, 282, 283. *See also* Germany

Berlin, Congress of (1878), 240

Berliner Revue, Die (periodical), 214

"Berlin Movement," 245, 262

Bible de l'humanité (Michelet), 130

Biblical tradition, 18, 36, 123, 130, 131; reinterpretation of, 15, 16, 132, 133, 165-166, 168; rationalist-Deist criticisms of, 25-30, 33, 35, 64, 65, 82, 137, 166, 208; Voltaire's view of, 37-43, 51, 72, 265; Schopenhauer's view of, 72. *See also* Old Testament

Biez, Jacques de, 297

Billroth, Theodor, 281, 283

Bismarck, Prince Otto von, 2, 210, 247, 252, 268, 271, 312; criticism of and opposition to, 251, 253, 256

Bleichröder, G. von, 252, 253, 254

Bloch, Samuel, 286

Blood libel, 140, 141; ritual murder and, 19, 20, 39, 96-97, 165-166, 228, 295; of Tiszaeszlár, 275-277, 278, 286, 292, 293

B'nai B'rith: formation of, 271

378

Index

379

Index

Index

Index

Index

Index

Hirsch, Jacob, 98, 99
Hirsch, Solomon, 98
Histoire du peuple d'Israel (Renan), 133, 136
Histoire générale et système comparé des langues sémitiques (Renan), 136
History, Jewish: vs. legend, 15, 17-20; and skepticism of Biblical tradition, 25-26; medieval interest in, 28; Voltaire's view of, 35-44; Greek and Roman versions of, 38; Rühs' use of, 76, 78; Leo's analysis of, 160-162; Bauer's conception of, 215-216. *See also* Biblical tradition
Hitler, Adolf, 304, 312-316, 325; *Mein Kampf*, 313
Holdheim, Samuel, 211
Holland: Jewish emancipation in, 2, 3, 52, 54, 223
Holocaust, the, 321, 326
Holst, Ludolf, 93-94, 151, 152, 154; *Über das Verhältniss der Juden zu den Christen . . .*, 92
Holubek, Franz, 285, 286
Holy Alliance, 86
Huguenots, 58. *See also* Protestantism
Humanism, 8, 198, 216, 233, 235
Humboldt, Alexander von, 233
Hungary: Jewish emancipation in, 3, 52, 107, 230-242, 275, 290, 320; anti-Semitism movement in, 9, 219, 237, 241-242, 273-280, 288, 296, 298, 303, (Tiszaeszlár affair) 275-277, 278, 286, 292, 293; Jewish immigration into, 230-231, 237-238, 275-276, 277; nationalism in, 231-236; Diets of (1838-1840, 1844), 231, 234; and Hungarian language, 233, 234, 235; -Austria relation, 236, 279; "Jewish Congress" in, 237; Germany and, 287. *See also* Austria-Hungary
Hungerpastor (Raabe), 203, 205

Image of Jews, *see* Stereotypes
Immigration of Jews: into Germany, 78, 268; into France, 120; into Hungary, 230-231, 237-238, 275-276, 277; prohibitions against, 268, 276, 277
Impossibility of the Emancipation of Jews in the Christian State, The (Fränkel), 195
Incitement, *see* Riots, incitement and

Independence, Party of (Hungary), 277-278
Indo-Europeans, 135, 137
Inquisition, the, 41
Intelligenzblatt (Wurzburg newspaper), 99
Intermarriage, *see* Assimilation
Isaac, Jules, 326; *The Teaching of Contempt*, 321
Islam, 14, 16
Israel: concept of (historical and legendary), 15, 16, 35-36, 37, 38, 115, 118, 130, 142, 165; Voltaire's view of people of, 39-42; state of, 327. *See also* Zionism
Istoczy, Györö, 9, 237-242, 273-280, 286, 292, 294, 303, 319
Italy: Jewish emancipation in, 52

Jellinek, Adolf, 286
Jesuit order, 295; disbanded, 58
Jesus Christ: Jewish rejection of, 24, 32, 125, 128, 151, 168, 180, 308, 323, (punished) 54, 115, 116, 266; Deist-rationalist view of, 28, 32, 37, 64, 155; as "enlightened philosopher," 64-65; Hegel's view of, 68-69, 70-71; Renan's view of, 133-134; second coming of, 211; Jewish acceptance of, 219, (Kant's theory of) 67; German "religion of future" view of, 305, 309; as "Aryan," 306, 308, 315. *See also* Christianity; Deicide; Messianic belief
"Jew Bill," *see* Naturalization ("Jew") Bill
"Jewish Congress" (Hungary), 237
Jewish festivals, *see* Sabbath-keeping and festival days
Jewish history, *see* History, Jewish
Jewish homeland, *see* Zionism
Jewish "nation," *see* "State within a state"
Jewish Question, The, as a Question of Race, Morals, and Culture with a World Historical Answer (Dühring), 265
Jewish Teachers Seminary (Münster), 219
Joseph II, emperor of Austria, 52, 53, 223, 224, 226, 230, 282, 290
Judaism: Christianity as outgrowth of, 7, 16, 25, 29-30, 37, 66, 70, 166, 308, 315, 326; "inferiority" of, 7, 20-21, 25, 30, 41, 47, 64-72, 82, 89, 118, 139, 140-142, 151-153, 158, 163-164, 166,

384

Index

Index

Index

Index

Index

Index

Saint-Simonism, 126

Sand, Karl Ludwig, 101

Sanhedrin (Napoleonic), *see* Napoleon Bonaparte

Saphir, Moritz Gottlieb, 176, 178

Sartorius, Georg, 103-104

Schacher, see Traders, Jews as

Schelling, Friedrich Wilhelm Joseph von, 83

Scheuring, Theodor A., 98-99

Schiller, Johann Christoph Friedrich von, 190

Schirnding, Count Ferdinand, 226; *Österreich im Jahre 1840,* 225

Schmidt-Phiseldeck, C. F., 149-150, 151, 152, 153-154, 196

Schöffler, Herbert, 33

Schönerer, Georg Ritter von, 287, 288, 289, 290, 291, 296, 314

Schopenhauer, Arthur, 72-73, 107, 326

Schulz, Johann Heinrich, 53, 58, 59, 64-65

Scripture, *see* Biblical tradition

Secret societies, 88-89

Secularization, 24, 81, 129, 191, 226, 326-327; and religious criterion, 1; in Germany, 97, 254; in France, 114, 212, 298; of Judaism, 212, 264; anti-Semitism and, 319, 320. *See also* Liberalism

"Semite" (as term for Jew), first use of, 261. *See also* Anti-Semitism

Semitic race, 135, 136-138, 295, 305, 307, 310, 314, 315, 324. *See also* Race and racism

Sephardim, 45, 118

Serbia, 280

Sessa, Karl Borromaus Alexander, 91

Shaftesbury, Anthony Ashley Cooper, 3rd earl of, 27, 28, 29, 35

Silberner, Edmund, 122

Simonyi, Ivan von, 279

Slavery, U.S., justification of, 132

Social contacts, 16, 54, 86, 103-104, 141-142, 233, 299; and social segregation, 56, 95-96, 155-156, 270-271, 272, 280, 283-284, 291, 299, 303, 321, 322-323; and Jewish solidarity as obstacle to emancipation, 58, 73, 87, 88, 109, 149-150, 176, 258-259, 264; and residential rights, 85, 147-148, 231, 320. *See also* Assimilation; Cultural life, Jewish participation in; Education; Language; Occupations, Jewish; "State within a state"

Social-Democratic party (Germany), 262, 289, 312

Socialism, 262, 268; and socialist hypothesis of anti-Semitism, 5-6, 119-128, 129, 133, 174, 294; radical thinkers and, 160, 174; Marx and, 173; and socialist activities curbed, 239; Jewish trend toward, 271; emergence of, 282; in postwar Germany, 312. *See also* Marx, Karl

Socrates, 68, 130

Sofer, Moses, 231

Soll und Haben (Freytag), 203-205, 206

Sonnenberg, Liebermann von, 280

Soviet Union: Christianity in, 326. *See also* Russia

Spinoza, Benedict, 26, 36, 67, 80, 168, 216, 266

Staats und Gesellschaftslexikon (encyclopedia), 214

"Stagnation" as characteristic, 149. *See also* Stereotypes

Stahl, Friedrich Julius, 198-201, 211, 266, 271, 319; *Der christliche Staat und sein Verhältniss zum Deismus und Judenthum* ("The Christian State and its Relation to Deism and Judaism"), 199

Stahr, Adolf, 248

"State within a state," 58-60, 62, 78-80, 81-82, 88, 108, 140, 156, 226; Zionism as solution for, 5; Church as, 60; and "collective mentality," 78; and "nation within a nation," 109-110, 126. *See also* Aliens, Jews as; Zionism

Stein, Baron Karl von, 84

Stereotypes: unscrupulous-amoral behavior toward non-Jews, 20, 32, 44, 55-56, 93, 111, 137, 152, 204, 213; Voltaire's acceptance of, 40-44, 47, 137; of Jewish "national character," 40, 81, 131, 156-157, 160-162, 176, 178, 181, 184, 208, 212; as "pariahs," 54, 118, 132, 141, 264, 272, 320, 327; as "parasites," "poisoners," 60, 125, 150-151, 180-181, 239, 296, 304, 314, 315; traditional Christian, 69-70, 78, 81, 82, 118, 121, 153-154, 197, 200-201, (Schopenhauer's acceptance of) 72-73, (Marx's acceptance of) 172, (revival of)

390

Index

Varnhagen, Rachel, 97
Vaterland (anti-Jewish weekly), 282
Vatican, the, 115, 326. *See also* Roman
 Catholicism
Veuillot, Louis, 140
Viau, Raphael, 297
Victory of Judaism over Germanism, The
 (Marr), 260
Vie de Jésus (Renan), 133-134
Vienna: Jewish status (and restrictions) in,
 52, 53, 223, 224, 250, 289; anti-Sem-
 itism movement in, 281, 284-285, 289,
 308, 314; Jewish students in, 281, 283;
 Jewish population in, 284; politics in,
 288-289; Hitler's years in, 314. *See also*
 Austria
Vienna, Congress of, 75-76, 84, 90, 98
Vogelsang, Karl von, 282-283, 287-288,
 319
Voltaire, François de, 10, 33, 112, 159,
 265, 319; as Deist, 34-40, 137, 208; as
 rationalist, 34-36, 39, 43, 74; ethnologi-
 cal-anthropological approach of, 35, 36-
 37, 41; *Essai sur les moeurs et l'esprit
 des nations*, 36, 46; portrayal by, of
 Jewish nation, 39-42, 124, 137, 224;
 attitude of, toward Jewish community in
 Europe, 43-47, 51-52, 59; and Voltairian tradition, 72, 131, 152, 158, 293
Voss, Julius, 91
Vrecourt, A., 292, 293

Wagener, Hermann, 212-213, 214, 215,
 217, 219, 248, 319; *Das Judenthum
 und der Staat*, 211
Wagner, Richard, 182, 184, 217, 306;
 anti-Jewish writings of, 185-194, 219,
 239
Wahrmund, Adolf, 314; *Babylonierthum,
 Judenthum und Christenthum*, 287
Waldegg, Egon, *see* Pinkert, Alexander
 Friedrich
War of Liberation (1813), 76, 179
Wasserman, Rabbi, 164
*Was soll bei der neuen Verfassung aus den
 Juden werden* (anon.), 88
Weber, Max, 132, 320
Weil, Jacob, 182
Weimar Republic, 296, 311, 312. *See also*
 Germany

Wellhausen, Julius, 308
Wenckheim, Béla, 239-240
Wertheimer, Samson, 14
Westfälischer Merkur (newspaper), 219
Wienbarg, Ludolf, 182
Wiener Kirchenzeitung (newspaper), 227,
 228, 229
Wiesinger, Albert, 228, 286; *Poor Chris-
 tians and Starvelings, Jewish Capitalists
 and Spendthrifts*, 229
William II, emperor of Germany, 309, 312
Wilmanns, C., 254, 255-256, 257, 269;
 The Golden International, 256, 261
Wolfart, Philip Ludwig, 195, 196, 197
Woolston, Thomas, 27, 28, 30
"World domination" by Jews, 43, 219,
 319; English view of, 32; German view
 of, 86, 94-95, 113, 181, 215-216, 252,
 254-255, 260, 261, 268, 287; French
 view of, 132, 140, 142, 143, 150, 212,
 294; Hungarian view of, 238-239, 241;
 Dresden conference view of, 279-280;
 "Jewish-Masonic conspiracy" and, 314.
 See also Stereotypes
Württemberg (German state): Jewish
 emancipation in, 52, 197

Yiddish dialect, *see* Language
Young Germany (writers' group), 177,
 181-182, 207; equated with "Young
 Palestine," 179-180
Young Hegelians, 160, 214. *See also*
 Hegel, Georg Wilhelm Friedrich von
"Young Palestine," *see* Young Germany
Young people, *see* Students

Zeitschrift für spekulative Theologie (Bauer,
 ed.), 165
Zerboni, Karl von, 279, 285
Zionism, 5, 6; resettlement proposals, 90,
 122; and Palestine as homeland, 122,
 156, 269, 273; and Jew as "eternal
 stranger," 149, 156; and establishment
 of Jewish state, 240, 327, (Voltaire's
 suggestion of) 46. *See also* "State within a state"
Zunz, Jomtov Lippman, 151

392